Religion, Race, and the American Presidency

D0162571

Religion, Race, and the American Presidency

Edited by
Gastón Espinosa

ROWMAN & LITTLEFIELD PUBLISHERS, INC.
Lanham • Boulder • New York • Toronto • Plymouth, UK

ROWMAN & LITTLEFIELD PUBLISHERS, INC.

Published in the United States of America
by Rowman & Littlefield Publishers, Inc.
A wholly owned subsidiary of The Rowman & Littlefield Publishing Group, Inc.
4501 Forbes Boulevard, Suite 200, Lanham, Maryland 20706
www.rowmanlittlefield.com

Estover Road
Plymouth PL6 7PY
United Kingdom

Copyright © 2008 by Rowman & Littlefield Publishers, Inc.
First paperback edition 2011

British Library Cataloguing in Publication Information Available

The hardback edition of this book was previously cataloged by the Library of Congress
as follows:

Library of Congress Cataloging-in-Publication Data:

Espinosa, Gastón
  Religion, race, and the American identity / Gastón Espinosa.
     p. cm.
  Includes bibliographical references and index.
  1. Religion and politics—United States. 2. United States—Race relations—Political
aspects. 3. Presidents—United States—Election. I. Title.
  BL2525.E78 2008
  322'.10973--dc22   2008016891

  ISBN: 978-0-7425-6321-6 (cloth : alk. paper)
  ISBN: 978-0-7425-6322-3 (pbk : alk. paper)
  ISBN: 978-0-7425-6348-3 (electronic)

Printed in the United States of America

∞ ™ The paper used in this publication meets the minimum requirements of American
National Standard for Information Sciences—Permanence of Paper for Printed Library
Materials, ANSI/NISO Z39.48-1992.

This book is dedicated to my bright and energetic children Gastón, María, and Carina.
"Care enough to be involved, be involved enough to care." —Dad

Table of Contents

List of Photographs

CHAPTER 1—Evangelicals and the American Presidency, Corwin Smidt
Ronald Reagan gives "Evil Empire" speech at the National Association of
Evangelicals (NAE) Convention, Orlando, Florida, March 8, 1983. (Courtesy: Ronald Reagan Presidential Library, C13322-21A)

CHAPTER 2—Mainline Protestants and the American Presidency, Laura
R. Olson and Adam L. Warber, Episcopal Priest, Reverend Billy Graham,
and George H. W. Bush at St. Anne's Episcopal Church, Kennebunkport,
Maine, September 2, 1990. (Courtesy: George Bush Presidential Library,
P15460-05)

CHAPTER 3—Catholics and the American Presidency, David C. Leege
John F. Kennedy standing with Roman Catholic Cardinal Francis Spellman,
Archbishop of New York, and Vice President Richard Nixon at the Al Smith
Memorial Dinner, 1960. (Photo: Jack Schildkraut) (Courtesy: John F. Kennedy Presidential Library & Museum, Photo No. Px88-7:3)

CHAPTER 6—Jews and the American Presidency, David G. Dalin
President Harry S. Truman is given Hebrew Torah Scroll by Dr. Chaim Weizmann, president of Israel, during a visit to the White House, May 25, 1948.
(Institutional Creator: Brown-Suarez Photo) (Courtesy: Harry S. Truman
Library & Museum, HTZ59848)

CHAPTER 7—Muslims and the American Presidency, Brian Calfano, Paul
A. Djupe, and John C. Green
Israeli Prime Minister Yitzhak Rabin, President Bill Clinton, and Palestinian

List of Tables

Acknowledgments

This book would not have been possible without the generous financial support of Stephen T. Davis and the Claremont McKenna College (CMC) Department of Philosophy and Religious Studies; Pamela Gann and the CMC Office of the President; Deans William Ascher, Jerome Garris, and Gregory Hess; Charles R. Kesler and The Salvatori Center for the Study of Individual Freedom in the Modern World; The Marian Miner Cook Athenaeum; Ronald Riggio and The Kravis Leadership Institute; Nicholas O. Warner and The Benjamin Z. Gould Center for Humanistic Studies; Cynthia Humes of the Teaching Resource Center; and Zayn Kassam and the Pomona Department of Religious Studies. I would also like to thank my student assistants: Alexei Laushkin, Evan Rutter, Julia DiIuliss, Miles Orton, Tess Mason-Elder, Taylor Smith, Benjamin Hunsaker, and Francis Nugent. I also wish to thank Benji Rolsky for his assistance.

Last, but not least, I thank my wife (Jeanette) and three children (Gastón, María, and Carina), without whose support and patience this book would not have been completed.

Introduction

The roles that race, ethnicity, gender, and religious pluralism play in the American presidency is attracting national media attention. The 2008 presidential campaigns of Barack Obama, Hillary Rodham Clinton, John McCain, Mitt Romney, and Mike Huckabee brought these themes into the national limelight. These candidates along with conflicts over 9/11, wars in Iraq and Afghanistan, debates over same-sex marriage, inner-city school vouchers, and faith-based initiatives make an understanding of religion and politics vital. Today's presidential candidates are reaching out as never before to major voting constituencies such as Catholics, Evangelicals, mainline Protestants, Jews, Muslims, Latinos, African Americans, Asian Americans, women, and seculars. Despite this, very little critical scholarly attention has been focused on the important intersection of religion, race, gender, pluralism, and the American presidency—with the notable exceptions of J. Matthew Wilson's *From Polling to Polling Places: Faith and Politics in the American Religious Mosaic*, David E. Campbell's *A Matter of Faith: Religion and the 2004 Presidential Election*, John C. Green's *The Faith Factor: How Religion Influences American Elections*, and several other publications.

Religion, Race, and the American Presidency explores how racial and religious groups and women have voted over the past forty years in general and in the last three elections (1996–2004) in particular. The contributors focus special attention on how Americans of different racial, ethnic, gender, and religious backgrounds voted in presidential elections by analyzing the most recent national survey data, historical research, and, in some cases, on-the-ground interviews. In particular, they examine the complicated and often tricky relationships between American presidents and Catholics, Evangelicals, mainline Protestants, Jews, Muslims, Latinos, African Americans, Asian Americans, women, and seculars.

Where data and the historical literature permitted, the contributors examined the historical relationship between past and current American presidents and their respective groups under consideration, followed by an examination of political party affiliation and voting trends. I then asked them to illustrate (if and when the literature permitted) these developments by exploring two case studies.

This book will explore a number of overlapping critical questions such as: How have presidents used religion as part of their leadership styles and outreach activities? What role have religious rhetoric, values, and symbols played in helping presidents to leverage diverse racial, ethnic, and religious constituencies? In what ways have presidents attempted to manipulate religious and racial-ethnic rhetoric, symbols, and domestic and foreign policy issues to win the White House? How have racial, ethnic, and religious minorities such as Catholics, Evangelicals, mainline Protestants, African Americans, Latinos, Asian Americans, Jews, Muslims, and seculars shifted in their political party affiliation and voting patterns over the last three presidential election cycles? Why? Trends? How have presidents responded? How have individual presidents attempted to reach out and win these voting blocks? Why did Catholics give a majority of their votes to a Republican candidate in 2004—the first time since Walter Mondale lost his bid for the White House in 1984? Why did Euro-American Catholics give Kerry only 47 percent of their vote while Latino Catholics gave him 69 percent of their vote? Why did 40 to 44 percent of Latinos vote for Bush in 2004? What role has the growth of evangelicalism played in American presidential elections? How are African American and Latino Catholics and Evangelicals voting? Why did Muslims support Bush in 2000 but then dramatically shift their support away from him in 2004? How are Asian Americans, who are now the fastest growing minority in the United States, voting? How are American women voting and why? How did American presidents like Bill Clinton and George W. Bush use religion to close the "gender gap"? What roles do faith, moral values, the economy, and foreign policy play in their voting decisions? Whose morals? Whose values?

CHAPTER ANALYSES

In chapter 1 on Evangelicals and the American presidency, Corwin Smidt draws on Alexis de Tocqueville to argue that the United States has a distinctive religious character that has had a profound impact on the way Americans think and act politically. This distinctive religious character has shaped the relationship between religion and the American presidency and helps explain why religion remains such a salient topic in presidential campaigns. This saliency is especially true for born-again, Bible-believing evangelical Protestants. After examining the historical evolution of evangelical Protestantism in America, he argues that it was the main Protestant tradition in American political life until the rise of slavery during the Civil War in the 1860s and the fundamentalist-modernist controversy in the 1920s split the movement into regional and liberal and conservative branches. He then analyzes the changing character of evangelical political engagement over the past four decades. He argues that it has moved from being "a relatively passive and divided bloc of voters" in the early twentieth-century to a "relatively engaged, largely unified, and critical voting bloc" in the post-1976 period. No single factor explains this shift, he argues. Rather, their growing influence and power is primarily the result of their size (one-fifth of the U.S. electorate) and transformation from a fragmented and diverse voting bloc to a more homogenous one concentrated in one political party. Their growing influence and Republican partisanship is also due to their political mobilization as a result of the candidacy of Catholic John F. Kennedy, Barry Goldwater's and Richard Nixon's southern strategies, the Jimmy Carter campaigns in 1976 and 1980, Ronald Reagan's support for Evangelical causes, Jerry Falwell's Moral Majority in 1979 and Pat Robertson's Christian Coalition in the 1980s, and the Democratic Party's decision to embrace a platform that supported a woman's right to choose and homosexual lifestyles.

Finally, the growing influence and power of Evangelicals in the Republican Party is also the result of the fact that their voting rates have increased by ten percentage points (56 percent to 66 percent) over the past four decades. In 2004, for example, 78 percent of Evangelicals voted for President George W. Bush. They also made up 40 percent of all Republican voters, in contrast to mainline Protestants (18 percent) and Roman Catholics (20 percent). Despite their overwhelming support for Bush (78 percent), more than one in five Evangelicals (12 percent) supported Kerry. They made up 12 percent of Kerry's vote totals, which was almost equivalent to Kerry's entire African American Protestant support (13 percent). Evangelicals are likely to remain solidly Republican because they tend to vote the party ticket across all national and state offices and because two-thirds of all Evangelicals self-identify as Republican. Although it is unlikely that Democrats will be able to make any significant inroads among Evangelicals today, Smidt argues, a center left Democratic candidate could win a presidential election by slicing off three or four percentage points of all Evangelical voters (something Obama did in 2008) because it would result in a two-point advantage in a presidential race, thus transforming a 51–49 Republican victory into a 51–49 Democratic victory.

Mainline Protestants are moving in just the opposite direction of American Evangelicals. Laura R. Olson and Adam L. Warber argue in chapter 2 on mainline Protestants and the American presidency that they are moving from a once largely Republican political partisanship to an increasingly divided partisan identity that may lean Democratic in the future. Although they represent a smaller political constituency than Evangelicals, their lower numbers are made up for by the fact that they vote at higher rates (75 percent) than their Evangelical counterparts (66 percent). This has enabled mainline Protestants to become a growing swing constituency in both parties. Despite their shrinking size in the American population, electorate, and in American Christianity, their denominations, colleges and universities, and other institutions still influence the halls of power in Washington, D.C. The vast majority of past and recent American presidents and congresspersons have affiliated with mainline Protestant traditions like the Presbyterians (Jackson, Polk, Wilson, Eisenhower), Methodists (Johnson, McKinley, Bush Jr.), Episcopalians (Washington, Jefferson, Madison, FDR, Ford, Bush Sr.), and the Disciples of Christ (Garfield, Reagan).

The present trend among mainline Protestants is that the less observant moderate-to-progressives are moving toward the Democratic Party, despite historically having given a sizable level of their support to Republican candidates. This trend makes them ripe for Democratic outreach and political mobilization. As a result of this trend in less observant mainline Protestants, Olson and Warber argue that denominational identity is no longer the best predictor of political partisanship or voting behavior.

However, the decision to avoid talking about faith and religion in past Democratic campaigns was "almost certainly . . . an electoral mistake" because many mainline Protestants still resonate with the language of faith and faith-based social justice. They argue that this lack of talk about faith may be one of the reasons why neither Gore nor Kerry could maintain Clinton's (a Southern Baptist) advantage with this constituency and is one of the main reasons why both lost their election bids in 2000 and 2004. Conversely, this is precisely why Bush attracted many mainline Protestant women voters, who tend to be more religious than their male counterparts. This is one of the reasons why Bush was able to close the gender gap. They also found that Democrats are increasingly attracting a higher percentage of older mainline Protestants who do not attend church on a regular basis and those at higher income levels, thus indicating a potential class, generation, and "God-gap" in the future, although Barack Obama's 2008 election run may have slowed or even reversed these trends.

The findings in Olson and Warber indicate that Democrats are attracting older, secular-minded, and wealthier people—three constituencies that have been historically associated with the Republican Party. This realignment could be effectively used against the Democratic Party. The positive side to this development for Democrats is that the once solidly mainline Protestant

Republican coalition may be at risk of losing secular leaning segments to the Democratic Party. However, even this shift toward the Democrats has to be tempered by the fact that most traditional mainline Protestants—and those with large families—tend to vote or lean Republican. Whatever the outcome, it is not likely to change the fact that many of America's presidents will continue to associate with mainline Protestant traditions, a pattern that was also the case in the 2008 presidential candidates such as John McCain (Episcopalian), Hillary Rodham Clinton (United Methodist), and Barack Obama (United Church of Christ).

At the same time mainline Protestants appear to be making a slight shift toward the Democratic Party, David Leege points out in chapter 4 on Catholics and the American presidency that Catholics were slightly trending toward the Republican Party in 2004. Like mainline Protestants, Catholics are fairly split between Democratic and Republican partisan identity. They also tend to hold a middle position between strict seperationists on the one hand, who want all vestiges of religion removed from public life, and many Evangelicals and conservative religionists on the other hand, who want religion to play a more robust role in American politics. This moderating impulse has been shaped by the discrimination that Catholics have faced throughout U.S. history. This began to change after American Catholics came into their own after Al Smith's presidential bid in 1928 and especially after John F. Kennedy's ascension to the White House in 1960. Kennedy's campaign not only mobilized Catholics to vote in unprecedented numbers, but it also persuaded them to give him more than 80 percent of their vote.

However, since Kennedy's election, Republicans have steadily chipped away at the Democratic hold on the Party's faithful. Republicans put a Catholic (William Miller) on the 1964 presidential ticket and Ronald Reagan was able to use his father's Irish Catholic background and Hollywood movie star role as the Notre Dame football star Knut Rockne (i.e., "the Gipper") to carve into the Catholic vote, a community's whose negative attitude toward Soviet "atheistic-communism" was matched only by the Gipper's. These factors, along with concerns about the civil rights movement, their rising economic and social status, and a revitalized Catholic hierarchy that opposed the Equal Rights Amendment, abortion, and homosexual relations, prompted a small but growing number of Catholics to self-identify as politically independent or Republican, Leege argues.

Buoyed along by Bill Clinton's progressive political agenda and widespread Catholic support, the Democratic Party was caught off guard by George W. Bush's political campaign, which successfully tapped into Catholic-sounding rhetoric like "compassionate conservatism" and its deeply held religio-social views on abortion and same-sex marriage to win the White House in 2000 and again in 2004. Bush proactively promoted faith-based initiatives and a limited partnership between the government and religious charities and social service agencies. He defined his policies in a language that resonated with Catholic sensibilities and persuaded Catholic leaders and organizations to adopt his partisan programs. This has made it very difficult for Democrats to secure their once decisive political advantage over Republicans. As a result, Leege argues that the Catholic vote will go to the political party that "out-analyzes, outsmarts, and out-hustles" their opponent.

Leege's analysis highlights the fact that Democrats came out of the 1990s too confident in their political and moral platform and underestimated the conservative Republican political ground game and mobilization strategy. These factors along with the perception by many Catholics that the Democratic Party was increasingly controlled by radical leftist ideologues that would not make room for pro-life Democrats like Bob Casey from Pennsylvania to speak at the national convention prompted many Catholics to shift their party allegiances. At the same time this was happening George W. Bush was working at top speed to reach out to the Catholics by having three meetings with the Pope during his first term. Although he received a number of stern rebukes for his aggressive foreign policy in Iraq, the larger perception was that Bush was friendly toward Catholics that largely supported many of his conservative social views. These factors, along with growing working-class Catholic support for Republican presidential candidates, do not bode well for the Democratic Party because they reinforce the perception that its working-class constituency is moving away from the party despite its consistent working-class message.

The growing secularization of the Democratic Party constituency between 1992 and 2004 is underscored in Lyman Kellstedt's analyses in chapter 4 on seculars and the American presidency. He argues that secular-minded voters—a group that gave a large segment of their vote to Ronald Reagan in the 1980s—are fast becoming a growing and powerful lobby in the Democratic Party. In 2004, they made up one-sixth of all Democratic voters.

Despite this shift, Kellstedt argues that scholars and politicians have inadvertently inflated the size of this constituency because it assumes that all nonreligiously affiliated Americans are secular or have no religion. Kellstedt found this problematic because not all of the four identifiable clusters of people in the group often described as secular or having no religion (atheists/agnostics, nonreligious affiliated, nominally religious, and religious unaffiliated) are in fact secular or without a religion. He found that although all four subgroups differ religiously and politically, the fourth group (religious but unaffiliated) differed so much from the other three groups that it is really inaccurate to include them in categories like "secular" or "nonreligious" because their religious identity, beliefs, and practices are very similar to the religious segment of the American population. This misclassification is based on the common practice by social scientists to use church attendance as the primary indicator of religious identity rather than beliefs and behavior, which Kellstedt believes are a much more accurate way to ascertain the religious identity of the American people.

He also argues that lack of church attendance does not necessarily imply lack of religious belief, behavior, and identity, because a person can believe fervently in God or a religion without attending religious services for numerous reasons. If the religious unaffiliated really do share more characteristics with the religious population than with seculars, then talk about growing secularization along with its political consequences in American presidential politics and civil society needs to be reanalyzed. The argument is further problematized because the religious unaffiliated segment of this group tend to be young, southern, mostly female, low income, and with a relatively high percentage of nonwhites—all variables that tend to favor high levels of religiosity and in some cases (e.g., southern, low income) Republican Party identity. In light of these factors, Kellstedt proposes a new classification for seculars and nonreligious that excludes religious unaffiliated. After controlling for this new classification, he found that the nonreligious unaffiliated, the nominally religious, and atheists/agnostics are all strongly Democratic in partisanship and voting behavior.

Kellstedt contends that there has been undeniable growth in the number of Americans that self-identify as secular or nonreligious, possibly due to the negative reaction to the rise of the Christian Right or because a small but growing number of mainline Protestants may now be self-identifying as nominally religious or some similar category. The first three secular groups do in fact hold liberal positions on church and state and moral issues. Seculars and nonreligious have to be taken very seriously by the Democratic Party because they make up a sizable segment of the U.S. population. They are as numerous as mainline Protestants or Euro-American Roman Catholics. The fact that seculars voted overwhelmingly for John Kerry also underscores their critical role in presidential politics. However, the three factors that potentially undermine their political strength are their lower voter turnout, mobilization difficulties due to their highly independent nature and lack of readily accessible mobilization sites, and because a significant segment are not as secular as previously believed.

Although it is a longstanding sociological fact that women tend to be religious at a higher rate than their male counterparts, Katherine Stenger found in chapter 5 on women, religion, and the American presidency that higher rates of religious affiliation do not automatically translate into Republican Party identity or presidential support on Election Day. She found that both religious women and nonreligious women gave a majority of their vote to Democratic candidates in 1992, 1996, 2000, and 2004, while religious men gave Republican candidates a majority of their vote in 1980, 1984, 1988, 1996, 2000, and 2004—only in 1992 did men give a Democratic candidate—Bill Clinton—a majority of their vote. Despite the seeming uniformity for Democratic candidates, when broken down further by Protestant, Catholic, Jewish, and other women, Stenger found that Protestants voted Republican, while Catholic, Jewish, and other women voted Democrat in 2000 and 2004. Although it might be easy to assume that this is because they are tied to religious and political conservatism, she also found that Protestant women supported Clinton in 1992 and 1996.

Women tend to vote differently than men. They also tend to vote for Democratic candidates at all levels of religious commitment. On matters of sex and faith, religious women hold views similar to their male counterparts in order to balance these two otherwise seemingly inconsistent parts of their lives. Thus, while a woman might hold conservative moral views, she may still swing over and vote Democrat. Women's political groups like Concerned Women for America, Eagle Forum, Catholics for a Free Choice, Church Women United, the National Council of Jewish Women, and the Muslim Women's League help to facilitate political empowerment and expression for both liberal and conservative religious women. These groups wield considerable symbolic and real influence.

Stenger's research challenges the notion that religious conservatism among women necessarily translates into Republican Party gains as Bill Clinton won a majority of religious women in the 1990s. She also shows the importance of women's religious organizations in empowering women and platforming their issues in American presidential politics.

David Dalin notes a similar influence of religious organizations and communal spokespersons in chapter 6 on Jews and the American presidency. He argues that the relationship between Jews and the American presidency is more than two centuries old and stretches all the way back to George Washington's affirming letter to the Jews of Newport, Rhode Island, in 1790. Although Jews were appointed to various ambassadorships and administrative posts in the nineteenth century and the early twentieth century, it was under Franklin Delano Roosevelt that presidential ties to the Jewish community reached unprecedented proportions—15 percent of his top-level appointments were Jewish despite constituting slightly more than 2 percent of the U.S. population. Dalin points out that Jimmy Carter and Bill Clinton appointed many Jews to national posts, cabinet positions, and the U.S. Supreme Court. Despite this fact, Republican presidents have been able to win a large segment of the Jewish vote. Ronald Reagan, for example, took 40 percent of the Jewish vote in 1980. This was due to the fact that Reagan was a staunch supporter of the State of Israel and because of his support for the Jews suffering in the Soviet Union. Reagan also appointed Jewish conservatives like Elliot Abrams, Paul Wolfowitz, and Richard Perle to high-level administration posts. The inroads that Reagan made into the Jewish community were largely washed away by Bill Clinton in 1992, after he took 80 percent of the Jewish vote. He was a strong supporter of the State of Israel, a close friend of Yitzhak Rabin, and the architect of the Oslo Peace Accords. President George W. Bush has been able to gain modest Jewish support, capturing 27 percent of the Jewish vote in 2004, although nowhere near the level of support enjoyed by Reagan.

The American Muslim community has undergone significant shifts in party preference between 2000 and 2004. In chapter 7 on Muslims and the American presidency, Brian Calfano, Paul Djupe, and John C. Green note that the Muslim community went from giving George W. Bush a plurality of its vote in 2000 (48 percent to Gore's 36 percent) to a minority of its vote in 2004 by an overwhelming margin (82 percent to 7 percent). This was the direct result of how Muslims perceived his handling of 9/11 and his decisions to invade Afghanistan and Iraq, which many Muslims interpreted as a war on Islam rather than a war on terrorism. Despite Bush's statements that "terror is not the true faith of Islam" and that "we welcome Islam in America," many Muslims saw these statements as a political ploy to secure their support. Interestingly enough, when broken down by race and nationality, Bush's support in 2000 was not unanimous across these variables as African American Muslims gave Al Gore rather than Bush a decisive majority of their vote, the only large segment of American Muslims to do so. Bush did well among other Muslims in 2000 not only because his pro-family traditional values message rang true in the community, but also because Gore chose as his running mate Senator Joseph Lieberman, an Orthodox Jew. The dramatic shift in Muslim political allegiance and voting patterns reveals the community's responsiveness to American foreign policy, racial profiling, and the growing intolerance toward Muslims, which many believe could have been avoided if Bush had reached out to Muslims more convincingly right after 9/11. The importance of Muslims is not only symbolic, but also very concrete as Muslims tend to congregate in key electoral rich states such as New York, Florida, Illinois, Michigan, Ohio, and California. Although 9/11 served as a rallying point for Muslim political mobilization and action much like John F. Kennedy did for Catholics and Jimmy Carter did for Evangelicals, Calfano, Djupe, and Green's study also reveal some of the fault lines and differences in ideology, and in voting patterns by region, race, gender, and country of origin.

So Young Kim points out in chapter 8 on the Asian Americans, religion, and the American presidency that Asian American Muslims followed their co-religionists in 2000 by giving George W. Bush a majority of their vote. In fact, they were the only Asian American group not to give Al Gore a majority of its vote. The rest voted Democrat by decisive margins. She points out that although the Asian American community is very religiously and culturally diverse, individual ethnic groups tend to be dominated by a single religion. Only 52 percent of Asian Americans self-identify as Christian (versus 76 to 82 percent of the U.S. population), 20 percent as secular or no religion, and the remaining 28 percent as practitioners of other world religions or traditions. Despite this religious diversity, many ethnic groups tend to be overwhelmingly associated with one religious tradition. Filipino and Korean communities are overwhelmingly Christian (89 percent and 85 percent, respectively). Kim argues that the high levels of secularism and immigration explain why Asian American political participation is lower than some other voting constituencies. For example, 37 percent of those who profess no religion also did not identify with a political party—something only true for 10 percent of nonbelievers nationwide. The high level of no religion in the Asian American community is in part driven by Chinese (almost 50 percent nonreligious) and Japanese (28 percent nonreligious) Americans.

Although Asian Americans, like other racial-ethnic minorities, tend to vote Democrat in the aggregate, Kim also found that political party identity and voting patterns differ significantly when broken down by ethnic or national subgroups. Furthermore, she found that 43 percent of Asian Americans said they were Democrat rather than Republican (17 percent) and 68 percent voted for Al Gore over George W. Bush (32 percent). She found that pan-ethnic Asian identity was positively linked to greater levels of political activism, although they are not more uniquely linked to the Democratic or Republican parties. Finally, she found that there was a strong positive relationship between pan-Asian identity and political interest and integration. The dominance of a single religion among some Asian American ethnic groups is a double-edged sword because it makes potential coalition building across ethnicities and national origin difficult. This kind of coalition building is also undercut by the high percentage of Asian Americans who self-identify as secular or as having no religion. Whether or not a refinement of this category would change these outcomes is uncertain, but possible. Regardless, the fact that a number of Asian American ethnic groups practice primarily one religious tradition also creates a certain level in internal cohesion that may allow them to exercise targeted and strategic political influence. Despite the limitations of pan-ethnic political cohesion, Asian Americans do tend to vote Democrat, as we saw in

2004 when exit polls indicated that they gave Kerry 56 percent of their vote compared to Bush's 44 percent.

This kind of pan-ethnic political diversity was not the case among African Americans who, as Melissa Harris-Lacewell points out in chapter 9 on African Americans, religion, and the American presidency, remain tied almost exclusively to the Democratic Party. She argues that the black church operates as a kind of "cultural training ground" for cultural norms that are later strategically employed in political action, decision making, and discursive ideological formations. These cultural norms are rooted in the community's Old Testament prophetic notions of social justice and equality, the "standard by which black America judges American presidents." For this reason, she argues that black religion mediates the relationship between African Americans and the presidency. This relationship between black intellectual and religious leaders and the American presidency has often manifested itself in the jeremiad tradition, which has been powerfully articulated by African American social prophets like Frederick Douglass. African Americans remained faithful to the Party of Lincoln until Franklin D. Roosevelt because of Lincoln's strategic emancipatory decisions and because they resonated with Lincoln's profuse use of scriptural allusions and moral critiques of the injustices of American society.

The inroads that FDR and especially Eleanor Roosevelt made were solidified by the work of Lyndon B. Johnson's historic voting and civil rights acts of 1964 and 1965. Franklin D. Roosevelt took 76 percent of the black vote in 1936, and African Americans have given 85 percent of their vote to the Democratic candidate since mid-century. This process of political solidification was spurred on by Johnson, who functioned in the black community like an Old Testament prophet. His prophetic moral language spoke truth to power by calling for dramatic social change. Bill Clinton's strategic outreach to African Americans along with his socially broken upbringing and ease in mixing with black culture led Toni Morrison to call him the nation's first black president. This commitment to Clinton resulted in his receiving 97 percent of the black vote in 1996 and Gore receiving 91 percent in 2000. Although Bush took 12 percent of the black vote in 2004 versus Kerry's 85 percent, Harris-Lacewell argues that this does not reflect any major shift in African American political allegiances but rather simply a return to the historic percentages Republicans received in the 1990s when even Dole took 16 percent against a popular second term Bill Clinton.

Harris-Lacewell argues that church-based political discussions have been an important variable in shaping political mobilization and guidance historically, as almost half of African Americans said that clergy members talked about the need for political involvement and almost a quarter reported helping in voter registration, giving a ride to the polls on election day, giving money to a political candidate, and attending a campaign fundraiser. Harris-Lacewell ends by arguing that the black community is shaped by two powerful impulses that may be at a crossroads: the progressive communitarian and Social Gospel movement that birthed the civil rights movement and the highly individualistic prosperity Gospel of the megachurches that emphasize individual rather than community empowerment. This shift in African American religiosity and spirituality may have a profound impact on the future of black political thought.

In a similar vein, Gastón Espinosa argues in chapter 10 on Latinos, religion, and the American presidency, that the growth of Latino Catholic and transdenominational Latino Evangelical and Pentecostal spirituality in the United States has influenced political partisanship and voting patterns. He found that the Latino Protestant community has blossomed to 8.8 million people in 2004, 88 percent of whom are born-again and 64 percent Pentecostal or Charismatic. All of this may help explain why Latino Protestant political support for George W. Bush grew by over 31 percentage points between 2000 and 2004. He points out that although Latinos have historically voted for Democratic presidential candidates across denominational and religious lines, the growth of conservative Christianity has given birth to a realignment among the once solidly Democratic Latino Protestant community, which in 2004 gave Bush a decisive majority of its vote. However, Latino Catholics that self-identified as born-again and/or Pentecostal, Charismatic, or Spirit-filled did not break from the traditional Latino Catholic voting patterns, except in a few cases but not to any significant degree.

Despite the fact that being born-again and Charismatic did not greatly alter Latino Catholic voting patterns, as an overall aggregate Latino Catholic support for the Democratic candidate did slip by seven percentage points between 2000 and 2004. However, not too much should be made of this because the Latino Catholic community still overwhelmingly voted for John Kerry in 2004. Still, the combined shifts in Latino Protestant and Catholic votes may have helped George W. Bush receive 40 to 44 percent of the Latino vote, a significant increase over the 35 percent he received in 2000.

One of the major reasons why Bush was able to make inroads among both Latino Protestants and Catholics is due to his systematic outreach efforts to both communities before, during, and after his presidential campaigns in 2000 and 2004. He did this through his faith-based initiatives, constitutional amendments to define marriage as a covenant between a man and a woman, promotion of family values, and more recently—and controversially—his promotion of comprehensive immigration reform, which resulted in a backlash by many conservative Republicans. Although Clinton made major efforts to reach

Latinos, Bush worked harder than any previous American president to attract, court, and win over Latinos in the faith community. He targeted not only Latino Catholic leaders, but also Latino Pentecostal, Evangelical, and mainline Protestant faith-based activists, clergy, and denominational leaders. His decision to target these communities between 2000 and 2004 helps explain why there was a dramatic shift in some of their voting patterns in 2004.

Many of the shifts in the 2004 election set the stage for Barack Obama's stunning victory in 2008. In chapter 11, Espinosa argues that Obama beat John McCain by increasing his margin of victory over John Kerry's 2004 results in almost every major religious and racial-ethnic minority group by 4 to 14 percentage points. Although Obama's economic recovery plan and hopeful optimism proved critical in helping people vote for him on Election Day, there was no single factor that explained his victory, although the economy came as close as any. Instead, his victory was due to his more persuasive plan for economic recovery, aggressive outreach to Catholics, Evangelicals, Latinos, and people of all faiths and none at all, and outreach to Latinos in key swing states. It is also due to the fact that he publicly supported traditional marriage (thus implying in the minds of many moderates and conservatives that he did not support gay marriage). This enabled him to thread the moral needle by splitting the two moral issues that often influence religious voters.

CONCLUSION

This book highlights a number of important developments and trends over the past forty years. Taken as a whole, these analyses offer a window into the dynamic changes taking place in the relationship between race, religious pluralism, women, and the American presidency. They demonstrate the subtle (Catholic, mainline Protestant) and momentous (Muslim, Latino Evangelicals) realignments that took place in 2004 and challenge a number of counterintuitive assumptions and findings in past research. These studies also reveal the important role that religion plays in shaping presidential campaigning, politics, and public policy. They also show why it would be unwise for future American presidential candidates and politicians to write off any religious or secular constituency because many of them are fluid and open to generational realignment. While these changes in presidential voting patterns may seem minor in some cases, given the remarkably close margins of victory in the 2000 and 2004 elections, even minor shifts in these constituencies can, as we have already seen, decide the next American president.

Ronald Reagan gives "Evil Empire" speech at the National Association of Evangelicals (NAE) Convention, Orlando, Florida, March 8, 1983.

Chapter 1

Evangelicals and the American Presidency

Corwin Smidt

Over the past two centuries, astute observers have noted the unique role of religion in American society. Alexis de Tocqueville, for example, wrote about the distinctive religious character of the American people upon his arrival in the United States in the early decades of the nineteenth century. Nor was he alone. Other European visitors throughout the last century also remarked about the religious nature of the American people. Even today, the religious beliefs and practices of the American people remain unique when compared to other Western industrial societies.

Moreover, not only is the role that religion plays in the nation relatively unique, but so also are its political consequences. If religion was simply something reflecting some relatively arbitrary preference or "taste" (e.g., whether one might simply prefer television sitcoms or soaps), then religion, despite its distinctive nature, could be ignored politically. However, the religious characteristics of the American people shape the way in which the American people think and act politically. And religion continues to play an important role in American politics, shaping expectations related to the kind of presidential candidates Americans are willing to support, the appropriateness of religious discussion within presidential campaigns, and the particular candidates for whom they ultimately cast their ballots.

This chapter examines the changing nature of how evangelical Protestants have related to the American political system since the celebration of the American bicentennial, particularly as the political system is symbolized in the occupant of the presidency. It seeks, first of all, to describe briefly the historical evolution of evangelical Protestantism as a religious tradition within American society. It addresses the changing nature of political engagement among evangelical Protestants over the past decades, and it examines the way

1

in which evangelical Protestants have related to American political parties, particularly in terms of their candidates for the office of the presidency.

EVANGELICAL PROTESTANTISM
AS A RELIGIOUS TRADITION

Evangelical Protestantism embodies a relatively continuous, deeply rooted, and fairly unified religious tradition within American political life.[1] It has been shaped by, and drawn from, a variety of religious movements with differing religious emphases (e.g., pietism, revivalism, and fundamentalism). However, at its core, evangelical Protestantism has represented that form of Christianity that affirms personal salvation through Jesus Christ, that calls individuals to conversion by turning from their old selves to being "a new creature in Christ," and that regards the Bible to be the final authority concerning all matters of faith and practice.[2]

In certain ways, evangelical Protestantism can be viewed to have preceded mainline Protestantism as well as to have arisen out of, or in response to, mainline Protestantism. During the nineteenth century, evangelicalism constituted the dominant religious expression in America,[3] as "white evangelical Protestants constituted the largest and most influential body of religious adherents in the United States."[4] In fact, evangelicalism's ethical and interpretative system permeated American culture to such an extent that it has been argued that "the story of American evangelicalism is the story of America itself in the years 1800 to 1900."[5] Thus, there has been an evangelical Protestant tradition within American religious life for several centuries, and it continues to exist today.

A division of American Protestantism into evangelical and "mainline" wings began to develop after the Civil War. These divisions did not take full institutional shape until the 1920s, when the fundamentalist-modernist debate ultimately led to denominational splits in the wake of the theological divisions associated with that debate. At that time many evangelical Protestants left historic denominations (e.g., the Northern Presbyterian Church) and formed new (e.g., the Orthodox Presbyterian Church), and what they deemed to be more orthodox, churches and denominations. In so doing, evangelical Protestants located themselves largely outside the mainstream of American society, a move that "greatly weakened the public presence of evangelicalism."[6]

Actually, the first wave of denominational splits that occurred within American Protestantism transpired prior to the Civil War, as many major Protestant denominations split regionally between the North and South over the issue of slavery. During Reconstruction and the first decades of the twentieth century, denominations in the South remained fairly theologically conservative and were less internally embroiled in the fundamentalist-modernist controversy. Thus, when the fundamentalist-modernist conflict led to denominational splits in the 1920s, it did so primarily in the North.

As a result, evangelical Protestantism was, from roughly 1925 to 1975, largely removed from the public eye. In part, this was a function of the fundamentalist strand of evangelicalism that advanced "separation" from the world, but it was also the consequence of the major effort at building an institutional infrastructure on the part of those who had withdrawn from the major denominations. During this period of time, fundamentalist and fundamentalist-oriented Evangelicals engaged in the construction of a growing number of self-contained networks of churches, book publishers, Christian colleges, Bible schools, seminaries, and radio broadcasters.[7] These efforts remained largely out of sight of the popular press, as did the rapid growth during the 1930s and 1940s of several evangelical denominations, such as the Southern Baptist Convention and the General Council of the Assemblies of God. In 1942, various religious leaders founded the National Association of Evangelicals in an effort to promote interdenominational cooperation within their ranks. During this same period of time, fundamentalists and Evangelicals began to seek and establish new connections with a number of smaller, largely ethnically-based immigrant denominations. Following World War II, these efforts began to produce fruit in evangelical efforts to forge institutional linkages across the vast denominational domain within American religious life.[8]

Still, in many ways, the American society in which fundamentalists lived was hardly threatening to their way of life. They continued to benefit indirectly from the legacy of the generic Christian culture that Protestants had labored to establish in the nineteenth century and that many mainline Protestants sought to keep patched together in the first half of the twentieth century. Prayer and Bible reading were permitted and practiced in public schools. The practice of abortion was illegal. The domestic role of women within family life was still held as the ideal. Even as late as the 1950s, the American government continued to practice what many religious conservatives now seek in politics today—namely, the upholding of standards of public decency and traditional values. Thus, if evangelical Protestants were not very politically active during the first half of the twentieth century, it was, in part, because they hardly needed to be.[9]

Building upon the institutional foundations established earlier, evangelical institutions began to flourish during the 1970s. The number of Christian schools increased, enrollment in evangelical colleges climbed, circulation of evangelical periodicals grew, and the production of radio and television programs sponsored by Evangelicals multiplied.[10] And, partly as a result of these changes, evangelical Christianity rose to a position of central importance within American Protestantism.[11]

Nevertheless, despite their growing institutional strength, Evangelicals continued socially to be somewhat less educated, less urban, and less affluent than Americans as a whole. Despite the social status they generally shared, evangelical Protestants continued to be divided politically. Evangelical Protestants in the South, given the region's post–Civil War political culture, continued to be predominantly Democratic in terms of their partisanship. Evangelicals in the North were somewhat less middle-class than mainline Protestants within the region, and they were more divided politically—leaning Democratic, but including a fair number of Republicans within their ranks.

Still, despite these social and political continuities, the number of Evangelicals seemingly had grown following World War II. As early as 1972, it had become evident that membership in "mainline" churches had been declining while membership in "conservative" churches had been growing,[12] and only a decade later, such evidence had become an undisputed sociological fact.[13]

These religious developments held several important political consequences for evangelical Protestants. First, while the fundamentalist-modernist controversy may have moved many Evangelicals to withdraw from cultural engagement in the middle portion of the twentieth century, there was an earlier, and longer, tradition of evangelical engagement with American political and cultural life. As a result, within the evangelical "cultural toolbox," there was a richer and deeper heritage from which Evangelicals could draw should they choose to become politically engaged once again.

Second, evangelical Protestants were a sizable constituency found in all regions of the country, though largely concentrated in the historic Bible Belt of the South and Midwest. Their size made them a potentially important voting bloc within American electoral politics, while their concentration made them potentially important in helping to deliver, given the "winner-take-all" system of voting in terms of a state's electoral college votes, a large number of electoral college votes to some presidential candidate on Election Day.

Third, despite this potential, there was much to preclude evangelical Protestants from being a politically significant bloc of voters. Evangelicals were institutionally fragmented into a myriad of distinct denominations and independent congregations. This decentralization and lack of organizational hierarchy created communication difficulties and made them hard to organize and mobilize politically.

Fourth, in addition to their institutional fragmentation, evangelical Protestants were hard to mobilize politically for other reasons—namely, the response of cultural withdrawal and disengagement tied to the fundamentalist-modernist controversy. This emphasis on cultural withdrawal and the pessimistic dispensationalist eschatology of Christ's Second Coming among the separatist fundamentalists in the North, coupled with one-party dominance in the South, moved many evangelical Protestants to be relatively passive in terms of their political engagement.

And finally, not only were evangelical Protestants relatively passive politically, they were also somewhat divided in terms of their partisanship. Evangelical Protestants in the South were predominantly Democratic politically. But their counterparts in the North were much more divided politically, as their ranks contained fair numbers of both Democrats and Republicans.

EVANGELICAL PROTESTANTISM AND THE AMERICAN PRESIDENCY: POST-1975

Given these particular characteristics among evangelical Protestants between roughly 1925 and 1975, what changes are evident within their ranks when one examines their political attitudes and behavior over the last quarter-century prior to the turn of the millennium? To what extent and in what ways have evangelical Protestants grown as a political force within American politics? Have such changes occurred gradually or rather dramatically? And how, if at all, are current patterns likely to change in the future?

In order to address these questions, we examine data drawn from the National Election Study's cumulative election file. These data are based on national election surveys conducted during each of the presidential election years since 1948, though the analysis of this paper is limited to the surveys conducted between 1972 and 2000. In order to make the analysis of these data more manageable, and to reduce some of the distinctiveness of particular elections, the national elections survey data are averaged together by decade.

Finally, since any changes among Evangelicals must be understood in relationship to changes evident within the ranks of other religious traditions, the analysis is based on comparing evangelical Protestants to the other major religious traditions within American society. Historically, members of six major religious traditions have dominated American political life: evangelical Protestants, mainline Protestants, black Protestants, Roman Catholics, Jews, and the religiously unaffiliated (the relatively secular component of the American electorate). Consequently, the patterns found among evangelical Protestants will be examined in light of the patterns found within these five other religious traditions.

Size and Growth of American Evangelicalism

One important characteristic contributing to the political significance of any social group relates to the size of that group. Obviously, everything else being

Table 1.1: Size of Religious Traditions over Time

Religious Tradition	1972–1980	1984–1988	1992–2000
Evangelical Protestant (whites only)	19.5%	20.0%	20.2%
High Attend*	*12.7*	*13.1*	*14.4*
Low Attend**	*6.8*	*6.9*	*5.8*
Mainline Protestant (whites only)	26.0%	20.9%	18.3%
High Attend	*14.7*	*11.5*	*10.4*
Low Attend	*11.3*	*9.4*	*7.9*
Black Protestant	7.7%	9.9%	10.4%
Roman Catholic (whites only)	19.3%	16.5%	17.2%
High Attend	13.1	11.2	11.9
Low Attend	6.2	5.3	5.3
Jewish	1.7	1.8	1.5
All Others***	5.6	8.9	11.0
Unaffiliated/Secular	21.1	21.9	21.4

Source: NES Cumulative File
* High church attendance = every week/once or twice a month.
** Low church attendance = seldom/never
*** This category includes Hispanic Catholics and Protestants, black Catholics, and
   Mormons, as well as numerous smaller groups.

equal, the larger the group, the more important it is politically. As can be seen in table 1.1, evangelical Protestants constitute, at the turn of the millennium, a sizable segment of the American electorate. They comprise about one-fifth of the electorate. But the relative size of evangelical Protestants is no greater than the size of the religiously unaffiliated, as they too comprise about one-fifth of the American electorate. Mainline Protestants and Roman Catholics each constitute a little less than one-fifth of the electorate, while black Protestants today constitute about one-tenth of the electorate.

Interestingly, despite all the theoretical anticipation of a secularization of American religion supposedly inherent in modernization, the relative size of each of the major religious traditions has remained relatively stable over the past three decades. The size of the religiously unaffiliated segment of the electorate has not grown over the last quarter-century,[14] while evangelical Protestants have continued to maintain, if not increase, their size of the religious "market share" in each of the last three decades of the twentieth century.

Only mainline Protestants have declined in terms of their particular market share, as they have moved from constituting about one-quarter of the American electorate in the 1970s to less than one-fifth in the last decade of the twentieth century. This loss has largely been at the expense of a growth in the "all others" category—reflecting, in part, the growth of Hispanic Catholics and Protestants, as well as other faiths outside the Christian tradition.

Thus, as table 1.1 shows, while evangelical Protestants remain a relatively sizable religious tradition, they hardly constitute a majority of potential voters. Nor have their numbers grown as a proportion of the total electorate, though they have grown somewhat as a proportion of all Protestants. Consequently, given the overall stability of their relative size as a proportion of the American electorate, any growth in the political significance of evangelical Protestants over the past several decades hardly stems from any major growth in their relative numbers.

Social Composition and Resources of the U.S. Evangelical Community

While Evangelicals may not have grown in terms of their relative numbers, it may be that important demographic changes have occurred within their ranks. Several factors could prove to be important politically. For example, growth in educational attainment among evangelical Protestants would have important political consequences, as greater educational attainment is directly linked to increased levels of political participation.[15] Likewise, if the number of young Evangelicals is insufficient to replace older Evangelicals whose ranks become increasingly depleted due to the natural processes of aging and dying, then the number of Evangelicals will decline, perhaps quickly so, with generational change.

Table 1.2 examines evangelical Protestants, along with members of the other major religious traditions, in terms of their changing demographic characteristics over the past three decades. Such changes are traced in terms of gender and regional composition, educational attainment, and age distribution.

Evangelical Protestants have been, and continue to be, predominantly female in terms of their gender composition, as approximately three of five Evangelicals are women. In this regard, they mirror mainline Protestants, who also exhibit a similar proportion of women within their ranks and a similar pattern of stability of gender composition over time. In terms of the percentage of women within their ranks, evangelical (and mainline) Protestants stand between black Protestants and Roman Catholics, as nearly two-thirds of all black Protestants are women, while the proportion of women among white Roman Catholics diminished to nearly one-half by the close of the twentieth century. Not surprisingly, given that women tend to be more religious than men, only the religiously unaffiliated exhibit a higher proportion of men than women.

Evangelical Protestants are largely southern in terms of geographical location. Basically one-half of all Evangelicals reside in the South,[16] and this

Corwin Smidt

Table 1.2: The Social Composition of Religious Traditions over Time

Religious Tradition	1972–1980	1984–1988	1992–2000
Evangelical Protestant (whites only)			
% Female	58	60	59
% South	49	51	51
% College graduate	8	12	21
% under 40 years of age	44	46	40
% 55+ years of age	34	32	34
Mainline Protestant (whites only)			
% Female	61	60	58
% South	18	20	29
% College graduate	20	25	34
% under 40 years of age	40	37	33
% 55+ years of age	37	40	39
Black Protestant			
% Female	66	66	64
% South	58	57	65
% College graduate	5	9	12
% under 40 years of age	47	50	47
% 55+ years of age	33	28	29
Roman Catholic (whites only)			
% Female	57	58	52
% South	11	9	14
% College graduate	13	19	32
% under 40 years of age	48	49	37
% 55+ years of age	27	29	37
Unaffiliated/Secular			
% Female	48	46	46
% South	19	21	22
% College graduate	15	18	28
% under 40 years of age	50	56	48
% 55+ years of age	29	28	23

Source: NES Cumulative File

proportion has not changed over the past three decades. Only black Protestants exhibit a higher percentage of southerners within their ranks. Less than one-third of mainline Protestants reside in the South, though the proportion of southerners among mainline Protestants has grown steadily over the past three decades. Roman Catholics are relatively rare in the South, as less than one in seven reside in southern states. On the other hand, more than one in five of the religiously unaffiliated reside in the South—a region known for its religiosity.

In terms of age composition, evangelical Protestants tend to be younger than mainline Protestants and white Roman Catholics, though older than black Protestants and the religiously unaffiliated. Overall, a higher percentage of Evangelicals continue to be relatively young (under forty years of age) than relatively old (fifty-five years of age or older)—40 percent versus 34 percent in the 1990s. Thus, over the next several decades, it would appear that among those adhering to the Christian faith, the percentage of evangelical Protestants is likely to increase relative to mainline Protestants and Roman Catholics, while the percentage of black Protestants is also likely to increase relative to each of the three other Christian traditions.

Over the past three decades, evangelical Protestants have exhibited a major increase in the percentage of college graduates found within their ranks. Whereas less than one in ten evangelical Protestants (8 percent) were college graduates in the 1970s, nearly three times as many (21 percent) reported that they were college graduates in the 1990s. Thus, the current generation of Evangelicals is better educated than the preceding generation.

However, when one compares the percentage of college graduates among evangelical Protestants to the percentage of such graduates found among members of the other major religious traditions, one sees that evangelical Protestants still trail mainline Protestants (34 percent), Roman Catholics (32 percent), and the religiously unaffiliated (28 percent) in terms of their relative number of college graduates, while exceeding only the percentage found among black Protestants (12 percent). Nevertheless, while evangelical Protestants still trailed most other religious traditions, they have narrowed that educational gap considerably over the past three decades. For example, whereas the ratio of college graduates among Evangelicals to mainline Protestants was basically 1 to 2.5 in the 1970s, it was approximately 1 to 1.5 in the 1990s. And whereas the ratio of college graduates among Evangelicals to the religiously unaffiliated was 1 to 2 in the 1970s, it was basically reduced to 1 to 1.3 in the 1990s.

Clearly, education is an important political resource, as it is more closely related to voting than either income or occupation.[17] Consequently, the growth in the percentage of college graduates among evangelical Protestants holds several political implications for that religious tradition. First, increased educational attainment among evangelical Protestants could well lead to a liberalization of social attitudes, something similar to that which has occurred among other religious groups with younger and better-educated members. Second, such increased educational attainment among evangelical Protestants serves to enhance the political resources and skills at the disposal of Evangelicals, which, in turn, can facilitate increased political participation within their ranks.

But Evangelicals have another important source of political resources at their disposal, as involvement in religious institutions serves as a significant source of civic skills that foster, in turn, political activity.[18] Such an acquisition of civic skills is not a function of education, but depends on frequency of church attendance and the kind of ecclesiastical structure of the denomination of the church one attends.[19] In particular, churches that are more congregational, than hierarchical in their governance are more likely to enhance the civic skills of their participants.[20] And the structure of Evangelical denominations and independent churches tend, as a whole, to be more congregational and less hierarchical in nature than the structure of other mainline Protestant or Roman Catholic churches. Moreover, evangelical Protestants exhibit a higher level of church/religious attendance than mainline Protestants, Roman Catholics, or Jews.[21] Thus, there are various reasons to expect that the level of voter turnout among evangelical Protestants has increased over time with the reported increase in their educational attainment over the past three decades and that the level of voter turnout would be somewhat greater than what one might expect simply based on levels of educational attainment achieved.

Voting Turnout from 1976–2004

Despite the relative numerical strength of evangelical Protestants today and their enhanced political resources, as well as their increased institutional capacities, Evangelicals would hardly be a significant bloc of voter if they chose to stay home on Election Day. Hence, we turn our attention to how, if at all, the level of voter turnout among evangelical Protestants has changed over the past three decades.

In the past, the electoral clout of Evangelicals has been limited, because evangelical Protestants have been rather passive politically. Even in the 1960s they voted in lower proportions than those in most other religious traditions.[22] But beginning in the late 1970s, a new wave of evangelical political engagement seemingly began, attempting to stem the perceived moral decline in the United States. This renewed involvement was first symbolized by the election of an Evangelical, Jimmy Carter, as president in 1976, as well as by *Newsweek's* designation of 1976 as The Year of the Evangelical. Institutionally, the reinvigorated evangelical forces were represented most visibly by the Reverend Jerry Falwell's Moral Majority, formed in 1979, and later by the formation of the Christian Coalition.

For many evangelical Protestants in America, the challenges and problems that confronted American society in the late decades of the twentieth century were replete with dangers, both internal and external. In addition to "godless communism," there appeared to be growing secularism within American society. Supreme Court decisions on school prayer and Bible reading basically removed such practices from public schools. "Family values" appeared to be eroding as issues related to sex permissiveness, homosexuality, and the role of women in society began to emerge on the national political stage. And the Supreme Court decision of *Roe v. Wade* in 1973 both reflected these changes and contributed to making abortion an issue of central concern among social conservatives.

Given these social and political changes, coupled with the enhanced political resources evident within their ranks, one might anticipate that evangelical Protestants, who historically have perceived themselves as the moral custodians of the nation, would have become more politically energized over the past several decades. Moreover, few if any analysts would likely deny that Evangelicals have become more politically oriented and involved at the turn of the millennium than they had been only decades earlier. In fact, by 1984, one important analyst contended that Evangelicals had seemingly come from nowhere to express "the most visible and assertive political position in American religion."[23]

Yet despite all these considerations, there are also reasons to suspect that voting turnout among evangelical Protestants may have only increased during the 1980s, only to decline again in the 1990s. At least in the eyes of some analysts, this third wave of evangelical political mobilization in the twentieth century only ended in disillusionment,[24] as the Moral Majority and similar organizations disbanded within a few years and as President Ronald Reagan, an Evangelical favorite who often spoke at the National Association of Evangelicals (NAE) convention, proved unable or unwilling to enact a conservative social agenda.[25]

Other factors also suggest that there may well have been a downturn in Evangelical political engagement over the past several elections: some widely known evangelical leaders have seemingly called for a "political retreat" (e.g., Thomas and Dobson 1999); the once politically formidable Christian Coalition has become simply a shell of its former self; and, during the 2004 election, there were claims made that four million fewer evangelical Protestants voted in the 2000 election than had voted in the 1996 election.

As can be seen in table 1.3, the historic patterns of differential levels of voter turnout among members of different religious traditions continue, for the most part, to be evident today. In the 1970s, slightly more than one-half of white evangelical Protestants (56 percent) reported having voted on Election Day, with Evangelicals trailing mainline Protestants (68 percent), Jews (66 percent), and Roman Catholics (65 percent) in terms of their reported level of turnout.[26] In fact, the rate at which white evangelical Protestants reported that they voted hardly exceeded that reported by black Protestants (54 per-

Table 1.3: Reported Voter Turnout by Religious Traditions over Time

Religious Tradition	1972–1980	1984–1988	1992–2000
Evangelical Protestant (whites only)	56%	58%	66%
*High Attend**	*61%*	*64%*	*72%*
*Low Attend***	*49%*	*53%*	*56%*
Mainline Protestant (whites only)	68%	71%	75%
High Attend	*76%*	*80%*	*82%*
Low Attend	*60%*	*66%*	*70%*
Black Protestant	54%	57%	59%
Roman Catholic (whites only)	65%	72%	76%
High Attend	*73%*	*76%*	*82%*
Low Attend	*54%*	*65%*	*70%*
Jewish	66%	69%	79%
Unaffiliated/Secular	51%	52%	59%
TOTALS	61%	63%	67%

* High church attendance = every week/once or twice a month.
** Low church attendance = seldom/never
Source: NES Cumulative File

cent), though it did exceed the rate reported by the religiously unaffiliated (51 percent).

Moreover, over the past several decades, turnout differences have diminished only slightly across the religious landscape. It is true that the reported levels of voting rates among Evangelicals have increased by ten percentage points over the past three decades—but so too have the reported levels of voting turnout among members of other religious traditions. As a result, the rate at which evangelical Protestants report they vote today (66 percent) still tends to lag behind the reported voting rates of mainline Protestants (75 percent), Jews (79 percent), and Roman Catholics (76 percent).

The rate at which evangelical Protestants now report that they vote (66 percent) approximates the rate reported by Americans as a whole (67 percent), whereas in the 1970s evangelical Protestants trailed the national average by about five percentage points. Thus, evangelical voting turnout rates have grown only in relationship to black Protestants and the religiously unaffiliated, though much more in relation to the former than the latter. Any growth, therefore, in the political significance of evangelical Protestants over the past three decades hardly stems from their enhanced level of voter turnout in recent elections.[27] While there may have been some increase in the level of voter turnout among evangelical Protestants over the past three decades, such increases hardly seem to be sufficient to diminish the higher levels of voter turnout exhibited by mainline Protestants, Roman Catholics, and Jews.

EVANGELICAL POLITICAL PARTISANSHIP

Since the advent of the New Deal, most analysts have viewed political cleavages in the United States as reflecting economic interests, though some analysts have recently begun to suggest that the major fault line within American politics today is a cultural rather than an economic division.[28] While the roots of such a new cultural politics could be varied, the social issues that rise from such cultural conflict frequently involve important questions related to moral values and, as a result, religious factors may come to play an important role in establishing the bases of such political cleavages.

During the immediate post–World War II era, evangelical Protestants were united politically in terms of their anticommunism and anti-Catholicism, but they remained relatively passive politically and divided in terms of their partisanship. Given their anti-Catholicism at the time, the presidential candidacy of John Kennedy, a Roman Catholic, temporarily brought evangelical Protestants together in their support of Republican Richard Nixon.

The southern strategy of Barry Goldwater also led to increased Republican voting among southern Evangelicals in 1964, though likely at the expense of some Republican defections among segments of northern Evangelicals. Nixon's courting of southern voters in 1968, the presidential candidacy of the southerner George Wallace, and the more sympathetic view of the Vietnam War in the South led to continued Democratic defections and possible growing GOP presidential voting among evangelical Protestants in the South, as did the candidacy of George McGovern in 1972. Thus, as the bicentennial of American independence approached in 1976, southern Evangelicals remained largely Democratic in terms of their partisan identifications, though many had over the course of several elections defected in terms of voting for the standard-bearer of the Democratic Party.

The candidacies of Southern Baptist Jimmy Carter in 1976 and 1980 likely slowed the Republican trend among Evangelicals, as Carter was the first president since James Garfield to be a member of an "evangelical" denomination. Still, as can be seen from table 1.4, nearly two-thirds of all Evangelicals cast a Republican ballot in the three presidential elections between 1972 and 1980. This level of voting for GOP presidential candidates increased to greater than 70 percent during the 1980s, only to return during the three elections between 1992 and 2000 essentially to the same level evident during

Table 1.4: Republican Vote for President by Religious Traditions over Time

Religious Tradition	1972–1980	1984–1988	1992–2000
Evangelical Protestant (whites only)	66%	71%	65%
*High Attend**	*68%*	*73%*	*70%*
*Low Attend***	*63%*	*65%*	*48%*
Mainline Protestant (whites only)	69%	69%	54%
High Attend	*72%*	*69%*	*59%*
Low Attend	*65%*	*68%*	*45%*
Black Protestant	11%	9%	5%
Roman Catholic (whites only)	54%	55%	49%
High Attend	*54%*	*54%*	*51%*
Low Attend	*54%*	*58%*	*43%*
Jewish	35%	29%	12%
Unaffiliated/Secular	49%	55%	30%
TOTALS	57%	56%	44%

* High church attendance = every week/once or twice a month.
** Low church attendance = seldom/never
Source: NES Cumulative File

the three presidential elections between 1972 and 1980. Thus, on the basis of the data presented in table 1.4, evangelical Protestants hardly appear to have exhibited any steady increase in Republican voting over the course of the past three decades.

However, there are other means by which to assess whether or not there has been any increase in Republican partisanship among Evangelicals over the past three decades. Voting for presidential candidates tends to be relatively volatile, given the two-term restriction on the office, as the choices offered voters vary considerably from one election to the next and as voting decisions are dependent, in part, on the nature of the candidates nominated. Consequently, "downticket" voting may be a better gauge than presidential voting of the level of changing partisanship evident among religious groups over time.

There has been a steady growth in the level of GOP voting for congressional candidates over the past three decades. This increase has basically amounted to an increase of ten percentage points in GOP voting for each successive decade and, as a result, the gap in voting for GOP presidential and congressional candidates among Evangelicals has declined considerably over time. By the turn of the millennium, the percentage of Evangelicals reporting

Table 1.5:   Partisan Identification of Religious Traditions over Time

Religious Tradition	1972–1980		1984–1988		1992–2000	
	Rep.	Dem.	Rep.	Dem.	Rep.	Dem.
Evangelical Protestant (whites only)	35%	49%	45%	41%	51%	38%
High Attend*	36%	51%	50%	39%	57%	34%
Low Attend**	33%	45%	37%	46%	36%	51%
Mainline Protestant (whites only)	51%	35%	55%	37%	51%	39%
High Attend	54%	35%	59%	33%	56%	35%
Low Attend	46%	35%	49%	40%	44%	46%
Black Protestant	10%	79%	11%	79%	7%	82%
Roman Catholic (whites only)	26%	61%	37%	50%	40%	50%
High Attend	25%	62%	37%	52%	43%	47%
Low Attend	27%	57%	38%	46%	35%	54%
Jewish	23%	68%	16%	74%	12%	78%
Unaffiliated/Secular	28%	52%	34%	48%	32%	51%
TOTALS	33%	51%	38%	49%	38%	50%

* High church attendance = every week/once or twice a month.
** Low church attendance = seldom/never
Republicans and Democrats include Strong and Weak Identifiers, coupled with those Independents who reported that the Leaned toward the party.
Source: NES Cumulative File

that they had voted for GOP congressional candidates for the three elections beginning in 1992 (61 percent) was nearly equivalent to the percentage reporting that they had voted for GOP presidential candidates (65 percent).

Given these patterns in congressional voting, it is not surprising that, over the course of the last three decades of the twentieth century, evangelical Protestants moved from being Democratic to Republican in terms of their partisan identifications. As is evident in table 1.5, only one-third of evangelical Protestants claimed to be Republican identifiers in the 1970s, while a majority identified as Democrats. However, by the end of the century, a majority of Evangelicals labeled themselves as Republicans in terms of their partisan identifications, while slightly more than one-third labeled themselves Democrats. In fact, evangelical Protestants today exhibit just as strong partisan affections for the Republican Party as mainline Protestants, long the dominant religious group in the GOP, do.

What were the bases for these party shifts? Two particular factors came into play.[29] First, during the course of this particular period of time, a new and powerful divide emerged with regard to social issues, with defenders of traditional values and social roles pitted against those advocating new values and lifestyles. In many ways, differences on matters of foreign policy paralleled this cultural divide. Second, during this period of time, many Americans experienced important gains in socioeconomic standing, with members of certain historically disadvantaged groups, such as Evangelicals and Catholics, tending, relatively speaking, to gain the most.

Among Evangelicals, these two trends combined to generate increased support for the GOP, though, of the two, cultural polarization clearly mattered most. But these same trends cross-pressured some mainline Protestants and Catholics to move more toward the GOP, and others more toward the Democrats. Religiously unaffiliated voters confronted a similar situation, but as social issues (e.g., abortion and gay rights) became increasingly important in presidential campaigns, more of them moved in a Democratic direction. Certainly, various social movements served to play a role in creating these new alignments, with the Christian Right and the pro-life movements moving some voters to the one side of the political divide, and feminist, gay, and civil rights movements moving other voters to the other side of that divide. But the extent to which they shaped the scope, form, and pace of these changes is far from clear.

EVANGELICALS AND RECENT PRESIDENTS: CLINTON AND BUSH, JR.

Because evangelical Protestants constitute a substantial bloc of voters, neither presidential candidates nor presidents can safely ignore Evangelical voters without potentially damaging their candidacy or presidency. At a minimum, the presence of Evangelicals must be taken into account politically. But given the swing to the Republican Party that has occurred among Evangelicals over the past quarter-century, the political strategies of Democratic and Republican presidential candidates and presidents in relation to Evangelicals are likely to vary.

As presidential candidates, the Democratic standard-bearer and the Republican standard-bearer have slightly different tasks when courting the evangelical vote. Democratic presidential candidates are not likely, at least in the near future, to capture a substantial portion of the evangelical vote. However, election campaigns tend to be won "at the margins." Therefore, in order to enhance the likelihood of their being elected, what Democratic presidential candidates seek is simply to capture a marginally larger proportion of the evangelical voter (e.g., 3 or 4 percent) than the Democratic candidate received in the previous campaign. In addition, the Democratic candidate ideally wants to adopt positions that will activate his or her base of voters without necessarily generating a larger countermobilization against his or her candidacy based on the adoption of these particular positions. The Republican candidate, on the other hand, wants to energize his or her evangelical base and enhance voter mobilization among them while not activating broader opposition to his or her candidacy because of such endeavors.

In so doing, presidential candidates and presidents court voters through a variety of means. First, such courting can transpire through the substantive content of campaign or public speeches and through the kind of rhetoric employed within them. Second, it can occur by means of invitations extended to plan campaign strategy meetings, to visit the White House, to attend briefings, or to meet with members of one's administration. And finally, such courting can take place through policy proposals by presidential candidates and by the policy proposals and executive orders made by the president.

President Bill Clinton

President Clinton's relationship with evangelical Christians was rather rocky in nature. Certainly, some of the support that Clinton received from Evangelicals in both the 1992 and 1996 presidential elections could be attributed to the fact that Clinton was raised as a southerner within the evangelical tradition. Clinton, known for his talent as a public speaker, employed a good deal of religious language during the campaign, and on many occasions asserted that the relationship between citizens and the government was one of a "covenant," a religious concept that resonated with many Evangelicals. While many Evangelicals continued to oppose Clinton because of the public policies he proposed, Clinton nevertheless won many crucial votes among Evangelicals in the 1992 election in a three-way race, as support for President Bush was relatively soft among Evangelicals and as other Evangelicals were also attracted to the candidacy of Perot.[30] Clinton's use of religious language in the 1992 presidential campaign certainly did not hurt his candidacy among Evangelicals, and in all likelihood helped to enhance his appeal among a crucial segment of evangelical voters who may have voted for President Bush in the previous election.

After his election, Clinton tried to reach out to the evangelical community by inviting twelve evangelical Christian leaders in October 1993 to a private breakfast at the White House. Clinton not only wanted to discuss the criticisms that his administration had received from many Christian leaders, but he wanted to try to find a way in which they could address these criticisms. Among those attending were: Richard J. Mouw, president of Fuller Seminary; Tony Campolo, founder of the Evangelical Association for the Promotion of Education; Jay Kessler, president of Taylor University; Bill Hybels, senior pastor of Willow Creek Community Church; Philip Yancy, *Christianity Today* columnist; Jack Hayford, Founder of Living Way Ministries; and, Bob Seiple, president of World Vision.[31]

Another way in which Clinton tried to reach out to evangelical Christians was through certain initiatives. For example, in 1993, Clinton helped pass the 1993 Religious Restoration Act, an effort to enhance religious rights within American society. In 1996, he set up an advisory committee to the Secretary of State on religious freedom abroad, a direct response to pressure from evangelical Christians regarding the plight of persecuted Christians around the world,[32] and signed into law the Defense of Marriage Act, which states that neither the federal government nor the states are required to recognize same-sex marriages even when such marriages are recognized by another state. Likewise, Clinton sought to address evangelical concerns about public misunderstandings related to church-state separation by instructing that public reports be issued outlining what current constitutional law permitted (rather than denied) related to the teaching of religion in public schools as well as the expressions of religious faith that could legally be made, whether by teachers or by students, in public schools.[33]

Nevertheless, despite these efforts, Clinton lost ground with Evangelicals in the 1996 election, as the percentage of Evangelicals casting their vote for him dropped from 28 to 25 percent across the two elections (with Perot included in the vote totals for both elections). But whatever support that existed among Evangelicals for Clinton diminished considerably in the wake of the Monica Lewinsky scandal, which broke in 1998. Clinton did publicly apologize for the affair at the White House Prayer Breakfast on September 11, 1998, stating at one point "I don't think there is a fancy way to say that I have sinned," a clear religious assessment of his behavior.[34] Following that breakfast, Clinton appointed Evangelicals Tony Campolo and Gordon MacDonald (senior pastor of Grace Chapel in Lexington, Massachusetts) to be his spiritual counselors.

During the closing days of his presidency, Clinton also appeared in front of an evangelical audience; this time it was in August 2000 at the Leadership Summit held at Willow Creek Community Church outside of Chicago. At this gathering, Clinton permitted himself to be interviewed by the organizer of the conference and pastor of the Willow Creek Community Church, Bill Hybels, who was a friend and had served as an advisor to Clinton since he entered office. There Clinton called his affair a "terrible mistake" and indicated that "I also learned a lot about forgiveness."[35]

Clearly, Clinton's relationship with Evangelicals was fairly bumpy. To a certain extent, this was not too surprising, given that the vast majority of evangelical Christians were conservative and Republican. Though he had close relationships with certain evangelical leaders during his presidency, these ties did little to translate into support at the mass level. President Clinton made several attempts to reach out to Evangelicals, both before and after the Lewinsky scandal, though much of this effort was largely through the use of renewed religious rhetoric and certain executive actions than through major policy initiatives. Following the Lewinsky scandal, Clinton especially employed the language of redemption and forgiveness, religious language frequently employed within the evangelical community.

President George W. Bush

During the course of the 2000 presidential election, Republican candidate George W. Bush made a concerted effort to court evangelical voters. In the initial stages of his campaign, Bush sought support through meetings with selected religious leaders as he assembled a "values defense team" who were to speak vigorously "in favor of abortion restrictions, school vouchers and more interaction between church and state."[36] Bush wanted to ensure that moral issues and values, for example, abortion and his emphasis on government funding for faith-based initiatives, would serve as important factors in evangelical decisions related to voter turnout and presidential choice. Members of this team include TV preachers John Hagee and James Robison, Kay Cole James of Pat Robertson's Regent University, Catholic priest Richard John Neuhaus, and several officials with the Southern Baptist Convention (SBC), including Richard Land and Paige Patterson, former SBC president.[37]

During the 2000 presidential campaign, Bush touted his own version of Bill Clinton's "charitable choice" legislation and stressed the importance of distributing public funds to appropriate faith-based organizations that provide important social programs (e.g., job training programs, food distribution programs, and programs that provide basic medical care services). In order to mobilize religious support for this policy proposal, Bush invited a group of religious leaders to meet with him. Among those attending the meeting was Ron Sider, president of the Philadelphia-based Evangelicals for Social Action. Though Sider did not publicly endorse Bush, he did express support for Bush's faith-based initiatives.[38]

In recent campaigns, presidential candidates have increasingly visited houses of worship during the course of the campaign. Bush actually visited fewer churches than Gore during the course of the 2000 campaign, but two days prior to Election Day, Bush attended a church in Jacksonville, Florida, where he was welcomed by Rev. Billy Graham, one of the most well-known religious leaders in America.[39] Polls at the time suggested that the race in Florida was extremely close and that Florida's twenty-five electoral college votes were up for grabs. Bush hoped that some last-minute involvement from church and religious figures might help sway any remaining undecided evangelical voters in Florida to vote in favor of him. At the church meeting, Rev. Graham expressed his respect for Bush's integrity and expressed support for the candidate's views on various matters of public policy.[40]

Bush also sought to woo evangelical voters, in part, through the nature of the political rhetoric he employed. He hired Michael Gerson, a man steeped in evangelical theology,[41] to be his chief speech writer. A self-described compassionate conservative, Gerson was instrumental in crafting "a social-policy language for Bush that touches evangelical hearts without alienating the suburban soccer moms and ethnic Catholics who react negatively to hard-edged culture-war rhetoric."[42]

Bush also hired Tim Goeglein as deputy director of the White House Office of Public Liaison. Goeglein's task, in part, has been to get the president's message out to the faith community, including Evangelicals.[43] With Goeglein's help, Evangelicals were "successful in lobbying Bush to push for abstinence-first funding to combat AIDS and speak out against the persecution of Christians in Sudan."[44]

As president, Bush was active in making visits to religious centers as well as faith-based organizations engaged in public service. The purpose of these visits was, in part, both to strengthen support among moderate suburban Republicans as well as to nurture support for his faith-based initiative policies within the African American community.[45]

The White House also hosted in 2004, as it has done since 1952, a gathering for the National Day of Prayer. However, this meeting was, for the first time, broadcast all over the country on Christian cable and satellite TV outlets. Millions of viewers could thereby participate in the National Day of Prayer and watch as President Bush joined evangelical Christian and other religious leaders at the White House for the celebration. Although the National Day of Prayer Task Force does not explicitly endorse any particular candidate, it provided President Bush with the opportunity to court conservative Christians.

As the 2004 presidential campaign approached, the Bush campaign also extended invitations to a number of evangelical activists to attend regular meetings at the White House. These meetings and discussions with evangelical leaders were designed to strengthen Bush support among evangelical voters and to strategize about how best to do so during the campaign. For example, the President's chief political adviser Karl Rove led regular strategy sessions with religious leaders during the 2004 campaign, and administration officials kept in continuous contact with social conservative leaders. And during the 2004 presidential campaign, the Bush-Cheney campaign sent to conservative Christian volunteers a sheet that listed twenty-two election duties to be carried out by certain dates. Volunteers were encouraged through e-mails and political newsletters, for example, to remind church members about voting, distribute voter guides, and recruit people to volunteer for the Bush-Cheney campaign as well.[46]

THE ELECTION OF 2004

To assess the role of Evangelicals in the 2004 election, data are used from the Fourth National Survey of Religion and Politics, conducted by the University of Akron and sponsored by the Pew Forum on Religion in Public Life. This survey has two major advantages for studying the role of religion in a presidential campaign: it has a much larger sample (4,000 respondents) and more religious questions than most election polls. The preelection survey was conducted during February and March of 2004, with a postelection "call-back" conducted in the weeks immediately following the presidential election.

As table 1.6 reports, more than three-fourths of all Evangelicals who cast their ballots did so for Bush, a proportion matched by no other tradition (although black Protestants, Jews, and the religiously unaffiliated showed similarly strong support for Kerry). Mainline Protestants and Roman Catholics were much more evenly split between the candidates. Nor did evangelical Protestants confine their Republican voting to Bush in 2004, as the level of Republican voting for congressional candidates among Evangelicals (75 percent) was virtually identical to the level of voting for Bush (78 percent). Clearly, whatever personal attraction Evangelicals may have felt toward Bush appears to have been readily transferred to other Republican candidates lower on the ticket.

Furthermore, nearly two out of three Evangelicals today identify as Republicans in partisan affiliation, while only a quarter report that they identify as Democrats. No other religious tradition exhibits such strong partisan affections for the Republican Party; in fact, no other religious tradition even has a majority expressing Republican partisan identifications. Thus, Evangelicals have now clearly replaced mainline Protestants at the center of the Republican coalition.

Strong evangelical turnout was critical to the strategy of the Bush campaign in 2004. And Evangelicals clearly did turn out at the polls at a higher rate than in previous elections, as almost two-thirds reported voting.[47] However, voting rates among Evangelicals still tend to lag behind those of mainline Protestants and Jews, though they are close to those of Roman Catholics and somewhat higher than those of black Protestants and the religiously unaffiliated.

Table 1.6:   The Republican Partisanship by Religious Traditions: The 2004 Election

Religious Tradition	Bush	GOP Cong.	GOP Party Id.	Voted
Evangelical Protestant (whites only)	78%	75%	67%	63%
*High Attend**	*81%*	*78%*	*70%*	*66%*
*Low Attend***	*61%*	*62%*	*53%*	*54%*
Mainline Protestant (whites only)	50%	54%	47%	69%
High Attend	*50%*	*52%*	*45%*	*78%*
Low Attend	*50%*	*57%*	*50%*	*59%*
Black Protestant	17%	20%	11%	50%
Roman Catholic (whites only)	53%	52%	46%	67%
High Attend	*61%*	*61%*	*53%*	*73%*
Low Attend	32%	32%	35%	55%
Jewish	27%	27%	20%	87%
Unaffiliated/Secular	28%	30%	22%	52%
TOTALS	51%	51%	43%	61%

* High church attendance = every week/once or twice a month.
** Low church attendance = seldom/never
Source: Fourth National Survey on Religion and Politics, University of Akron

PARTY COALITIONS

Another way in which to assess the relations between evangelical Protestants and the contemporary American party system is to examine the percentage that Evangelicals comprise of the total votes cast for each of the standard-bearers of the two major parties, and how these percentages may have changed over time. Table 1.7 presents the data related to such an analysis, and it provides the summary statistics for each of the three decades prior to the advent of the millennium (as reflected in the National Election Study's cumulative file) as well as the results for the 2004 elections (as reflected in the Fourth National Survey of Religion and Politics conducted by the University of Akron).

Clearly, evangelical Protestants have grown in importance in terms of their proportionate contribution to the total votes received by Republican presidential candidates, while their proportionate contribution to the Democratic presidential coalition of votes has declined somewhat. Between 1972 and 1980, the votes of evangelical Protestants constituted a little more than one-fifth (22 percent) of all the votes cast for GOP presidential candidates. But that proportion has consistently increased over time to a little more than

Table 1.7: Presidential Vote Coalition by Religious Traditions over Time

Religious Tradition	1972–1980 Rep.	Dem.	1984–1988 Rep.	Dem.	1992–2000 Rep.	Dem.	2004 Rep.	Dem.
Evan. Protestant (whites only)	22%	15%	26%	12%	31%	13%	40%	12%
*High Attend**	*16%*	*6%*	*16%*	*6%*	*21%*	*6%*	*34%*	*8%*
*Low Attend***	*6%*	*9%*	*6%*	*6%*	*10%*	*7%*	*6%*	*4%*
Main. Protestant (whites only)	36%	20%	30%	18%	26%	17%	18%	19%
High Attend	*17%*	*8%*	*14%*	*8%*	*13%*	*6%*	*11%*	*12%*
Low Attend	*19%*	*12%*	*16%*	*10%*	*13%*	*11%*	*7%*	*7%*
Black Protestant	1%	16%	2%	18%	1%	16%	3%	13%
Rom. Catholic (whites only)	20%	22%	19%	20%	22%	18%	20%	19%
High Attend	*13%*	*14%*	*10%*	*12%*	*14%*	*10%*	*17%*	*11%*
Low Attend	*7%*	*8%*	*9%*	*8%*	*8%*	*8%*	*3%*	*8%*
Jewish	1%	3%	1%	3%	1%	3%	1%	4%
All Other Religions	5%	6%	7%	11%	7%	11%	10%	11%
Unaffiliated/Secular	15%	19%	17%	18%	13%	22%	8%	22%
TOTALS	100%	101%	101%	100%	101%	100%	100%	100%

* High church attendance = every week/once or twice a month.
** Low church attendance = seldom/never
Sources: 1972–2000 NES Cumulative File; 2004: Fourth National Survey on Religion and Politics, University of Akron

one-quarter (26 percent) in the 1984 and 1988 elections, to nearly one-third (31 percent) in the 1992–2000 period, and to two-fifths (40 percent) in 2004. Thus, evangelical Protestants have grown steadily in terms of their political importance to the GOP, though, at the same time, it should be noted that evangelical Protestants still contribute a sizable number of votes to the Democratic nominee for president. Even in 2004, more than one of ten (12 percent) of all votes cast for John Kerry were cast by evangelical Protestants—and this level of total support was basically equivalent to the level of total support provided Kerry by black Protestants (13 percent).

Over the same period of time, the importance of mainline Protestants, historically the core of the GOP coalition of voters, has steadily declined in terms of their overall contribution to the GOP vote total. During the 1970s, mainline Protestants contributed more than one-third of all the votes secured by the GOP nominee for president, whereas in 2004, that number had dwindled to less than one-fifth (18 percent). This overall decline is a function of two different factors: declining GOP voting coupled with the declining size of mainline Protestantism overall.

The contribution of white Roman Catholics has, interestingly, hardly changed at all since the early 1970s. White Catholics cast basically one of out every five votes for GOP candidates for president between 1972 and 1980, and they continued to do so during the 1980s and 1990s. In 2004, their proportional contribution to the GOP vote total was the same (20 percent) as it had been in the elections during the 1970s. Over the same span of time, they have also continued to contribute a relatively equivalent, and equally steady proportion, to the Democratic candidate. White Catholics provided a little more than one out of every five (22 percent) votes cast for Democratic presidential nominees in the 1970s, their contribution continued to hover around that same level during the 1980s and the 1990s, and, in 2004, white Catholics provided approximately one out of every five votes Kerry received on Election Day (19 percent).

Finally, those who are religiously unaffiliated have grown somewhat in importance as a component of the Democratic voting bloc, while they have clearly declined in importance within the Republican voting bloc. Whereas in the 1970s and 1980s, the religiously unaffiliated were a relatively important component within the coalition of voters supporting GOP candidates (15 percent to 17 percent of all GOP votes for president), their contribution to the GOP coalition of voters declined in the 1990s, and they provided less than one in ten of all votes cast for Bush in 2004 (8 percent). The overall contribution of votes provided by the religiously unaffiliated for Democratic presidential candidates has increased slightly over the same period time, so that today nearly one in four (22 percent) of all votes cast for the Democratic nominee are cast by those without any religious affiliation.

CONCLUSION

Since the mid-1970s, evangelical Protestants have moved from being a relatively passive and largely politically divided bloc of voters, to a relatively engaged, largely unified, and critical voting bloc within the American presidential elections. The growth in the political significance of Evangelicals over the past quarter-century does not stem from any major increase in the numbers of Evangelicals, or from any major increase in political resources at the disposal of Evangelicals, or from any major increase in levels of political engagement evident within their ranks. Rather, their growing political importance stems primarily from the shifting partisanship that has occurred over the past three decades, as they have moved from being fairly divided in terms of their partisan support to being largely Republican today. With this shift, evangelical Protestants have become a crucial, and core, component of the coalition of voters supporting Republican presidential candidates on Election Day.

Given the strong connections of Evangelicals to the GOP in general today, it is worth asking: What prospects do the Democrats have in wooing evangelical votes? The answer is somewhat uncertain. Nevertheless, it seems unlikely that any Republican presidential candidate who emerges in 2008 will resonate with Evangelicals quite as well as Bush has. And should those Democratic strategists who are insistent on moving the party to the cultural center ultimately win that battle and nominate a candidate in 2008 reflecting such centrism, many Evangelicals may see less reason to reject the Democratic nominee out of hand. Thus, on both grounds, one could argue that it is unlikely that Evangelicals will be as solidly Republican in 2008 as they were in 2004.

Certainly, all is not lost for the Democrats. First, evangelical Protestants comprise a sizable segment of the American electorate, and despite the general Republicanism among Evangelicals, there remains a sizable number of evangelical Protestants who vote Democratic. Even though evangelical Protestants overwhelmingly supported Bush in the 2004, it must be remembered that basically one out of every ten votes cast for Kerry in 2004 did come from evangelical Protestants. Second, election campaigns tend to be won at the margins. Democratic presidential candidates do not need to win a majority of evangelical Protestant voters; they need simply to slice off 3 or 4 percent of all evangelical voters from supporting the Republican candidate. To do so would provide an overall shift in vote totals of about 2 percent,[48] thereby moving, for example, the 51 to 49 percent vote total for Republican candidate (such as Bush in 2004) to a 51 to 49 percent vote total for the Democratic candidate.

Yet, despite such considerations, there is considerable evidence to suggest that Evangelicals will continue to be at the center of future Republican presidential coalitions. First, Evangelicals do not, as they once did, largely confine their Republican voting simply to the presidential nominee of the party, as there is virtually no fall-off in Republican voting for congressional candidates. Second, nearly two-thirds of all Evangelicals today identify themselves as Republicans. These numbers suggest that it will be difficult for Democratic presidential candidates to make significant inroads among evangelical Protestant voters in the near future. Thus, even with generational replacement of leaders within American Evangelicalism, it is likely that Evangelicals will remain at the center of the Republican presidential coalitions for some time to come.

Episcopal Priest, Rev. Billy Graham, and George H. W. Bush at St. Anne's Episcopal Church, Kennebunkport, Maine, September 2, 1990.

Chapter 2

Mainline Protestants and the American Presidency

Laura R. Olson and Adam L. Warber

The framers of the United States Constitution created three separate branches of government that share and compete for political power.[1] The president must come to terms with this constitutional reality and utilize formal and informal means of influence over the Congress and federal judiciary. One way in which presidents attempt to influence the federal policy process is by reaching out to key constituencies and earning their trust and support. Conventional wisdom holds that when a president is able to convince members of Congress that he is popular among their constituents, they should be more likely to defer to the president's wishes and enact legislation pursuant to his policy agenda.[2] However, presidents confront an array of obstacles when seeking public support, such as the extent of their own rhetorical skills, the media's coverage of their administrations, the saliency of various public policy issues, the political mood of the country, and the party composition of Congress.

During the last several decades, religion has continued to take on an important role in presidential elections. It also has shaped fundamental debates about public policy. Mainline Protestants are one of many religious groups that have participated actively in both political processes. However, our knowledge about the political relationship between mainline Protestantism—or any religious group, for that matter[3]—and the American presidency is extremely limited. Presidents are strategic actors who serve a vast constituency. Religion is just one of many political tools that presidents may use to reach specific groups of citizens in their efforts to gain public support. In essence, chief executives might incorporate religion into their "going public" strategies to bolster public support on certain public policy issues and to maintain that support for future elections.[4] Although Protestant presidents might seek to preserve their support from fellow Protestants once in office, they cannot afford to reach out exclusively to just one religious constituency. Presidential politics does not operate in a political vacuum but rather within a dynamic political environment in which the political winds in Washington can change at a moment's notice. Presidents must remain acutely aware of the influence that such an environment can have on their ability to govern. As a result, if presidents are to develop "religious strategies," they must build broad coalitions of support from people across religious traditions.

This chapter examines the relationship between American presidents and mainline Protestants since 1988. We begin by providing a historical background regarding mainline Protestantism and its general approach to politics. We proceed to analyze survey data on mainline Protestant voters to assess trends in their partisanship and presidential voting behavior in recent elections. We conclude with two case studies of direct, personal interactions between mainline Protestantism and two American presidents: Bill Clinton and George W. Bush.

THE BACKDROP: MAINLINE PROTESTANTISM IN THE UNITED STATES

Protestantism in the United States comes in three principal varieties: mainline, evangelical, and African American. The story of mainline Protestantism and the presidency—and indeed the story of mainline Protestantism and any avenue to political or social power in the United States—historically has been one of great advantage, access, and privilege. Mainline Protestants were quite hegemonic in American society over many generations; historically, many of America's socioeconomic elites have been mainline Protestants.[5]

Generally speaking, mainline Protestants today remain better educated than the general population, and they tend to occupy higher-paying and higher-status jobs than the average American.[6] These socioeconomic advantages have meant that mainline Protestants not only have access to the channels of political power in this country, but that they often occupy those channels of power themselves. Twenty-six of the forty-three American presidents have been at least nominally affiliated with mainline Protestantism. A remarkable ten of the chief executives who are classified as mainline Protestants have been Episcopalians (and 2008 Republican presidential nominee Senator John McCain would become the eleventh); six presidents have either held membership or attended services during their administrations at Presbyterian churches.

In recent decades, however, mainline Protestantism has encountered significant membership challenges. Evangelical Protestantism has thrived and emerged as a stronger religious market than mainline Protestantism for a range of reasons.[7] Roman Catholicism has flourished because of the assimilation of Catholic immigrant groups.[8] Increasing numbers of Americans also have turned to secularism, new religious movements, and non-Western religious traditions.[9] Indeed, cynics and detractors now refer to mainline Protestant denominations as "oldline" Protestantism.[10] In the last decade of the twentieth century, for example, the United Church of Christ lost 14.8 percent of its membership, while the Presbyterian Church (USA) experienced an 11.6 percent reduction in its membership.[11] Nonetheless, mainline Protestantism has not disappeared, and as Robert Wuthnow argues, it continues to exert a "quiet" influence on American society and politics.[12] Whether the membership decline facing mainline Protestants has precipitated political challenges, especially with regard to the mainline's relationship to the White House, is unclear.

THE STRUCTURE AND ORGANIZATION OF MAINLINE PROTESTANTISM

American Protestantism came to a crossroads in the 1920s with the dawn of industrialism and Darwinism. Protestants disagreed strongly about the extent to which religious beliefs ought to reconcile themselves with expanding scientific knowledge and with modernity in general. Most of the old Protestant establishment adapted successfully (and often enthusiastically) to modernity. Many traditional religious perspectives were cast aside, including literal scriptural interpretation, which drove away church members who wished to preserve established and customary worldviews.[13] Mainline Protestantism today retains this open approach to scriptural interpretation. Clergy are not seen as the authoritative or final voice on either theology or politics. This outlook is clearly exemplified by television advertisements run by the United Methodist Church since 2003 advertising itself as a denomination of "open hearts, open minds, open doors."

Approximately 18 percent of all Americans are classified as mainline Protestants.[14] These individuals are part of a religious tradition that is distinctive for its strong adherence to hierarchical denominationalism. Mainline Protestant denominations tend to feature clear lines of organization and authority, while many evangelical and African-American Protestants favor the more independent, congregational model of religious organization.

The major denominations of mainline Protestantism include the American Baptist Churches, USA; the Christian Church (Disciples of Christ); the Episcopal Church; the Evangelical Lutheran Church in America; the Presbyterian Church (USA); the Reformed Church in America; the United Church of Christ; and the United Methodist Church. American Baptists trace their roots to American frontier revivalism, much like their Southern Baptist cousins, but they diverged from Southern Baptists during the Civil War era in ways that have had long-lasting theological and political ramifications. The Disciples of Christ share the American Baptists' revivalist roots but are more theologically and politically liberal than the Baptists. The Episcopal Church is the American branch of the Anglican Church. Episcopalians, many of whom cherish high-church religious rituals, have long been more socioeconomically advantaged than other mainline denominations. The Evangelical Lutheran Church in America (ELCA) was the result of a 1987 merger of three smaller Lutheran synods that grew out of Scandinavian state churches. Its greatest numeric strength today lies in the Midwest. Despite its roots in the theological teachings of John Calvin, the Presbyterian Church (USA), is now one of the more liberal Protestant denominations in the United States. Also steeped in Calvinism is the Reformed Church in America, whose early adherents were Dutch immigrants. The most liberal mainline Protestant denomination is the United Church of Christ, which was the result of a merger of five denominations in 1957, including (ironically) the historic Congregational churches originally founded by the Puritans. Finally, the most diverse of the mainline denominations is the United Methodist Church, which began as an eighteenth-century revival movement in the Episcopal Church.[15]

MAINLINE PROTESTANTISM AND AMERICAN POLITICS

Politically speaking, mainline Protestantism is characterized by a long-standing emphasis on social justice and an equally long history of Republican voting preferences and party identification on the part of those in the pews. Many mainline Protestant laity opposed President Franklin D. Roosevelt's New Deal Coalition, in part because of mainline leaders' staunch anti-Catholicism during the first half of the twentieth century.[16] This official anti-Catholic sentiment fell away both as Catholics assimilated into American society and as mainline leaders embraced equality and tolerance. As the twentieth century progressed, the politics of mainline leaders in general grew increasingly liberal, in part because of the liberalization of mainline Protestant seminaries.[17] Scholars began identifying and evaluating a "new breed" of leftist mainline clergy.[18] Yet, for the most part, mainline laity remained solidly behind the Republican Party.

A much touted clergy-laity political "gap" emerged in the second half of the twentieth century, frustrating many liberal mainline clergy who found their rank-and-file congregation members markedly conservative and unwilling to be mobilized for social justice–oriented political causes.[19] Nonetheless, generations of mainline Protestants have agreed about the value of civic engagement despite their ideological disagreements.[20] In many congregations, social—and even political—action is not just tolerated; it is celebrated.[21]

The modernist-fundamentalist split of the 1920s gave rise to mainline Protestantism's general sociopolitical outlook.[22] It was in the 1920s that mainline Protestant denominations became associated with a movement known as the Social Gospel. The Social Gospel was a theological and political perspective that stressed structural reform—not just spiritual conversion and personal sanctification—as the best means for social change. The modernist faithful rallied to the cause of social reform, emphasizing the need to "bring the Kingdom of God to earth" by helping the poor and disadvantaged in this world, rather than bringing the people of the earth to the Kingdom of God via individual sanctification and focus on the next world.[23] Mainline Protestants favored adapting their faith to the modern world and uniformly eschewed strict adherence to traditional scriptural interpretation.

This imperative to reform society was given new life in the 1950s and 1960s when thousands of mainline Protestants, particularly from the North, linked arms with African Americans to demand justice and equality in the South.[24] This activism was anchored in a widely accepted image of Jesus Christ as a champion for the poor and disadvantaged. When northern mainline Protestants, many of whom were Republicans, went to the South to aid in the civil rights movement, they encountered a white power structure run by the Democratic Party. Thus many mainline activists retained their ties to the Republican Party while still fighting for what some perceived to be a "liberal" cause. Civil rights activism gave way to antiwar protest by mainline clergy in the 1970s,[25] which later led to organized activism against the foreign policies of President Ronald Reagan in the 1980s (e.g., fomenting rebellion against communist governments in Latin America).[26]

Since the 1980s, mainline Protestants have been less visible nationally than they were a generation ago, but they do maintain an active hand in American politics.[27] For decades each mainline denomination has staffed a national lobbying office in Washington, D.C.[28] At the state and local level, mainline Protestant political and social outreach increasingly has focused on addressing the causes and consequences of poverty on the ground.[29] Here we see the continuing legacy of the Social Gospel, with its emphasis on the high ideals of working for social justice, being actively involved in secular society, and addressing the problems of the less fortunate in a Christlike manner.

To some extent we are even beginning to see a drift among mainline Protestant laity toward the Democratic Party,[30] most likely as a reaction against the strong alliance between the Republican Party and evangelical Protestants in recent decades. Mainline Protestants seem to be reevaluating their ties to the Republican Party as it has come to emphasize moral issues under Presidents

Ronald Reagan and George W. Bush. Mainline Protestants traditionally have favored the economic conservatism of Presidents Dwight D. Eisenhower and Richard M. Nixon, but not necessarily strict moral conservatism. Mainline Protestants now make up an important swing constituency, even if they are not collectively mobilized as such. They remain a significant electoral force despite their declining numbers because they are well educated and have a strong commitment to civic participation (both of which make them likely voters).

MAINLINE PROTESTANTS AND
PRESIDENTIAL POLITICS, 1988–2004

We now assess mainline Protestants' recent orientations toward presidential politics at the mass level based on their party affiliation and presidential vote choice in recent presidential elections. Our analysis focuses on mainline Protestants drawn from survey data that the American National Election Studies (ANES) collected for the years of 1988, 1992, 1996, 2000, and 2004.[31] We excluded all respondents who did not identify themselves as members of one of the eight mainline Protestant denominations (the American Baptist Churches, USA; Disciples of Christ; the Episcopal Church; the Evangelical Lutheran Church in America; Presbyterian Church (USA); the Reformed Church in America; the United Church of Christ; and the United Methodist Church). As a result, we created mainline Protestant subsamples for each year's analysis.[32] It is important to note that in 1988, ANES did not include all of the questions about denominational affiliation required for precise categorization that were later added to subsequent surveys.[33] Therefore, the validity of our findings for 1988 is somewhat challenged because American Baptists and members of the Reformed Church in America were excluded, and Lutherans and Presbyterians from nonmainline denominations (primarily the Lutheran Church–Missouri Synod, the Wisconsin Evangelical Lutheran Synod, the Associate Reformed Presbyterian Church, and the Presbyterian Church in America) were included. We also employed the proper weighting procedures recommended by ANES in our data for each year.

   The first question we analyze is whether mainline Protestant partisanship and voting behavior are related to race. The results in table 2.1 show that each year's sample includes very small numbers of nonwhite respondents, as mainline Protestantism is known for being homogeneously white despite concerted efforts by denominational leaders to diversify its racial and ethnic makeup.[34] Race's high degree of salience in American politics is evident in our mainline Protestant subsamples for each of the five years, as is the case in the American population at large.[35] Specifically, nonwhite mainline Prot-

Table 2.1: Race by Party Identification and Presidential Vote Choice, Mainline Protestants, 1988–2004

	White	Nonwhite	Full Sample
1988			
Party ID***			
Republican	188 (40.1%)	3 (8.3%)	191 (37.8%)
Democrat	129 (27.5%)	20 (55.6%)	149 (29.5%)
Independent/Other	152 (32.4%)	13 (36.1%)	165 (32.7%)
Vote***			
Bush	210 (62.9%)	3 (16.7%)	213 (60.5%)
Dukakis	121 (36.2%)	15 (83.3%)	136 (38.6%)
1992			
Party ID***			
Republican	168 (40.3%)	5 (11.4%)	173 (37.5%)
Democrat	96 (23.0%)	29 (65.9%)	125 (27.1%)
Independent/Other	153 (36.7%)	10 (22.7%)	163 (35.4%)
Vote***			
Bush	129 (40.8%)	3 (10.3%)	132 (38.3%)
Clinton	108 (34.2%)	26 (89.7%)	134 (38.8%)
Perot	79 (25.0%)	0 (0.0%)	79 (22.9%)
1996			
Party ID***			
Republican	123 (42.0%)	2 (6.3%)	125 (38.5%)
Democrat	76 (25.9%)	19 (59.4%)	95 (29.2%)
Independent/Other	94 (32.1%)	11 (34.4%)	105 (32.3%)
Vote**			
Dole	107 (49.1%)	1 (5.6%)	108 (45.8%)
Clinton	101 (46.3%)	15 (83.3%)	116 (49.2%)
2000			
Party ID***			
Republican	82 (37.8%)	2 (5.7%)	84 (33.3%)
Democrat	66 (30.4%)	21 (60.0%)	87 (34.5%)
Independent/Other	69 (31.8%)	12 (34.3%)	81 (32.1%)
Vote**			
Bush	91 (52.0%)	5 (17.9%)	96 (47.3%)
Gore	84 (48.0%)	23 (82.1%)	107 (52.7%)
2004			
Party ID**			
Republican	59 (41.5%)	3 (11.5%)	62 (36.9%)
Democrat	39 (27.5%)	13 (50.0%)	52 (31.0%)
Independent/Other	44 (31.0%)	10 (38.5%)	54 (32.1%)
Vote			
Bush	61 (59.8%)	4 (33.3%)	65 (57.0%)
Kerry	41 (40.2%)	8 (66.7%)	49 (43.0%)

***p<0.001; **p<0.01; *p<0.05.
Source: American National Election Studies (ANES), 1988, 1992, 1996, 2000, 2004

estants are significantly more likely to identify as Democrats and to vote for Democratic presidential candidates. The one exception occurs in 2004, when the difference between the voting behavior of whites and nonwhites fails to attain statistical significance. This finding supports the conventional wisdom that George W. Bush did better than most recent Republican presidential candidates in attracting the votes of African Americans and Latinos.[36]

In table 2.2, we assess the role of gender in mainline Protestant political party affiliation and presidential voting behavior. Despite a well-established gender gap in American politics on the whole dating back to the presidential election of 1980,[37] mainline Protestants' partisanship and vote choice is cleaved significantly by gender only in 1988, 1996, and 2000. Surprisingly, Bill Clinton did markedly better among women in his reelection campaign than he did in 1992. This edge among mainline Protestant women did not transfer over to Al Gore in 2000—even though women were more likely to identify as Democrats that year—or to John Kerry in 2004. Many of the "soccer moms" whose votes Clinton aggressively sought in 1996 were likely mainline Protestant suburbanites.[38] The fact that neither Gore nor Kerry could maintain Clinton's advantage with this constituency is one likely reason why neither candidate won the presidency. These findings also suggest that George W. Bush became a surprisingly attractive candidate to many women voters (including those within mainline Protestantism) in 2004. By and large, the gender gap among mainline Protestants in presidential elections appears to have waned since 1996.[39]

We turn to the question of whether marital status plays a role in structuring mainline Protestants' partisanship and vote choice. Marital status might be especially important to examine because of the increased attention to homosexuality and same-sex marriage, particularly within mainline Protestantism, over the past several decades.[40] People who are married may be viewed as more traditional than those who are single, separated, or divorced.[41] For the most part, however, there are not many significant relationships between marital status and these two political variables, with the noteworthy exception of 1992, when married people were substantially more likely to identify as Republicans and to vote for George H. W. Bush. Married people again emerged as significantly more Republican in 2000, but this cleavage did not spill over into voting behavior that year.

Age is another important demographic variable that tends to structure partisanship and voting behavior in the United States. Consistent with most previous research on the generation gap, our results in table 2.3 suggest that age itself is not determinative of political orientations and presidential vote choices.[42] Instead, life-course socialization experiences are what affect people of different ages most profoundly when it comes to politics.[43] We clas-

Table 2.2:   Gender by Party Identification and Presidential Vote Choice, Mainline Protestants, 1988–2004

	Male	Female	Full Sample
1988			
Party ID**			
Republican	84 (41.2%)	107 (35.4%)	191 (37.7%)
Democrat	41 (20.1%)	108 (35.8%)	149 (29.4%)
Independent/Other	79 (38.7%)	87 (28.8%)	166 (32.8%)
Vote **			
Bush	102 (70.8%)	112 (53.6%)	214 (60.6%)
Dukakis	41 (28.5%)	95 (45.5%)	136 (38.5%)
1992			
Party ID			
Republican	82 (37.8%)	91 (37.4%)	173 (37.6%)
Democrat	56 (25.8%)	69 (28.4%)	125 (27.2%)
Independent/Other	79 (36.4%)	83 (34.2%)	162 (35.2%)
Vote			
Bush	60 (35.7%)	73 (41.0%)	133 (38.4%)
Clinton	62 (36.9%)	72 (40.4%)	134 (38.7%)
Perot	46 (27.4%)	33 (18.5%)	79 (22.8%)
1996			
Party ID**			
Republican	63 (49.6%)	62 (31.3%)	125 (38.5%)
Democrat	25 (19.7%)	71 (35.9%)	96 (29.5%)
Independent/Other	39 (30.7%)	65 (32.8%)	104 (32.0%)
Vote**			
Dole	56 (53.8%)	52 (39.1%)	108 (45.6%)
Clinton	39 (37.5%)	78 (58.6%)	117 (49.4%)
2000			
Party ID*			
Republican	42 (40.8%)	42 (27.6%)	84 (32.9%)
Democrat	36 (35.0%)	53 (34.9%)	89 (34.9%)
Independent/Other	25 (24.3%)	57 (37.5%)	82 (32.2%)
Vote			
Bush	39 (46.4%)	56 (47.5%)	95 (47.0%)
Gore	45 (53.6%)	62 (52.5%)	107 (53.0%)
2004			
Party ID			
Republican	32 (41.6%)	31 (34.1%)	63 (37.5%)
Democrat	19 (24.7%)	32 (35.2%)	51 (30.4%)
Independent/Other	26 (33.8%)	28 (30.8%)	54 (32.1%)
Vote			
Bush	31 (63.3%)	34 (53.1%)	65 (57.5%)
Kerry	18 (36.7%)	30 (46.9%)	48 (42.5%)

***p<0.001; **p<0.01; *p<0.05.
Source: American National Election Studies (ANES), 1988, 1992, 1996, 2000, 2004

sified age into four distinct life-course categories: young adults aged 18–29, early-career adults aged 30–49, late-career adults aged 50–64, and retired adults aged 65 and older. In our analysis of the relationship between age and the two political variables for mainline Protestants, few significant findings emerge except for 1992. In that election, young people were far more likely to identify themselves as Independents or affiliates of third parties, which reflects the general trend among younger Americans to eschew identification with either of the two major parties.[44] This general trend continues across subsequent election years but does not attain statistical significance.

Education and income have long been gold-standard predictors of partisanship and vote choice.[45] We examine the extent to which education and income levels differentiate among mainline Protestants in terms of their party identification and voting behavior. Historically, mainline Protestants have held higher socioeconomic status than other religious groups.[46] However, we do find some variation on both dimensions in our mainline Protestant subsamples for each of the election years. We categorized education into four categories (did not finish high school; high school diploma; some college; college degree or higher). We also stratified income levels for each of the five election years into four quartiles. The results indicate that education is significantly associated with partisanship only in 1992 and 1996 (the most educated mainline Protestants are the most Republican). Higher levels of education are also associated with greater support for Bob Dole in the 1996 presidential election, and slightly greater support for George W. Bush in 2004. Mainline Protestants of different income levels were politically distinct from one another in 1988 and 1992. These differences vanish, however, by 1996. As the twenty-first century dawned, higher-income mainline Protestants appear to have been moving away from the Republican Party ever so slightly.

In table 2.4 we turn to the question of whether region might differentiate mainline Protestants' political orientations.[47] Mainline Protestantism is not a faith tradition that historically has been hegemonic in the South,[48] so it may be the case that mainline Protestants in the South are politically distinct from their counterparts in other regions of the United States. The American South, of course, has long been politically unique,[49] and in recent years, the region has undergone a profound electoral realignment. Specifically, what was once considered the solid Democratic South is now the solid Republican South.[50] Nonetheless, the only significant finding in the entirety of table 2.4 indicates that Bob Dole did substantially better among southerners than did Bill Clinton in 1996. Southern mainline Protestants do not appear to differ substantially from their counterparts in other regions in terms of partisanship or presidential voting behavior.

Table 2.3:   Age by Party Identification and Presidential Vote Choice, Mainline
Protestants, 1988–2004

	18–29	*30–49*	*50–64*	*65+*	*Full Sample*
1988					
Party ID					
Republican	26 (36.6%)	58 (31.5%)	54 (46.6%)	52 (39.1%)	190 (37.7%)
Democrat	19 (26.8%)	55 (29.9%)	32 (27.6%)	43 (32.3%)	149 (29.6%)
Ind./Other	26 (36.6%)	71 (38.6%)	30 (25.9%)	38 (28.6%)	165 (32.7%)
Vote*					
Bush	20 (54.1%)	74 (58.3%)	64 (70.3%)	55 (56.7%)	213 (60.5%)
Dukakis	17 (45.9%)	53 (41.7%)	27 (29.7%)	39 (40.2%)	136 (38.6%)
1992					
Party ID***					
Republican	17 (21.5%)	71 (35.3%)	37 (45.1%)	48 (48.0%)	173 (37.4%)
Democrat	16 (20.3%)	59 (29.4%)	23 (28.0%)	27 (27.0%)	125 (27.1%)
Ind./Other	46 (58.2%)	71 (35.3%)	22 (26.8%)	25 (25.0%)	164 (35.5%)
Vote*					
Bush	12 (22.2%)	60 (39.5%)	31 (46.3%)	30 (41.1%)	133 (38.4%)
Clinton	21 (38.9%)	56 (36.8%)	27 (40.3%)	29 (39.7%)	133 (38.4%)
Perot	21 (38.9%)	36 (23.7%)	9 (13.4%)	14 (19.2%)	80 (23.1%)
1996					
Party ID					
Republican	12 (32.4%)	58 (38.9%)	22 (35.5%)	34 (43.6%)	126 (38.7%)
Democrat	10 (27.0%)	41 (27.5%)	22 (35.5%)	23 (29.5%)	96 (29.4%)
Ind./Other	15 (40.5%)	50 (33.6%)	18 (29.0%)	21 (26.9%)	104 (31.9%)
Vote					
Dole	8 (42.1%)	51 (48.1%)	19 (40.4%)	30 (46.2%)	108 (45.6%)
Clinton	9 (47.4%)	50 (47.2%)	27 (57.4%)	31 (47.7%)	117 (49.4%)
2000					
Party ID					
Republican	6 (17.6%)	32 (36.4%)	19 (32.2%)	22 (33.3%)	79 (32.0%)
Democrat	11 (32.4%)	33 (37.5%)	24 (40.7%)	20 (30.3%)	88 (35.6%)
Ind./Other	17 (50.0%)	23 (26.1%)	16 (27.1%)	24 (36.4%)	80 (32.4%)
Vote					
Bush	6 (33.3%)	35 (46.1%)	21 (43.8%)	30 (54.5%)	92 (46.7%)
Gore	12 (66.7%)	41 (53.9%)	27 (56.3%)	25 (45.5%)	105 (53.3%)
2004					
Party ID					
Republican	3 (30.0%)	23 (38.3%)	19 (42.2%)	17 (32.7%)	62 (37.1%)
Democrat	5 (50.0%)	14 (23.3%)	10 (22.2%)	23 (44.2%)	52 (31.1%)
Ind./Other	2 (20.0%)	23 (38.3%)	16 (35.6%)	12 (23.1%)	53 (31.7%)
Vote					
Bush	3 (60.0%)	27 (65.9%)	18 (60.0%)	17 (43.6%)	65 (56.5%)
Kerry	2 (40.0%)	14 (34.1%)	12 (40.0%)	22 (56.4%)	50 (43.5%)

***$p<0.001$; **$p<0.01$; *$p<0.05$.
Source: American National Election Studies (ANES), 1988, 1992, 1996, 2000, 2004

Table 2.4:   Region by Party Identification and Presidential Vote Choice, Mainline Protestants, 1988–2004

	South	*Non-South*	*Full Sample*
1988			
Party ID			
Republican	30 (28.3%)	161 (40.3%)	191 (37.7%)
Democrat	39 (36.8%)	110 (27.5%)	149 (29.4%)
Ind./Other	37 (34.9%)	129 (32.3%)	166 (32.8%)
Vote			
Bush	37 (56.1%)	177 (61.7%)	214 (60.6%)
Dukakis	29 (43.9%)	107 (37.3%)	136 (38.5%)
1992			
Party ID			
Republican	33 (30.3%)	140 (39.8%)	173 (37.5%)
Democrat	35 (32.1%)	90 (25.6%)	125 (27.1%)
Ind./Other	41 (37.6%)	122 (34.7%)	163 (35.4%)
Vote			
Bush	33 (41.8%)	100 (37.5%)	133 (38.4%)
Clinton	32 (40.5%)	101 (37.8%)	133 (38.4%)
Perot	14 (17.7%)	66 (24.7%)	80 (23.1%)
1996			
Party ID			
Republican	39 (37.9%)	76 (38.0%)	115 (38.0%)
Democrat	24 (23.3%)	66 (33.0%)	90 (29.7%)
Ind./Other	40 (38.8%)	58 (29.0%)	98 (32.3%)
Vote*			
Dole	43 (56.6%)	57 (39.3%)	100 (45.2%)
Clinton	30 (39.5%)	80 (55.2%)	110 (49.8%)
2000			
Party ID			
Republican	20 (29.0%)	63 (34.2%)	83 (32.8%)
Democrat	25 (36.2%)	64 (34.8%)	89 (35.2%)
Ind./Other	24 (34.8%)	57 (31.0%)	81 (32.0%)
Vote			
Bush	25 (49.0%)	69 (45.7%)	94 (46.5%)
Gore	26 (51.0%)	82 (54.3%)	108 (53.5%)
2004			
Party ID			
Republican			
Democrat			
Ind./Other	Data	Data	Data
Vote	Not	Not	Not
Bush	Available	Available	Available
Kerry			

***$p<0.001$; **$p<0.01$; *$p<0.05$.
Source: American National Election Studies (ANES), 1988, 1992, 1996, 2000, 2004

Finally we turn to two key measures of religiosity: the self-reported importance of religion in one's life and church attendance. Studies have shown that in recent years, citizens who are most involved and invested in religious communities are more politically conservative than citizens who are either nominally religious or secular.[51] Therefore, we expect to observe political differences between observant and nonobservant mainline Protestants, particularly in recent election years. Table 2.5 illustrates the relationship between religion's importance in respondents' lives and their partisanship and voting behavior. We find that by 2004, observant mainline Protestants were voting significantly more Republican than nonobservant mainline Protestants. George W. Bush did substantially better among this constituency than did John Kerry. Table 2.6 reveals a similar pattern. In 1996, infrequent church attendees were significantly more likely to vote for Bill Clinton. In 2000, infrequent attendees were significantly more likely to identify as Democrats. They also voted in larger numbers for Al Gore, although that relationship does not achieve statistical significance.

On the whole, our results suggest that mainline Protestants are emerging as a key swing constituency in American presidential politics. Each of our tables shows that mainline voters are gravitating away from the Republican Party and its candidates to some extent. Especially noteworthy is the drift of higher-income mainline Protestants toward the Democrats, which suggests a perceived difference between today's Republican Party (allied as it is with conservative evangelical Protestantism) and the economically conservative Republicanism of Eisenhower and Nixon.[52] We also see striking evidence of the "God gap" in contemporary American politics. Traditionalist mainline voters appear to be maintaining their ties to the Republican Party, while more nominal mainline voters increasingly favor the Democrats. Despite the fact that they are not mobilized as a cohesive voting bloc (as are evangelical Protestants), presidential candidates need to think about mainline Protestants strategically. Mainline Protestants are especially important politically because they participate in politics more than most other religious groups because of their comparatively high socioeconomic status and their long-standing commitment to civic engagement.

MAINLINE PROTESTANTISM AND THE PRESIDENCY: TWO CASE STUDIES—BILL CLINTON AND GEORGE W. BUSH

To what extent does mainline Protestantism exert a direct, personal influence on the American presidency? To explore this question we present two case studies of two recent presidents and their encounters—both personal and strategic—with mainline Protestantism.

Table 2.5: Importance of Religion by Party Identification and Presidential Vote Choice, Mainline Protestants, 1988–2004

	Religion is Important	Religion is not Important	Full Sample
1988			
Party ID			
Republican	141 (38.6%)	39 (41.5%)	180 (39.2%)
Democrat	113 (31.0%)	21 (22.3%)	134 (29.2%)
Independent/Other	111 (30.4%)	34 (36.2%)	145 (31.6%)
Vote			
Bush	171 (60.4%)	41 (63.1%)	212 (60.9%)
Dukakis	109 (38.5%)	24 (36.9%)	133 (38.2%)
1992			
Party ID			
Republican	125 (37.0%)	36 (39.1%)	161 (37.4%)
Democrat	97 (28.7%)	20 (21.7%)	117 (27.2%)
Independent/Other	116 (34.3%)	36 (39.1%)	152 (35.3%)
Vote			
Bush	98 (38.1%)	23 (33.8%)	121 (37.2%)
Clinton	106 (41.2%)	23 (33.8%)	129 (39.7%)
Perot	53 (20.6%)	22 (32.4%)	75 (23.1%)
1996			
Party ID			
Republican	95 (37.3%)	30 (42.3%)	125 (38.3%)
Democrat	79 (31.0%)	17 (23.9%)	96 (29.4%)
Independent/Other	81 (31.8%)	24 (33.8%)	105 (32.2%)
Vote			
Dole	89 (48.1%)	19 (36.5%)	108 (45.6%)
Clinton	89 (48.1%)	28 (53.8%)	117 (49.4%)
2000			
Party ID			
Republican	76 (35.7%)	7 (17.9%)	83 (32.9%)
Democrat	70 (32.9%)	18 (46.2%)	88 (34.9%)
Independent/Other	67 (31.5%)	14 (35.9%)	81 (32.1%)
Vote*			
Bush	86 (49.7%)	9 (30.0%)	95 (46.8%)
Gore	87 (50.3%)	21 (70.0%)	108 (53.2%)
2004			
Party ID			
Republican	55 (37.2%)	7 (35.0%)	62 (36.9%)
Democrat	44 (29.7%)	8 (40.0%)	52 (31.0%)
Independent/Other	49 (33.1%)	4 (25.0%)	54 (32.1%)
Vote*			
Bush	60 (61.2%)	4 (28.6%)	64 (57.1%)
Kerry	38 (38.8%)	10 (71.4%)	48 (42.9%)

***$p<0.001$; **$p<0.01$; *$p<0.05$.
Source: American National Election Studies (ANES), 1988, 1992, 1996, 2000, 2004

Table 2.6: Church Attendance by Party Identification and Presidential Vote Choice, Mainline Protestants, 1988–2004

	Every Week	Almost Every Week	Once or Twice a Month	A Few Times a Year	Never	Full Sample
1988						
Party ID						
Republican	42 (45.2%)	31 (40.3%)	27 (37.5%)	61 (33.7%)	30 (36.6%)	191 (37.8%)
Democrat	30 (32.3%)	26 (33.8%)	19 (26.4%)	48 (26.5%)	26 (31.7%)	149 (29.5%)
Ind./Other	21 (22.6%)	20 (26.0%)	26 (36.1%)	72 (39.8%)	26 (31.7%)	165 (32.7%)
Vote Choice						
Bush	50 (60.2%)	36 (64.3%)	29 (60.4%)	69 (59.0%)	29 (60.4%)	213 (60.5%)
Dukakis	31 (37.3%)	20 (35.7%)	18 (37.5%)	48 (41.0%)	19 (39.6%)	136 (38.6%)
1992						
Party ID						
Republican	41 (42.7%)	24 (42.1%)	22 (27.2%)	36 (41.4%)	50 (36.2%)	173 (37.7%)
Democrat	27 (28.1%)	19 (33.3%)	23 (28.4%)	18 (20.7%)	36 (26.1%)	123 (26.8%)
Ind./Other	28 (29.2%)	14 (24.6%)	36 (44.4%)	33 (37.9%)	52 (37.7%)	163 (35.5%)
Vote Choice						
Bush	33 (43.4%)	20 (40.0%)	24 (41.4%)	28 (41.8%)	28 (30.1%)	133 (38.7%)
Clinton	29 (38.2%)	19 (38.0%)	21 (36.2%)	27 (40.3%)	36 (38.7%)	132 (38.4%)
Perot	14 (18.4%)	11 (22.0%)	13 (22.4%)	12 (17.9%)	29 (31.2%)	79 (23.0%)
1996						
Party ID						
Republican	27 (42.2%)	27 (55.1%)	20 (35.7%)	27 (31.8%)	24 (33.8%)	125 (38.5%)
Democrat	19 (29.7%)	13 (26.5%)	17 (30.4%)	28 (32.9%)	19 (26.8%)	96 (29.5%)
Ind./Other	18 (28.1%)	9 (18.4%)	19 (33.9%)	30 (35.3%)	28 (39.4%)	104 (32.0%)
Vote Choice*						
Dole	24 (46.2%)	28 (68.3%)	17 (43.6%)	23 (39.7%)	16 (34.8%)	108 (45.8%)
Clinton	27 (51.9%)	13 (31.7%)	20 (51.3%)	32 (55.2%)	24 (52.2%)	116 (49.2%)
2000						
Party ID*						
Republican	27 (37.5%)	12 (34.3%)	15 (25.9%)	15 (30.6%)	14 (35.0%)	83 (32.7%)
Democrat	21 (29.2%)	9 (25.7%)	19 (32.8%)	18 (36.7%)	22 (55.0%)	89 (35.0%)
Ind./Other	24 (33.3%)	14 (40.0%)	24 (41.4%)	16 (32.7%)	4 (10.0%)	82 (32.3%)
Vote Choice						
Bush	36 (62.1%)	14 (45.2%)	17 (39.5%)	15 (38.5%)	12 (38.7%)	94 (46.5%)
Gore	22 (37.9%)	17 (54.8%)	26 (60.5%)	24 (61.5%)	19 (61.3%)	108 (53.5%)
2004						
Party ID						
Republican	15 (38.5%)	14 (42.4%)	6 (28.6%)	10 (45.5%)	17 (34.0%)	62 (37.6%)
Democrat	14 (35.9%)	7 (21.2%)	6 (28.6%)	9 (40.9%)	14 (28.0%)	50 (30.3%)
Ind./Other	10 (25.6%)	12 (36.4%)	9 (42.9%)	3 (13.6%)	19 (38.0%)	53 (32.1%)
Vote Choice						
Bush	17 (58.6%)	15 (62.5%)	11 (68.8%)	6 (40.0%)	16 (55.2%)	65 (57.5%)
Kerry	12 (41.4%)	9 (37.5%)	5 (31.3%)	9 (60.0%)	13 (44.8%)	48 (42.5%)

***p<0.001; **p<0.01; *p<0.05.
Source: American National Election Studies, 1988, 1992, 1996, 2000, 2004

A Port in the Storm: Reverend J. Philip Wogaman and President Bill Clinton

In January 1998, the American press began reporting a sexual scandal between President Bill Clinton and a former White House intern, Monica Lewinsky. Lewinsky had filed an affidavit in sexual harassment litigation that Paula Corbin Jones was pursuing against Clinton. Clinton quickly and repeatedly denied having an affair with Lewinsky, most memorably with this January 28, 1998 statement: "I did not have sexual relations with that woman, Ms. Lewinsky." After Clinton's attempt to invoke executive privilege was denied in federal court, he became the first sitting president to testify before a grand jury investigating his conduct on August 17, 1998. Immediately following his deposition in the White House, Clinton admitted to having an inappropriate relationship with Lewinsky before a national television audience. Independent counsel Kenneth Starr, who had been appointed to investigate possible wrongdoing by the president in the infamous Whitewater real estate venture in Arkansas, delivered a report to Congress in which he argued that there was "substantial and credible information that President . . . Clinton committed acts that may constitute grounds for an impeachment."[53] The full House of Representatives subsequently voted on December 16, 1998 to bring four articles of impeachment against Clinton on the grounds that he had perjured himself before the grand jury. After the Senate trial, Clinton was acquitted of all charges on February 12, 1999.[54]

Even before the Lewinsky matter became public, questions about Bill Clinton's moral rectitude had cast a shadow over his presidency. Despite such questions, Clinton had tremendous appeal to many people of faith, in part because he had grown up attending Baptist churches and could therefore offer chapter-and-verse quotations from scripture. Religion was an important part of Clinton's formative years. Clinton recounts in his autobiography that in 1955 "I had absorbed enough of the church's teachings to know that I was a sinner and to want Jesus to save me. So I came down the aisle at the end of Sunday service, professed my faith in Christ, and asked to be baptized."[55] Religion remained a vital element of Clinton's personal life after he reached adulthood and embarked on his political career.

Despite the fact that Clinton was raised as an evangelical Protestant, his early socialization experiences imbued him with the deep and abiding mainline Protestant concern for (as he writes in the dedication of his autobiography) "people [whom] others [look] down on, because we're not so different after all."[56] Once Clinton married Hillary Rodham in 1975, this Social Gospel impetus was strengthened because of Mrs. Clinton's intense lifelong involvement in the United Methodist Church.[57] In Washington, D.C., the Clintons attended Foundry United Methodist Church.[58] As Clinton notes in his autobiography, "we liked Foundry's pastor, Phil Wogaman, and the fact that the church included people of various races, cultures, incomes, and political affiliations, and openly welcomed gays."[59] Both Clintons are long-standing proponents of a politically and theologically liberal interpretation of scripture.

Given his lifelong involvement in organized religion, it should come as no surprise that Clinton turned to his faith both publicly and privately when he encountered the gravest crisis of his presidency. After the Lewinsky affair unfolded, Clinton invited three Protestant clergy—his own mainline Protestant pastor, Rev. J. Philip Wogaman; Rev. Tony Campolo, a liberal Evangelical and close personal friend; and the nondenominational Rev. Gordon MacDonald—to comprise an "accountability group" that would "counsel me at least once a month for an indefinite period . . . . They would . . . [come] to the White House together, sometimes separately. We would pray, read scripture, and discuss some things I had never really talked about before."[60]

Clinton's deep and abiding connection to mainline Protestantism is exemplified by his close relationship with Rev. Wogaman, who served as senior pastor of Foundry United Methodist Church, one of the denomination's most influential American congregations, from 1992 until his retirement in 2002.[61] Wogaman, the author of seventeen books, is one of mainline Protestantism's leading intellectuals. He has also drawn his share of criticism from conservatives,[62] in part because Foundry has long been active in grassroots social justice activism. In fact, former senator Robert Dole (R-Kansas) and Senator Elizabeth Dole (R-North Carolina) attended Foundry for fifteen years until criticism of Wogaman began appearing in conservative publications.[63]

Indeed, Wogaman is an unapologetic champion of both liberal theology and politics.[64] Heavily steeped in mainline Protestantism's Social Gospel legacy, Wogaman is the former president of the liberal interest group Interfaith Alliance, which portrays itself as the polar opposite of the religious right.[65] He is an exemplar of the "new breed" of clergy who gained prominence in the 1960s for their desire to work for structural changes to ameliorate poverty and inequality.[66] In fact, as a seminary professor at Wesley Theological Seminary (a United Methodist institution in Washington, D.C.), Wogaman trained clergy to think in precisely this way about politics.[67] As he writes in his book on the Clinton scandal, "to put it in biblical language, part of our task is to care for the sheep—and part of it is to keep the wolves at bay! Thus, a pastor can want to help poor people directly, but it is also important for him or her to be an advocate for social policies that help to wipe out poverty."[68]

Wogaman's general political outlook has emphasized the value of working for social justice and inclusiveness, particularly for African Americans, women, gay and lesbian people, oppressed people in developing countries, the homeless, and other groups that face discrimination.[69] Unlike many main-

line Protestant clergy, Wogaman says he had the luxury of preaching to a primarily receptive audience in this regard: "Most Foundry people appreciated
having a preacher who engaged the issues. Some even went out of their way
to tell me that that is what attracted them to the church in the first place."[70]

Wogaman's academic specialty is Christian social ethics. On September
13, 1998, the first Sunday after the release of the Starr Report, he drew upon
this background in asking:

> Are we going to take one person and heap the sins of the nation on him, and feel
> free of those sins ourselves? Or, are we going to do the harder work of corporate
> repentance that draws all of us in, and helps us all to grow in love? Without the
> prospect of forgiveness and love, there can be no real repentance or change.
> The essence of all morality is love. We cannot deal with evils in society on a
> foundation other than love. That is the prophetic word we all need to hear. The
> greatest of the prophets in the biblical tradition were people who did not point
> at somebody else and say, "There is the sinner." The greatest were the ones who
> went to God and said, "O God, have mercy on *us*, a nation of sinners."[71]

These words reveal Wogaman's commitment to the broad concepts of egal-
itarianism and tolerance, hallmarks of liberal mainline Protestant thought.
Wogaman argued steadfastly throughout the Clinton scandal against remov-
ing the president from office, because in his view, compassion and corporate
love should predominate over the judgmental pettiness he perceived in the
Starr Report.[72]

It is important to note that Clinton's connection to Wogaman likely did not
affect electoral politics in any substantial way. Conservatives launched attacks against Wogaman before Clinton was reelected,[73] but the president was
already in his second term when Wogaman emerged as a more public figure
at the time of the Lewinsky scandal. Average American voters may have
known that Clinton was consulting with clergy, but they are unlikely to have
known many specific details about Wogaman himself (nor, for that matter,
would most Americans have known much about either Rev. Campolo or Rev.
MacDonald, the other two ministers with whom Clinton met).

Even though the relationship between Clinton and Wogaman had few
electoral consequences, the fact that the president selected a liberal mainline
Protestant as a spiritual advisor was not lost on Washington insiders. Wogaman seems to have played a symbolic role for Clinton during the period of
scandal, softening the blow that Clinton might have taken from religious
Americans who were disappointed by his lack of moral behavior. Clinton's
policy effectiveness was limited in his second term by the impeachment scandal and the fact that the Republican Party controlled Congress, but his public
affiliation with Wogaman (and the other two members of his "accountability

team") helped Clinton to maintain some measure of respectability in Washington and beyond. In this sense, Clinton was able to benefit both personally and politically from the counsel that Wogaman provided.

Meanwhile, during the second term of the Clinton administration liberal interest groups undoubtedly enjoyed good access to the White House—and felt generally empowered in the policy process. As an illustration, consider the major victory earned by a liberal religious coalition at the end of Clinton's second term, when Congress voted to appropriate over $400 million for international debt relief in response to the Jubilee 2000 antipoverty campaign. Liberal Protestants (and members of other faith traditions, including Catholics and Jews) were inspired by a scriptural reference to the jubilee year ("Consecrate the fiftieth year and proclaim liberty throughout the land to all its inhabitants. It shall be a jubilee for you; each one of you is to return to his family property and each to his own clan." Leviticus 25:10 [New International Version]). They allied to request one-time forgiveness of the debts owed by developing countries to the United States. Eventually, conservative religious voices joined the alliance demanding debt relief as well. Having a sympathetic president in the White House, one who was closely connected to the social justice imperative of mainline Protestantism, was helpful in pushing for Jubilee 2000.[74]

Pitting Religion against Politics: George W. Bush and Faith-Based Governance

As of this writing, President George W. Bush is concluding his second term in office. Although a few months of the Bush presidency remain, scholars, political pundits, and the media already have portrayed him as a leader who relies heavily on his faith and religious convictions to govern the nation.[75] Yet some claim that Bush's personal faith has no bearing on how he governs from the Oval Office and that it instead serves as a source of personal strength for Bush as he copes with the realities associated with serving as president.[76] On the surface, it does appear that religion has influenced the direction of White House policy making during the George W. Bush administration. Despite this perception, scholars have failed to account systematically for this phenomenon. To their credit, it will take years after Bush leaves office before scholars can assess with any degree of accuracy the importance that his personal faith and religion may have had on his presidency.

As we approach the conclusion of Bush's time in office, there are early indications that suggest religion has played a key role in Bush's "going public" strategies.[77] Specifically, tentative evidence indicates that religion was highly politicized within the Bush White House. Presidents are strategic and rational actors who seek to enact their policy agendas and maintain public support once they capture control of the White House. In the case of George W. Bush, personal faith and strong religious convictions are core components of his political persona. Bush's religious appeal is broad-based. He has personal connections to mainline Protestantism, as he was raised an Episcopalian and is now a committed United Methodist. He also has spoken about his personal conversion experience, which endeared him to the vast majority of evangelical Protestants. During his years in office, Bush sought to stabilize support with his base constituency of evangelical Protestants and devout mainline Protestants, and he also made important new inroads with members of other religious faiths, particularly traditional Catholics.[78]

However, presidents govern within a dynamic political environment that frequently requires them to rethink and refine their political strategies. The September 11, 2001 attacks on the World Trade Center and the Pentagon significantly shaped the role that religion would play in the Bush White House. Although these catastrophic events allowed President Bush to infuse more of his religious faith and values into his administration, the White House also was forced to contend with the need to display tolerance toward a multitude of religious faiths, especially Islam.

During Bush's early years, personal faith and religiosity contributed to the moral glue that held the George H. W. Bush family together. George W. Bush's parents immersed their children in the values and beliefs of the Episcopalian faith. As privileged, educated, wealthy northeasterners, the Bush family was well acquainted with the mainline Protestant virtue of noblesse oblige. This value was exemplified by George H. W. Bush's emphasis on volunteerism during his presidency. However, George W. Bush's personal faith has been formed by his experience with several Protestant traditions, including evangelicalism. Bush attended worship services at the First Presbyterian Church as a child while growing up in Midland, Texas. Once the Bush family moved to Houston in 1959, George W. Bush attended St. Martin's Episcopal Church.[79] Eventually, Bush followed his wife Laura Welch Bush's Methodist faith by becoming a member of the First United Methodist Church of Midland.[80] Today, Bush remains a United Methodist, but when he speaks of his personal faith, he uses the terminology and style of evangelical Protestantism, not mainline Protestantism. Just as the Southern Baptist Bill Clinton did not resemble most evangelical Protestants, it is dubious whether George W. Bush should be perceived as an exemplar of mainline Protestantism. In fact, in 2003 the United Methodist Church ran television advertisements before the beginning of the war in Iraq in which it specifically stated its opposition to Bush's foreign policy.

Biographers of George W. Bush frequently note two major events in Bush's adult years that strengthened his personal faith in God. One of these milestones occurred in the summer of 1985 when Bush's father invited the noted Evangelical Rev. Billy Graham to speak at St. Ann's by the Sea Episcopal Church in Kennebunkport, Maine, and to talk with members of the Bush family after the service.[81] George W. Bush spent time discussing issues of faith with Rev. Graham during the next day of his visit. This encounter with Rev. Graham redirected Bush's spiritual life. Bush later recounted:

> Over the course of that weekend, Reverend Graham planted a mustard seed in my soul, a seed that grew over the next year. He led me to the path, and I began walking. And it was the beginning of a change in my life. I had always been a religious person, had regularly attended church, even taught Sunday school and served as an altar boy. But that weekend my faith took on new meaning. It was the beginning of a new walk where I would recommit my heart to Jesus.[82]

These words indicate an incipient evangelicalism in Bush's personal faith, which could be interpreted as a movement away from the mainline Protestantism of his youth. The encounter with Rev. Graham did not instantly change Bush's personal faith, however. His journey toward a more spiritual lifestyle would continue until it reached a second milestone in 1986 on the day after his fortieth birthday, when Bush struggled with a hangover from the night before. It was at this point that Bush decided to quit drinking alcohol for the rest of his life.[83] A question that scholars will continue to debate is whether these two events in Bush's life dramatically shaped his future political career. For example, Fred Greenstein is rather cautious about concluding that Bush's informal visit with Billy Graham set Bush on a new course in life that led religious views to guide his politics.[84] Instead, Greenstein suggests that Bush's encounter with Graham and his struggles with alcohol further disciplined Bush as a person. This discipline has manifested itself in Bush's presidential style, which is marked by strict loyalty and a very strong will. Greenstein explains that Graham's visit with Bush "was an important experience in disciplining Bush to live life he hoped to live. However, it is much truer to say that Bush's was a drawn-out journey, political and personal, with no single Damascus Road experience."[85]

George W. Bush's political career has often pitted his religious faith against politics, from the time when he was governor of Texas through his two-term presidency. During the 2000 presidential election campaign, candidate Bush promised to incorporate the ideals of "compassionate conservatism" formulated by Marvin Olasky, a Bush supporter and journalism professor at the University of Texas. One of the pillars of Bush's version of compassionate conservatism was the idea that the contemporary social welfare state (first enacted during the Franklin Roosevelt administration and later developed during Lyndon Johnson's War on Poverty) was outmoded. Olasky and Bush

felt that religious institutions (which they termed "faith-based organizations") could assist government in dispensing social welfare programs more
effectively and efficiently. Faith-based organizations also could serve as core
repositories for "spiritual and intellectual empowerment" that might break a
recipient's reliance on welfare in the long term.[86] Although compassionate
conservatism does resonate with the virtue of noblesse oblige, it is inconsistent with mainline Protestantism's more recent view that government should
take responsibility for the poor and dispossessed.[87] In this sense, Bush's connection of religion to politics is not reflective of contemporary mainline Protestant social and political thought. It also breaks with the more long-standing
Social Gospel imperative of mainline Protestantism.

It is quite clear that Bush's overall religious strategy has not been defined
solely by his personal experience with mainline Protestantism. This fact,
however, is neither unusual nor unexpected. As a rational and strategic political actor, Bush was required to reach out to a variety of religious denominations during the beginning of his first term in office for political support,
especially if he had hoped to gain greater electoral and popular support in the
2004 presidential election than he had in 2000. Indeed, Bush relied on a wide
variety of religious leaders for policy advice during his administration, while
maintaining special informal ties with Rev. Mark Craig, pastor of Highland
Park United Methodist Church in Dallas.[88] There is no doubt that Bush made
sure to court mainline Protestants during his presidency, especially when
he named Dick Cheney, a fellow United Methodist, as his running mate in
2000.[89] Bush also appointed other mainline Protestants to key leadership
positions in his administration, including National Security Adviser and
later Secretary of State Condoleezza Rice, whose father was a Presbyterian
minister; former chief of staff Andrew Card, whose wife is a United Methodist minister; and former counselor to the president, Karen Hughes, who has
served as an elder in her Presbyterian church.[90]

Apart from his political appointments, one of Bush's main efforts at the
beginning of his first term was the development of faith-based programs
that would form a stronger relationship between the federal government
and religious institutions. Bush's faith-based ideas were not entirely new
to the American political landscape; they were in part extensions of the
"Charitable Choice" provisions of the Welfare Reform Act of 1996, passed
by Congress during the Clinton administration.[91] These particular laws were
established to provide a more level playing field between religious and
secular nonprofit institutions that sought to participate in delivering federal
social welfare programs to the public.[92] However, what set Bush apart from
previous presidents was the fact that he was the first chief executive to
develop an organizational unit within the White House dealing exclusively

with religious issues: the White House Office of Faith-Based and Community Initiatives.[93]

The George W. Bush administration considered faith-based programs a core component of its domestic agenda right from the beginning. Bush signed his first two executive orders as president on January 29, 2001. Both were devoted to giving life to his faith-based ideas. Executive Order 13198 called for the creation of a Center for Faith-Based and Community Initiatives in the Departments of Justice, Education, Labor, Health and Human Services, and Housing and Urban Development. The main responsibilities of these centers were to identify major bureaucratic hurdles in the executive branch that would hinder Bush's faith-based programs and to cut through that red tape. In addition, these centers were instructed to promote the president's faith-based initiatives among the various religious institutions that might be eligible to participate in delivering social welfare to target populations in society.[94]

The White House Office of Faith-Based and Community Initiatives (OFBCI) was created by Bush's second directive, Executive Order 13199, and it was housed in the Executive Office of the President. OFBCI was designed to be the main organization in the executive branch that centralizes faith-based policy-making and implementation responsibilities.[95] John DiIulio, Jr., a professor of political science at the University of Pennsylvania, a conservative, Democratic Catholic, and a strong advocate of aiding the poor, was appointed by President Bush as the first head of the Office of Faith-Based and Community Initiatives.

Bush's religious intentions regarding faith-based initiatives were no match for the nature of politics that pervades Washington. As a result, OFBCI struggled and fell victim to the influence of politics throughout the first term of the Bush presidency. For example, DiIulio resigned as head of OFBCI in August 2001, and a new director was not named until February 2002, when Bush appointed Jim Towey, who is, like his predecessor, Catholic.[96] The long period of time that passed between the tenures of DiIulio and Towey further underscored the serious political problems and lack of attention that the White House actually placed on the administrative operations of OFBCI. Furthermore, all but one senior member serving within OFBCI had resigned within this office's first operating year.[97]

There were additional political problems associated with OFBCI from the very beginning. For example, DiIulio took over the job of director at the OFBCI at a time when the Bush White House already had put a set of staff members (all of whom supported the president's policy agenda) in place to work under DiIulio's leadership. DiIulio was able to add several members whom he personally sought to work in OFBCI; however, he presided over an organization that the White House had attempted to politicize and control from the start.[98]

Another problem that Bush encountered with OFBCI was that at the beginning, DiIulio failed to reach out to the full spectrum of religious leaders. For example, Rev. Jerry Falwell criticized DiIulio in the summer of 2001 for overlooking key constituencies within the religious community, especially conservative Evangelicals. The Southern Baptist Convention was concerned that the faith-based programs might violate the Establishment Clause of the First Amendment.[99] In contrast, the White House perceived DiIulio as a director who was not sufficiently aggressive in implementing Bush's faith-based programs. Instead, he became perceived as more of an advocate for the Democratic Party rather than Republican Party based on his moderate approach in promoting the role of religious institutions in delivering social welfare programs to the public.[100]

Personal frustrations between DiIulio and the White House added to the conflictual environment at OFBCI. In addition, Bush's faith-based programs and their overall missions were not clearly defined. As a result, OFCBI often found it difficult to implement Bush's policies because of ambiguous policy mandates. DiIulio was so dismayed with the internal political conflicts between the White House and OFCBI that he eventually claimed: "What you've got is everything, and I mean everything, being run by the political arm. It's the reign of the Mayberry Machiavellis."[101]

We should not be surprised that politics trumped Bush's efforts to incorporate his religious ideals into his faith-based programs. It is clear that politics influenced how the Bush White House handled the faith-based initiative. During Bush's first term in office, tax cuts and education reform overshadowed and replaced faith-based programs as the top items on the domestic agenda.[102] Another tentative observation that we might make about Bush's domestic policy is that he was more interested in setting the policy agenda and developing policies than he was in following them through during the stages of implementation. On the other hand, OFCBI was a powerful political symbol for the Bush administration. Its very existence served as a cue to religious voters and organizations that the White House deemed them a critical constituency of the Republican Party. During the 2002 midterm elections, OFBCI became a strategic tool used by the White House to increase political support for Republican candidates running for Congress in selected districts.[103]

Furthermore, presidential scholars have noted that presidents are much more interested in quantity rather than quality with regard to public policies, because a list of many policy achievements is much more useful to chief executives running for reelection than any claim of achievements regarding actual policy implementation. Voters are not adept at understanding the mundane and complex details of policy implementation, nor are most even aware of this type of policy function.[104] As a result, they are more likely to judge presidents on the number and types of policies that they have created during their administrations. Despite administrative and political problems associated with implementing the faith-based initiative, the mere fact that Bush created OFCBI at all sends a signal to a variety of religious groups that Bush considers them to be an important constituency.

Religion and politics in American government often make for strange bedfellows. Although at this writing we can reach only tentative conclusions regarding the Bush presidency, there are indications that his White House has struggled to define its religious strategies, and that religion has taken a back-seat to politics with respect to the president's policy agenda. There is no doubt that the doctrines and beliefs of mainline Protestantism inform George W. Bush's personal faith. Yet these same mainline Protestant values remain elusive within the Bush White House as Bush increasingly favored evangelical Protestant spirituality and politics, both for personal and political reasons.

CONCLUSION

Mainline Protestantism is hardly a monolith in American politics. Our analysis indicates that mainline voters have increasingly constituted a swing constituency. Mainline voters, particularly those who are least observant and traditionalist, are moving toward the Democratic Party. This partisan shift is both significant in its own right and indicative of several other important trends in American politics.

First, increasingly it has become clear that denominationalism is not an especially good predictor of partisanship or political behavior.[105] Until the post–World War II era, it was reasonably safe to assume that white Protestants of all varieties would vote for Republican candidates, whereas Catholics, Jews, and African American Protestants would vote for Democrats.[106] In recent times, however, a loss of collective identity has left large religious groups, particularly mainline Protestants and Catholics, open to mobilization by either party.[107]

Strategically speaking, this suggests a second trend, which is that moderate-to-progressive mainline Protestants may be ripe for mobilization by Democratic candidates who can connect their policy goals with mainline priorities, especially the struggle for social justice.[108] Our data show that there are at least some mainline Protestants who have grown disenchanted with the Republican Party and its emphasis on morality politics. Such individuals could become an important constituency for the Democratic Party if Democratic candidates can reach them with strategic rhetoric. Vice presidential candidate John Edwards spoke briefly of the immorality of poverty in his acceptance speech at the 2004 Democratic National Convention. However, the Kerry/Edwards campaign's "religious strategy" largely consisted of avoiding the topic of religion altogether. This lack of attention almost certainly was an electoral mistake, at least in terms of attracting the votes of liberal mainline Protestants. There is not much of an organized "religious left" in the United States today, but neither was there an organized religious right until Ronald Reagan mobilized evangelical Protestants with conservative religious rhetoric in 1980.[109]

The third trend we see is the effort by presidents to appeal to a wide range of religious groups simultaneously. Our case studies of Presidents Clinton and Bush illustrate two different ways in which presidents have steered clear of presenting themselves as representatives of one specific religious tradition alone. Bill Clinton's personal ties are to the evangelicalism of the Southern Baptist Convention, yet he worshipped with a United Methodist congregation in Washington and reflected some of the social justice agenda of mainline Protestantism in his policy initiatives. He sought the counsel of clergy from both mainline (including Rev. J. Philip Wogaman) and evangelical (including Rev. Tony Campolo) Protestantism, partly to temper the effect of the Lewinsky affair on his support from religious Americans. George W. Bush also exemplifies the trend away from religious particularlism in the White House. He retains ties to the mainline Protestant United Methodist Church even while his own spirituality is more evangelical in nature. His faith-based initiative was designed to have appeal for—and to benefit—congregations across religious traditions that wish to participate in federally funded social service delivery programs. Bush has also attracted large numbers of votes from observant Christians, regardless of their specific religious affiliation. Religion therefore appears to be a valuable strategic tool in the president's political arsenal, and recent presidents have been utilizing this tool as broadly as possible.

Religion and politics have always been profoundly intertwined in the United States. Religious values, attitudes, and discourses continue to play powerful roles in shaping American politics, as they have since the founding era. The institution of the presidency is no exception to this rule. Presidents are widely viewed as the "high priests" of America's "civil religion," or the widely shared perception among Americans that the United States is specially blessed by God among all nations.[110] The occupant of the White House undoubtedly will continue to use religious strategies to great advantage, for both electoral gain and policy influence, in the twenty-first century and beyond.

John F. Kennedy standing with Roman Catholic Cardinal Francis Spellman, Archbishop of New York, and Vice President Richard Nixon address at the Al Smith Memorial Dinner, 1960.

Chapter 3

Catholics and the American Presidency

David C. Leege

Chiseled into the stone above a door to the Basilica of the Sacred Heart at the University of Notre Dame are the words, "God, Country, Notre Dame." This is the door closest to the administration building, whose fabled golden dome is peaked by the patroness, Notre Dame du Lac, Our Lady of the Lake. The order of the words tells a great deal about devout but upwardly mobile Catholics in the United States. While "proudly in the heavens," as sung in the alma mater, Our Lady pleads for the university, down on terra firma where we live and work, study and worship. American Catholics owe first loyalty to God, second to country, and third to the tools for successful living honed at an alma mater.

Under the distant uplifted arms of "Touchdown Jesus," as the Hesburgh Library mural is dubbed, football fans take a moment before the game to pay obeisance to God and country. This quasi-religious patriotic ritual invokes the Divine through the singing of *America the Beautiful*, the reading of the Preamble to the Constitution, the presenting of colors, and singing of the national anthem. No doubts here—before Catholics enter combat in this Saturday ritual, they reassert their Americanism.

Notre Dame resembles the melting pot that is the Roman Catholic Church in the United States. Each Catholic reflects a different ethnic history and political journey, encompassing persecution, assimilation, and upward mobility. In the 1960s, mimicking parental affiliations, Notre Dame could be 70 percent Democrat, but in the first decade of the twenty-first century it could be 70 percent Republican. The GOP's Gipper is an enduring hero, but so are former president Carter and Father Hesburgh, whose parallel goals for the world are embodied in a research and teaching institute. There is nothing retreatist about this venue—the struggles for the soul of Catholicism, for the values of

American culture, for the policy directives of White House and Capitol Hill, the Pentagon, State, and the UN all are enjoined at Notre Dame.

Notre Dame is a metaphor for the political history of successive streams of Catholic ethnic groups in the United States. The American presidents who speak at her commencements and the presidential wannabes who crave the six-second sound byte of a campaign visit are perhaps the strongest testimony to the evolution of Catholics in American political history and particularly to the path ambitious people take to the White House. This chapter (1) offers a cultural and political history that draws conclusions from American Catholic political experiences, (2) analyzes Catholic voting patterns over the last half-century, (3) illustrates three types of relationships between prelates and politicians, and (4) summarizes evidence about Catholic opinion on church/state and religion/politics intersections.

ORIGINS OF THE DIVERSE PATTERNS

Much of Catholic political history in the United States is grounded in European migrations from many countries interacting with a host culture drawn from Anglo and Protestant sources. American Catholic political history in the twenty-first century will become increasingly the study of Hispanic, African, and Asian peoples being taken seriously in the direction of the country. Throughout, several forces operate: (1) Catholics tried to put distance between church and state when dominant groups could use the power of the state to oppress them; (2) Catholics tried to use the powers of the state when other forces threatened the fundamental values of human life, dignity, and compassion, and the privilege to worship according to one's beliefs; (3) Catholics enhanced their power as a swing electorate operating within the nuances of the electoral college; (4) Catholics, operating the widest range and largest number of institutions in the civil society, had to be taken seriously as providers of education and social services; and (5) Catholics residing in the United States at least share affinity with an international system of churches and political actors and are socialized, however imperfectly, with a substantial body of ideas and teachings about the proper human life, and thus have become a force in the conduct of domestic and foreign policy. All of these link Catholics, the largest single organized church body in the United States (about one-fourth of the adult population) to the American presidency.

Maryland, which textbooks call the *Catholic* colony, was not founded as a haven for Catholics. Unlike Massachusetts and more like colonies to its immediate north, Maryland's purpose was commercial; "profit, not religion (was) the primary impulse."[1] The "Maryland Design" of Catholic Cecil Calvert, Lord

Baltimore, welcomed colonists of all religious persuasions, so long as religion did not dominate commercial and civic life. Jesuits, and eventually Quakers, Anglicans, and others, worked its settlements. Fearing that religious conflict could impede commercial pursuits as it had in the old country, the Maryland Assembly enacted assurances of religious freedom in 1639. A decade later, the Assembly enacted an "Act Concerning Religion," which codified religious diversity. While it included many religious proscriptions, the slightest violation of which was punishable by death or public whipping, it ensured tolerance of different religious groups so long as they did not interfere with the role of the government. A year earlier, Calvert had squelched the desire of Jesuits for state-recognized privileges for clergy. Protestants streamed into a colony where wealthy Catholics were recognized as economic and civic leaders.

Even Maryland could not withstand the Revolution of 1688 in England. By 1718, the Maryland Assembly voted to disenfranchise Catholics. In the French and Indian War, Catholics had to pay double taxation. By the time of the American Revolution, however, the climate of religious toleration was restored. Wealthy planter and European-educated aristocrat Charles Carroll of Carrollton was a signer of the Declaration of Independence and was admired as "a flaming patriot." Daniel Carroll signed the Constitution. John Carroll became the first Catholic bishop of the colonies. Interestingly, the Carrolls along with other Catholic gentry had become slave owners like the Anglican and Presbyterian planters to their south. Even the Jesuits owned slaves on their farms. Both in economic practices and in the common struggle for independence, Catholics and Protestants were united. As Dolan observes, "The [American] revolution hardly destroyed the spirit of anti-Catholicism, but it dealt bigotry a severe blow."[2] George Washington, first commanding general and president, acknowledged with respect the "patriotic part" Catholics took in the Revolution.

Something else of significance happened in Maryland. Not only was Father John Carroll appointed the first bishop (superior) of the Vatican's mission in the thirteen colonies, but he had earlier been appointed by the Continental Congress to a delegation seeking the support of Canada during the Revolutionary War. Carroll gained the respect of Benjamin Franklin, and Franklin himself intervened in the Vatican on behalf of Carroll's investiture. Carroll had written that the Catholic Church in the United States must avoid "any dependence on foreign jurisdiction" and should acknowledge only that the Bishop at Rome (Pope) is *spiritual* head of the Church.[3] This was also an important "declaration of independence" that has surfaced many times in American Catholic political history, especially in Senator John F. Kennedy's address to the Houston Ministerial Alliance in 1960; not surprisingly, it was one reason American Catholics were chastised by the Vatican for the heresy of Americanism late in the nineteenth century. This same combination of spiritual oneness along with national independence and religious freedom became embedded in the central documents of Vatican II through the efforts of American Jesuit John Courtney Murray and Francis Cardinal Spellman of New York. Early roots yield significant fruits. Throughout his life, Carroll remained comfortable among political leaders, but wary about coziness between church and state.

He remained wary with good reason: the United States remained a Protestant nation and a Calvinist culture. Tsunamis of Catholic immigrants, first from Germany and Ireland, then from Italy, Poland, and other parts of southern and eastern Europe, fit neither characteristic. Many of the immigrants were from rural peasant cultures and had little experience with either democracy or economic self-sufficiency. Often, the Catholic Church became a solidary mechanism of last resort. But in northeastern states for two decades following 1830, Catholics could not get jobs and their churches were desecrated. The American Protestant Association and the Know Nothings organized anti-Catholic sentiment politically. Anti-Catholic riots and widespread nativism in public circles grew across the entire country, so that by the mid-1850s, Know Nothings and nativists among the Whigs and Democrats carried the majority of the U.S. Congress.

Public schools were regarded as Protestant educational institutions. Clinics and hospitals did not take well to the lifestyles of Catholic immigrants. Settlement house workers and reformers wanted to make sure that the English language replaced other tongues, that democracy was embraced, and that dominant Calvinist values about righteousness supplanted Catholic notions of sin and grace. Faced with what they viewed as both cultural imperialism and second-class citizenship, Catholics organized a system of parochial schools, welfare and ethnic betterment societies, hospitals, colleges and universities, newspapers, and presses. This system was a forerunner to the parallel institutions organized by Southern and later Northern Evangelicals in the final three decades of the twentieth century. With such massive institutional interests, Catholics developed close liaisons with politicians and government agencies to ensure favorable tax and regulatory treatment. Into the late twentieth century, this meant that Roman Catholics and evangelical Protestants who warred over alleged religious and cultural differences could find common ground on the protection of institutional interests.

New political forces converged in the 1850s. Nominally Protestant politicians expanded the franchise and courted Catholic voters, seeking political gain. Catholics turned ethnic parish "betterment societies" into urban political machines. Each provided welfare assistance, job access, language and citizenship training, brokering skills, and often the financial rewards from rackets and honest graft—in return for voter mobilization. Observers often forget that Boss Tweed, the legendary founder of Tammany Hall in New York, was a Scot Presbyterian. Many of the sachems and later leaders of Tammany were Irish and later Italian. Often machine leaders and Irish priests alike advised support of the Democratic Party; Democrats were antigovernment, anti-Yankee, and anti-Protestant elite and showed respect for the ways minorities organized their own affairs. Ironically, this Democratic bias ignored the fact that several prominent Catholics had served in Federalist and Whig administrations.[4] In 1852 the Whigs made appeals to Catholic voters, charging Franklin Pierce, the Democratic nominee, with nativism. Once elected, however, Pierce was the first to appoint a prominent Catholic as postmaster general, a patronage-rich practice followed by later presidents of both parties. Thus, here we see competition for Catholic votes not only in voter appeals but also in the symbolic politics of appointments and "Cabinet balance."

The most critical election for American Catholics in the nineteenth century was its last, 1896. The Irish in the cities continued to align with the Democratic Party. Italian households were often split—the women, who were devout, were Democrats as their Irish priests advised, but the men, who were anticlerical, became Republican. To this day, many eastern urban/suburban Republican machines are led by Italian Catholics. Much of the church, however, was not in the cities but in the small towns and farms of the Midwest and Great Plains, settled by Germans and Central Europeans. In church politics, the German Catholics had lost their worship practices to the Irish hierarchy. But in party politics, German Catholics often became what the Protestant commercial leaders weren't. If the Protestants were Republican, the Germans were Democrats; if the Protestants were Democrats, the Germans were Republican. Outside the eastern cities, many Catholics from the British Isles and Ireland had fully assimilated, were part of local business and professional elites, and were Republican. Following the Civil War and the failures of Reconstruction onward into the 1920s, many nativists had allied with the Ku Klux Klan, which was not only anti-black, but anti-Catholic and anti-Jewish, and more likely to be Democratic. So Catholics had large entourages of voters in both parties for historical, self-protection, and self-promotion reasons.

In 1896, a strong Midwestern evangelical pietistic movement swept the Democratic Party and nominated Senator William Jennings Bryan, a gifted orator from Nebraska. Republicans under the leadership of Cleveland steel magnate, Mark Hanna, nominated Governor William McKinley of Ohio. Historian Paul Kleppner and others have described elections of the final two decades of the nineteenth century as religious wars between two "political churches."[5]

Democrats this time had chosen a supporter of Prohibition and Sunday closing laws, an opponent of foreign languages and parochial schools, an aggressively evangelical Protestant with strong nativist overtones. Hanna saw great opportunities to attract Republican votes from big-city labor circles, appealing to active government and corporate capitalism as the engine of jobs for all—in contrast to the financial panic of 1893 under a Democratic administration. Prominent Archbishop John Ireland, a visible Republican activist (in contrast to the advice of first bishop John Carroll a century earlier to put distance between religion and politics) was alarmed by the direction Democrats were taking and he denounced their convention. A major realignment followed as many urban Catholic workers joined their small-town and rural coreligionists in the Republican Party. In time, progressive reforms chipped away at the patronage powers of urban Democratic machines and reduced the turnout of newer ethnic immigrants. Bryan continued to be the standard-bearer for the Democrats. Anti-German and pro-British bigotry during World War I, "Wilson's War," drove still more Catholics to realign Republican. Catholics again were seen as a swing sector of the electorate, cultivated by non-Catholic politicians who coveted the presidency. Catholic religious and political leaders moved to protect Catholics from politicians who threatened Catholic values or ways of life. Even more important, however, the Bryan candidacy was itself a wedge issue used to distance many Catholics from their inherited political affiliation. Wedge issues aimed at religious groups did not begin in the late twentieth century, but have a long American pedigree. They are often the basis for new electoral majorities.

Al Smith's nomination as the Democratic presidential candidate in 1928 again reshuffled the Catholic political landscape. Smith, "New York Governor, a product of the tenements, urban wage slavery, anti-Prohibition, anti-Catholic persecution, and Tammany Hall collected the aspirations of Catholics in the Eastern cities."[6] The Democrats cared enough about Catholic voters to break a taboo in American politics. While Herbert Hoover defeated Smith in a landslide, Franklin Delano Roosevelt, the first post-Depression Democrat, could reap the harvest of Catholic voter mobilization and realignment from 1932 onward. Gradually in the later 1940s and 1950s, Catholic voting patterns returned to normalcy as part of the swing electorate.

In 1960, religious affinity and the poignant memory of anti-Catholic bigotry in 1928 fueled over 80 percent of Catholics to vote for John F. Kennedy. Their presence in key electoral college states carried Kennedy to the White House. But it did more than that: it told *both* parties that they needed to compete for Catholic voters. In the 1964 election, Republicans for the first time placed a Catholic, Rep. William Miller, on the ticket. In 1980, Catholics recognized the similarities between the Gipper, Ronald Reagan, and a long line of Irish Catholic politicians; Reagan's life story as the son of a hard-drinking apostate Catholic, but still an optimistic American, resembled that of many Catholics. To some observers he was the nation's second Catholic president, the equalizer for the GOP. He appointed more Catholics to prominent posts than had recent Democratic presidents. He took pains to court Catholic leaders with policy promises, and renewed the Gipper tie to Notre Dame and Catholics generally.

Equally important things were happening to the Catholic voter base. The American dream and the New Deal had worked. Greeley has documented how most Catholic ethnic groups were equaling or surpassing most Protestant denominations in their educational attainment and economic success.[7] World War II and the GI Bill had plucked Catholics out of ethnic ghettoes to the leading college campuses; eventually, top jobs in Fortune 500 companies; and family and church lives in suburbia. The solidarity of old patterns began to weaken as Catholics gained the capacity to make choices. Kennedy's election was like a coronation for this generation of autonomous Catholics. Political parties could no longer gain advantage through nativist appeals. The tight control Protestant elites exercised over community life gave way to the formation of coalitions and shared responsibility. No sooner did leadership welcome Catholic partners than African Americans were insisting on civil rights and economic opportunity and the women's movement was calling for cultural change toward true equality between the sexes. The pressures to adapt were squeezed into less than two decades.

While many priests and devout laity were at the forefront of the civil rights movement, some Catholics did not take well to sharing jobs, power, and neighborhoods with African Americans. Trade unions had developed closed apprentice systems that favored children of members. Urban renewal and highway building programs, the products of elite planners, often gutted old ethnic neighborhoods. Urban riots and looting came to the edge of white ethnic neighborhoods. When Martin Luther King Jr. charted northern marches, they often traversed "our ground," old Catholic neighborhoods, and drew out the ugliness of bigoted responses. When the McGovern-Fraser reforms swept the Democratic Party, the delegation led by urban ethnic *Catholic* politician Richard J. Daley was unseated at the 1972 convention by upstart blacks, women, and elite reformers. There was a widespread perception, fueled by racial code words devised by Republican presidential candidates, that Great Society programs had transferred the hard-earned tax dollars of middle Americans (Catholics) to unworthy black welfare cheats and to people who met quotas but were unqualified for jobs or educational slots.[8] Reagan was particularly adept at sanctifying wedge racial and gender issues with the language of egalitarian individualism. Later analyses will show that massive Catholic, especially male, defections to Nixon and realignment as Republicans during Reagan were responses to racial wedges. In a gripping multigenerational account of three Catholic families, Freedman shows how the firm commitment of ethnic Catholics to the party of Smith, the New Deal, and Kennedy gave way to commitment to and leadership of the current conservative Republican Party based on rationalized wedge issues.[9]

This is not the way Catholic social teaching would have had it. Vatican II urged the formation of national bishops' councils that not only addressed "church" matters but also were a strong leaven in national public policy. In the United States, the National Conference of Catholic Bishops developed study committees and issued pastoral letters advising the flock on a variety of public issues. The teaching is largely prescriptive but on some human life issues it is proscriptive. Perhaps the most significant of these are (1) a sequence of letters on abortion and other human life issues such as capital punishment and euthanasia, (2) the economy, (3) nuclear war and peace, and (4) race relations.

The response to these letters tells a great deal about Catholics and American politicians. On abortion, while not as opposed as Evangelicals, Catholic laity are more likely than the general public to seek its outlawing or to limit its frequency. They follow general trends in intergenerational acceptance that there are circumstances in which abortion should be an available option. On the economy, Catholic neoconservative Michael Novak and former Reagan cabinet official William Simon issued a conservative counter-pastoral before the bishops had even promulgated their teaching; still, it is often unclear on complex economic issues, such as how the "preferential option for the poor" and the quest for dignity, opportunity, and subsidiarity translates into specific domestic and foreign policies. American Catholics are accustomed to seeking both private and public solutions, but increasingly resemble Calvinists in their quest for personal responsibility and private charity. On nuclear war and peace, the Reagan administration made many attempts to counter this letter, but Catholics have become increasingly willing to apply "just war" tests to national defense actions and are more hesitant than others to rush into war or deploy certain weapons systems—as was shown at the time George W. Bush formulated his doctrine of "preemptive strikes" to justify invading Iraq. "Sons and Daughters in Christ," the principal letter on race relations, recently received a twenty-five-year review, and slow progress was documented, despite the presence of well over two million blacks in the Catholic Church in the United States. Joseph Cardinal Bernardin formulated a "seamless garment" of human life and social justice issues that is held up as a model of consistency in Catholic social teaching. Studies show that only about 10 percent of Catholics embrace it. Clerical leaders and laity decry "cafeteria-style Catholicism," often castigating political liberals; yet beyond abortion, political conservatives are likely to be inconsistent with church teaching on far more issues.[10]

The fundamental problem for Catholics who wish to vote for presidential candidates consistent with church teaching is that the two-party system offers bigger tents, and the candidates themselves obfuscate their positions and misrepresent the opponent's record. As E. J. Dionne argues, Catholics can be a leaven within their respective parties, but if they tried to follow either their party line or Catholic teaching, they would quickly compromise one or the other.[11] And so, for example, a handful of Catholic bishops urged withholding communion from Senator John Kerry in the 2004 campaign for his abortion position (with the apparent support of Cardinal Ratzinger, now Pope Benedict XVI), but raised no protest against President Bush's decision to invade Iraq in 2003 over Pope John Paul II's formal presentation against it. Partisan politics also makes one pick and choose, based less on consistent application of principles and more on priorities. Partisan politics exposes the human frailties of magisterial notions of the holy Catholic Church. That is why many devout Catholic voters turn to their "ordination of baptism" and to notions of "informed conscience" to make political choices.

PRESIDENTIAL VOTING OVER THE LAST HALF-CENTURY

Since the advent of sample survey research and political polling in the 1930s, many data sources are available to scholars who wish to study the political behavior of identifiable groups like Catholics. We will use time-series data from 1952 to 2000 generated by the American National Election Studies (ANES). ANES, based at the University of Michigan, uses the Survey Research Center's system of national probability samples and face-to-face interviewing with high quality control. We prefer it to its equal quality competitor, the National Opinion Research Center's General Social Survey, only because it usually has a wider range of political variables. Both are superior to random digit dial (RDD) telephone interviews (such as Gallup) because of response biases. Few survey houses conduct nine to thirteen efforts to reach a respondent; therefore on key religious variables they have samples unrepresentative of the American public because of substitutions after only four or five attempts.[12] Even RDD surveys are far superior to immediate exit polls because the latter have unestimated biases. In some states, 25 to 100 percent of the electorate has not voted at a polling place and therefore do not receive questionnaires. Response is voluntary but is likely to overrepresent the highly committed, who in effect "vote" a second time through the exit poll. Items are selected based on a less demanding pretest, and their meaning to the respondent is sometimes vague and confusing. Field representatives make choices of respondents that are often stereotypical and done with limited supervision. The survey is paper-and-pencil without interaction with an interviewer. The drawback with ANES data, unfortunately, is that it often takes half a year before defensible analysis can be done, whereas exit polls are almost instantaneously available.

Table 3.1 shows the partisan political behavior of non-Hispanic white Catholics from 1952 to 2000. Updated from ANES data presented in Leege, Wald, Krueger, and Mueller,[13] the figure presents a politician's calculus of the vote. It matters little to the campaign handler what the distribution of partisanship is within a particular group. More important is whether Democrats or Republicans actually *vote* in a given election, and if so, whether they remain loyal or defect to the opposition. In an era characterized by the politics of cultural differences, a minority party may neutralize the identifier advantage owned by the majority party by creating disappointment and disinterest; people fail to turn out. Or they may create sufficient anxiety to stimulate crossover voting. In much of the post–New Deal era, the campaign strategy of the minority Republican Party was *to control the size and composition of the electorate* through negative appeals to vulnerable groups in the Democratic coalition on race, patriotism, gender, and religion. From 1952 onward, white Catholic Democrats were seen as a vulnerable group whose turnout could be depressed or whose anxiety could be heightened into defection. Eventually defection becomes a learned behavior and leads to realignment. As the culture of partisanship within the group is changed, young people consider it natural that they, as Catholics, would align with the new party when they enter the electorate.

The upper 40 percent of table 3.1 presents data for white non-Latino Catholics who identify themselves as Democrats, and the second 40 percent provides similar information on Catholic Republicans.

Row 1: *Democratic Party identification*—the proportion of the sample of white non-Latino Catholics who call themselves strong Democrats, not so strong Democrats, and Independent leaning Democrat in each presidential election year, as noted on the columns.

Row 2: *Proportion loyal to party*—the proportion of Catholic Democrats who turn out and select the Democratic candidate for president.

Row 3: *Proportion not voting*—the proportion of Catholic Democrats who fail to vote for President.

Row 4: *Proportion defecting to opposition candidates(s)*—the proportion of Catholic Democrats who turn out but select the Republican or other candidate.

Row 5: *Democratic partisan yield*—the proportion of white non-Latino Catholics who are both Democratic and loyal to the party, that is, Catholic Democrats who turned out and voted Democratic.

Rows 6–10: The same sets of measures for white non-Latino Catholic Republicans.

Row 11: *Democratic partisan advantage*—the difference between the Democratic partisan yield and the Republican partisan yield. (A positive number favors Democrats, while a negative number favors Republicans.)

Table 3.1: Partisan Patterns of White, Non-Latino Catholics, 1952–2000

Political Characteristics	1952	1956	1960	1964	1968	1972	1976	1980	1984	1988	1992	1996	2000
Democratic Party ID[a]	68	59	73	69	63	62	61	54	52	45	53	52	46
Proportion Loyal to Party[b]	61	57	87	79	61	39	58	45	60	67	64	65	50
Proportion not voting	15	18	6	14	19	19	22	24	17	17	14	20	11
Proportion defecting to opposition candidate(s)	24	25	6	7	20	42	21	31	23	16	23	15	13
Democratic Partisan Yield[c]	41	34	64	55	39	24	35	25	31	30	33	33	23
Republican Party ID	25	27	19	22	25	25	26	31	36	45	36	41	45
Proportion Loyal to Party	83	83	60	65	72	77	66	68	83	73	60	67	56
Proportion not voting	12	14	13	9	10	11	22	19	13	19	11	11	7
Proportion defecting to opposition candidate(s)	5	3	28	26	18	12	12	13	4	8	29	23	10
Republican Partisan Yield	21	22	11	14	18	19	17	21	30	33	22	27	25
Dem. Partisan Advantage[d]	20	11	53	40	21	5	18	4	1	-3	12	6	-2
"True" Independent[e]	7	11	8	9	11	12	12	15	11	10	11	7	5
Apolitical	0	3	1	0	1	1	1	1	1	1	0	1	0
Number in Sample	376	360	215	333	313	595	494	316	428	343	432	330	365

[a] Includes percent strong Democrat, not so strong Democrat, and Independent leaning Democrat.
[b] Proportion of Democrats who turn out and select the Democratic candidate for President.
[c] Product of Democratic party identification and reported vote for Democratic candidate.
[d] Subtract Republican partisan yield from Democratic partisan yield to calculate partisan advantage.
[e] Respondents who claim to be Independents but do not lean to either party.

Source: ANES Cumulative File

Row 12: *"True" Independent*—the proportion of white non-Latino Catholics who claim to be Independents and lean to neither party.

Row 13: *Apolitical*—the proportion of white non-Latino Catholics who claim not to be Democrats, Republicans, or Independents.

Row 14: *Number in sample*—the number of white non-Latino Catholics in the sample during each presidential election year.

Several conclusions can be drawn from inspection of table 3.1:

(1) The culture of Catholic party identification has favored Democrats until very recently. (Row 1)
(2) White, non-Latino Catholics have either heavily favored Democratic candidates for president or slightly favored Democrats. (Row 11)
(3) Catholics, while identifying as Democrats, are quite willing to defect to Republican presidential candidates. Democratic defections were massive in 1972 in the Nixon-McGovern race, but were also quite high in the Eisenhower and Reagan races. White Catholic Republicans are less likely to defect, but their highest rate of crossover voting was to Clinton. (Rows 4 and 8)
(4) Failure to vote is often as common among Catholic Democrats as is crossover voting. It was relatively high among Catholic Republicans only in 1988. (Rows 3 and 7)
(5) The greatest partisan loyalty and highest turnout among Catholic Democrats came in 1960 with a fellow Catholic on the ticket. (Row 2) In data not shown here, the high turnout/high Democratic loyalty pattern of white Catholics was not replicated with John Kerry, a fellow Catholic, in 2004.
(6) There has been a gradual realignment of Catholics over the time span. Part of what appears as realignment is simply the move back to normalcy after the extraordinary Kennedy election. It reached a plateau in the 1970s. Realignment or Republican alignment accelerated steeply in the Reagan years. Now Democrats have a narrow advantage among white Catholic party identifiers and no partisan advantage at all in actual vote. (Rows 1 and 6)

Scholars have argued that a strong cultural identification kept Catholics in the Democratic fold longer than their rising class status would have predicted. Further, as wedge issues moved to the forefront, we should expect that some of the perturbations and general trends evident in table 3.1 should reflect value differences. We turn to the latter first.

In research presented elsewhere, we have analyzed the forces that led to low turnout and defection among white, non-Hispanic Catholic Democrats from 1960–1996. Sufficient data are not available for this analysis in 1952–1956 and the factor structure changed enough in 2000 not to be included in the source. This work makes fairly complex analyses of why Catholic Democrats did not remain loyal partisans during the post–New Deal period.[14] We extracted explanatory factors from respondents' feelings toward groups and positions on issues in any given presidential election. There is basic continuity in the factor structure from 1964 to 1996. The coefficients that account for turnout failure and defection are based on multinomial probit analysis. They tell us that the substantial defections of white Catholic Democrats to Nixon or Wallace in 1968 were based on negative feelings toward African Americans and toward government policies presumably aimed at enhancing equality of opportunity. They tell us that in 1980 Catholic Democratic defection to Reagan was far less the result of his conservative family values policies (abortion, women's rights, etc.) and far more the result of negative feelings on race and the role of government. Family values were not an independently important factor in Catholic Democratic defection until after four years of the Clintons. Throughout the entire post–New Deal period and especially from 1964 to 1992, Democrats lost adherents among Catholics because Republicans were able to find an acceptable language that rubbed open the wounds of racial grievances and created a sense of relative deprivation among whites. Family values issues merged with the dominant race-based party ideology factor in 1972, 1992, and 2000. In both 1964 and 1992, appeals to patriotism were also sources of instability in Democratic loyalty.

These findings have to be disappointing to those who argue that Catholics are generally more progressive on racial issues than Protestants. They are. But Republicans were able to tap into the discontent that exists and to destabilize partisan loyalties. The findings also challenge the notion that Reagan's verbal championing of family values captured the loyalty of Catholics (after a record of signing into law the most permissive abortion policy in the United States and a lengthy religious apostasy). It attracted some, but not on the magnitude of race until well after Reagan in the 1990s. Catholics have been historically slow to embrace politicians who publicly flaunt piety—a reminder of Calvert's position in Maryland. Yet, there is evidence that in the last three elections, abortion-related appeals have been implicated in Democratic defections.

In a manner reminiscent of the effects of Bryan on Catholics, Democrats have shot themselves in the foot on abortion-related issues in recent presidential elections. Sample surveys of the 1970s and 1980s ironically have shown a higher proportion of abortion opponents among Democrats than among Republicans. Reagan and Bush were both originally pro-choice, but after the

Equal Rights Amendment (ERA) ratification wars they realized there was a large base among Evangelicals that was restless in the Democratic Party and that could be mobilized. The presidents-to-be switched, following their new base. Democrats, however, were doing increasingly well in a traditional Republican base—business and professional women. Feminist leaders became an important interest group in the party. Young, educated, professional women were seeking autonomy from male control, and the notion that women should be free to decide about their sexuality and whether and when to have a baby captured their sentiment. Abortion was seen as the outer boundary for birth control. But for others, it was seen as a compassionate option for terrible circumstances leading to problem pregnancies. For Democratic candidates, this took the form of "a woman's right to choose." While Republican presidential candidates made appeals to code words like "pro-life" or "culture of life" to mobilize their base, they always stopped short of a constitutional amendment to ban abortion. Rather, they spoke of nominating judges who "respected life" and "the original intent of the Founders." They retained much of their pro-choice base.

Democrats, while accusing Republicans of an antiabortion litmus test for judicial appointments, developed their own pro-choice litmus test. In 1988, they dropped a platform acknowledgment recognizing "the religious and ethical concerns many Americans have about abortion." In 1992, they refused to allow popular Catholic governor Robert Casey of Pennsylvania to address the convention with a minority report challenging the party's acceptance of government funding for abortion as a "fundamental right." They drew a line in the sand, opposing instances where abortion was defined as a medical issue rather than a privacy issue for fear that it would move the country toward a definition of life in the womb. And in their opposition to a late-term procedure that extracts a viable fetus from the womb, they failed to develop a counter language to the Republican label "partial-birth abortion."

Successive presidential candidates Clinton, Gore, and Kerry described their abortion policies as "safe, available and rare," which comes close to the mediating positions of most Catholics and, in fact, most Americans. Yet in recent elections, the party has continued to suffer modest erosion in Catholic support, where abortion can be painted by Republicans as symptomatic of a broader range of cultural issue positions. In the post-2004 self-examination of the Democratic loss, Senator Hillary Clinton and many others urged the party to adopt more effective language to describe a "compassionate" abortion policy. At the same time Democratic women's groups saw the candidacy of pro-life ex-Congressman Timothy Roemer for chair of the Democratic National Committee as a nonstarter, and criticized new

Senate minority leader Harry Reid for his pro-life positions, which they charged would impede unified opposition to Bush's judicial nominations. While "rights" language has long outlived its political utility, Democrats seem powerless to find a language that again resonates with Catholics who care about church teachings. We expect the family values factor to grow as a source of defection or realignment so long as Republican White Houses continue to outsmart Democrats.

The other source of change in the Democratic-favoring culture is the diminishing distinctiveness of Catholic life. Earlier, we spoke about the process of assimilation and upward mobility. Here it is more important to note the drastic change in mass-attendance patterns.[15] At the end of the time series, frequency of mass attendance in all Catholic age cohorts was greatly reduced. Attendance dropped precipitously in the 1970s, and only among Catholics who came of age during the New Deal was it partially restored. Ironically, this is the age cohort that is both most conservative on family values and has remained the most loyal to the Democrats. Attendance among others never recovered and it is lowest among Catholics under age forty-five. Yet this is where the greatest growth in Republican affinity has occurred. The growth is disproportionately among the young men, who again show weaker attendance than the younger women. Neither young men nor young women are especially inclined to buy into Republican appeals on family values and abortion. The men prefer Republican economic and racial policies. The women prefer Democratic economic and social justice policies. In that, neither group is greatly distinctive from their age cohorts outside Catholicism. There is slightly more recognition and acceptance of Catholic social teaching among the young women, but they too show more frequent mass attendance.

These kinds of findings have led Leege, Wald, Krueger, and Mueller; Abramowitz and Saunders; Wilson; and Mockabee to suggest that Catholics are gradually moving away from a system of partisanship based on group identity, toward partisanship based on liberal-conservative ideology.[16] In that respect, they may be approximating the political momentum that divides mainline and evangelical Protestants. We do not accept all of the "culture wars" argument because (1) Catholic social teaching is a leaven, and (2) the diminution in Catholic cultural distinctiveness is a more powerful macro explanation. Mainly, we do not buy into the "culture wars" argument because politicians themselves exercise autonomy in deciding when to heat up or cool down value differences to their own advantage.

We have not addressed trends in the partisan loyalties of Hispanic Catholics. The basic problem is the lack of time-series data. Starting in the 1990s, we had sufficient sample sizes in ANES to start making defensible generalizations. When supplemented by specialized surveys of Hispanic groups, we could say that about two-thirds of Mexican Americans and Puerto Ricans voted Democratic for president and about three-quarters of Cuban Americans voted Republican. However, scholars are only beginning to give sufficient attention to whether these patterns differ according to Catholicism, evangelical Protestantism, and mainline Protestantism. There are knotty measurement problems in deciding when a Hispanic is actually a Catholic, although in the country of origin they may have been baptized Catholic and imbibed Catholic culture. We have enough of a baseline to claim that in 2004, there was substantial movement by Hispanics in a Republican direction. The magnitude is in dispute. Preelection surveys and trend data during the campaign cannot sustain the 44 percent Republican claim of the exit polls.[17] The National Annenberg Election Study of 2004 can support a 39 percent figure. It also observes more movement in the Republican direction among Hispanic Evangelicals than among Hispanic Catholics. The former tend to resemble the movement in the last two decades of non-Hispanic Evangelicals. We see these measurement issues as challenging over the next two decades, because answers to them will have consequences both for presidential campaign strategy and for postelection interpretations. Further, there is potential for the test of rich theories about reference groups, competing identities, processes of assimilation, and social mobility. We underanalyze Hispanics—whether Catholics or Evangelicals—at our continuing scholarly peril.

INTERACTIONS BETWEEN POLITICIANS AND PRELATES: THE CASES OF KENNEDY, REAGAN, AND GEORGE W. BUSH

We will use three recent illustrations of the complex nature of interactions between ambitious politicians and Catholic leadership. They include passivity on both sides, proactivity by the prelate, and proactivity by the politician.

The relationship between Richard Cardinal Cushing of Boston and the Kennedy family is almost a classic study of the private rather than public dimension of religion. Cushing has been described as the Kennedy family's cardinal, not unlike the relationships that characterized prelates and princes in medieval times. The merger of Joseph Kennedy's lust for wealth and power with Rose Fitzgerald's political lineage could have produced nothing but the expectation of high political office for successive sons. Joseph Sr. got his wealth in the gray areas of transition from Prohibition to legal liquor. He exercised his power over Washington politicians and Hollywood women. Rose practiced pre–Vatican II daily devotions and learned to live with deceit and tragedy. It was a family of destiny, but much in need of grace. The Church offers forgiveness to sinners through its sacraments.

Cushing also had an Irish power broker's vision for the American Church. He was part of the group of American bishops and theologians who sought accommodation between church and state through mutual respect for the legitimate sphere of action for each.

John F. Kennedy was a New Deal Democrat and a cold warrior with no tolerance for communist expansion. He did not see conflict between the claims of church and the claims of state because he was an *American* Catholic. Some have argued that he was never obsessed with the notion that his Catholic beliefs and practices should alter what he wanted to do; although far more urbane and sophisticated, he was his father's son. There probably would not have been much basis for conflict between Cushing and JFK. They understood sin and grace, human frailty, and magnificent accomplishment. They found communists abhorrent and they saw government as legitimately designed to improve the lot of the poor. Probably Kennedy's first moral crisis as president was in what to do about the civil rights movement. He hardly had credentials as a desegregationist. But the white segregationists' response to the peaceful claims of blacks in the early 1960s appeared to strike a moral nerve, and for the first time he cast a government response to a racial issue as a moral imperative. Then he was slain. It was up to Lyndon Johnson to use all of his legislative acumen to enact systems for racial justice into law.

The Kennedy presidency preceded the public conflicts over gender rights, changes in family structure, abortion, homosexuality, drugs, and other issues. In fact, we cannot really be sure what Kennedy would have done about Vietnam withdrawal. Cushing's prelature preceded the expectation that the National Conference of Catholic Bishops would issue pastoral letters on public issues. Below the Pope, the Catholic leadership structure was highly Balkanized, each bishop choosing to define church-state matters as he saw fit. Both Kennedy and Cushing saw Kennedy's Catholicism as a political advantage in the large swing states. Neither seemed to have the expectation that it would mandate certain kinds of policies. With the exception of state aid to parochial schools, sectarian conflict did not dominate the public agenda. Kennedy opposed parochial aid, fearing charges of being a tool of Rome. Prelate-politician interaction was passive.

The second set of interactions—between John Cardinal O'Connor and other prelates and Ronald Reagan and other Republicans—exhibits more proactive behavior by the prelate, followed by opportunistic behavior by the politician.

O'Connor was chosen to lead New York. It was the most powerful arch-diocese in the United States in the most powerful city in the world. From that see, Francis Cardinal Spellman had been a highly influential spokesman for Catholics in America. Presidents chose not to ignore him, in part because they needed to co-opt his influence for national purposes. The Archbishop of New York also holds the titular mission to the American military.

O'Connor had been bishop of Scranton, hardly a powerhouse diocese in Catholic circles. Both by personality and sense of vocation, O'Connor welcomed public visibility and a fight for a worthy cause. Some of his col-leagues among the bishops had reservations about his appointment to New York, and some were probably jealous for their own advancement. Never-theless, he was faithful to the Pope, and the Papal Nuncio thought he was right for New York. Before he had his feet wet on the new assignment and even before investiture as a cardinal, O'Connor plunged into the middle of the 1984 political campaign. Apparently unlike Cushing, O'Connor was de-termined that powerful Catholic politicians would act politically according to church teachings. The case in point was Governor Mario Cuomo, who had signed legislation providing state funding for abortions. In response to a reporter's question, O'Connor said that he would look into the excom-munication of Cuomo.[18] Cuomo, a lifelong student of St. Thomas Aquinas, shrank neither from political nor theological conflict. In a widely publi-cized speech at Notre Dame that summer, Cuomo argued that rival claims between faith and public stewardship could be mediated only through con-science-informed prudential judgments. He thought he had found common ground with O'Connor, who was willing to use prudential judgments on justice and life issues outside abortion. But conservative publicists quickly reduced Cuomo's argument to the familiar language—I am personally op-posed to abortion but I am sworn to uphold the law.

What the nation saw here, however, was two relatively new directions in Catholic church-state relations: (1) a Catholic politician of presidential stature was willing to challenge a prelate on *theological* grounds and (2) an American prelate felt comfortable holding a Catholic politician to higher standards of behavior than any other politician. The latter opened new terrain for non-Catholic politicians and leadership in the Evangelical right: attack the Catholic politician through his/her own church leadership for not being Catholic enough. Political opportunity had taken the country a long way from the traditional charge that a Catholic was unfit for the presidency because he would be too Catholic.

While the Cuomo-O'Connor controversy simmered, Democrats were choosing candidates. Women's groups had set as their highest priority in 1984 placing a woman on the presidential ticket. The convention settled on

Congresswoman Geraldine Ferraro of New York, a pro-choice Italian Catholic who ran in both congressional and feminist leadership circles. She had joined hands with a small but aggressive Catholic pro-choice group that had challenged the bishops. Immediately, and many Catholics feel justifiably, O'Connor took after Ferraro. Never accused of theological acumen, Ferraro was unable to mount a defense in the Church. O'Connor was now attracting an intellectual entourage among New York's influential neoconservatives, many of whom had left the Democratic Party over the issues that Ferraro and her feminist supporters symbolized. O'Connor escalated the language, telling devout Catholics that they could not vote for a presidential ticket including a candidate who supported abortion. When put together with pastoral letters on the responsibility of Catholic citizens to vote, this came dangerously close to an endorsement of the Reagan-Bush ticket.

Other bishops turned to damage control. Bishop Malone of Youngstown, president of the National Conference of Catholic Bishops, placed an advertisement in the *New York Times* that reiterated both the obligations of citizenship and the obligation of bishops not to endorse (or disendorse) candidates. Influential Joseph Cardinal Bernardin of Chicago spoke on church-state matters at Georgetown; he took pains to distinguish differences between Catholic approaches to politics and the Evangelical right's approaches, but his central argument about the position of Catholic leadership was somewhat similar to Cuomo's: "There is a distinction between a moral principle and the best political or legal strategy for realizing it in public life."[19]

The Reagan administration had been bruised by the 1983 bishops' pastoral letter, "The Challenge of Peace." Already there were plans for another pastoral letter on the U.S. economy that did not bode well. But here was an opportunity to divide and conquer, to exploit differences among American bishops. The Reagan White House and conservative foundations developed a strategy of consulting and courting friendly prelates, of funding think tanks with visible Catholic intellectual presence, of subsidizing books and conferences that established the reputations of conservative Catholic authors, and of funding endowed chairs and programs at Catholic universities. Catholic diversity and personal ambition, among both the leadership and laity, did much to create political opportunity. Reagan strengthened this growing relationship by having a positive and friendly meeting with Pope John Paul II on May 2, 1984 in Washington, D.C.

Although Cardinal O'Connor comes off as the heavy in this narrative, it must be stressed that O'Connor was committed to the full range of Catholic teaching on human life and social justice questions. He did not shrink from criticizing conservative domestic policies, particularly as a conservative Republican movement with harsh edges took control of Congress after 1994. At his death, he was eulogized as a consistent advocate both for Church teaching and compassionate government responses for the poor. That too offers a lesson: a political party that thinks it can capture Catholic leadership often learns otherwise.

The third case study is one where most of the initiative toward Catholics comes from the politician, in this case George W. Bush and his handlers. It takes several forms: sanitizing the candidate, visibly courting Catholic leaders and using divide-and-conquer techniques, addressing a limited range of hot-button moral topics, "speaking Catholic," studying the Catholic electorate for its loyal partisan bases and vulnerable segments, and occupying vacuums in the Church's mobilization structures with partisan front organizations that appear to have the tacit endorsement of Catholic leaders.

The first thing that Governor Bush had to do was perform damage control on his past. He knew there was a record of profligate behavior, inveterate drunkenness including a DUI, job failure, and military irresponsibility. These behaviors had changed for the good after a religious conversion experience at the age of forty. Bush and his political manager, Karl Rove, realized that if Bush were planning to run against the sleaziness and shame of Clinton's White House and if he planned to mobilize Evangelicals as his base, he needed to select a religious language that forgave his past. No parable is more powerful in Christian families than the prodigal son. Once the sinner recognizes his life of sin and turns his life over to the mercy of God, God will forgive, strengthen, and bring new life. Bush's record post-forty seemed to attest to that scriptural truth. In his acceptance address to the Republican convention, then, he spoke not only of turning his life over to a Higher Power but drew in others of the profligate Baby Boom generation who had seen the light. A "prodigal generation" now offered leadership to the country. This stroke of genius inoculated Bush from later revelations, and suggested to some premillenial dispensationalists that he was chosen by God to lead our country through these times of testing. As a born-again Christian, he would not deliberately mislead the public. Bush deserved the benefit of the doubt.

President Bush traces his most important political learning experiences to his father's 1988 campaign for the White House. Young Bush and Rove worked with Lee Atwater, the master of wedge issues. In the Iowa caucuses, George W. marveled at how the Reverend Pat Robertson was able to gain the support and mobilize Evangelicals with a language that mixed religious pietism and patriotism. In a segment caught on tape, Bush, who had had a recent conversion experience, said, "I can do that. I can speak that language." And he did—in South Carolina and in other venues. He also had observed how Atwater attached homosexual innuendoes to political opponents and how he had crafted the Willie Horton ad, which mixed fear of crime and fear that black males seek to assault white women with his opponent's civil libertarian position. Rove thought that his sidekick, W. Bush, was so good at the pietistic-patriotic language that he had a future in Texas politics. Bush himself was a seeker engaged in daily Bible study; scriptural turns of phrase rolled easily from his lips.

By the time Bush was governor and seriously exploring a presidential bid, Deal Hudson, editor of *Crisis*, a conservative Catholic fortnightly, and Steve Wagner, a Catholic and Republican pollster, had convinced Rove that restless Catholic Democrats could complete a winning Republican coalition. Catholics, who were attracted by Reagan's American religion, had been frightened away by the Republicans' relentless pietistic sectarian attacks during the 1990s. Hudson and Wagner also argued that Bush would have to "speak Catholic," that is, instead of treating government as the enemy, find ways that it could enhance compassionate partnerships with churches to alleviate human suffering.

For 2000, Bush fashioned the overarching theme "compassionate conservatism" and made the faith-based initiative the centerpiece of his domestic program. He adopted Marian Wright Edelman's slogan "Leave No Child Behind" to sell his school reforms. Looking toward his reelection in 2004, President Bush cut taxes, but equally important, vetoed no government spending bill despite its impact on the mounting deficit. Government was no longer the enemy, a position that resonated with many Catholics. Bush called for massive American response to the AIDS pandemic in Africa. He later asked Congress to liberalize immigration policies toward Mexicans who entered the United States illegally but were gainfully employed. Both were policies that appealed to Catholic sensitivities. Both drew criticism from conservatives in the party, but that again showed Catholics how compassionate Bush was.

President Bush also used visible contacts with Catholic leaders to show his respect for their moral guidance. He had three meetings with the Pope during his first term, the last in election summer 2004. Although each time the Pope expressed displeasure with Bush's conservative domestic positions and aggressive war policies, these were lost on much of the Catholic public; Bush had sought counsel from the Holy Father. He appeared to select moral issues and tend them with deep gravitas. On stem cell research, he already occupied the Catholic position—but spent weeks of announcing to the public that he was seeking the advice of Catholic ethicists, among others. After staff members say he had already made up his mind to invade Iraq, and after refusal to see mainline Protestants who opposed a preemptive strike against Saddam Hussein, Bush, with much public attention, received the Papal Nuncio to present the Holy Father's opposition to war at this time. Although his decision was contrary to the Pope's position, he had heard the Holy Father out. Shortly thereafter, President Bush dispatched General Colin Powell, a respected moral leader, to the United Nations to establish that the "facts of the case" made war the only moral alternative. Facts are needed to make prudential moral judgments, and perhaps the Holy Father did not have access to the facts.

Placing gay marriage onto the 2004 election agenda was a classic case of President Bush co-opting the initiative from Catholic—and Evangelical—leaders. At a hastily called press conference in August 2003, President Bush responded to barbed queries about duplicity leading up to the war in Iraq. The Rose Garden was uncomfortably hot. At one point in the questioning, however, the President stepped aside from the podium, placed his hand on his heart, and in his most earnest persona made a plea. He said, in brief, that he believed marriage is a sacred bond between a man and a woman. Then, the tough questioning on Iraq resumed. In its feeding frenzy, the press reported how they had trapped the President on Iraq. They missed the reason Bush and Rove had called the press conference, in itself a rare event. Shortly thereafter, Pope John Paul II released a Vatican teaching on marriage, in particular gay marriage. A terrible wrong, he called it, and called on all officials and, in particular, Catholic legislators and jurists to resist pressures to authorize it.

To that point in August 2003, no legislative or judicial action had approved gay marriage. In the Defense of Marriage Act of 1996, with support from President Clinton, Congress had defined marriage as a partnership between a man and a woman. States, including California, had banned gay marriage. The only related item on the agenda was whether states should recognize health care benefits and hospital visitation privileges for committed partners in a same-sex union. Recently, the Texas court had declared a longtime ban on sodomy unconstitutional. The Massachusetts court ruling on gay marriage was still many months off. The response in San Francisco with many illegal marriages had not occurred.

In effect, the President had escalated the partner benefits issue into a gay-marriage issue. Polls had shown that over half of the public supported same-sex benefits, but nearly three-quarters opposed gay marriage. Bush had done more: in heating up a new wedge issue for the 2004 campaign, he had occupied a Catholic position *before* the strong proscription was released by the Pope. Once again, Catholics could say, "He is one of us."

In successive months, the President continued to heat up the issue. In his State of the Union address, he framed it in *cultural populism* terms, naming the enemy—activist judges who are out of touch with the moral values of the public. He tried hard to pin the issue on Democrats, but John Kerry and John Edwards had also expressed opposition to gay marriage. Both sets of campaigners were careful not to target gays and lesbians themselves. In the final debate, Kerry got caught in a trap set by the Cheneys. Vice President John and Lynne Cheney's daughter is a lesbian; she was also an aide in the campaign. In Iowa late in the campaign, Cheney acknowledged her lifestyle and expressed the family's love for her. In the vice presidential debate, John Edwards spoke positively of this acknowledgment. In the final presidential debate, Kerry also expressed warm feelings, saying that we are all God's children and that he respected that the Cheneys could show such love for the daughter, whom he named. Within hours, Lynne Cheney blasted Kerry for exploiting this issue and charged him as someone who would do anything to get elected. This, of course, was the culmination of a campaign against Kerry as the ultimate political opportunist. The press gave the exchange a long life right up to Election Day.

On the Catholic front, the Bush campaign made major institutional efforts to exploit the gay marriage issue. Although the Catholic hierarchy and parish priests are prohibited from endorsing candidates, into this vacuum a network of nationally funded but parish-based organizations of "Catholics for. . ." was established by the Bush campaign and friends. They stressed not only church teaching on abortion but also gay lifestyle issues. As mentioned earlier, several bishops said they would refuse communion to Kerry. Republican and conservative front organizations distributed this information. The press paid attention to them rather than to most bishops, who reiterated the Church's position on religion and politics adopted in 1984.

The difference from Reagan in 1984 and Bush in 2004 was in the way the issue was created, timed, and played. In 1984, a prelate took the initiative. The politicians followed. In 2004, the politician took the initiative, and he played the press and prelates for advantage among Catholics. In 1984, the nation had a large number of visible and influential Catholic prelates. The bishop's conference was diverse but still able to unite on pastoral letters. Even thoughtful non-Catholics looked to them for moral teaching on pressing public issues. In 2004, many of the nation's visible, powerful bishops had been brought low by the pedophile scandal, hush money, and charges of homosexual behavior. Not only was there insufficient unity to agree on pastoral letters beyond abortion and gay marriage, but in the eyes of many, Catholic and non-Catholic alike, they had forfeited their moral authority to teach on *any* public issue, least of all human sexuality. Further, leaders of the Evangelical religious right had become politically so prominent in the intervening decades, that Catholic prelates were developing an inferiority complex and avoided a variety of social justice issues important in 2004. Some feared internal criticism if they did not stick to the abortion/gay marriage priority.

The situation was opportune for the Bush organization's Catholic Voter Project. Few people would visit the Bishop's Conference website, where lengthy and carefully nuanced statements on religion and politics appeared. Instead, they would pay attention to the statements of self-designated leaders among bishops, as enhanced by campaign front organizations, the Republican National Committee itself, and Clear Channel, Sinclair, and Fox. While survey data show no nationwide groundswell in support for Bush among Catholics, even the modest movement in states like Ohio, Florida, and others was all it took. Careful research has documented how microtargeting reached vulnerable groups in battleground states and how, in particular, the gay marriage issue enhanced Republican turnout in key electoral college states.[20]

THE CHURCH/STATE, RELIGION/POLITICS DIVIDE

Much of this chapter has addressed the uneasy push and tug between the obligation to witness to the state and to shape its policies and the caution that state powers could disadvantage the Catholic Church and violate religious liberty. Although Catholics and Evangelicals both have many institutional interests to protect and they share some policy values, Catholics with any memory are wary about too much state power in the hands of Evangelicals, their historic persecutors. It is interesting to note that the Christian Coalition has made little more progress with organizing Catholic affiliates than it has among African American Christians and Jews.[21]

A number of studies have addressed this spate of issues, either by looking at Catholics alone or comparatively with other religious traditions. Leege and Welch, Leege, Wald, and Kellstedt have found that parish-connected Catholics expect prelates and priests to offer teaching on political issues, but the overwhelming majority place the teaching into a calculus of conscience where they will make their own prudential judgments.[22] Unlike Evangelicals but more like mainline Protestants, the overwhelming majority of Catholics feel it is inappropriate for clergy to endorse candidates or parties or even to appear to endorse. Wilcox and Jelen have shown that Catholics occupy the middle ranges in issues of church-state separation. Mainline Protestants seek a "high wall," Jews like the high wall but encourage assistance for all religious groups, Evangelicals seek government protection and assistance to all groups, and Catholics are split between the high wall position and the protection/assistance options.[23] Current American Catholic opinion resembles the dilemmas of the Maryland colony in the 1640s.

Kohut, Green, Keeter, and Toth find that Evangelicals and black Protestants are most likely to want the government to take special steps to preserve the nation's religious heritage, Catholics are evenly split between this position and maintaining a high degree of separation between church and state, mainline Protestants are more supportive of the high wall position, and Jews are heavily supportive of it.[24] Two-thirds of Catholics do not feel the United States should declare itself a Christian nation, perhaps recalling that in American history "Christian" meant "Protestant." Nevertheless, a solid majority of Catholics, only a few points less than Evangelicals, feel it important to protect Christian values through political action. In all of these findings, more religiously committed members of the tradition are more likely to embrace the position that draws a less fine line between religion and politics. Among Catholics, Kohut, Green, Keeter, and Toth point out that support for Church involvement in politics has grown over the last quarter century, but not as rapidly as it has among Evangelicals. Catholics note the largest increase in contact by political parties in presidential elections, even larger than partisan contacts reported by Evangelicals.

These patterns suggest that historical precedent plays a large part in the way Catholics approach church-state matters, but that there is also a willingness to contend on matters of faith, values, and practices, and some willingness to consider Church teaching but primarily to inform conscience. It further suggests that Catholics, as a recognizable swing electorate, are increasingly targeted by the parties in presidential elections. What the data do not show is any increase in the willingness of Catholics to be told for whom to vote. Exacerbating the problem is the steady decline in the unity and moral authority of American Catholic leadership since its peak in the 1980s. Given these characteristics, it is little surprise that the Bush organization developed its Catholic Voter Project, put thought into the management and timing of positions, defined policies in a language comfortable to Catholics, co-opted Catholic leadership agendas, and filled vacuums in Catholic organizational design with partisan fronts and media attention. It is also clear that Democrats are a long way from recapturing their presidential campaign advantages in the old political culture of Catholicism. Until that occurs, the spoils belong to the organization that outanalyzes, outsmarts, and outhustles the opponent.

Chapter 4

Seculars and the American Presidency[1]

Lyman A. Kellstedt

Religion and politics is a growth industry. Much of the talk has been about Evangelicals and their emergence as the key constituency of the Republican Party. Other foci have included the decline in the size of mainline Protestantism or the movement of Roman Catholics from their leadership position in the Democratic Party coalition to a group that is "up for grabs" today. Attention has also been given to the key role of religious minorities such as black Protestants or Hispanic Catholics. However, the secular population, those with no religious preference or commitments, has remained under the radar, so to speak. This is unfortunate. For despite the difficulty in assessing the size of the secular community, there is no doubt that it is large and it is reasonably clear that it is growing. In addition, the evidence indicates a growing affinity between seculars and the Democratic Party. Yet, as suggested above, seculars remain an afterthought in most religion and politics research. This chapter is a modest effort to change that situation.

Specifically, this chapter examines the secular or nonreligious community—its size, its social-demographic character, its religious characteristics, and its political behavior. The analysis begins with a look back in time before turning to the 2004 election. In survey research, "secular" (or "no religion") tends to be used as an undifferentiated concept. In contrast, this chapter argues that the secular population has numerous components, including atheists and agnostics, who are often militant opponents of religion; the nonreligious unaffiliated, who tend to be indifferent to religion; and, potentially, the nominally religious, who claim an affiliation but show no signs of religiosity. This last group is rarely, if ever, considered secular in recent scholarship. These three subgroups differ not only religiously, but also politically. In addition, there is an unaffiliated but religious group that in most studies is considered secular, but does not belong in that category. This misclassification occurs because analysts focus on the absence of religious affiliation for this group, rather than examining its religious beliefs and behaviors.

Why is an accurate mapping of the secular population important? First, we need to know the size of this segment of the society, and this can only be done by establishing meaningful membership criteria. Should only non-affiliates be included? Or should affiliates without religious commitments be incorporated? What about the unaffiliated who nevertheless hold orthodox beliefs and relatively high levels of religious practice? Can we distinguish among groups that are potentially secular? For example, do atheists and agnostics stand out from other secular groups? And, finally, how does the secular population, however determined, differ from the religious affiliated in social-demographic characteristics, social and political attitudes, and political behavior? We address these questions in what follows in this chapter.

ARE THERE A VARIETY OF SECULARS?

Almost forty years ago, the sociologist Glenn Vernon argued, "Those who study religion scientifically have tended to ignore a category of religious phenomenon which appears to be of significance and an understanding of which provides a more complete understanding of religious behavior. That category is the religious 'nones.'"[2] In an extensive review of prior literature, Vernon showed that few scholars had tackled the problem. Leading sociologists of religion like Gerhard Lenski as well as Charles Glock and Rodney Stark had begun to explore religion using in-depth surveys,[3] but had not dealt in any detail with the size of the secular or unaffiliated population. Vernon's work pointed out the problem, but suffered from the lack of a national sample, making it impossible for him to estimate the size of the "nones." Gallup surveys going back to the 1930s collected data on affiliation, beliefs, and religious practices, but scholars did not assess these data for their bearing on the size of the secular population until a review article appeared by John Benson, followed by work by Norval Glenn, and Andrew Greeley.[4] Glenn's focus did not go beyond those who claimed no religious affiliation, Vernon's nones. Greeley's work, however, was somewhat off target for the main concerns of this chapter. His purpose was to refute the "secularization hypothesis," the assumption that modern societies would inevitably lose their religious flavor.[5] He concluded that "religion does not seem to have been notably weakened in the United States during the past half-century, insofar as we are able to measure its strength from survey items."[6] But his extensive analysis was more concerned with the *presence* of beliefs and practices rather than the *absence* of religion. As a result, he did not examine the possible disparate types of seculars or even give much attention to religious nones.

The inattention to seculars is somewhat paradoxical given the focus in the literature on secularization.[7] In this literature, little attention was given to seculars themselves. If secularization is on the increase in American society, the size of the secular population should be growing. It turns out that the evidence for this growth from opinion surveys conducted over the past sixty years is difficult to assess at times.[8] Generally, scholars have classified individuals as secular on the basis of absence of affiliation.[9] Gallup surveys conducted over the past sixty years provide us with some evidence about the size of the unaffiliated population. Immediately after World War II, Gallup found that 6 percent said "none" in response to a religious preference question. This figure decreased to about 2 percent in the 1950s and early 1960s, as many veterans of the war began to raise families and participate in a religious revitalization noted by some scholars.[10] Kohut and colleagues classified about 10 percent of the population in 1965 as secular, combining both unaffiliated and the nominally religious.[11] Since the 1960s, the percentage of unaffiliated increased to around 9 percent. Kosmin and Lachman found about the same percentage.[12] In recent work, Hout and Fischer show that the figure has risen significantly in the past decade to about 14 percent.[13] Even more recently, the Pew Forum on Religion and Public Life finds the size of the unaffiliated population to have reached 16 percent in 2007.[14] So there is evidence that the unaffiliated population has grown significantly, especially in recent years.

But is the absence of affiliation the only basis for assigning a person to a secular category? Some individuals give an affiliation response based on family history but do not show any evidence of religious belief or practice. Others may claim an affiliation because of the pervasive religiosity in the United States (which makes it easier to give a religious preference than to say "none"). In addition, many affiliation questions assume a religious "preference," a problem noted by several scholars.[15] Conversely, absence of affiliation is not a foolproof indicator of secularity. Some respondents without a current affiliation may have strong religious beliefs and regular religious practices. They simply may not be "affiliated" at the time of the survey, "in between" churches as a result of a geographical move, or in the process of changing churches for some other reason. This group's lack of religious "preference" should not be taken as evidence of secular status.

In addition, some respondents—the nominal religionists—name an affiliation but lack basic beliefs or practices, do not believe in God or life after death, or never darken the door of a house of worship or engage in prayer. They may resemble the unaffiliated in social and political attitudes and behavior in that they pick up few, if any, religious cues. It is reasonable to assume that the "nominal" group is sizeable. Assuming the existence of a nominal group is one thing, but deciding which variables determine membership in such a group is another. Failure to believe in God and life after death are good possibilities as are the absence of church attendance and prayer. Or those who regard religion as unimportant in their lives might also be "nominal," despite claiming an affiliation. Generally speaking, nominal religionists have been ignored in scholarly research, although Kohut and colleagues (2000) combine them with no affiliation.[16]

So far, our discussion suggests two groups of seculars and an important third group of respondents: (1) the religiously unaffiliated with little or no religiosity, (2) the nominal religionists, and (3) the religiously unaffiliated with high religiosity. Ideally, the first group should be separated into three categories: (1) atheists, (2) agnostics, and (3) the remaining unaffiliated, who simply have no religious affiliation.[17]

Why are these distinctions important? In a society where the public role of religion is under such scrutiny, it is crucial to ascertain the political attitudes and behaviors for those for whom religious cues are minimal or nonexistent. Can the distinctions noted above be sustained empirically, and, if so, are the different groups of seculars similar or different in their political attitudes and behaviors? How greatly do they differ from those who affiliate with a religion and who hold at least a modicum of religious beliefs and engage in some religious practices?

LOCATING THE SECULARS OVER TIME

For the portion of the analysis that deals with change over time, we make use of the General Social Surveys (GSS). The religious preference question, despite its limitations, allows us to examine changes in the no affiliation category over time. In addition, a church attendance item was included in each of the years the GSS conducted a survey. For most years, a dichotomous item on belief in life after death was included as well. Respondents who claimed an affiliation, attended church once per year or less, *and* said they did not believe in life after death (or gave a "don't know" response) were placed in the nominal religion category.[18] This allows for comparisons between nominals and those with no affiliation, as well as with the remainder of the sample.

For 2004, we rely on the National Survey of Religion and Politics (NSRP), funded by the Pew Forum on Religion and Public Life. This survey interviewed four thousand respondents, using random digit dialing (RDD) procedures. Both preelection and postelection surveys were conducted. A large battery of religious measures was included in the survey, allowing us to compare five groups of potential seculars: (1) atheists and agnostics;[19] (2) unaffiliated nonreligious; (3) unaffiliated religious; (4) nominal religionists; and (5) religious modernists, who are less than orthodox in belief and low in levels of religious practice.[20] The first portion of our analysis examines change over time using the categories from the GSS surveys. The latter part of the analysis involves an in-depth look at results from the 2004 NSRP using the broader set of categories created from those data.

The analysis begins by estimating the size of the unaffiliated or secular population and comparing it with other religious groups over the years from 1972 to 2004. Table 4.1 demonstrates that the proportion of the public with no religious affiliation (labeled "No Affiliation") remained fairly stable from 1973 to 1994, increasing by only one percentage point, well within the margin of sampling error. However, the size of this group increased significantly in the 1996–2002 time period and continued to rise in 2004. This is not the place to attempt an in-depth assessment of the causes for this sudden rise. Social-demographic explanations for the shift appear unlikely, for the changes in education levels, to use but one example, tend to occur gradually, as would general secularization. Hout and Fischer suggest that the spurt of nonaffiliation is the result of negative reactions to the activities of the Christian Right, leading individuals to eschew their faith, although such a causal link is difficult to establish. Given the significant decline in the percentage of mainline Protestants from the early 1970s through 2004, it is likely that part of the increase in nonaffiliation comes from that tradition. The decreasing percentage of nominal religionists raises another possibility—that many former nominals simply abandoned any pretense of religious affiliation and joined the ranks of the unaffiliated. Whatever the explanation, the recent upsurge in nonaffiliation in the GSS data is impossible to deny, as is the decline in the percentages in the nominal category.

Who are the "secular" groups in terms of social demographics? Table 4.2 addresses the question. Those with no affiliation tend to be younger than both the nominal religionists and the religious affiliated. Here the two groups of potential seculars differ greatly. The former fits the stereotype of the young who may return to the religion of their youth as they marry and have children or simply come to religious faith for the first time as adults. The latter claim an affiliation but do not associate themselves with the beliefs and practices of organized religion. Turning to gender differences, the unaffiliated are more likely to be male than the other two groups, with the nominals falling in the middle (until 2004, when they resemble the unaffiliated), while the religious affiliated are more likely to be female. The unaffiliated are the most educated of the three groups until 2004 when they are edged out by the nominals. At the end of the time period, both groups of potential seculars are more likely to have graduated from college than the religious affiliated. Both potential

Table 4.1:   Size of Religious Traditions over Time

Religious Tradition:	1973-1980	1983-1987	1988-1994	1996-2002	2004	Gain or Loss Over Time
White Evangelical Protestant	20.2%	22.9%	24.6%	23.9%	24.2%	+3.6%
White Mainline Protestant	25.1	20.5	19.2	16.8	14.0	-11.1
Black Protestant	8.0	9.6	9.6	8.3	9.0	+1.0
Hispanic Protestant	0.4	0.6	0.9	1.2	1.0	+0.6
White Roman Catholic	19.8	19.9	19.2	17.7	16.4	-3.4
Hispanic Catholic	1.8	2.4	2.8	3.7	4.3	+2.5
Mormon	0.7	2.1	1.6	0.6	1.4	+0.7
Jewish	1.3	1.5	1.5	1.6	1.5	+0.2
All Others*	1.2	1.3	1.2	2.6	5.1	+3.9
No Affiliation	7.3	7.1	8.3	13.4	15.3	+8.0
Nominal Religionists **	13.6	11.6	10.4	9.6	7.6	-6.0

* Includes all non-Judeo Christian religions, black Catholics, and various Eastern Orthodox denominations.
** Includes those who claim an affiliation but do not believe in life after death *and* who attend religious services once per year or less.
Source: General Social Survey 1973–2002. National Survey of Religion and Politics, 2004.

secular groups are more likely to be white than those with religious affiliations.[21] Finally, in data not shown, the two potential secular groups tend to reside outside the South, not surprising given the high levels of religiosity in that region. In sum, Table 4.2 demonstrates that there are significant differences between the religious affiliated and the two "secular" groups. Do these differences carry over into politics?

Table 4.3 examines voter turnout rates and partisan identification for the three groups over time. The unaffiliated have the lowest turnout rates in each time period. Despite being disproportionately non-Southern, male, highly educated, and white—characteristics usually associated with high turnout—the unaffiliated are less likely to go to the polls. In contrast, the religiously affiliated have the highest turnout rates, although they are caught by the nominals in 2004, the highest year for turnout in the time series. With the exception of 2004, the nominals resemble the unaffiliated. Hence, historically, both potential secular groups have not contributed to the electorate in proportion to their numbers. Affiliation plus at least minimal levels of religiosity appear to be essential ingredients of high turnout.

Table 4.2:　Social-Demographic Characteristics of Nonreligious Groups over Time

Social Demographic Variables:	1973– 1980	1983– 1987	1988– 1994	1996– 2002	2004
Mean Age:					
No Affiliation	35.42	37.17	38.94	39.02	39.69
Nominal Religionists	44.05	46.17	46.13	46.90	41.25
Religious Affiliated	45.48	45.26	46.42	46.65	42.87
Male:					
No Affiliation	60.0	56.0	59.1	55.9	56.9
Nominal Religionists	52.5	51.8	50.3	48.1	57.5
Religious Affiliated	41.5	40.0	40.4	41.4	44.4
Education-College Graduate:					
No Affiliation	26.3	30.0	29.8	28.9	27.5
Nominal Religionists	14.3	18.5	22.2	24.5	31.5
Religious Affiliated	13.4	18.1	22.0	25.3	22.7
White Race:					
No Affiliation	91.4	87.6	85.8	81.7	73.8
Nominal Religionists	92.3	88.1	88.5	85.2	78.0
Religious Affiliated	88.2	84.8	82.9	78.9	74.1

Source:　General Social Survey 1973–2002. National Survey of Religion and Politics, 2004

The partisan identification of individuals is critical to an understanding of American politics. Evaluations of candidates and vote preferences are tied to partisanship, and issue positions are compatible with partisanship as well. Table 4.3 shows that both the unaffiliated and the nominals are strongly Democratic in leaning, and rather consistently so over time.[22] In contrast, the religiously affiliated start off the time period with Democratic proclivities, although not matching those of the potential secular groups, but move in a Republican direction beginning in the late 1980s. In 2004, they joined the GOP bandwagon. This partisan division somewhat resembles the clerical/anticlerical divide prevalent historically in continental Europe. At least three of the religiously affiliated groups—Jews, black Protestants, and Hispanic Catholics—lean strongly Democratic. Remove them from the religiously affiliated in table 4.3 and the partisan differences between them and the two potential secular groups are even more dramatic.

Table 4.3: Vote Turnout and Party Identification by Nonreligious Groups over Time

Political Variables:	1973–1980	1983–1987	1988–1994	1996–2002	2004
Vote Turnout:					
No Affiliation	57.6%	54.6%	56.4%	57.9%	74.1%
Nominal Religionists	59.3	58.8	60.3	60.2	85.6
Religious Affiliated	67.8	70.5	70.4	69.6	84.6
Party Identification:					
No Affiliation:					
Republican	19.5	25.8	26.9	21.2	21.6
Democratic	53.9	50.3	47.8	46.5	49.5
Nominal Religionists:					
Republican	27.2	35.1	34.9	28.2	30.5
Democratic	54.4	48.1	45.2	45.4	51.5
Religious Affiliated:					
Republican	32.2	36.6	41.5	38.0	44.6
Democratic	53.4	51.8	46.4	44.7	38.8

Source: General Social Survey 1973–2002. National Survey of Religion and Politics, 2004.

In presidential voting, table 4.4 shows that the unaffiliated voted Democratic in every presidential election since 1972, with the exception of 1980. The tendency grew more pronounced beginning in 1992.[23] Given the rather low turnout for this group, they do not contribute as much to the Democratic vote as they would if they were more involved. Nominal religionists have been much less consistent in providing votes for Democratic presidential candidates. At times, they voted like the unaffiliated, but at other times resembled the religiously committed. In 2004, however, they voted overwhelmingly for John Kerry, and their turnout rates matched those of the religiously affiliated.

There are some important implications in these findings. There are two relatively large potential secular groups, but their numbers do not translate into comparable proportions of the actual vote, given their low turnout.[24] On religious grounds at least, they are impossible to mobilize, for they are not in the pews and, as a result, do not have the strong social ties that heightened religiosity can bring. Given their partisan leanings and strong support for Democratic candidates, this poses a problem for Democratic candidates. In close elections at the national level, such as 2000 and 2004, lower turnout rates among seculars contributed to the defeats of both Al Gore and John Kerry.

Table 4.4: Presidential Vote by Nonreligious Groups over Time: Percent Republican of the Two-Party Vote

	1972	1976	1980	1984	1988	1992	1996	2000	2004
No Affiliation	38.3%	27.8%	50.0%	46.9%	41.4%	25.0%	19.6%	32.8%	27.3%
Nominal Religionists	53.7	40.2	49.5	64.6	53.9	37.1	34.3	50.9	32.5
Religious Affiliated	64.3	46.0	49.7	61.5	60.2	45.8	39.8	56.1	56.8

Source: General Social Survey 1973–2002. National Survey of Religion and Politics, 2004.

THE SECULAR POPULATION IN 2004

So far, the argument has treated seculars as a group composed of the religious unaffiliated and the nominal religionists. The remainder of the analysis, using data from the 2004 NSRP survey, examines four groups of potential seculars: (1) the unaffiliated but religious, (4.9 percent of the sample), (2) the unaffiliated and nonreligious (a larger 8.9 percent), (3) the affiliated but nonreligious (the so-called "nominals," 3.6 percent), and (4) atheists or agnostics (unaffiliated and antireligious, 3.4 percent).

A fifth group, religious modernists, is also examined. These are individuals in religious traditions who are heterodox in belief and relatively uninvolved in religious practices. They make up a sizeable 9.4 percent of the sample. This exercise assists in a decision as to where to draw the line between the secular and religious. The analysis begins with an examination of the religious characteristics of the groups. The results in table 4.5 are clear-cut—nominals have religious perspectives that are much closer to the atheists and agnostics or to the unaffiliated nonreligious than to those of the religious modernists. They clearly belong in some type of secular classification and should not be combined with the religious modernist category.

Of the four groups of potential seculars remaining, the unaffiliated and religious category stands out as different. As Andrew Greeley has noted: "not all the unaffiliated are unreligious."[25] A number of factors could account for the combination of religious beliefs and practices with the absence of affiliation. If they are not "members" of a particular congregation, respondents may not claim an affiliation despite reasonable levels of religiosity. Second, they may not be "joiners." Third, as noted above, they may have left a local church but not hooked up with another at the time of the interview, have moved from one community to another, or left a former church for whatever reason and not yet reaffiliated. Unfortunately, these possibilities cannot be checked out

Table 4.5: Subgroups of Potential Seculars and Religious Variables in 2004

Religious Variables:	Unaffiliated & Religious	Unaffiliated Nonreligious	Nominally Religious	Atheists/ Agnostics	Religious Modernists	Religious Affiliated
Religion is not important in my life	39.4%	73.7%	88.2%	93.4%	32.5	3.8%
I consider myself a spiritual person	63.3	43.6	35.2	37.0	67.4	90.2
No life after death	13.1	42.9	55.2	73.0	23.2	8.3
Doubts God's existence	5.1	69.0	82.1	90,0	34.2	4.4
Never attends Church	31.4	43.8	24.8	55.1	9.9	2.6
Never Prays	20.3	50.4	48.6	77.2	12.5	1.6
There are absolute moral standards *	51.0	59.6	61.7	52.5	70.8	77.3
Too much emphasis on religion in the campaign *	33.7	51.4	60.0	71.9	40.1	19.3
It is important that a president have strong religious beliefs *	53.4	25.3	26.9	8.6	47.5	82.9
% of Sample	4.9	8.9	3.6	3.4	9.4	69.8
Column Ns	198	355	145	138	374	2,781

*Percents on these items are those who strongly agree or agree.
Source: National Survey of Religion and Politics, 2004.

with the NSRP data, but all are plausible reasons for such responses. The data show the importance of distinguishing this group from the others. The religious unaffiliated are clearly more religious (usually much more so) than the nonreligious unaffiliated, the nominals, and the atheists/agnostics. On numerous measures, they are more religious than even the religious modernists, and clearly both groups do not belong in a secular category, at least based on religious measures. In most survey analysis, the religious unaffiliated are classified as secular, and this should not be the case.[26]

The results in table 4.5 for the unaffiliated nonreligious, the nominally religious, and atheists/agnostics suggest another important conclusion—the atheist/agnostic category is predictably the least religious, in some instances much more so than the unaffiliated nonreligious. The nominally religious group falls in between, holding apparently secular outlooks. The three groups differ significantly, and a discriminant analysis confirms that these differences are statistically significant (data not shown). Why are the atheists and agnostics so different? One possible answer is that when a person answers a religious preference question with "atheist" or "agnostic," he or she is signifying that they are antireligious. In contrast, an individual who responds "no preference," "nothing in particular," or "none" is not necessarily communicating antireligious sentiments. The point here is that atheists and agnostics should be separated from respondents who are unaffiliated and nonreligious.[27]

In summary, most research on religion employs one category for the so-called secular population. But, rather than one group, it is composed of three: the nominally religious, the nonreligious unaffiliated, and the atheists/agnostics. Most scholarship fails to include the nominally religious category in a secular grouping, but the results in table 4.5 suggest that it is a mistake not to do so. However, the proof in the pudding, so to speak, is whether these secular categories differ in social-demographic characteristics and, in particular, political behavior. These matters are considered in what follows.

Table 4.6 compares four groups in terms of their social-demographic characteristics. Earlier analysis, using GSS data, showed that the unaffiliated were more likely to reside outside the South, to be younger, and more likely to be single and male than the religiously affiliated. Generally speaking, the nominal religionists fell in between the above groups. When we break the potential secular groups apart on these social-demographic variables, the religious unaffiliated stand out. They tend to be young, the most female, low in education and income (data not shown for the latter), have a relatively high proportion of nonwhites and reside in the South (again, data not shown). In sum, they don't resemble the other three groups of potential seculars, but on many measures they look like the religious affiliated. Second, the atheist/agnostic category also differs in significant ways from the other groups. They are less likely to reside in the South (data not shown), where expressing an agnostic or atheist position even in a confidential interview situation would not be easy, are disproportionately male, with high levels of education and income (again, data not shown for the latter), and white. Third, the nonreligious unaffiliated group is very different from the atheists and agnostics in social demographics, with nominal religion-

Table 4.6:   Subgroups of Potential Seculars and Social-Demographic Variables, 2004

Social-Demographic Variables:	Unaffiliated & Religious	Unaffiliated Nonreligious	Nominally Religious	Atheists/ Agnostics	Religious Affiliated
Age: Less than 40	53.3	54.9	39.7	46.0	37.6
Greater than 54	11.7	16.3	22.7	21.2	30.8
Percent Male	48.5	58.9	60.7	63.5	44.6
Education: High School Grad or Less	69.0	47.3	35.2	27.3	47.6
College Grad or More	8.1	31.0	41.4	43.9	22.7
Race: Percent White	69.5	82.2	88.9	90.5	76.1

Source: National Survey of Religion and Politics, 2004.

ists falling in between. And yet all three secular groups differ significantly from the religious affiliated. In sum, the results in table 4.6 make a strong case for differentiating various groups of seculars. But for purposes of political behavior, the case has not yet been made. Despite religious and social-demographic differences, if the secular groups act similarly in terms of political behavior, then differentiating them may not be necessary for political analysis.

Table 4.7 shows that such distinctions are important politically. First, the religious unaffiliated differ significantly from the other groups. In terms of political involvement, they are very much *uninvolved*. Their turnout rates are much lower than other groups and far below those of the religious affiliated. In addition, they did not follow the 2004 campaign closely, seldom or never talk politics, have very low levels of political knowledge, and rarely engage in political acts beyond voting. They are disproportionately Independent in their partisan leanings, and although they tend to vote Democratic, their voting behavior appears to be based on social-demographic characteristics rather than partisan or ideological leanings. In ideological self-identification, they resemble the three secular groups and differ significantly from the religious affiliated. They also look like the unaffiliated nonreligious and the nominal religionists in evaluating Bush job performance. Quite simply, combining this group with the nonreligious unaffiliated and the atheists and agnostics, the common survey research practice, is a mistake. The religious unaffiliated do not belong in a secular category.

Among the three remaining secular groups in table 4.7, the nonreligious unaffiliated are the least active politically (although they do outpace the

Table 4.7: Subgroups of Potential Seculars and Political Variables, 2004

Political Variables:	Unaffiliated & Religious	Unaffiliated Nonreligious	Nominally Religious	Atheists/ Agnostics	Religious Affiliated
Vote Turnout *	43.7%	52.9%	67.6%	60.8%	63.2%
Seldom/Never Talk Politics	45.4	31.3	28.4	16.7	29.5
Engage in 2+ Campaign Acts	21.8	30.7	35.0	37.5	31.7
Party ID: Republican	25.6	22.0	24.3	21.5	44.5
Democratic	36.3	50.4	62.6	57.9	38.8
GOP Presidential Vote	38.0	28.2	25.7	20.6	56.6
Group Percent of Bush Vote	2.3	4.4	2.1	1.5	89.7
Group Percent of Kerry Vote	3.9	11.7	6.5	6.2	71.8
Conservative Ideology	26.7	26.5	30.5	19.5	43.6
Bush Job Performance Poor/Very Poor	42.2	40.0	43.4	52.6	27.3

* In contrast to the earlier table, turnout rates are corrected here to match the national turnout figure. This corrects for the overreporting of turnout found in survey results. Details of the correction procedure are available from the author.
Source: National Survey of Religion and Politics, 2004.

religious unaffiliated). Their turnout rates are below those of the nominally religious and the atheists/agnostics. Their frequency of talking politics and engaging in acts of participation beyond voting are also less than the nominal religionists and atheists/agnostics. All three secular groups are strongly Democratic in party identification, particularly when compared with the religious affiliated, but the ratio of Democratic to Republican is higher for the nominally religious and the atheists/agnostics. The same three groups voted overwhelmingly for Kerry (with atheists/agnostics providing strongest support), and provided almost one-quarter of the total Democratic vote as compared with only 8 percent of the votes for Bush. Voting for House candidates closely resembles the vote for president. In addition, self-identification as a "conservative" is low for all three groups, but lowest for the atheists/ agnostics. Similarly, Bush job performance ratings are low, with, again, the atheists/agnostics standing out as the most negative. The latter are the most involved of the secular categories and the most Democratic and liberal as well as the most negative on Bush job performance.

What are the implications of these findings? The results suggest that an atheist/agnostic category should be included in any religious classification scheme. Beyond that conclusion, does it make sense to combine the nonreligious unaffiliated with the nominally religious? A discriminant analysis (data not shown) shows that there are statistically significant differences between these two groups as well, suggesting that they not be combined.

Table 4.8:   Subgroups of Potential Seculars and Issue Positions

Issue Positions:	*Unaffiliated & Religious*	*Unaffiliated Nonreligious*	*Nominally Religious*	*Atheists/ Agnostics*	*Religious Affiliated*
Abortion Should Be Solely a Woman's Choice	34.2	57.7	62.1	63.8	29.8%
Favor Traditional Marriage	53.6	27.4	27.1	10.2	61.2
Favor Same-Sex Marriage	33.0	50.9	49.3	69.3	21.4
Favor Equal Rights for Gays	57.5	78.7	79.2	85.5	53.1
Favor Display of 10 Commandments	58.3	44.9	38.2	27.7	71.5
Favor Ban on Stem Cell Research	35.5	16.7	20.6	6.5	35.8
Iraq War Justified	50.0	47.5	51.0	30.5	60.7
Favors Supporting Israel not Palestinians	21.2	24.1	28.4	14.5	40.1

Source: National Survey of Religion and Politics, 2004.

Table 4.8 looks in depth at the issue positions of these groups. In most instances, the unaffiliated and religious look like the religious affiliated. The three secular groups differ in dramatic fashion from the religious unaffiliated (and the religious affiliated) on the "social" or "moral" issue items at the top of the table.[28] These groups are strongly pro-choice on abortion, favor gay marriage and equal rights for gays, oppose the display of the Ten Commandments, and favor greater stem cell research. When we turn to foreign policy, the differences emerge again. In particular, the atheists and agnostics stand out as unabashed opponents of the Bush foreign policy doctrine.[29] The unaffiliated nonreligious and the nominally religious are also opposed, but to a lesser extent. The religious affiliated agree that the Iraq War can be justified (at least they did in 2004). U.S. support for Israel over the Palestinians is viewed unfavorably by all the groups in the table, but gets most approval from the religious affiliated. In sum, the pattern in table 4.8 is clear: the three groups of seculars—the nonreligious unaffiliated, the nominally religious, and the atheist/agnostics—differ significantly from the religious affiliated and religious unaffiliated groups, but also from each other on some issues. It is invariably the atheist and agnostic category that is the most liberal, matching their strong Democratic partisanship and voting propensities.[30]

As a result, one would expect a similar pattern to emerge when attitudes toward interest groups active in the political process and in political campaigns are examined (see table 4.9 for results). First, we examine attitudes toward conservative groups—the Christian Right and the National Rifle Association. Even the religious affiliated tend to feel "far from" these two groups, while the secular groups have decidedly negative feelings toward both. The atheists and agnostics are in the vanguard of opposition. Attitudes are reversed when we look at gay rights and environmental groups. Atheists and agnostics are

Table 4.9 Subgroups of Potential Seculars and Attitudes toward Interest Groups, 2004

Percent Far from:	*Unaffiliated & Religious*	*Unaffiliated Nonreligious*	*Nominally Religious*	*Atheists/ Agnostics*	*Religious Affiliated*
Christian Right	55.1%	77.8%	83.8%	93.4%	44.1%
NRA	43.0	59.0	67.6	73.2	51.3
Environmental Groups	27.8	22.2	27.4	17.8	33.0
Gay Rights Groups	58.9	40.9	44.8	30.3	69.5

Source: National Survey of Religion and Politics, 2004.

the most positive, although all of the groups—secular and religious—have positive attitudes toward environmental groups.

Table 4.10 considers the contacts with voters made by candidates, parties, and interest groups during the 2004 campaign. Earlier analysis (table 4.7) showed that the unaffiliated religious and the unaffiliated nonreligious groups were quite inactive and uninvolved in the campaign. Hence, it is reasonable to assume that they would receive fewer contacts than the other groups. The results in table 4.10 confirm this hypothesis.[31] In most instances, the contact levels for these two groups fall below those for the religious affiliated. The nominally religious resemble the religious affiliated but have slightly more contacts from liberal groups and fewer contacts from the right-leaning conservative issue and moral/religious groups. The atheists and agnostics, however, had more contacts than the religious affiliated from all but moral/religious groups. These findings support a rather consistent pattern found throughout the chapter—that atheists and agnostics were a very involved group in 2004, much more so than the unaffiliated nonreligious and the nominally religious and generally even more so than the religious affiliated.

THE IMPACT OF THE SECULAR GROUPS
ON PARTISAN IDENTIFICATION

Three groups of seculars have been identified—the nonreligious unaffiliated, the nominally religious, and the atheist/agnostic category—that are different enough to warrant separate categorization. In addition, the religious unaffiliated, usually placed in secular category, are clearly different from the three groups above. To see if these four categories have explanatory power, dummy variables were created for each of them, as well as for other religious groups, and used to predict party identification in a multiple regression analysis (table 4.11). A series of social-demographic variables were also included in the equation. Two religious groups stand out as having the biggest impact on partisan identities: traditionalist Evangelicals, who are very orthodox in belief and highly active in terms of religious behaviors, and black Protestants, whose commitment to the Democratic Party has been extremely high since the 1960s, but whose religious beliefs and practices resemble white Evangelicals. But close behind in terms of impact were the nonreligious unaffiliated, the atheist-agnostic, and the nominally religious. All three groups had strong statistically significant relationships with Democratic Party identification, even with other religious groups (mainline Protestants, Anglo and Latino Catholics, and Jews) as well as a number of social-demographic variables included in the regression equation. In addition, the coefficients for both the nominally religious category

Table 4.10: Subgroups of Potential Seculars and Political Contact Variables, 2004

Percent Contacts from:	Unaffiliated & Religious	Unaffiliated Nonreligious	Nominally Religious	Atheists/ Agnostics	Religious Affiliated
Candidates	25.0%	35.1%	31.4%	47.6%	34.8%
Political Parties	25.2	37.4	42.5	56.5	43.4
Liberal Issue Groups	5.4	11.3	8.0	11.7	7.2
Conservative Groups	3.6	2.1	2.8	5.8	4.4
Environmental Groups	7.0	14.3	11.7	25.5	8.4
Moral/Religious Groups	7.9	5.6	8.5	7.7	15.4

Source: National Survey of Religion and Politics, 2004.

and the religious unaffiliated group reached statistical significance (although the latter barely did so). In sum, the results support the inclusion of these differentiated categories of seculars in political behavior research.

SECULARS AND POLITICAL BEHAVIOR: WHAT DOES THE FUTURE HOLD?

Beyond demonstrating the importance of differentiating groups of seculars in future research, what do the results in this chapter offer substantively? Not surprisingly, we have shown that the nonreligious unaffiliated, the nominally religious, and the atheists/agnostics are not very religious, and it is the atheists and agnostics who are the least so. We have also shown that this latter group has social-demographic characteristics that differ from the other secular groups. Politically, the nonreligious unaffiliated, the nominally religious, and the atheists/agnostics are strongly Democratic in both partisanship and voting behavior with the latter group again in the lead. Somewhat to our surprise, we found the atheists and agnostics to be quite involved politically and to have been contacted in the campaign by all kinds of interest groups other than the moral and religious. One reason for this is that this group has social-demographic characteristics that are generally associated with high involvement. In addition, both the nominally religious and the atheist/agnostic groups were at or above the national mean for vote turnout. All three secular groups

Table 4.11: Predicting Party Identification with Religious and Social-Demographic Variables—OLS Regression

Religious Group:	Beta	Significance Level
Traditionalist Evangelical	-.199	.000
Mormon	-.092	.000
Traditionalist Catholic	-.069	.000
Traditionalist Mainline	-.065	.001
Religious Unaffiliated	.041	.035
Jewish	.076	.000
Hispanic Catholic	.078	.000
Other Religions	.079	.000
Nominal Religionists	.080	.000
Modernist Religionists	.095	.000
Atheists or Agnostics	.102	.000
Nonreligious Unaffiliated	.113	.000
Black Protestants	.209	.000
Social Demographic Variables:		
Age	-.080	.000
Gender	.067	.000
Income	-.064	.006
Marital Status	-.026	.194
South versus other Regions	-.016	.395
Education	.001	.976

R =.434. Adjusted R Square = .182

Minus scores indicate Republican Party leanings, while, conversely, positive scores reflect Democratic Party preferences. The religious measures are dummy variables. Modernist and nominal religionists include evangelical and mainline Protestants, as well as Anglo Catholics. Low income respondents lean Democratic as do women and older respondents. Education, region, and marital status are not significant predictors of party identification. Centrist religionists are the suppressed reference category.
Source: National Survey of Religion and Politics, 2004.

hold liberal opinions on the issues examined with, again, the atheists and agnostics being the most liberal. Finally, all three secular groups felt far from leading conservative interest groups and relatively close to liberal groups.

In conclusion, political scientists need to sharpen their research instruments and pay closer attention to these secular groups. Their numbers are large and growing. The three clearly secular groups that we have identified constitute about one-sixth of the population, making them as large as the declining mainline Protestant population and about the same size as the white Catholic tradition. It is hard to imagine a political campaign that would ignore any group this large. Yet they are hard to reach. They don't sit around in "secular" pews. But they have become increasingly important in deciding the outcome of American elections. If candidates and parties can't find them, maybe political scientists can, but only if our research instruments begin to pick them out and subject them to intensive analysis.

Chapter 5

Women, Religion, and the American Presidency

Katherine E. Stenger

During the 1997 national convention of Hadassah, an association of Jewish women, then Secretary of Health and Human Services Donna Shalala remarked that, "one day a Hadassah member will be president of the United States."[1] This quip alludes to the growing power of religious women in politics. No women, and thus no women of faith, have yet been elected president of the United States. However, women of faith across the political spectrum have been active and influential participants in presidential politics at the individual level as voters and at the group level as members of organized interest groups. While much research addresses the impact of sex on political behavior and opinion,[2] and a growing body of research examines the role of faith in politics,[3] little research explores the convergence of these two important aspects of identity as they relate to political opinion and behavior. This chapter examines the impact of faith and gender on voting behavior in presidential elections. In addition, it explores the ways in which women of faith are represented in the policy process through organized groups using case studies of several national women's religious interest groups.

PRESIDENTIAL VOTING AND WOMEN OF FAITH

In 1980, President Jimmy Carter was in a heated battle against actor-turned-governor Ronald Reagan. In postelection analyses, two blocs of voters emerged as having played notable roles in the election—women and religious conservatives. Female voters noticeably favored Carter, and this difference between male and female voting patterns was termed the "gender gap." Although some scholars note that the gender gap trend emerged as early as the election of 1952,[4] the 1980 election was the first time this phenomenon received widespread public attention.[5] Scholars propose a number of factors that account for the difference in voting preferences between men and women, including their views on economic and social issues,[6] factors associated with marital status,[7] participation in the workforce,[8] and trends in voter turnout.[9] Other scholars argue that the gender gap has less to do with changes among female voters and more to do with male voters, who have become more conservative over time.[10] Whatever its cause, the gender gap is an important strategic consideration for presidential candidates because women tend to vote at higher rates than men.[11]

In addition to recognition of the gender gap, the 1980 election also reflected growth in the power of conservative Christian groups.[12] Recently mobilized by the Supreme Court decision to legalize abortion (*Roe v. Wade*, 1973), the persistent debate over teaching evolution in schools, and the successful battle against the proposed Equal Rights Amendment, conservative Christian groups channeled their energies into electing Reagan (despite Carter's evangelical credentials). The combined efforts of Christian Right groups, including the newly formed Moral Majority and Christian Voice, yielded approximately two million new voters in the 1980 election.[13] Perhaps as a result of these groups' efforts, white Protestant and Catholic voters switched allegiance from Carter to Reagan in this election. The perceived impact of religious conservatives was evident when, shortly after the 1980 election, Jerry Falwell appeared on a variety of television programs to claim that Evangelicals had provided the votes behind Reagan's victory.[14]

The electoral impact of women and conservative Christians was highlighted in the 1980 elections and has received continued attention in subsequent elections. These groups are also interesting because they are not mutually exclusive categories. In fact, a majority of people professing religious beliefs are women. This creates an interesting puzzle: studies find that women are more likely than men to hold liberal views on political issues and to vote for Democrats,[15] but women are also more likely than men to say they are religious, and research suggests that religious people tend to hold more conservative views and vote for Republicans.[16]

The question posed by this paradox is what happens when these two facets of identity—sex and religious beliefs—are combined in a single voter? Do religious women support different presidential candidates than religious men or nonreligious women? How do religious women differ from nonreligious women or religious men in their views on critical issues where faith and sex are in tension such as abortion and women's rights? What differences, if any, exist between women of different religious traditions or levels of religiosity when it comes to voting in presidential elections?

Some of these questions are partially addressed in studies of specific segments of the religious population. For example, a group of scholars examined the political beliefs of female clergy in a handful of mainline Protestant denominations and found that clergywomen are generally more liberal, more politically active, and have different policy priorities than clergymen.[17] Other interesting research examines the negotiation of faith and gender among women in conservative religious traditions and among Jewish women who call themselves feminists.[18] However, there is no research that directly examines the political beliefs of nonelite religious women across religious traditions.

Using data collected from the National Election Survey (NES) between 1980 and 2004,[19] I examine the above questions regarding the voting behavior of religious women.[20] The NES is especially useful in addressing these questions because it provides comparable questions that address both political and religious characteristics of voters. While changes to the religion questions in 1989 have greatly improved our ability to "measure" religion, even the earlier versions of these questions allow for a comparison across time. Other comparable variables used to address these questions include the presidential candidate preference, the respondent's political ideology, and the respondent's position on the issues of women's equality and abortion rights.

To answer the questions outlined above, I created four categories of survey respondents: religious women, nonreligious women, religious men, and nonreligious men. These variables were created using the respondent's sex and their response to the statement, "religion is an important part of my life." While this question dramatically oversimplifies the nature of religious beliefs, it provides a benchmark to separate the clearly nonreligious from those professing any sort of religious belief. As is the case in other national surveys, most respondents claim to be religious. Religious women make up the largest bloc of the population and therefore the largest potential group of voters. Between 1980 and 2000, religious women comprise approximately 43 percent of voters. Religious men make up the next largest group, averaging 29 percent of the population. Nonreligious women represent slightly over 7 percent of the population and nonreligious men make up 12 percent of the population. The percentage of religious women has increased slightly over the past twenty years, but even in 1980, religious women comprised almost 40 percent of the population.

Party Voting, Religion, and Sex

The most important issue in terms of influence is identifying whether religious women intend to vote differently in the presidential election than nonreligious women, religious men, or nonreligious men. Table 5.1 indicates the expected vote breakdown between the Democratic and Republican candidates for each of these categories of voters.[21] In 1980, religious women favored Jimmy Carter, as did nonreligious women. However, in 1984, both religious and nonreligious women shifted their support from the Democratic candidate, Walter Mondale, to the Republican candidate, Ronald Reagan. This is especially surprising given that Mondale's running mate was a woman, Geraldine Ferraro. The only woman to be nominated for a spot on a major party ticket failed to gain the support of both religious and nonreligious female voters. During both of these elections (1980 and 1984), religious and nonreligious men favored the Republican candidate. Religious men slightly favored Reagan in 1980 and overwhelmingly favored Reagan in 1984. In terms of candidate choice, religious women since 1992 have strongly favored Democratic candidates for president.

Table 5.1:   The Impact of Sex and Religion on Presidential Voting

	Religious Women		Nonreligious Women		Religious Men		Nonreligious Men	
	Dem	Rep	Dem	Rep	Dem	Rep	Dem	Rep
2000 Gore / Bush	54%	41.7%	64.4%	23.7%	43.4%	47.2%	46%	36.9%
1996 Clinton / Dole	57.6	35.9	66.0	20.2	42.2	47.8	56.5	32.8
1992 Clinton / Bush	57.2	35.8	60.8	31.1	51.9	39.4	56.7	29.9
1988 Dukakis / Bush	49	49.4	51.4	46.5	41.7	56.4	43.9	53
1984 Mondale / Reagan	44.4	55	43.9	54.7	36.4	61.9	34.5	63.2
1980 Carter / Reagan	49.9	40.7	46.5	36	43.7	46.5	35.3	47.6

Notes: Percentages do not total 100 because of votes for third-party candidates; Differences between religious women and other categories are statistically significant at the 0.05 level in 1984, 1996, and 2000; when these variables are compared with standard determinants of vote choice (such as party identification, political ideology, race, class, age, etc.) in a regression model, these variables are no longer statistically significant.

In the 1988 election between Democratic candidate Michael Dukakis and Republican candidate George H. W. Bush, religious women split evenly between the candidates. In this election, nonreligious women favored Dukakis, while religious and nonreligious men favored Bush. President Clinton was elected in 1992 with high levels of support from both religious and nonreligious women. Nearly 60 percent of religious women supported him in both 1992 and 1996, and over 60 percent of nonreligious women supported him in 1996. In the 1992 election, even a majority of religious men expressed a preference for Clinton. By the 1996 election, religious men had tentatively shifted their support to the Republican candidate, Robert Dole.

In the 2000 election, religious women favored Gore 54 percent to 42 percent. Nonreligious women supported Gore even more strongly. Bush's greatest support came from religious men, who favored him by a margin of 47 percent to 43 percent. Bush won the election despite these numbers, which indicate a general lack of support for his candidacy. The difference between the electoral outcome and these results can be explained by accounting for the impact of turnout, the electoral college (which Bush won despite losing the popular vote), and voters' changing preferences in the final days of the campaign.

These results indicate that religious women display consistently more in common with nonreligious women than they do with religious men, indicating that sex may carry greater weight than religion in presidential voting decisions. Furthermore, religious women have been more likely to support Democratic candidates than Republican candidates, a pattern growing stronger in the last three elections.

Ideology, Issue Positions, Religion, and Sex

Religious women may be similar to nonreligious women in presidential vote choice, but do these women also share commonalities in terms of political ideology and positions on key political issues? The connection between party strength, political ideology, and the rise in candidate-centered campaigns may affect the position religious women take on important social issues. Political parties in America display much less ideological coherence than do parties in other countries. Scholars also point to a rising trend in candidate-centered, as opposed to party-centered, campaigns.[22] These trends suggests that even very conservative voters might be persuaded to vote for a Democratic candidate who appeals to them on an individual level or on the basis of particular issues.[23]

In figures 5.1 to 5.3, I compare religious and nonreligious women and men according to their reported political ideology and positions on two political issues that involve both faith and sex. The figures chart the mean score of each demographic group for ideology, view of women's equality, and opinion on abortion over time. In each case, a lower number indicates a more liberal opinion, while a higher number indicates a more conservative opinion. The ideology and women's equality scales ranges from one to seven. The abortion scale ranges from one to four. A score of one indicates that the respondent thinks that abortions should be legal, while a score of four indicates that the respondent does not think abortion should be allowed under any circumstances.

As displayed in figure 5.1, nonreligious women are consistently the most politically liberal of the four groups. In this figure, a lower number indicates a more liberal political ideology while a higher number indicates a more conservative political ideology. The difference between nonreligious women and other groups has become even more pronounced since 1992. Nonreligious men make up the next most liberal group, although they have become steadily more conservative since 1988. Religious men are the most conservative

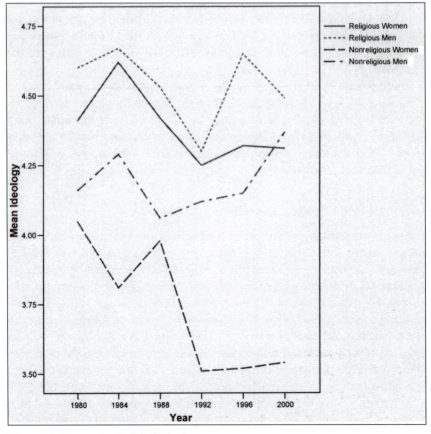

Figure 5.1: Comparing Political Ideology

group, but they are only slightly more conservative than religious women. This is especially surprising given the degree to which religious women tend to vote for Democratic candidates.

Over the past twenty years, all four groups have become more liberal in terms of their view of women's equality. Figure 5.2 compares the views of the four categories of respondents across time. A lower number indicates a more liberal position on the issue of women's equality while a higher number indicates a more conservative position on the issue. Again, nonreligious women and men tend to be more liberal in their view of women's equality than religious women and men. Between 1992 and 2000, religious women did become much more liberal; however, there is still a large gap between religious and nonreligious women. Views on the issue of women's equality are interesting because the feminist movement inspired a strong backlash from conservative religious groups. As discussed in the latter half of this chapter, several reli-

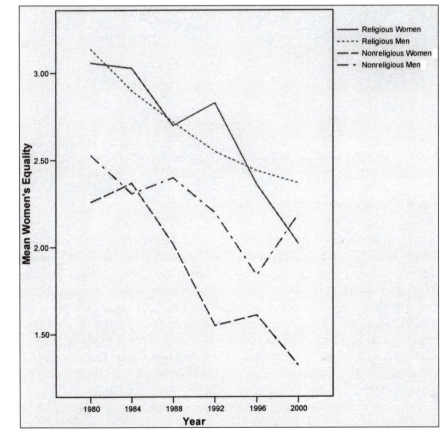

Figure 5.2: Comparing Beliefs About Women's Equality

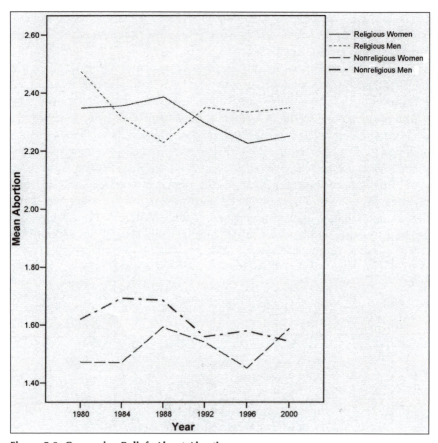

Figure 5.3: Comparing Beliefs About Abortion

gious interest groups formed specifically in response to the proposed Equal Rights Amendment. Lakoff argues that the connection between conservatism and opposition to women's rights is grounded in metaphorical understandings of the proper role of families.[24] For religious conservatives, who tend to support a metaphor of the family that emphasizes hierarchy and respect for tradition, the move for women's equality embodied in the campaign for the Equal Rights Amendment was a threat not only to family life, but to the stability of social and political life as well. Thus, while religious women may support the individual rights of women, the strong pull of the dominant family metaphor may cause them to align more closely with the views of religious men.

The issue of abortion is where we see the greatest impact of faith and the most dramatic difference between religious and nonreligious citizens regardless of sex. Figure 5.3 shows the differences between the groups on the issue of abortion, with lower numbers indicating a more liberal position and higher numbers indicating a more conservative position. Both religious women and men tend to hold more conservative opinions regarding abortion. Nonreligious women and men hold much more liberal opinions on the issue. Again, this is an issue over which there has been intense debate between religious groups and the feminist movement and even within religious communities. Feminists view the issue as one involving the constitutionally protected right to privacy for the women while many in religious circles express a need to protect the rights of unborn children. Much like the movement for women's equality, the campaign to legalize abortion and to protect legal abortions inspired the mobilization of a number of religious-based groups opposed to abortion. Today, the issue of abortion has become a major fault line in politics, with both sides unwilling to compromise. It should be noted, however, that not all conservatives are opposed to abortion rights, while not all liberals support full access to abortion.

Religious women tend to vote in ways that are similar to nonreligious women. However, when asked about their political ideology or their views on issues that activate both aspects of their identity, religious women tend to have much more in common with religious men. What explains this discrepancy? While this might indicate that religious women are ideologically inconsistent, the finding more likely reflects the negotiation of identity in real-world contexts. When making a decision, voters are asked to consider a number of relevant factors, including the candidates, political predispositions, and situational factors.[25] For women of faith, this means a conscious or unconscious consideration of both sex and faith in addition to a variety of other factors when making a decision. When asked issue by issue, religious women may hold more conservative positions; however, when asked to aggregate these opinions with other salient factors, these issues may be relegated to a less important role. In her study of Jewish feminists, Dufour refers to this process as "sifting."[26] In other words, women take the aspects of faith and gender that are relevant to a particular decision and sift out those factors that are irrelevant. In regard to political decisions, it appears as though women of faith take into account faith and sex along with other factors such as education level, socioeconomic status, and race in making political decisions.[27]

Religious Tradition and Religious Commitment

Thus far, the data indicate that religious women tend to vote much like nonreligious women (for Democratic candidates), but hold more conservative views on issues such as abortion and women's rights, which are similar to religious men. These findings, however, mask potential differences between

religious women of different religious traditions and between religious
women of different levels of religious commitment.

As evidenced by several of the chapters in this volume, scholars find
significant differences among voters of different religious traditions. Denominational families comprising religious traditions share a history and
basic beliefs.[28] Scholars generally identify six major religious traditions:
evangelical Protestant, mainline Protestant, black Protestant, Catholic, Jewish, and secular. In addition to the distinction between religious traditions,
scholars also identify an important difference between religious persons
holding traditional, or orthodox, beliefs, and those holding modernist
beliefs.[29] Ideally, we would be able to compare the political behavior of
religious women across belief structure in all of the presidential elections,
however, questions that tap into these concepts were not asked in all of
the surveys (the religion questions in the NES were redesigned in 1989).
Instead, to gauge some of the differences that exist among religious women
in terms of candidate preference, we can look at differences between Protestant, Catholic, and Jewish women as well as differences between women
of varying religiosity (defined in terms of aspects of belief, belonging, and
behavior) for available years.

Table 5.2 reflects the voting tendencies of religious women from different religious traditions. Jewish and Catholic women tend to vote for Democratic presidents. Although the number of Jewish women in the sample
is quite small, with the exception of the 1980 election, they have heavily
favored the Democratic candidate. Catholic women also favor Democrats,
although the margin of support is not as pronounced. Among Protestant
women, support for candidates is fairly evenly split. With the exception of
the 1980 election, Protestant women as a whole have supported the eventual winning candidate rather than aligning more strongly with a particular
party. These trends are statistically significant for the 2000, 1996, 1988, and
1984 elections.

Religiosity, or strength of religious commitment, is a difficult concept to
measure. A person may hold very deep and meaningful spiritual beliefs, but
his or her religious commitment may not be reflected accurately in a single
survey question. At a minimum, a measure of comparative religiosity should
include aspects of belief structure, sense of belonging to a religious community, and evidence of behavior that indicates religious commitment. The
scholars responsible for redesigning the religious questions on the National
Election Study survey in 1989 recognized the importance of variables addressing these components of faith. Thus, in the surveys from 1992 on, we
can examine differences in voting behavior among religious women of different levels of commitment, or religiosity.

Table 5.2: Presidential Votes and Religious Tradition

	Protestant Women		Catholic Women		Jewish Women		Other Women	
	Dem.	Rep.	Dem.	Rep.	Dem.	Rep.	Dem.	Rep.
2000 Gore / Bush	45.1% (114)	53% (134)	57.9% (92)	37.7% (60)	100% (13)	0% (0)	59.4% (79)	34.6% (46)
1996 Clinton / Dole	49 (125)	45.5 (116)	57 (73)	36.7 (47)	77.8 (7)	11.1 (1)	69.6 (32)	17.4 (8)
1992 Clinton / Bush	51.5 (121)	41.3 (97)	61.7 (71)	31.3 (36)	90 (9)	0 (0)	59.4 (41)	33.3 (23)
1988 Dukakis / Bush	46.5 (245)	52.2 (275)	55.1 (97)	43.8 (77)	75 (3)	25 (1)	58.8 (10)	29.4 (5)
1984 Mondale / Reagan	41.8 (222)	57.8 (307)	48 (107)	50.7 (113)	73.3 (11)	26.7 (4)	50 (13)	50 (13)
1980 Carter / Reagan	50.4 (184)	42.5 (155)	49.3 (68)	37 (51)	42.9 (3)	42.9 (3)	47.6 (10)	33.3 (7)

Notes: Number of cases in parentheses; percentages do not total 100 because of votes for third-party candidates; relationship between religious tradition and vote choice is statistically significant at the 0.05 level in 1988, 1996, and 2000.

The religiosity scale for this analysis is built with questions regarding the respondent's view of the Bible (belief),[30] the frequency of attendance at religious services (behavior), and membership in a religious community regardless of attendance (belonging). Responses to these questions are combined into a six-point religiosity scale, with a higher number indicating a stronger degree of religious commitment across these three dimensions. A score of six means that the respondent believes in the inerrancy of the Bible, attends religious services almost every week, and is a member of a religious congregation. A score of zero indicates that the respondent believes the Bible was written by men, never attends religious services, and does not belong to a religious congregation. Since this analysis focuses on women who report that religion is an important part of their lives, the number of respondents in the bottom category is very small.

In 1992, Bill Clinton received more support than George Bush among women in most of the categories of religious commitment. Only in the highest two levels of religiosity did Bush receive slightly more support from religious women. In 1996, Clinton received more support than Bob Dole among women in all six categories of religiosity. Dole received no support from women in the lowest levels of the scale, and performed best among religious women with the strongest level of religious commitment, even though Clinton still beat him in this category. In 2000, Al Gore received more support from religious women than did George W. Bush in nearly every category. It was only among women in the strongest level of religious commitment that Bush received more support. Generally, though, among religious women, Republicans enjoy no significant advantage at even the highest levels of religious commitment.

Between 1976 and 2000, religious women were more likely to support Democratic candidates for president. Data from 1992, 1996, and 2000 indicates that this pattern holds true for women from different religious traditions and for women at all levels of religious commitment. This trend in candidate preference is quite different from the comparable category of religious men, who tend to support Republican presidential candidates. Despite this, when we look at reported political ideology and opinions on women's rights and abortion, religious women tend to be a bit more conservative and have more in common with religious men than with nonreligious women.

WOMEN, RELIGION, AND THE 2004 ELECTION

Religion, more than gender, played a major role in the 2004 presidential election between incumbent Republican George W. Bush and Democrat John Kerry. Both candidates courted religious voting blocs and many observers commented that the 2004 campaign was one of the most religiously-infused campaigns in American history.[31] Bush pursued the support of evangelical and Catholic voters, in particular, and incorporated faith-based language into his campaign rhetoric. Kerry, the first Catholic nominee to run for president since John F. Kennedy, tried to avoid the topic of religion claiming that his Catholic faith was a private matter. Eventually Kerry was forced to confront the topic directly when it was raised on the campaign trail and when several Catholic leaders, such as St. Louis archbishop Raymond Burke, publicly suggested that he should be denied communion because some of his policy views were inconsistent with Church teachings.

The year 2004 saw a slight increase in the percentage of men and women who claimed that religion was an important part of their life compared with the average percentages between 1980 and 2000. Religious women comprised 45 percent of the general population, while their male counterparts comprised 33 percent. This change reflects a national shift toward spiritual beliefs following the September 11 terrorist attacks as well as the salient role religion played in the 2004 election as evidenced by eleven state ballot initiatives to ban same sex marriage.[32]

While the percentage of religious respondents increased slightly, the vote choices of the four groups changed dramatically. In 2004, women favored Kerry to Bush (51 percent to 48 percent), while men favored Bush (55 percent to 44 percent). Protestants strongly favored Bush (59 percent to 40 percent), while Catholics narrowly favored Bush (52 percent to 47 percent). Jewish voters favored Kerry (74 percent to 25 percent).[33] These general trends were not significantly different from patterns in 2000, however the patterns created by the overlap between sex and religious belief did change considerably. Between 1980 and 2000, religious women were similar to nonreligious women in their vote choice, but in 2004, religious women were evenly split between Kerry and Bush (49 percent voted for each). Nonreligious women, in contrast, overwhelmingly supported Kerry (63 percent compared to 35 percent supporting Bush). Religious men supported Bush over Kerry (57 percent to 39 percent), while nonreligious men supported Kerry over Bush (54 percent to 41 percent). These findings indicate that religious women were torn by competing factors. As a group, they did not vote the same way as either nonreligious women or religious men.

New patterns also emerged among women of different religious traditions. Protestant women overwhelmingly supported Bush over Kerry. Protestant women shifted support between Democratic and Republican candidates over the years, but in 2004, Bush won over this category of voters, with 58 percent of Protestant women expressing support for the incumbent. Another factor that contributed to Kerry's loss was his dwindling support from Catholic women. In 2000, Gore won the support of nearly 58 percent of Catholic women. In fact, Catholic women supported the Democratic candidate in 1980, 1988, 1992, and 1996 as well. In 2004, however, Kerry only won the support of 47 percent of Catholic women, while Bush won the support of 52 percent of Catholic women. In short, Kerry's loss of both Protestant and Catholic women, traditional supporters of Democratic candidates, contributed to his loss in the election.

The vote choice of religious women in the 2004 presidential election represents a change from established patterns of voting behavior. While in past elections, religious women seem to be more aligned with the voting behavior of other women, in 2004, these women were much more closely aligned with the voting behavior of religious men. This suggests that in 2004, the salience of religion created a strong pull on religious women; a pull that may have overshadowed the sex-based solidarity that existed in past election cycles.

ORGANIZED INTERESTS AND WOMEN OF FAITH

In addition to their role in electing presidents as individual voters, religious women are also active players in national politics through organized interest groups.[34] Similar to the role religion has played in the civil rights movement as discussed in this volume by Melissa Harris-Lacewell, religion also plays an important role in women's activism.[35] Baxter and Lansing argue that the greatest impact on politics from women has been through organized interest groups.[36] Religious women have a long history of participating in interest group politics and social movements, only some of which fall into the subset of groups examined in this analysis.[37] Much of the access of women's religious groups is limited to Congress and state and local governments, but these groups have, on occasion, had opportunities to influence presidents as well.

The Women's Christian Temperance Union (WCTU), founded in 1874 and most prominently led by Francis Willard, is perhaps one of the most well-known women's religious interest groups. By the late 1880s, the WCTU grew into the largest women's political organization, mobilizing religious women in support of prohibition.[38] The group was also an active supporter of women's suffrage, and campaigned vigorously on behalf of the Nineteenth Amendment. The group was successful in spearheading the passage of the Eighteenth Amendment in 1919 to ban the sale of alcohol. Despite the major setback of the Twenty-first Amendment repealing prohibition, "at the close of the nineteenth century, the WCTU was one of the most powerful vehicles in the United States for addressing women's issues and producing strong, independent women, who entered the public world, determined to change it."[39] Although it is not as visible today, the WCTU is still active, claiming over six thousand current members and still requiring new members to sign a pledge of abstinence from alcohol.

Other contemporary women's religious interest groups are just as active. They have been at the forefront of recent debates over abortion, women's rights, education, social justice, and international affairs. In thinking about religious women's interest groups, groups representing the Christian Right are often the first to come to mind. Concerned Women for America and the Eagle Forum are two examples of groups that have received much attention from the media and politicians over the past thirty years. However, there are a number of other groups reflecting a diversity of religious and political beliefs. In the section that follows, I explore a few of the groups representing religious women in national politics. Some of the groups are more overtly political than others, some have weaker religious ties than others, and some are open to members of both sexes. I have included these groups that are more marginal to an analysis of women's religious interest groups because they provide much-needed perspective on the activities of groups outside the evangelical tradition. I begin with the groups with Christian roots, followed by Jewish and then Muslim groups.

Christian Groups

Women's groups with a Christian heritage span the ideological spectrum, ranging from the conservative Concerned Women for America (CWA) and Eagle Forum (EF) to the politically liberal Catholics for a Free Choice (CFFC) and Church Women United (CWU). Though these groups share a common commitment to faith, their different theological interpretations of Christianity impact their approach to politics. CWA and EF are more overtly political than CWU and CFFC. Both groups (CWA and EF) operate active headquarters in Washington, D.C., and have goals of impacting government policies. In contrast, CFFC targets most of its efforts toward changing the position of the Roman Catholic Church on the issue of abortion, but through these efforts, the group is undeniably political. CWU is committed to the ecumenical movement and their political activities stem from their positions on social justice issues.

Through the presidencies of Ronald Reagan and George W. Bush, Concerned Women for America, a conservative Christian group, has experienced a high level of presidential access and policy success, leading President Ronald Reagan to refer to the group as one of the "powerhouses on the political scene."[40] Concerned Women for America (CWA) was formed in 1979 by Beverly LaHaye in response to the potential passage of the Equal Rights Amendment and the growing feminist movement.[41] Within the first year, there were over six hundred members, and today CWA identifies itself as the "largest public policy women's organization," claiming five hundred thousand members. Over the years, this focus has expanded to include concern for education, protecting a traditional definition of the family, marriage, religious liberty, the sanctity of human life, opposition to pornography, and national sovereignty. According to the CWA website, "the mission of CWA is to protect and promote Biblical values among all citizens—first through prayer, then education, and finally by influencing society—thereby reversing the decline in moral values in our nation."

During its first year of existence, CWA joined forces to oppose the passage of the Equal Rights Amendment and two years later, joined a campaign to address television content. In 1983, CWA opened a branch in Washington, D.C., which it shared with two other groups, Christian Voice and the American Coalition for Traditional Values. Through this office, CWA maintains a legislative action committee and member lobbying campaign (Project 535).

CWA is also active in electoral politics, offering financial support to Republican candidates through its political action committee. CWA frames its mission in sharp contrast to secular liberals. The CWA website encourages volunteer lobbyists to represent the group's conservative viewpoints, saying, "We should be storming Capitol Hill, letting our government know how we feel." In 1991, during the Supreme Court confirmation hearings for Clarence Thomas, group founder Beverly LaHaye discussed the topic on her weekly syndicated call-in radio program, *Beverly LaHaye Live*. During the discussion, she broadcast the phone number for the congressional switchboard. In response, hundreds of listeners phoned their representatives voicing support for Thomas.[42] The CWA has displayed similar patterns of mobilization in other confirmation battles over other presidential nominees.[43] In 1996, the CWA lobbied successfully in support of the Defense of Marriage Act, signed by President Clinton, which allowed states to deny recognition of same-sex marriage licenses from other states.[44]

The Eagle Forum shares many political beliefs with CWA. Led by Phyllis Schafly, it developed out of the STOP-ERA coalition, a loose coalition of state and local groups also opposed to the ratification of the Equal Rights Amendment (ERA).[45] Members of the Eagle Forum were opposed to the ERA because "they were convinced that feminism, the ERA, sex education in schools, and the increased openness of homosexuality were all part of the same phenomenon," which ran in stark opposition to traditional values.[46] In the spring of 1972, ratification of the ERA seemed inevitable, however, in just a few short months (and eventually by 1982), the STOP-ERA coalition and the newly formed Eagle Forum (1972) had ended the ratification momentum. Schafly's role in defeating the ERA was recognized throughout Washington. Through the influential writing of Schafly and the mobilization of state and local branches of the groups, the Eagle Forum rose to a place of political power. After leading the movement to defeat the ERA, the Eagle Forum turned its attention to the Supreme Court's decision to legalize abortion in *Roe v. Wade*.

The Eagle Forum is a strongly conservative organization that appeals to religious women who hold traditional values. Schafly herself is a practicing Catholic but the group does not restrict members based on religion. However, Schafly's Catholic affiliation helped to differentiate the Eagle Forum from Concerned Women for America, which is primarily comprised of conservative evangelical Protestant women.[47] In later years, the Eagle Forum also differentiated itself from CWA by focusing more on international issues.[48] Though it lost some momentum and membership after the ERA was defeated, the group currently claims eighty thousand members and is open to both men and women.[49]

In contrast to these conservative groups, politically liberal groups such as Catholics for a Free Choice and Church Women United have had more restricted access to, and less recognition from, modern presidents. CWU was founded in 1941 as a racially, culturally, and theologically inclusive women's movement. Over the years, CWU has partnered with the United Nations, the National Council of Churches of Christ, and the World Council of Churches on a number of different initiatives and projects.[50] Today CWU claims 500,000 members in 1,400 local groups. The mission of CWU, according to their website, is to bring "Christian women together for spiritual nourishment and faith-based advocacy. CWU local and state units are active in a broad spectrum of community ministries, including social justice advocacy and action, prison ministries, food pantries, tutoring and child care, and job skills training. On national and global levels, CWU works in coalition with partner groups around common issues and emphases."

With its focus on social justice and human rights, CWU is the largest politically liberal women's religious organization. CWU established offices in Washington, D.C., and at the United Nations to advance its policy goals. One of its first attempts to influence government policy was to gather signatures on a petition urging the U.S. government to full participation in the newly formed United Nations. First Lady Eleanor Roosevelt personally responded to the petition with a note of thanks. Recognizing the theological diversity of group members, CWU refrains from taking official policy positions on the issues of abortion, homosexuality, and same-sex marriage.

New policy priorities are outlined by the group every four years. Civil rights, global justice, poverty, race relations, and health care are a few of the issues CWU has prioritized over the years. CWU pursues their policy priorities in a number of ways. For example, in 1994, CWU hosted a televised question and answer forum on the topic of health care with First Lady Hillary Rodham Clinton.

The development of Church Women United corresponds with, and was inspired by, the feminist movement. As scholars note, "It is clear that CWU women were pioneers in, were affected by, and brought considerable insight to the larger women's movement and the second wave of feminism that came to life with the publication of Betty Friedan's book (*The Feminine Mystique*, 1963) in the early sixties."[51] In addition to fighting political battles, CWU has also struggled with finding its role in the male-dominated world of religious interest groups. In its association with the National Council of Churches, leaders of CWU found they were confined in terms of decision making over finances and membership.[52] "As was typical of most bureaucratic institutions of this time, patriarchy was painfully evident."[53] In response, by 1970, CWU became completely independent from the National Council of Churches.

Another group, Catholics for a Free Choice, has also experienced tension with a related religious organization. CFFC was formed in 1973 to represent pro-choice Catholics but has no official connection with the Catholic Church because their position on abortion contrasts so strongly with the official position of the Catholic Church. CFFC has no formal membership, only a mailing list of donors and supporters divided into three categories—supporters, who give money and are active in group activities on a regular basis; spokespersons/ activists, who are the main organizers of local events; and associates, who pay thirty dollars a year in dues. The group claims approximately fifteen supporters, fifty spokespersons, and eight thousand associates in addition to the thirty thousand people on their mailing list. Instead of recruiting new members, CFFC focuses on attracting Catholic opinion leaders such as leaders of organizations and professors and works on building ties with progressive Catholic and women's groups.

Although the group primarily views itself as an educational association rather than a lobbying organization, they maintain a full-time staff in Washington, D.C., to lobby on behalf of reproductive rights and often testify in congressional hearings. Republican moves to limit abortion, presidential executive orders regarding abortion rights, and the sex abuse scandal in the Catholic Church have all contributed to increased visibility and interest in the group, although this visibility does not necessarily lead to increased access to policy makers or presidents.

Jewish Groups

Jewish women's interest groups have a long history of involvement in American politics. All three of the major Jewish groups for women are primarily service organizations, but they all have strong histories of political involvement, especially regarding issues of social justice and U.S. policy toward Israel. The National Council of Jewish Women (NCJW) was the first of the three to form, in 1893. Jewish Women International (JWI) emerged shortly after, and Hadassah formed in the early 1900s.

The National Council of Jewish Women was founded in New York in by Hannah Greenbaum Solomon. The NCJW is primarily a volunteer organization and it takes a progressive stance on a variety of public policy issues including social justice and individual rights. Being one of the first associations of religious women, the NCJW opened up new paths for Jewish women in America by providing women with a venue for political and social action outside of the home, while still respecting the religious and cultural beliefs of members and their families.[54] The organization is comprised of more than one hundred chapters around the country and has offices in New York, Washington, D.C., and Israel. After World War II, the NCJW became more politically active, taking an active interest in defending civil rights and liberties. The group developed a program, the School for Community Action, to train women in lobbying techniques.[55] After participating in the 1962 Commission on the Status of Women established by President John F. Kennedy, the group took a more active stand in defense of reproductive rights, and later in support of the Equal Rights Amendment.[56]

Today the National Council of Jewish Women claims more than ninety thousand members. Through these members and the group's policy office in Washington, the NCJW has played an active role in contemporary presidential politics. In 1998, President Bill Clinton addressed a meeting of the NCJW to speak to members about a variety of issues such as education, patients' rights, campaign finance reform, and international security. As governor of Arkansas, Clinton interacted with the NCJW when they introduced him to a program designed to aid educationally disadvantaged children, which he later successfully implemented in Arkansas. The NCJW was also active in its support for the passage of the Family and Medical Leave Act. In addition to lobbying on legislative proposals, the NCJW also sponsors the BenchMark program, the goal of which is to mobilize members to support federal judges who defend abortion rights.

Jewish Women International also strongly supports abortion rights. Formed in 1897 as B'nai B'rith Women, an organization devoted primarily to service, it is an independent and self-governing group affiliated with B'nai B'rith International.[57] In 1995, B'nai B'rith Women changed its name to Jewish Women International to reflect the growing autonomy of the group. With headquarters in Washington, D.C., the group claims approximately seventy-five thousand members in the United States and Canada. Jewish Women International advocates for women's rights such as access to abortion, affirmative action, childcare, homeless assistance, health care, and campaign reform. As part of these interests, JWI has been particularly involved in combating domestic violence through organizing national conferences on the topic and leading related activities during the annual Domestic Violence Awareness Month. JWI is also an active lobbyist on behalf of gun control.

Hadassah was founded in 1912 by Henrietta Szold and a group of women devoted to Judaism, Zionism, and American ideals. Originally organized under the Federation of American Zionists, the group became independent in 1921.[58] Like the other Jewish groups, the organization is primarily a service group but also has a strong policy focus, including several programs devoted to lobbying government officials. The group exists to "promote the unity of the Jewish people," and is concerned with healthcare, education, and hate crimes, among other issues. Hadassah claims 306,000 members in over 1,300 local groups.

The group's original presence in Washington functioned to ensure that the organization would be able to ship supplies to the Jewish community in European war zones during World War II. To regulate shipping during war time, the White House set up the President's Advisory Committee for Foreign Voluntary Aid. Hadassah was a charter member of this committee.[59] During the first two decades of Hadassah's existence, the group focused solely on international affairs and was not involved in domestic politics. In 1940, the group created the American Affairs Department and devoted attention to issues of civil rights, reproductive freedom, and other domestic policies. According to its website, Hadassah opened its Washington Action Office in 1997 in Washington, D.C., to "maximize Hadassah's activism, implement Hadassah's commitments on international and domestic issues, and encourage membership participation in the democratic process." The Hadassah Washington Action Office sponsors the Day on the Hill program, which brings Hadassah members to Washington, and issues public policy statements on issues of concern to the group. At the local level, members can be involved in the Date with the State program, an initiative to establish connections with local and state-level government leaders. In 2000, members of Hadassah were active participants in the Million Mom March, a rally in support of gun control legislation.

Muslim Groups

In contrast to Jewish groups with their long histories, Muslim women's interest groups are relatively new organizations. This is due both to theological differences between the religious traditions and to social factors impacting group formation. Theologically speaking, the conservative nature of the Muslim faith has made women's mobilization difficult. In many ways, the emergence of Muslim women's groups in the 1990s is analogous to the challenges to patriarchal religion made by Jewish women in the late 1800s and Christian women in the mid-1900s. As scholars of Muslim feminism point out, some aspects of Islam limit the political, social, and economic participation of Muslim women even though the theological basis for women's equality in Islam clearly exists.[60] In addition to theological reasons for the late development of Muslim groups, there are a variety of social factors that inhibited the development of these groups. To begin with, the Muslim population in the United States is relatively small compared to Catholics and Protestants, with a high estimate of five to eight million Muslims living in the United States.[61] Developments in the social-political world over the past twenty years facilitated the recent emergence of Muslim groups. In his work on interest groups, David Truman argued that groups tend to form in response to threats.[62] Recent political developments moved the Muslim faith into the spotlight and resulted in many cases of harassment and claims of discrimination in the United States in addition to increased negative attention to the treatment of women in Muslim cultures. Similar to groups from other religious traditions in their early years, both of the major Muslim women's groups are primarily service and religious organizations, but their actions in the private sphere have consequences in the public sphere.

The Muslim Women's League was founded in 1992 in response to the sexual violence and ethnic cleansing of the Bosnian War. With headquarters in Los Angeles, the MWL website identifies the group as "a nonprofit American Muslim organization working to implement the values of Islam and thereby reclaim the status of women as free, equal and vital contributors to society." The group identifies itself as a feminist organization strongly grounded in the Muslim faith. As a primarily educational organization, the MWL is not directly involved in political campaigns, although many members are individually politically active.

The Muslim Women's League served as a part of the official U.S. delegation to the United Nation's Fourth World Conference on Women.[63] Members of the MWL were the only Muslim women representatives in the U.S. delegation. Members have been asked to sit on a variety of committees regarding religious freedom and human rights. In 1996, the group made headlines by hosting First Lady Hillary Rodham Clinton at a luncheon. This was the first time a first lady had addressed a U.S. Islamic group outside the White House.[64] Clinton challenged the members and a larger audience to become involved in the political process. However, the willingness of Hillary Clinton to participate in an event sponsored by the MWL did not translate into presidential access. The group reports low access to the administration of President Clinton and low to nonexistent access to the Bush administration.

Kamilat, an Arabic term meaning "those who are perfect," is a nonprofit organization created to reach underserved women and their families within the Muslim community. The group was founded by religious scholars, academics, and community activists in 1997, led primarily by Shaykh Muhammad Hisham Kabbani and his wife Hajjah Naziha Adil. Kamilat opened a Washington office in 2000 in addition to regional offices in New York, Michigan, California, and New Mexico. Kamilat is the only women's interest group included in this sample of groups to be led by a man, although most of the work done by the group is volunteer-driven and managed by an all-female executive staff.[65] As the Muslim world has moved more into focus for U.S. policy makers, members of Kamilat have been called upon to consult with policy makers in Washington, playing a similar role to the Muslim Women's League.

Comparing Women's Religious Group Characteristics

Although religious values are often associated with conservatism, most of the groups representing religious women are politically liberal even as they retain devout religious beliefs (see table 5.3). Most religious interest groups representing women take their faith quite seriously but draw from it a more progressive understanding of the political world. Thus, for groups such as Church Women United and Hadassah, religious beliefs inspire a moral and spiritual imperative to work on behalf of racial minorities, the poor, and disempowered women. The media often draws a connection between religiosity and political ideology typified by the religious right, but that stereotype dramatically oversimplifies the nuanced relationship between faith and politics and the development of a number of liberal groups.

Groups representing Christian traditions have the largest reported membership levels (see table 5.4). Since Catholics and Protestants comprise the largest share of religious traditions in the United States, it is understandable that this is reflected in group membership. While it is interesting to compare membership levels, it is important to remember that membership numbers are often inflated by groups and are difficult to compare between groups because of different standards of membership. For example, members of the Women's Christian Temperance Union must take a pledge of abstinence from alcohol, while members of Church Women United only have to be a member of a participating church. Interest groups have an incentive to boast of large memberships because the potential for mobilizing voters provides groups with added leverage over policymakers.

Assessing the Influence of Women's Religious Interest Groups

Presidential access and influence over presidential decision making can be divided into two types—direct influence and symbolic influence. To exert direct influence, groups must first have access to presidents or must be able to mobilize group members to affect presidential decisions. Conservative Protestant groups, such as Concerned Women for America and the Eagle Forum, have had the most direct access to presidents since 1976. Republican presidents can actively court these groups without fear of reprisal from other members of the Republican coalition. Democratic presidents, in contrast, have not granted the same degree of policy access to religious women's groups. As Jim Wallis points out, Democrats are often hesitant to include a religious perspective in official policy business.[66] In addition to access, religious groups can exert influence through their support or opposition of presidential nominees. Both CWA and the NCJW are active in this through either actively supporting the president through lobbying on behalf of his nominees or actively oppos-

Table 5.3: Political Ideology of Groups

Group	Political Ideology
Catholics for a Free Choice	Progressive
Church Women United	Progressive
Hadassah	Progressive
Jewish Women International	Progressive
Kamilat	Progressive
Muslim Women's League	Progressive
National Council of Jewish Women	Progressive
Concerned Women for America	Conservative
Eagle Forum	Conservative
Women's Christian Temperance Union	Conservative

Table 5.4: Group Membership

Group	Current Membership
Catholics for a Free Choice	Mailing list only
Kamilat	—
Muslim Women's League	—
Women's Christian Temperance Union	6,000
Jewish Women International	75,000
Eagle Forum	80,000
National Council of Jewish Women	90,000
Hadassah	306,000
Church Women United	500,000
Concerned Women for America	500,000

ing the president through leading opposition to Senate confirmation of the nominee. For example, the NCJW has a program entirely dedicated to opposing presidential judicial nominees that oppose reproductive rights. Similarly, CWA is credited with mobilizing much of the support for the confirmation of Clarence Thomas to the Supreme Court.

Group interactions with presidents can also be symbolic displays of influence. Groups outside of the conservative Christian tradition have been successful in gaining symbolic access to presidents through serving on presidential commissions or through inviting the president or his spouse to group functions. Both the NCJW and Hadassah have served on presidential commissions, representing the views of Jewish women to various presidents.

Church Women United and the Muslim Women's League have both hosted First Lady Hillary Clinton at group events. Presidents Reagan and Bush spoke at Concerned Women for America events and President Clinton addressed a group of the National Council for Jewish Women. Although these events are largely symbolic, they are significant because they may open the door to further group access and eventual direct influence. In addition to these forms of influence over presidents, religious women's interest groups exert influence over members of Congress, state legislators, local government officials, and through other organizations such as the United Nations. The involvement of groups in these arenas certainly merits further study.

CONCLUSION

The connections between faith, sex, and politics are both interesting and important. "Many women's historians have assumed that feminism and religion were mutually exclusive terms, although some have claimed a heroic role for religion in conferring a gospel freedom upon women. More and more, however, scholars have come to recognize a complex and often fraught relationship between the two."[67] This complex relationship described by Bendroth and Brereton extends to the political world as well. Women of religious faith make up a significant portion of the electorate (45 percent in 2004) and often vote differently than religious men. In the past twenty years, religious women have primarily used this voting power on behalf of Democratic candidates. This is especially true for Jewish and Catholic women, although Protestant women also supported Democratic candidates in some elections. Furthermore, religious women of all levels of religious commitment tend to support Democratic candidates for president.

In contrast, on individual political issues that touch on aspects of sex and faith, religious women hold opinions that are more similar to those held by religious men than those held by nonreligious women. I suggest that, rather than indicating a lack of political sophistication or inconsistency on the part of religious women, religious women find the need to balance these two aspects of identity along with a variety of other considerations when choosing which president to support. While religious beliefs may drive political opinions on single issues in a more conservative direction, these opinions do not automatically translate into support for conservative presidential candidates.

A number of interest groups exist to facilitate the political expression of religious women. These groups represent the political views of women from different religious traditions at both liberal and conservative ends of the political spectrum. As a whole, these groups have access to the president through direct and symbolic channels. Conservative religious groups are credited with influencing Republican presidents, and groups across the ideological spectrum are actively involved in confirmation debates over presidential nominees. Progressive religious groups, in particular, have earned symbolic access to presidents through service on presidential commissions or through invitations to presidents or their wives to group events. These forms of symbolic influence have the potential to influence policy as the relationships between presidents and groups are strengthened.

As we move into the twenty-first century, groups representing the political views of religious women will continue to challenge conventional assumptions of the intersection of religion and politics. The 2008 contest in the Democratic primary between senators Hillary Clinton and Barack Obama is an excellent example of how the dimensions of sex and religion, coupled with race, interact in American politics. It remains to be seen which aspect of identity will play as stronger role in decision making in this case, though it is clear that presidents and presidential candidates will need to garner support from religious women if they hope to be successful in campaigning, agenda-setting, or policy making. Though no women of faith have ever served as president, religious women across the political and theological spectrum clearly play a vibrant role in national politics and will continue to do so in the future.

APPENDIX A

The groups included in this analysis have a political focus arising from religious beliefs and are primarily targeted to women (the exception to this is Catholics for a Free Choice, which targets both men and women), though they may be open to male members. The degree to which the primary focus of the group is political differs substantially. For some groups, their attention to politics is fairly marginal but they are heavily involved in social issues that have political ramifications. Other groups were formed specifically for political involvement. In choosing to highlight these ten organizations, I have left out a number of other organizations that meet some of the criteria outlined above. For example, many religious denominations have women's organizations, and these groups are not included in this analysis (e.g., Presbyterian Women, part of the PCUSA denomination). Special thanks to leaders of several groups who responded to my questions regarding their political involvement.

- Catholics for a Free Choice (Catholic) www.catholicsforchoice.org
- Church Women United (Christian Ecumenical) www.churchwomen.org

- Concerned Women for America (Christian Evangelical) www.cwfa.org
- Eagle Forum (Catholic) www.eagleforum.org
- Hadassah (Jewish) www.hadassah.org
- Jewish Women International (Jewish) www.jewishwomen.org
- Kamilat (Muslim) www.kamilat.org
- Muslim Women's League (Muslim) www.mwlusa.org
- National Council of Jewish Women (Jewish) www.ncjw.org
- Women's Christian Temperance Union (Christian Ecumenical) www.wctu.org

President Harry S. Truman given Hebrew Torah Scroll by Dr. Chaim Weizmann, President of Israel, during a visit to the White House, May 25, 1948

Chapter 6

Jews and the American Presidency

David G. Dalin

A great deal has been written about the history of the American-Jewish experience generally, but little has been written on the subject of Jews and the American presidency. In our recent book *The Presidents of the United States and the Jews*,[1] Alfred J. Kolatch and I examined the role and experience of Jews in each administration from George Washington to Bill Clinton, and discussed the relationship of each of the presidents to the American Jewish community at large and to individual American Jews.

The history of Jewish-presidential relations begins in the early republic, with the presidency of George Washington, who was the first president to visit a synagogue in the United States and to correspond with American Jews. The famed correspondence between Jews and George Washington, as Jonathan D. Sarna has noted, went far to define "the place of Judaism in the new nation."[2] The historic letter of the "Hebrew Congregation in Newport" to the president, composed for his visit to that city on August 17, 1790 following Rhode Island's ratification of the Constitution, "paralleled other letters that Washington received from religious bodies of different denominations and followed a custom long associated with the ascension of kings."[3] In their letter to George Washington, the Jews of Newport noted past discrimination against Jews, praised the new government for "generously affording to all liberty of conscience and immunities of citizenship," and thanked God "for all of the blessings of civil and religious liberty" that Jews now enjoyed under the Constitution.[4] President Washington, in his oft-quoted reply, reassured the Jewish community about what he correctly viewed as its central concern—religious liberty. Appropriating a phrase contained in the Newport congregation's original letter, he famously characterized the United States government as one that "gives to bigotry no sanction, to persecution no assistance."[5] He described religious liberty, "following Thomas Jefferson," as an inherent natural right, distinct from the "indulgent" toleration practiced by the British and much of enlightened Europe, where Jewish emancipation was so often linked with demands for Jewish "improvement."[6] Finally, echoing the language of Micah 4:4, as Sarna has pointed out, Washington hinted that America itself might prove something of a Promised Land for Jews, a place where they would "merit and enjoy the good will of the other inhabitants, while every one shall sit in safety under his own vine and fig tree and there shall be none to make him afraid."[7]

Beginning in the early republic, and throughout the nineteenth century, American Jews looked to the presidency for significant presidential statements and policy positions relating to anti-Semitism abroad and to the plight of Jews denied religious and political freedom in Eastern Europe and elsewhere. Presidents Ulysses S. Grant and Benjamin Harrison, for example, both expressed public concern and sympathy for the worsening predicament of the Jews in czarist Russia and were willing to protest to the czarist government in Saint Petersburg on their behalf. In 1869, when Jewish leaders brought to Grant's attention the fact that the expulsion of twenty thousand Jews from an area in southwestern Russia was being contemplated, he intervened with the czarist government and the expulsion order was rescinded.[8] As the pogroms and anti-Semitic expulsions of Jews in czarist Russia escalated in 1890 and 1891, a delegation of Jewish leaders met with President Harrison in the White House in April 1891 "to discuss the state of czarist anti-Semitism and what the United States government might do to alleviate the plight of Russian Jews."[9] President Harrison subsequently requested that Congress adopt a strong resolution calling upon the U.S. State Department to officially protest Russia's anti-Jewish persecutions. In his Annual Message to Congress on December 9, 1891, moreover, Harrison expressed "his sympathy for the Jews of Russia in the most unequivocal of terms."[10]

Beginning in the early republic, American Jews also looked to the presidency for political recognition in the form of presidential appointments to diplomatic posts and, much later, to the president's cabinet and White House staff.

The tradition of Jews receiving presidential appointments in America is almost as old as the nation itself. Presidents James Madison and James Monroe, for example, appointed Jews to several consular posts, including Scotland and St. Thomas.[11] The best known of President Madison's Jewish appointments was that of the Jewish political journalist and playwright Mordecai Noah who, in 1813, was appointed U.S. consul to Tunis. Noah had lobbied for the job as a Jew and won appointment, in part, "because it was hoped that he might establish beneficial ties with North Africa's powerful Jewish community."[12] The Muslim rulers of Tunis, however, later protested his appointment, because they did not want to deal with a Jew. As a result, the State Department decided to recall Noah. "At the time of your appointment as Consul at Tunis," Secretary of State Monroe wrote Noah, "it was not known that the religion which you profess would form any obstacle to the exercise of your Consular functions. Recent information, however. . . proves that it would produce a very unfavorable effect."[13] Despite the fact that, as Jonathan D. Sarna has noted, the Madison administration had other compelling reasons for wanting to recall Noah, President Madison explained his reason for rescinding Noah's appointment as being "the ascertained prejudice of the Turks against his Religion, and it having become public that he was a Jew."[14] Most Jews took President Madison at his word, believing that anti-Jewish prejudice lay behind Noah's recall. To this day, Madison's recall of Noah remains the only instance in American history in which anti-Semitism was a factor in the rescinding or rejection of a presidential appointment of a Jew.

The next major Jewish presidential appointment was made by Franklin Pierce when he named August Belmont, the influential Jewish financier and Democratic Party fundraiser, to the post of U.S. minister to The Hague. As the first Jew to hold this high rank in the American diplomatic service, Belmont represented the United States in the Netherlands from 1853 to 1857. Throughout his long career in Democratic Party politics, Belmont would raise more money for presidential candidates than any other nineteenth-century Jew. From 1860 to 1872, he would also serve as chairman of the Democratic National Committee, the first Jew to do so.[15]

A few months later, in the fall of 1852, President Millard Fillmore had offered Judah P. Benjamin a seat on the U.S. Supreme Court. In February of 1852, Benjamin, a Louisiana attorney and politician, had entered national politics, winning a seat in the United States Senate, the first professing Jew to do so. Benjamin declined Fillmore's Supreme Court appointment, preferring to remain in the Senate, where he soon established a reputation as one of the chamber's greatest orators, often compared to Daniel Webster and John C. Calhoun. Similarly, in 1857, Benjamin turned down an offer from President James Buchanan to appoint him U.S. minister to Spain. When Louisiana seceded from the Union in February 1861, however, Benjamin, a passionate Southerner, resigned his Senate seat. Soon thereafter, Confederate President Jefferson Davis appointed Benjamin attorney general of the Confederacy, making him the first Jew to hold a cabinet-level office in an American government. Benjamin subsequently served as the Confederacy's secretary of war and secretary of state.[16]

In 1881, President James A. Garfield appointed the eminent Jewish communal leader Simon Wolf as U.S. consul general in Egypt. Wolf, a Washington, D.C., attorney and power broker who was widely acknowledged to be the spokesman for American Jewry in the nation's capital, was a political confidant of every Republican president from Abraham Lincoln to William Howard Taft.[17] Wolf, who had actively campaigned for Garfield, as he had earlier for Ulysses S. Grant and Rutherford B. Hayes, was rewarded for his many years of service to the Republican Party when he was named consul general to Egypt by President Garfield on July 1, 1881, just one day before the chief executive was to fall mortally wounded to an assassin's bullet.

Between the Civil War and the turn of the century, all Jews who received presidential appointments were nominated for diplomatic posts. In 1887, President Grover Cleveland appointed Oscar S. Straus U.S. minister to Turkey, the second Jew to hold this rank in the American diplomatic service. Born in Bavaria on December 23, 1850, Straus was the youngest of three sons of Lazarus and Sara Straus, who had immigrated to the United States with their family in the early 1850s. After graduating from Columbia College and Columbia University Law School, Straus practiced law for a while before joining L. Straus and Sons, his family's growing china and glassware business. With the financial help of his brothers Isidor and Nathan (who in 1888 became partners in and later sole owners of New York City's famed R. H. Macy's department store, which they built into the largest department store in the world), Straus was able to devote his life to public service. In 1882, he entered politics as leader of a citizen's movement dedicated to municipal reform, which worked to reelect William R. Grace mayor of New York. Two years later, Straus played an active role in the presidential campaign of Grover Cleveland, speaking widely on behalf of Cleveland's candidacy.[18]

Straus was an immensely successful and popular minister to Turkey. His gift for diplomacy enabled him to win an invitation from the sultan to arbitrate a business dispute between the Turkish government and Baron Maurice de Hirsch, the Jewish financier and philanthropist who had built the first railroad connecting Constantinople and the cities of Europe.

In appointing Oscar Straus the first Jewish U.S. minister to Turkey in 1887, President Cleveland established a precedent that every president—Republican and Democrat alike—would follow during the next thirty years. Presidents Cleveland, Benjamin Harrison, William McKinley, Theodore Roosevelt, William Howard Taft, and Woodrow Wilson each appointed Jewish ministers (and later, ambassadors) to Constantinople. American presidents recognized the symbolic importance of the Turkish embassy for American Jews, and especially for the growing number of Zionists within the American Jewish electorate, since the Jewish homeland of Palestine (and its holy city of Jerusalem) remained under direct control of the Turkish government throughout this era. Indeed, it can be said without exaggeration that, during this era, the ambassadorship to Turkey came to be considered a quasi-

Jewish domain. Thus, when Oscar Straus resigned his diplomatic post in 1890, President Benjamin Harrison invited Simon Wolf to the White House and told him of his desire "to appoint a representative American citizen of the Jewish faith to Turkey."[19] Upon Wolf's recommendation, Benjamin Harrison appointed Solomon Hirsch, a Republican merchant and state legislator from Oregon, to succeed Oscar Straus as U.S. minister to Turkey. Hirsch served as U.S. minister to Turkey from 1889 to 1892.

Although Straus had resigned his ambassadorship following Cleveland's defeat for reelection in 1888, he remained a close friend and political confidant of President Cleveland, helping to renominate him at the Democratic National Convention of 1892 and serving as a member of Cleveland's "kitchen cabinet" during his second term of office. He was a frequent guest at the White House during the second Cleveland administration, advising the president on monetary policy and on immigration issues of Jewish concern. As an advocate of sound money and of the gold standard that the Republican Party upheld, Straus opposed the nomination of William Jennings Bryan and broke with the Democratic Party by actively campaigning for William McKinley in 1896.

With McKinley's election, Straus had easy access to the White House and advised McKinley on a variety of issues relating to international diplomacy and foreign affairs. In 1898, McKinley asked Straus to accept appointment as U.S. minister to Turkey, the same diplomatic post Straus had held under Cleveland. In the aftermath of the Turkish massacre of Armenians, which had shocked the civilized world the previous year, American relations with Turkey had deteriorated, with the Turkish sultan refusing American claims for property destroyed during the massacres and American citizens in Turkey calling for American warships to back up their claims. In offering him the appointment, McKinley told Straus, who enjoyed the respect of the Turkish sultan, that it was his duty to return to Turkey as the American minister, as he was "the only man in the United States who could save the situation."[20] The Senate quickly confirmed his nomination on June 3, and Straus remained as U.S. minister to Turkey for more than two years, until December of 1900.

A HISTORIC FIRST: THE CABINET
APPOINTMENT OF OSCAR S. STRAUS

In 1906, President Theodore Roosevelt appointed Oscar S. Straus as secretary of commerce and labor, the first Jew named to a president's cabinet. More than any other chief executive, Theodore Roosevelt introduced religious diversity into presidential cabinetmaking. Roosevelt was the first president to appoint a Catholic as well as a Jew to be members of his cabinet. The year before his appointment of Oscar Straus, Roosevelt had nominated the first Catholic, Charles J. Bonaparte, as secretary of the navy. Bonaparte, a grand-nephew of Napoleon and an ardent champion of civil service reform, served as navy secretary until 1906, when he was appointed attorney general, a position that he would hold for the rest of the Roosevelt administration.

When Theodore Roosevelt assumed the presidency after the McKinley assassination, Straus, who had known Roosevelt for several years, soon became a close political adviser and confidant of the new president. A few months after the election of 1904, during which Straus had actively campaigned for Roosevelt and the Republican ticket, Straus first learned of the president's intention to appoint him to the cabinet. Public and private speculation that Roosevelt planned to name Straus to the post of commerce and labor continued throughout 1905 and, when Straus visited the White House in January 1906, the president confirmed the report. While Straus's ability and experience were factors in Roosevelt's decision to name him to the cabinet, so was his religion. "I don't know whether you know it or not," Roosevelt told Straus over lunch at the White House, "but I want you to become a member of my cabinet. I have a very high estimate of your character, your judgment and your ability, and I want you for personal reasons. There is still a further reason: I want to show Russia and some other countries what we think of Jews in this country."[21]

As Richard F. Fenno Jr. and others have suggested,[22] a number of factors are involved in presidential cabinet appointments, as in judicial appointments made by the president. The criteria of objective merit or ability often compete with the need for achieving both geographic and religious "representation" or balance in the presidential selection process. In the case of Roosevelt's selection of Straus, there was considerable debate and varying interpretations as to whether the Jewish appointee was selected primarily on the basis solely of merit, ability, and/or professionalism or, rather, primarily because of the fact that he was a Jew. The latter interpretation of why Roosevelt made the first Jewish cabinet appointment has often been advanced. As Straus's biographer Naomi W. Cohen has noted, in 1912, newspaper reports circulated that at a public dinner the previous year at which both Roosevelt and Straus were speakers, the Jewish financier and philanthropist Jacob Schiff, one of the preeminent Jewish Republicans in America, had introduced Roosevelt, remarking that American Jews owed him a debt of gratitude because of his historic appointment of Straus. In his remarks, Roosevelt had stated that Straus had been appointed on the basis of merit and ability alone, and that the fact that he was Jewish had played no part in Roosevelt's decision to appoint him. A few minutes later, in introducing Straus, Schiff, who was a bit deaf, and had evidently not heard Roosevelt's remarks, recounted how Roosevelt had sought his advice as to who would be the most suitable and eminent Jewish leader to appoint to his cabinet![23]

It is quite probable that in Roosevelt's selection of Straus both the nominee's proven ability as a successful businessman, diplomat, and public servant, as well as his religion and reputation as a respected Jewish communal leader, were important factors in his historic appointment. It is indisputable that Roosevelt wanted to make a Jewish appointment in 1906. He had appointed Charles Bonaparte, a Catholic, to his cabinet the year before, and now sought an opportunity to appoint a Jew. As Naomi W. Cohen has concluded, while he upheld the Progressive ideal of appointments on the basis of merit and ability alone, he had an "equally strong. . . .desire to show American Catholics and American Jews that they had the same opportunities as others."[24]

Theodore Roosevelt's appointment of Oscar Straus received wide coverage in the nation's press, and was generally praised. As the first Jewish cabinet member, Straus's religion evoked more press comment than it had on the occasion of his other appointments. As his biographer has noted, many newspapers used his appointment "as a point of departure to praise the contributions of the Jews to the United States, to express surprise that no Jew had filled a cabinet post heretofore, to laud T. R.'s liberalism, and to discuss the official posts filled by Jews in America and in foreign countries."[25] The *Washington Star*, in applauding Roosevelt's appointment, eloquently labeled Straus "America's Disraeli."[26]

In the twenty-eight years between Theodore Roosevelt's appointment of Oscar Straus and Franklin D. Roosevelt's appointment of Henry J. Morgenthau Jr. as secretary of the treasury in 1934, there were no Jewish appointments to presidential cabinets.

Throughout his presidency, Franklin D. Roosevelt enjoyed extraordinary support throughout the American Jewish community. "The Jews," as Arthur Hertzberg has so aptly put it, "loved Franklin Delano Roosevelt with singular and unparalleled passion."[27] Indeed, American Jews had constituted "the most loyal and loving" of FDR's constituencies.[28] A vast majority of American Jews voted for Roosevelt in each of his four campaigns for the presidency. In 1932, 82 percent of the Jewish vote went to Roosevelt while only 18 percent went to Herbert Hoover. In 1936, running against Alfred M. Landon, FDR received 85 percent of the Jewish vote. In the elections of 1940 and 1944, 90 percent of American Jews voted for Roosevelt, the largest Jewish vote for a presidential candidate in American history. The elation felt by most Jews over Roosevelt's presidency was best expressed by New York judge Jonah Goldstein, who concluded that "the Jews have three *velten* [worlds]: *die velt* [this world], *yeneh velt* [the world to come], and Roosevelt."[29]

Table 6.1: American Presidential Vote, 1944

Religious Tradition	Republican	Democrat
Evangelical Protestant	44.1	55.9
Mainline Protestant	57.9	42.1
Black Protestants	30.2	69.8
Roman Catholics	31.6	68.4
Other Christians	48.5	51.5
Jews	7.3	92.7

Source: John C. Green, *The Faith Factor* (Westport, CT: Praeger Publishers, 2007), 39.

During his twelve years in the White House, Roosevelt appointed more Jews to public office than had any previous president. Although he only named one Jew to his cabinet, more than 15 percent of Roosevelt's top-level appointees were Jews."[30] Harvard Law Professor Felix Frankfurter, whom he appointed to the Supreme Court in 1939, had been an important Roosevelt adviser and political confidant since the beginning of his administration. Jews were especially prominent in the Department of the Interior, where they held many top-level presidential appointments. Abe Fortas, who would be appointed to the Supreme Court by President Lyndon B. Johnson in 1965, began his public career in the 1930s as a young lawyer in the Interior Department, serving first as director of the department's Division of Manpower and later as undersecretary. Jewish attorneys were also appointed to influential positions in the Department of Labor, the Security and Exchange Commission, the Tennessee Valley Authority, the Social Security Administration, and several other New Deal agencies. Among the several Jews who were appointed to ambassadorships by FDR, Jesse Isidor Straus, the nephew of Oscar Straus, was named ambassador to France, where he served from 1933 to 1936. FDR's one Jewish cabinet appointee, his Hyde Park neighbor and closest Jewish friend, Henry Morgenthau Jr., who served as secretary of the treasury from 1934 to 1945, was the longest-serving treasury secretary and the longest-serving Jewish cabinet member in U.S. history.

While President Harry S. Truman had several Jewish advisers on his White House staff, he did not appoint any Jews to his cabinet, the only Democratic president after FDR not to do so. President Kennedy was the first American president to name two Jews to his cabinet, Abraham Ribicoff as secretary of health, education, and welfare and Arthur Goldberg as secretary of labor. In 1962, when Felix Frankfurter announced his retirement from the Supreme Court, President Kennedy appointed Goldberg to fill the vacancy.

The Jewish presence in the federal government grew enormously in the post–World War II era, and especially beginning with the Kennedy administration, as presidents appointed more and more Jews to cabinet and subcabinet positions and to positions in the upper echelons of the White House staff. Presidents Kennedy through Carter made no less than twelve Jewish cabinet appointments, while naming two Jews assistants to the president for National Security Affairs, two Jewish chairmen of the Council of Economic Advisors, three Jewish special counsels to the president and, for the first time, a Jewish ambassador to the Court of St. James.

The relationship between President Richard Nixon's personal view of Jews, on the one hand, and his appointment of several Jews to important positions in his administration, on the other, remains paradoxical. The more than four hundred hours of Nixon White House tapes, made public in the summer of 1999, reveal a level of anti-Semitic prejudice and antipathy unique among American presidents. And yet despite Nixon's uncomplimentary comments about Jews as a whole, his personal dealings with individual Jews were highly cordial, and he reached out to several Jewish appointees to serve in his administration. Arthur Burns, a respected Columbia University economics professor who had served as President Eisenhower's chairman of the Council of Economic Advisors, was appointed chairman of the Federal Reserve Board. Walter Annenberg was named ambassador to England, the first Jew to be appointed to this most prestigious of diplomatic posts. Leonard Garment served in the White House as Nixon's Special Counsel, and William Safire served as one of the president's most trusted speechwriters on the White House staff.

Of course, his best known and, arguably, most influential Jewish appointee was Henry Kissinger.[31] Kissinger, the foreign policy adviser upon whom Richard Nixon relied upon more than any other, had been appointed President Nixon's Special Assistant for National Security Affairs in January 1969. In August 1973, replacing William P. Rogers, Kissinger was appointed secretary of state, the first Jew to serve in the cabinet position. While secretary of state, he retained the title of special assistant to the president for National Security Affairs, the only secretary of state to do so. No Jew has done so much to shape and determine U.S. foreign policy as Kissinger, who was unquestionably the most powerful and influential Jewish cabinet member or White House adviser in American history. As one journalist has aptly commented, "No Jew in modern times has wielded greater power on the world stage than Kissinger."[32]

During his administration, President Jimmy Carter appointed four Jews to cabinet positions, more than had been appointed by any president until that time: Harold Brown as secretary of defense, W. Michael Blumenthal as secretary of the treasury, Neil Goldschmidt as transportation secretary, and Philip Klutznick as secretary of commerce. In appointing Klutznick as the 1980 presidential elections were rapidly approaching, Carter was reaching out to a Democratic Party constituency that he had heretofore ignored—America's Jewish voters. Carter's November 1979 appointment of Klutznick, one of the preeminent Jewish communal leaders and philanthropists of his generation, was widely acclaimed throughout the American Jewish community. Not since Theodore Roosevelt's appointment of Oscar Straus in 1906 had a Jewish cabinet appointee been able to boast of such impressive credentials as a recognized and representative leader of American Jewry. One of the foremost figures in post–World War II American Jewish life, Klutznick had served as international president of B'nai B'rith, as general chairman of the United Jewish Appeal, and as president of the World Jewish Congress. A growing number of Jewish Democrats who had voted for Carter in 1976 were reassessing their support for the Carter ticket because of their dissatisfaction with the Carter administration's policies toward Israel and because of other administration policies of particular concern to the Jewish community. With the 1980 presidential election less than a year away, some political observers were already predicting that fewer Jewish voters would vote for the Democratic presidential candidate than in any election in recent memory, and that President Carter might well receive less than 50 percent of the Jewish vote. In the Carter White House, looking toward the campaign ahead, it was hoped that Klutznick being in the cabinet, and thus part of the official presidential team, would reassure those Jewish Democratic voters who were wavering in their support of the president's reelection.

THE REAGAN PRESIDENCY AND THE JEWS

As it turned out, however, despite Klutznick's presence in the Carter cabinet, these predictions about the Jewish vote in the 1980 presidential election proved to be correct. In the November 1980 election, Ronald Reagan won a landslide victory, defeating Jimmy Carter by more than eight million popular votes and receiving 489 electoral votes to Carter's 49. American Jews, increasingly concerned over the Carter administration's policies toward Israel, were less supportive of Carter's reelection than they had been of any recent Democratic presidential candidate. In the 1980 election, Jimmy Carter received only 45 percent of the Jewish vote, an unusually low proportion of Jewish electoral support for a Democratic presidential candidate.

Throughout his long and remarkable campaign for the presidency in 1975 and 1976, Carter had stressed his commitment to preserving the "integrity" of Israel and, in promising strong support for the Jewish state, had declared that "the United States will never support any agreement or any action that places Israel's security in jeopardy."[33] Moreover, the signing of the Camp

David Accords during his presidency, which led to the peace treaty ending the thirty-one-year-old state of war between Israel and Egypt, was hailed throughout the world as a monumental diplomatic accomplishment. For Carter, who had brought Egyptian president Anwar Sadat and Israeli prime minister Menachem Begin together and then had been instrumental in hammering out an agreement, the accords reached were a personal triumph and his administration's crowning foreign policy achievement.

Despite the euphoria of the moment, however, American Jews had been skeptical of the sincerity of Jimmy Carter's professed support for Israel and distrustful of his administration's increasingly "pro-Arab" policies. Carter's plan for a "reassessment" of Middle East policy had aroused suspicions early in his presidency. On March 8, 1977, Carter had indicated that Israel should withdraw from territories acquired in the Six-Day War of 1967, a position that neither presidents Johnson nor Nixon had taken. When, ten days later, Carter spoke publicly in favor of a "Palestinian homeland," Israeli foreign minister Yitzhak Rabin termed this "a further dramatic change in traditional U.S. policy." In his support for a Palestinian state, wrote George Ball, former undersecretary of state and no friend of Israel, Carter remained "more Arab than the Egyptians."[34] In the last two years of his presidency, Carter had become especially vocal of Israeli settlements on the West Bank and had gone so far as to personally order a "yes" vote by the United States on a UN Security Council resolution deploring new settlements in Judea and Samaria. Moreover, a 1978 Carter administration decision to sell advanced weapons to Saudi Arabia and Egypt had convinced a growing minority of Jewish Democrats that Carter was ready to abandon Israel. "If another presidential election were held today," *Newsweek* wrote at the time, "some experts report that disaffected Jews might turn the tide against Carter in crucial states such as New York, California, Illinois, and Michigan."[35]

And so they did in part in 1980, when Ronald Reagan, a staunch supporter of the State of Israel, received close to 40 percent of the Jewish vote. In the 1980 election, as noted above, only 45 percent of Jewish voters opted for Jimmy Carter. Indeed, in his unsuccessful bid for reelection, Carter became the only Democratic presidential candidate since the 1920s to receive less than 50 percent of the Jewish vote.

Ronald Reagan entered the White House with a strong record of support for Israel. As early as 1967, during the Six-Day War, while governor of California, Reagan had begun speaking at rallies for Israel. At a rally held at the Hollywood Bowl in Los Angeles the day after the war ended, Reagan received a standing ovation from the thirty thousand people in attendance for his stirring appeal on behalf of Israel's safety and security. In 1971, Reagan was instrumental in getting the California State Legislature to sign into law a bill authorizing banks and savings institutions to buy and invest in Israel bonds. This was the first such law in the United States and would become the model for similar laws passed in other states.[36]

During his emergence as a presidential candidate in the late 1970s, Reagan's thinking on foreign affairs was strongly influenced by a group of mostly Jewish neoconservative intellectuals and foreign policy analysts centered around *Commentary* magazine, who reinforced his commitment to the safety and security of Israel as an important strategic ally whose special relationship with the United States needed to be preserved.[37] Once in office, Reagan appointed several of these Jewish neoconservatives—including Elliot Abrams, Eugene Rostow, Max Kampelman, Paul Wolfowitz, Richard Pipes, Dov Zakheim, Kenneth Adelman, Douglas Feith, and Richard Perle—to positions in his new administration.[38]

Although President Reagan did not appoint any Jews to his cabinet, the first American president since Harry Truman not to do so, Reagan appointed several Jews to important subcabinet policymaking positions, especially in the State and Defense Departments. At the age of thirty-two, Elliot Abrams was appointed assistant secretary of state for international organization affairs, becoming the youngest assistant secretary of state in the twentieth century. Abrams worked in the State Department for all eight years of the Reagan administration, serving subsequently as assistant secretary of state for human rights and as assistant secretary of state for inter-American affairs.[39] Eugene Rostow, former dean of the Yale Law School, who had served as an undersecretary of state in the Johnson administration, was named director of the Arms Control and Disarmament Agency by President Reagan. He was succeeded by Kenneth Adelman, who had served as a deputy ambassador on Jeane Kirkpatrick's staff at the United Nations and was the Arms Control and Disarmament Agency director from 1983 to 1987.

Richard Perle, who had been a top aide to Senator Henry Jackson of Washington state from 1969 to 1980, was appointed assistant secretary of defense for international security policy in the Reagan administration, serving from 1981 to 1987. Douglas Feith, a young Washington, D.C., attorney and Jewish communal leader, served on Perle's staff as a deputy assistant secretary of defense for negotiations policy and as a Middle East specialist on the National Security Council as well. Richard Pipes, the Baird Professor of History at Harvard University and former director of Harvard's Russian Research Center, was appointed director of the East European and Soviet Affairs division of the National Security Council. Paul Wolfowitz, who had taught political science at Yale and worked for the Arms Control and Disarmament Agency during the 1970s, served first as director of the State Department's Policy Planning Bureau and subsequently as ambassador to Indonesia in the Reagan administration.[40]

Other Jews were appointed to important economic policymaking positions in the Reagan administration as well. Alan Greenspan, the influential Wall Street investment analyst who had served as chairman of the President's Council of Economic Advisers during the Nixon and Ford administrations, and who advised Reagan on economic policy throughout his presidency, was appointed chairman of the Federal Reserve Board in 1987. Also, one of President Reagan's closest and most trusted economic advisers was the distinguished University of Chicago economist Milton Friedman. Friedman, who had received the Nobel Prize for Economics in 1976 and had been an adviser to both British prime minister Margaret Thatcher and Israeli prime minister Menachem Begin, served as a member of President Reagan's Council of Economic Advisers and had easy access to the White House throughout the Reagan presidency.

REAGAN, ISRAEL, AND SOVIET JEWRY

During the 1980 presidential campaign, Reagan had left little doubt about his pro-Israel views. He denounced the Palestine Liberation Organization (PLO) as a terrorist organization and described Israel as a "strategic asset," a "stabilizing force," and a military offset to Soviet influence.[41] Throughout the campaign, Reagan made a point of differentiating his views on Israel from those of President Carter. As he reminded Jewish audiences, he had been appalled by the Carter administration's decision to abstain rather than veto a UN resolution condemning Israel's proclamation of Jerusalem as its capital. "Jerusalem is now, and should continue to be, undivided," declared Reagan. "An undivided city of Jerusalem means sovereignty of Israel over the city." He also publicly disagreed with the Carter administration's efforts to characterize Israel's West Bank settlements as illegal and was quick to reaffirm this position shortly after the election.[42]

American Jews were further encouraged by Reagan's appointment of Jeane Kirkpatrick as the new ambassador to the United Nations. Known to be a friend of the Jewish community and a strong supporter of Israel, Kirkpatrick shared Reagan's belief, reiterated throughout the 1980 presidential campaign, that "resolutions in the United Nations which undermine Israel's positions and isolate her people should be vetoed because they undermine progress toward peace."[43] Her mostly Jewish staff—which included deputy ambassadors Charles Lichenstein and Kenneth Adelman; her chief political adviser, Carl Gershman; and her legal counsel to the UN Mission, Allan Gerson[44]—also were friends of and strong supporters of Israel.

Despite this overt support for Israel, once Reagan was in office, his administration encountered issues that caused strains and tensions with the Jewish community. In particular, the administration's controversial decision to sell AWACS (airborne warning and control system), aerial surveillance aircraft, and other advanced weaponry to Saudi Arabia angered many Jewish leaders and touched off an eleven-month "battle" between the American Jewish community and the Reagan White House.[45] Indeed, as one political observer has noted, the Reagan administration's decision to sell AWACS jets to Saudi Arabia in 1981 precipitated "the sharpest clash between Washington and Jerusalem in the fifty-plus years of their relationship."[46]

Although the AWACS presumably were intended to monitor Iranian air operations, they could be used against Israel as well. Virtually all segments of the Jewish community were strongly opposed to the AWACS deal, while it was also questioned or opposed by some Jewish foreign policy officials within the Reagan administration itself. Paul Wolfowitz, for example, the director of the State Department's Policy Planning Bureau, "raised questions about the wisdom of selling AWACS aircraft to Saudi Arabia," and in so doing "demonstrated himself to be one of Israel's strongest supporters in the Reagan administration."[47] An influential group of Jewish Republicans even spoke out publicly against the AWACS sale, but to no avail. Despite intense lobbying by the American Israel Public Affairs Committee and other Jewish organizations, the Reagan administration won the AWACS battle, and the U.S. Senate narrowly approved the arms sale to Saudi Arabia in October 1981.[48]

Even with the tensions generated over the AWACS, overall relations between American Jewish leaders and the Reagan White House remained unimpaired. Jewish leaders were grateful that the Reagan administration had not condemned the Israeli bombing of an Iraqi nuclear reactor the previous June. So, too, they were pleased that the United States did not "overreact" to Israel's incursion into Lebanon and the bombing of Beirut in 1982, and that President Reagan had reassured Israel's ambassador that the United States did not "anticipate any change" or "fundamental reevaluation" of their relationship as a result of these incidents. During his first term, Reagan also became the first American president to formally authorize the signing of a "strategic cooperation agreement" between the United States and Israel, aimed at thwarting greater Soviet influence in the Middle East and affirming the Reagan administration's intention of enhancing Israel's special relationship with the United States; there was no corresponding strategic pact signed with any Arab state.[49]

Jewish leaders were also grateful to the Reagan White House for its financial assistance to Israel. United States financial aid to Israel increased steadily throughout the Reagan years, reaching an unprecedented $3 billion a year in loans and grants beginning in 1986.[50] In 1988, Israeli prime minister Yitzhak Shamir declared to reporters, "This is the most friendly administration we have ever worked with. They are determined that the strong friendship and cooperation will continue and even be strengthened despite differences that crop up from time to time." This statement seems to reflect the reality of the basic relationship between Israel and the United States during the Reagan era: despite some strains, relations between America and Israel were stronger at the end of the Reagan tenure than before Reagan took office. In Ronald Reagan, "most observers concur, the Jewish state had a reliable friend in the White House."[51] As one former Jewish official in the Reagan administration would later put it, "His [Reagan's] instinctive feeling that the Jewish state was a friend and ally that should be supported was pervasive in all his decision-making. . . . It was during the Reagan years that the view of Israel as a strategic asset to the United States, rather than as a moral burden, became a lodestar of American policy."[52]

During the 1980 presidential campaign, Reagan spoke out frequently on the issue of Soviet Jewry, attacking the Soviet Union for its imprisonment of Jewish dissidents and its curtailment of Jewish emigration. In a major address before B'nai B'rith in Washington, D.C., on September 3, 1980, Reagan declared: "The long agony of Jews in the Soviet Union is never far from our minds and hearts. All these suffering people ask is that their families get the chance to work as they choose, in freedom and peace. They will not be forgotten in a Reagan Administration."[53]

Within four months of his inauguration, on May 28, 1981, Reagan met in the White House with Avital Sharansky to discuss the plight of her husband, Anatoly, the Soviet Jewish activist and spokesman for the Soviet dissident movement who had been imprisoned in Moscow since 1977. Sharansky's plight became a major human rights cause for Secretary of State George Shultz and for Reagan, who successfully pressed for the dissident's release with Soviet prime minister Mikhail Gorbachev in Geneva on November 19, 1985. Sharansky's plight, and that of other Soviet Jewish dissidents, also became a major human rights cause for Elliott Abrams, who, during his four-year tenure as assistant secretary of state for human rights, made Soviet Jewry "a central issue on the agenda of the State Department's Human Rights Bureau, over which he presided."[54] Between 1981 and 1985, Abrams, "who cared passionately about the issue of Soviet Jewry," met regularly with Secretary of State Shultz to strategize and formulate ways to help secure visas for Jews wishing to leave the Soviet Union. Abrams also met regularly with American Jewish communal leaders and with Avital Sharansky to discuss Soviet Jewish emigration and the plight of her husband and other individual Jewish dissidents imprisoned in the USSR. On official visits to Moscow, Abrams, like Shultz, met with various Jewish dissidents and gave Soviet officials lists of those Jewish dissidents, such as Sharansky, that the Reagan administration hoped would be released.[55] Shultz and Abrams were assisted in these efforts by Max Kampelman, who had headed the U.S. delegation to the 1983 Conference on Human Rights held in Madrid and who served as a counselor to the State Department during President Reagan's second term.[56] Their efforts on Sharansky's behalf were eventually successful. On February 11, 1986, Sharansky was released from prison as part of a "prisoner exchange" and emigrated immediately to Israel, "where he became a spokesman for Soviet Jews living in Israel, as well as a major political figure," who presently serves as a cabinet member in the Israeli government.[57] When Sharansky arrived in Israel shortly after his release from prison on February 11, 1986, one of the first calls he received was from President Reagan, "welcoming him to a land of freedom."[58]

At his subsequent Reykjavik, Iceland summit with Gorbachev in October 1986, Reagan would again raise the issue of Soviet Jewry and the importance of the Jewish immigration issue to the people of the United States, telling Gorbachev that "because Jews want to freely practice their religion," their freedom to emigrate was imperative. "Reagan's interest in Soviet Jewry," as Israeli prime minister would later recall, "was immense; it was close to the first issue on the American agenda [at Reykjavik] and was part of the confrontation between the to superpowers."[59] The Soviet Jewry issue was woven, intrinsically, into the Reagan administration's view of the Soviet Union as an "evil empire" whose mistreatment and imprisonment of Jews was one of the most visible manifestations. At Reagan's behest, Secretary of State Shultz, who once attended a Passover seder organized by Jewish refuseniks in Moscow, would frequently raise the issue of the Soviet government imprisonment of Jewish dissidents. When Secretary of State Shultz met with Kremlin leaders, the Soviet Jewry issue "was not an item to touch on before lunch, but one of the first and longest items on the agenda. And he always named specific names, using his influence time and again to get specific individuals out of the Soviet Union."[60] As Elliott Abrams would later put it, "The Reagan Administration kept beating the Soviet Union over the issue of Soviet Jews and kept telling them, 'You have to deal with this question. You will not be able to establish the kind of relationship you want with us unless you have dealt with this question—the question of emigration and the question of what you are doing internally.'"[61] Reagan will be remembered for his "abiding support" of the cause of Soviet Jewry. "Too often," as Marshall Breger, a special assistant to the president and White House liaison to the Jewish community during the Reagan administration, has recently recalled, "politicians make perfunctory nods toward human rights issues and then go on with the business of realpolitik. The Reagan administration, in contrast, made Soviet Jewry a core issue."[62]

THE CLINTON PRESIDENCY AND THE JEWS

As Seymour Martin Lipset and Earl Raab have pointed out, the "American government's support for Israel" has for decades been "the top public affairs item" on the American Jewish political agenda.[63] U.S. political and financial support of Israel has been, and remains, the key policy concern for American Jewish voters. As such, in one presidential election after another since the establishment of the State of Israel in 1948, Jewish voting behavior has been shaped primarily by a candidate or administration's Middle East policies, and by Jewish perceptions of their support (or nonsupport) for the Jewish state.[64] In the presidential campaign of 1992, as in the campaign of 1980, perceptions of the incumbent administration's views and policies toward the State of Israel were a significant factor in shaping and determining the Jewish vote. Like Ronald Reagan, prior to his election as president, Bill Clinton had been known as a staunch supporter of the State of Israel and its political security and survival. During the presidential campaign of 1992, Clinton left little doubt about his pro-Israel views, and received over 80 percent of the Jewish vote in his race against George H. W. Bush. President Bush, however, left many such doubts, and the Bush administration's track record on Israel was decidedly less reassuring to American Jews. After George H. W. Bush assumed the presidency, as Steven L. Spiegel has argued, "the Jewish community was unable to prevent him from returning to a modified Carter perspective," on the Middle East, "marked by a willingness to pressure Israel for its own good and to improve America's relations with the Arabs."[65] For American Jews at least, Bush's nonsupportive "approach to Israel was most notable for his decision in the fall of 1991 not to approve loan guarantees for Israel as long as the Shamir government continued to expand settlements in the West Bank."[66] In the summer of 1991, Israel had sought $10 million in loan guarantees from the United States "to facilitate the construction of housing for Russian Jewish emigrants flooding into Israel." In August, the Bush administration "had decided to postpone the Israeli request. . . .in order to force the Israelis to stop building new settlements in occupied Arab territories and to ensure the Shamir government's cooperation with American efforts to arrange a Middle East peace conference"[67] in November. As Benjamin Ginsberg has pointed out, the Bush administration "forced Israel to participate in the conference though the Israeli government felt that it had little or nothing to gain and stood only to lose territory."[68] The Bush administration's "anti-Israel posture" became so pronounced that the *Wall Street Journal* in March 1992 observed that the White House had obviously adopted what it termed a pro-Arab policy. "The White House seems to be veering to the view that in the post–Cold War world Israel has diminished strategic importance, and the Arab regimes have increased importance."[69]

Throughout the Bush presidency and the 1992 campaign, American Jews were thus increasingly concerned about the Bush administration's professed support for Israel. American Jews were especially distrustful of the Middle East policies being advocated by Bush's secretary of state, James Baker, and his foreign policy team, who were viewed as pro-Arab and lukewarm (at best) in their support for the Jewish state. At the same time, pro-Israel groups in the Jewish community pointed to the prominence of Jews "and other staunch allies of Israel" such as Samuel "Sandy" Berger and former Reagan State Department official Richard Schifter on Clinton's campaign staff and among his key foreign policy advisers "as indicating the likelihood" that Democratic policy would be more favorable to Israel.[70] As a result, as Spiegel has concluded, "American Jews turned against Bush and his secretary of state, James Baker, in passionate form in the 1992 election campaign."[71] Many Jewish Republicans, including some prominent neoconservatives, shifted their support to Clinton and the Democrats in 1992, refusing to back Bush.[72] In the November election, only one out of ten Jews backed George Bush in his campaign for reelection, "a third of the Jewish vote he had received in 1988."[73]

As president, Clinton visited Israel four times, more than any other chief executive in American history, and he enjoyed an especially close friendship with Israeli prime minister Yitzhak Rabin, a friendship that evolved through their shared efforts to initiate and conclude a new Middle East peace process and agreement between Israel and the Palestinians. These efforts were facilitated, in large part, by Dennis Ross, a Jewish diplomat with extensive Defense and State Department experience who, throughout the first and second Clinton administration, served as the president's special Middle East coordinator and negotiator, with the rank of ambassador. As President Clinton's Middle East negotiator, Ross served as the point man for the president and the secretary of state in shaping U.S. involvement in the Middle East peace process.[74]

After the November 1991 Madrid Peace Conference, when efforts to establish a peaceful arrangement between the Palestinians and Israelis had all but collapsed, a new attempt was made in Oslo, Norway, which came to be known as the Oslo Accords. Ross was as instrumental in assisting the Israelis and Palestinians in negotiating the September 1995 agreement concluding the first stage of the Oslo Accords as he had earlier been, through intensive shuttle diplomacy, in brokering the historic Israeli-Jordanian peace treaty of October 1994, the second such document Israel had signed since its independence. On September 28, 1995, four days after the Oslo Accords were signed in Taba, Egypt, an elaborate ceremony was held on the White House lawn at which Yitzhak Rabin and Palestine Liberation Organization president Yasser Arafat signed official documents ratifying the Oslo agreement. At the prompting of President Clinton, Arafat and Rabin shook hands, a historic moment in the Clinton administration's ongoing (albeit ultimately unsuccessful) efforts to bring about peace in the Middle East.[75]

Then, shockingly, less than six weeks later, on November 4, 1995, immediately after addressing a peace rally in Tel Aviv's Municipal Square attended by an overflow crowd of more than one hundred thousand people, Yitzhak Rabin was assassinated. Two days later, Rabin was buried in Jerusalem at a state funeral attended by leading statesmen and political leaders from around the world. Among the many tributes to Israel's fallen leader, President's Clinton eulogy was most heartwarming and deeply felt, and widely praised and appreciated by American Jewish leaders, especially Democrats, who often spoke with pride of the Rabin-Clinton friendship. Indeed, Steve Grossman, a prominent Jewish communal leader who also served as chairman of the Democratic National Committee during the Clinton administration, believed that the president did not have a closer and more intimate relationship with any world leader than he had with Rabin.[76]

President Clinton's continuing support for Israel and a revitalized Middle East peace process, and well-known friendship with Rabin, were widely popular within the American Jewish community and, as the 1996 presidential election approached, American Jews generally assumed that Clinton's policies would be more favorable to Israel than that of his Republican opponent Robert Dole. Most Jews agreed with the assessment of former Democratic congressman Mel Levine of Los Angeles, who asserted while campaigning for Clinton in June 1996: "I wouldn't call Senator Dole an enemy of Israel," but "President Clinton has been a strong and consistent friend of Israel. And in a word, Dole has not."[77] In the November 1996 election, Clinton increased his electoral support within the Jewish community, receiving well over 80 percent of the Jewish vote to Senator Dole's 13 percent.

Table 6.2: Presidential Votes of Jews, 1976–2000

Year	Democrat	Republican	Independent
1976	64	36	—
1980	45	39	15 (Anderson)
1984	67	31	—
1988	64	35	—
1992	80	11	9 (Perot)
1996	78	16	3 (Perot)
2000	79	19	1 (Nader)

Source: Ira N. Forman, "The Politics of Minority Consciousness: The Historical Voting Behavior of American Jews," in L. Sandy Maisel, *Jews in American Politics* (Lanham, MD: Rowman & Littlefield, 2001), 153; Robert Booth Fowler, Allen D. Hertzke, Laura R. Olson, and Kevin R. Den Dulk, *Religion and Politics in America*, 3rd ed. (Boulder, CO: Westview Press, 2004), 98.

JEWISH APPOINTMENTS DURING
THE CLINTON ADMINISTRATION

President Clinton's great popularity and electoral support within the American Jewish community were not a result of his pro-Israel policies alone. They were also attributable to his presidential appointment policies, which seemed to reflect his genuine friendship with the Jewish community and his commitment to increasing Jewish political recognition and representation in American government and public life. In their continuing (and increasing) support for President Clinton throughout his presidency, Jews were especially appreciative of the unprecedented number of Jewish appointments made by President Clinton during the 1990s.

More Jews have served in prominent White House staff positions in the Clinton administration than at any time since the New Deal. Samuel "Sandy" Berger, who had served as deputy director of the State Department's Policy Planning Staff during the Carter administration, was appointed deputy assistant to the president for National Security Affairs. Following Clinton's reelection in 1996, Berger was elevated to special assistant to the president, thus becoming the third Jew in American history to serve as the president's chief national security policy advisor on the White House staff. Three Jewish attorneys, Bernard Nussbaum, Lloyd Cutler, and former congressman and federal judge Abner Mikva, served on the White House staff as special counsels to President Clinton. Numerous other Jews, including Rahm Emanuel, Ira Magaziner, Dick Morris, Ann Lewis, Maria Echaveste, and Sidney Blumenthal, served in a variety of advisory capacities on the White House staff during the Clinton administration. In 1998, Maria Echaveste was appointed deputy chief of staff, an influential White House job that involved coordinating the State of the Union speech and planning the Wye River Summit to negotiate the Clinton administration's Middle East peace effort. Echaveste, who had converted to Judaism in 1991, was the first Jew to be appointed deputy chief of staff to a U.S. president.[78]

During his eight years in the White House, Bill Clinton also appointed more Jews to cabinet posts than any other president. Two Jews, Robert E. Rubin and Lawrence Summers, served as secretaries of the treasury. Madeleine Albright, who was born a Jew but raised as a Roman Catholic and later became Episcopalian, became secretary of state in 1997, after having served as UN ambassador (with cabinet rank) during the first Clinton administration. Richard C. Holbroke, who had earlier served as the Clinton administration's ambassador to Germany and as its special envoy to Kosovo, was nominated as ambassador to the United Nations in October 1998 and confirmed the following year. Robert Reich was named secretary of labor, the third Jew in

American history to head the Labor Department. Dan Glickman, formerly a nine-term Democratic congressman from Iowa and a longtime member of the House Agriculture Committee, became secretary of agriculture, the first Jew ever to serve in that cabinet position. Mickey Kantor became the third Jew to serve as secretary of commerce in a presidential cabinet. Jacob Lew was named director of the cabinet-level Office of Management and the Budget.[79]

Shortly after his election in 1992, President Clinton had also sought to appoint a Jewish attorney general, Zoe Baird. One of his earliest cabinet nominees, Baird soon encountered problems when it was revealed that she and her husband had hired a Peruvian woman, who did not have the proper immigration papers permitting her to work in the United States, as a domestic worker in their home, in violation of the 1986 immigration law that made it illegal to hire undocumented workers. The fact that the Immigration and Naturalization Service, the government agency that enforced this law, was part of the Justice Department, which Baird had been chosen to administer, made the prospects of her Senate confirmation seem increasingly unlikely, and her nomination was eventually withdrawn.[80]

The problems the Clinton administration encountered with the nomination of Zoe Baird, however, were entirely unrelated to her Jewishness. It is of more than passing historical significance that anti-Semitic prejudice had no role in the public debate over, or the eventual withdrawal of, her nomination. Throughout American history, with the singular exception of Mordecai Noah's recall as U.S. consul to Tunis in the early nineteenth century, anti-Semitism has played no role in the presidential appointments and/or confirmation of Jews. There was not even any hint of anti-Jewish prejudice in President Nixon's approach to appointments. Richard Nixon's fondness for anti-Semitic statements and innuendo, as revealed in the Nixon White House tapes, did not deter him from appointing several Jews—including Henry Kissinger, Arthur Burns, Walter Annenberg, Alan Greenspan, Leonard Garment, and William Safire—to important positions in his administration. Indeed, allegations of anti-Semitic prejudice notwithstanding, no other Republican president, before or since, has appointed as many Jews to the cabinet and White House staff.

For the first time in American history, moreover, a president, Bill Clinton, appointed two Jews to the United States Supreme Court, a historic milestone in presidential-Jewish relations. As Robert A. Burt has noted, "of the 108 Justices who have served on the United States Supreme Court since its founding, seven have been Jews."[81] Prior to the Clinton presidency, five Jewish justices had been appointed to the Supreme Court.[82] President Woodrow Wilson appointed the first, Louis D. Brandeis, in 1917. Benjamin Cardozo, the second Jew to serve on the Court, was appointed by President Hoover in 1932 and served until his death in 1938. When Brandeis retired a few weeks later, Franklin D. Roosevelt appointed Harvard Law School professor Felix Frankfurter, the third Jewish justice, who would serve on the Supreme Court from 1939 until 1962. Upon his resignation that year, President Kennedy appointed his secretary of labor, Arthur Goldberg, the fourth Jewish appointee to the Court, who served until 1965, when he resigned to accept Lyndon Johnson's appointment as U.S. ambassador to the United Nations. President Johnson then appointed Abe Fortas, the fifth American Jew to serve as a member of the Supreme Court. For twenty-four years after Fortas's resignation in 1969, there were no Jewish members of the Supreme Court, until President Clinton appointed Ruth Bader Ginsburg, the first Jewish woman to serve on the Court, in 1993. The following year, President Clinton appointed U.S. federal judge (and former Harvard Law School professor) Stephen G. Breyer to a seat on the Court.[83]

In the sixty-four years between Millard Fillmore's offer of a Supreme Court nomination to Judah P. Benjamin in 1852 to Woodrow Wilson's nomination of Louis D. Brandeis in 1916, no president had seriously considered appointing a Jew to the Court. Wilson's appointment of Brandeis, like Theodore Roosevelt's earlier appointment of Oscar Straus to his cabinet, was thus a historic event in American Jewish political history. So, too, was Bill Clinton's appointment of two Jewish justices, Ginsburg and Breyer, in the early 1990s. Although two Jews, Benjamin Cardozo and Louis D. Brandeis, had served on the Supreme Court simultaneously between 1932 and 1938, they had been appointed by different presidents. Never before the Clinton presidency had two Jews appointed by the same president served simultaneously on the Court. In appointing Felix Frankfurter following Brandeis's retirement in 1939, Franklin D. Roosevelt established the precedent of there being a "Jewish seat" on the Court, a precedent that presidents Kennedy and Johnson would follow in making their appointments: This "informally" designated Jewish seat was thus occupied by justices Brandeis, Frankfurter, Goldberg, and Fortas, who served for fifty-three years in succession between 1916 and 1969. This tradition of there being a Jewish seat on the Court was, however, broken by President Nixon when he appointed Fortas's successor. Over the next two decades, there was much speculation that presidents Ford and Reagan might appoint a Jewish justice to fill this Jewish seat, and many Jewish political observers, journalists, and pundits urged presidents Reagan and Ford to do so. Although Ronald Reagan had in fact named a Jewish nominee, Douglas H. Ginsburg, a U.S. Court of Appeals judge and former Harvard Law professor, in 1987, Ginsburg withdrew his candidacy after "the startling disclosure of his past marijuana use, both as a student and law professor"[84] made his Senate confirmation unlikely. It was thus not until Bill Clinton's appointment of Ruth Bader Ginsburg twenty-four years after Fortas's resignation that another Jew would join the Court. The accession of a second Jew, Stephen G. Breyer, appointed by the same president, notes Robert A. Burt, "clearly denoted a new conception of the Jewish presence on the Court—not only the end of the apparent political understanding between 1939 and 1969 that there was room on the Court for only one Jew at a time but, more significantly, the disappearance of the Jewish seat as such."[85] In contrast to the appointments of Frankfurter, Goldberg, and Fortas, "no one regarded Ginsburg and Breyer as filling a Jewish seat."[86]

CONCLUSION

Since the nineteenth century, American Jews have looked to the presidency and to individual presidents for political recognition and representation in the form of presidential appointments to diplomatic posts, to the White House staff, to the president's cabinet, and (more recently) to the Supreme Court. And they were not disappointed in their expectations of the White House. During the twentieth century, from President Theodore Roosevelt's historic appointment of Oscar Straus as secretary of commerce and labor in 1906 and Woodrow Wilson's equally historic appointment of Louis Brandeis to the Supreme Court in 1916, to the extraordinary and unprecedented number of Jewish appointments made by President Bill Clinton during the 1990s, American Jews have received ever greater political recognition through presidential appointments, which have been one of the most important vehicles for Jewish representation and participation in American government and public life. In many respects, the 1990s were a historic—indeed, a golden—era for Jewish participation in American politics and government. More Jews won election to the U.S. Congress and Senate than at any other time in American history. During the 1950s, there was only one Jewish member of the U.S. Senate; during the 1990s, there were eleven. In the eight years of his presidency, Bill Clinton appointed almost as many Jews to cabinet posts as did all of his predecessors combined. During the Clinton presidency, Jews received more ambassadorial appointments than in any other administration in American history. Jews served by presidential appointment as ambassadors to many of the world's capitals, including, for the first time, to the State of Israel. Indeed, Martin Indyk, who from 1993 to 1995 served as special assistant to the president and senior director of Near East and South Asian Affairs on the National Security Council, would subsequently serve two stints as U.S. ambassador to Israel during the Clinton administration. In 1997, President Clinton also enjoyed the distinction of appointing the first religiously Orthodox Jew as an ambassador to an Arab country, Egypt. Soon after Ambassador Daniel Kurtzer arrived in Cairo, moreover, a kosher kitchen was installed for him at the Cairo embassy.[87] And in August 2000, Senator Joseph Lieberman, an Orthodox Jew who did not campaign on the Sabbath, became the first Jewish candidate for vice president. Each of these developments would have been unpredictable during the 1950s. Collectively they suggest that during the 1990s, as never before, Jews were politically at home in America.

Although it has been hardly remarked upon, a distinctive legacy of the Clinton presidency has been his two Jewish appointments to the Supreme Court and, especially, the extraordinary number of Jewish appointees to important policymaking and advisory positions throughout the executive branch of the federal government. Indeed, through appointments to his White House staff, cabinet, and a variety of subcabinet and diplomatic posts, President Bill Clinton brought more Jews into high-level positions in government than any other president since FDR, and perhaps more than any president of all time. Through these presidential appointments, American Jews have received an unprecedented degree of political recognition and influence in American government and public life that would have been unimagined in an earlier generation.

Israeli Prime Minister Yitzhak Rabin, President Bill Clinton, and Palestinian Liberation Organization (PLO) Chairman Yasser Arafat meet at the White House to sign the Oslo Peace Accords, September 13, 1993.

Chapter 7

Muslims and the American Presidency

Brian Robert Calfano, Paul A. Djupe, and John C. Green[1]

Although present in the United States for centuries, American Muslims have only recently started to receive scholarly attention as a distinct political and religious community in national surveys.[2] The community's relative size has likely contributed to the historical oversight by demographers and political analysts.[3] This oversight is unfortunate because, as social identity theory would suggest, the American Muslim community likely encountered biases and pressures attributable to its status as both a political and religious "out-group" long before the popular fixation on Islam took hold in the wake of September 11.[4] In addition, the U.S. policy emphasis on combating terrorism and interdicting perceived threats to national interest in the Middle East has encouraged the political study of Islam and its followers. However, existing work, which has generally not focused on quantitative assessment of the characteristics and political concerns of American Muslims, often paints the followers of Muhammad, irrespective of national identity, with the broadest of strokes.[5] Also largely overlooked are the attempts by political leaders to reach out to the American Muslim community in a manner that helps to ameliorate their out-group status. As such, the American Muslim community's experience with presidential politics is ripe for investigation.

This chapter fills a void in the literature by examining data generated through three special surveys of American Muslim political attitudes and behavior and assessing the efforts of presidents Bill Clinton and George W. Bush in reaching out to American Muslims in an attempt to demonstrate political responsiveness to this political community. From a theoretical standpoint, examining presidential efforts to respond to community needs extends understanding of how successful political leaders are in relating to out-group constituencies. Of course, the American Muslim community is not simply an out-group in the textbook sense of being in the numerical minority. The stereotypical equation of Islam with support for terrorism makes the Muslim political experience in the United States unique, arguably requiring a response from democratic institutions—including and especially the presidency—that affirms both national and Muslim community interests.[6]

We begin with an overview of the American Muslim community's size and diversity. Importantly, American Muslims are no less diverse than Christians or Jews, and, like the latter, their minority status has recently produced a high degree of political solidarity. On balance, American Muslims are Democrats and moderates, with a strong commitment to political engagement. Although they gave a plurality of their votes to George W. Bush in 2000, they overwhelmingly backed Democrat John Kerry in 2004. One reason for this dramatic change is reported discrimination since September 11 and a sense of hostility from the American government, which we juxtapose with discussion of recent presidential efforts at responsiveness. We then conduct a statistical analysis of selected factors determining the presidential vote among American Muslims. Throughout the chapter, interview data from members of the Muslim community in Pittsburgh, Pennsylvania, will be used to supplement the statistical analysis.

THE SURVEYS

In this chapter, we use two surveys commissioned by Project MAPS, funded by the Pew Charitable Trusts, and conducted by Zogby International. These surveys are the first to seek nationally representative samples of Muslims.[7] These surveys are worth describing in some detail. Zogby International began by constructing a sample with a random selection of Islamic centers, matching the zip code to local telephone exchanges, and then calling individuals within these areas with common Muslim surnames. Since many African American Muslims do not have common Muslim surnames, face-to-face interviews were conducted in and around four cities (Detroit, New York, Washington, and Atlanta). In the end, 1,781 self-identified Muslims over the age of 18 were surveyed in November and December of 2001; in August and September of 2004, 1,846 respondents were surveyed. The two samples have very similar demographic traits, revealing a high degree of consistency in the sampling methodology.

While the MAPS surveys are a great resource, it is important to note the limitations of this data. The most significant limitation is that the "mosqued" population of Muslims is probably overrepresented. As Leonard reviews the literature, the most quoted figure of those who are mosqued is a strikingly low 10 to 20 percent,[8] though she notes the figure is controversial.[9] The proportion of the MAPS samples affiliated with a mosque is significantly higher—one-half reported attending *weekly* or more often. Since religious commitment varies by ethnicity, certain groups, such as Turks and Iranians, who tend to have lower levels of religiosity, may be underrepresented.[10] Furthermore, the dataset pegs the proportion of African American Muslims at 20 percent of the total without any clear empirical justification.[11] Nevertheless, these systematically gathered data and large samples provide an unequaled opportunity to explore the politics of American Muslims and to help to shed individual light on the concerns that preoccupy the daily activities of persons caught up in the complex political, social, and religious crosscurrents that are part of the reality of Islamic life in the United States.

Though not, by far, the largest Muslim community in the country, the ten thousand-strong Islamic community in Pittsburgh represents almost 3 percent of the city's 325,000 residents.[12] Though membership estimates of local Muslim communities are not as reliable as we would prefer, Ghayur's approximation of Muslim populations in major American cities suggests that the Pittsburgh community is one of the twelve largest in the United States.[13] Though the Pittsburgh community is not necessarily representative of the ethnic diversity present among Muslims across the United States, it is both small enough to understand the realities of being a political out-group and large enough to have developed a group identity and local points of contact. As such, the perceptions of twenty-two of its members, as brought to light through long-form interviews, provide important personal context to findings from the national surveys as well as presidential attempts at responsiveness.

AMERICAN MUSLIMS: SIZE AND DIVERSITY

Any discussion of the involvement of American Muslims in presidential politics must begin with the size of the American Muslim population. On this crucial matter there has been considerable debate. On the one hand, the American Muslim Council and other Muslim organizations have offered the largest estimates for the number of Muslims in the United States—seven to eight million—based on immigration figures, local studies, and congregational canvasses.[14] Such figures translate into around 3 percent of the total population. However, no independent estimates support such figures. For example, the 2000 census of Religious Congregations and Membership estimated 1.6 million Muslim adherents or about 0.6 percent of the total population.[15] These lower estimates have been supported by survey researchers. For example, Tom Smith of the National Opinion Research Center estimated 1.8 million

Muslims or 0.67 percent of the population.[16] Smith concluded that American Muslims were unlikely to comprise more than 1 percent of the population, so a high estimate of their size is 2.8 million people. In 2007, a special survey by the Pew Research Center estimated that there were about 2.4 million Muslims in the United States.[17]

Of course, for political purposes, the most important figure is the number of Muslim adults. Smith's best estimate is 1.4 million, or about 0.7 percent of the voting age population. This figure is supported by the 2004 exit polls, where Muslims made up 0.7 percent of voters (the exit polls themselves constitute a rough estimate of the percentage of Muslims who voted in 2004—826,345 of the 118,049,259 votes cast).[18] The 2001 Annual Report Information Survey (ARIS) found 1.1 million Muslim adults, or about 0.5 percent of the voting age population; the 2004 National Survey of Religion and Politics, 0.5 percent; the 2004 Zogby postelection survey and the pooled 2004 Pew Research Center surveys, each 0.4 percent; and the 2007 Pew Muslim study found 0.6 percent.[19] These multiple data sources give considerable validity to the smaller estimates offered by scholars. These figures suggest that the politically active, visible part of the Muslim community is between one-quarter and one-third the size of its American Jewish counterpart.

Although Muslims make up only a small portion of the electorate overall, they, like other religious minorities, can matter in politics due to geographic concentration and high levels of political activity. For example, one estimate of the American Jewish community finds that Jews comprise 1.3 percent of the population (making the community larger than the Episcopal Church or the United Church of Christ).[20] However, since the Jewish community is concentrated in electoral vote–rich states such as New York, Florida, Illinois, Ohio, Michigan, and California, and is heavily involved politically in those places, Jews may enjoy political influence that is disproportionate to their relative population size. Muslims are also concentrated in vote-rich states, including New York, California, Illinois, and Texas.[21] A study commissioned by the Council on American-Islamic Relations (CAIR) found that 20 percent of respondents to their national survey reside in California, 9 percent in New York and Illinois, and 7 percent in Michigan, Texas, and New Jersey.[22]

The CAIR study employed a randomized sample of one thousand adult Muslim respondents. This means that the survey sample CAIR used must be representative enough of the American Muslim population to have confidence in the state percentage breakdowns.[23] Unfortunately, no survey organization endorses state-level estimates of the Muslim electorate (which may be attributable to the difficulties in obtaining representative population samples). Thus, if we wish to estimate the percentage of Muslims in a particular state, it is important to recognize that our extrapolations are based on population estimates that may be inherently flawed. Having acknowledged this, if we start with Smith's estimate of the American Muslim community at 1.4 million, and assume that the CAIR state-level estimates are accurate, California contains approximately 280,000 Muslims. Since the California electorate has approximately twenty-three million eligible voters, the California Muslim community constitutes approximately 1.2 percent of the state's electorate.[24] If we start with the high-end estimate of eight million American Muslims (not all of whom will be of voting age), the California percentage should be around 6 percent (accounting for an exclusion of those not eligible to vote). As stated, despite its relatively small size, the community's dense concentration in important electoral states provides it a potentially effective political platform. Moreover, there is considerable evidence that Muslim political engagement was increasing, at least until September 11, 2001.[25]

AMERICAN MUSLIMS: SIZE, DIVERSITY, AND HISTORY

Though an out-group in political and religious terms, the American Muslim community is experiencing significant growth. Scholars consider it the fastest-growing faith in the United States, and expect the number of American Muslims to surpass American Jews in the next several decades.[26] As it grows, the community's ethnic diversity may become more pronounced. While conventional stereotypes couple Islamic faith with Arab ethnicity, the migration histories of American Muslims demonstrate that the community is quite diverse. Based on the community's most predominant ethnic characteristics, we have separated respondents from the MAPS surveys into five categories based on race/ethnicity and national origin: African Americans, South Asians (e.g., Pakistanis and Indians), Africans, Arabs (e.g., Saudis and Yemenis), and a catchall "other" category comprised of those not covered by the preceding four. These classifications are hardly trivial. Indeed, to the extent that they help to define the political realities confronting certain subgroups in the Muslim community, separating members according to ethnic ties may shed additional light on the community's experiences with presidential politics. Not surprisingly, the experiences of certain ethnic groups are intertwined with precipitous events in the nation's historical development.

African American Muslims first came to the United States as slaves, though Islam really took hold in the African American community in the early decades of the twentieth century in urban areas, spurred by contact with immigrant Arab and South Asian Muslims.[27] Ghayur documents that the first voluntary Muslim migration to North America occurred among Turks, Lebanese, Palestinians, Syrians, Russians, and Albanians in the nineteenth century. The last wave of Muslim migration in the twentieth century may be characterized as a student-centered one, in which large numbers of Muslim students began study at American academic institutions and elected to stay in the United States.[28] The circumstances by which certain Muslim groups arrived in the United States may have important ramifications for how Islam and cultural realities interact. For instance, the character of Islam was altered to fit African American culture, with traditions and symbols borrowed from other American religions.[29] Early African American Muslims, such as members of the Nation of Islam, were part of a black nationalist movement seeking out identities independent from connections to slavery. True to their roots, African American Muslim organizations have an agenda based in eradicating racism and its legacy of poverty, crime, drug use, and supporting rights for prisoners, as prisons remain important recruiting grounds for their movement.[30]

Although there were early immigrants to America from colonial India, the rate was heavily circumscribed by U.S. immigration laws. After the laws were liberalized in 1965, much larger numbers came to the United States, particularly after Bangladeshi independence in the early 1970s and the Soviet invasion of Afghanistan in 1979. Though South Asian immigrants are divided by the politics that created their homelands, they are united in their high social class and probably constitute the largest group within the American Muslim community.[31]

Arab Muslims, too, are divided by their national histories, languages, and Muslim sects, though these have been considered more national than religious groups until recently. Early Arab Muslims left the Ottoman Empire when freedoms were limited and before access to the United States closed after World War I. Families of these early immigrants largely defined the immigration from World War I to 1965, when immigration policy was relaxed. Many post-1965 Arab immigrants were educated and looking for economic opportunities and advancement.[32] Less is known about African Muslims. Diouf suggests they are largely invisible—except that they were the first American Muslims (as slaves) and also the newest immigrants.[33] In addition, they do not have the stereotypical Islamic appearance—veils, headscarves, long dresses, and skullcaps.[34] Some are students, and many are not well off; most studies of African Muslims describe the lives of day laborers and other low-wage workers.[35]

AMERICAN MUSLIMS: POLITICAL POSITIONS, IDENTIFICATION, AND ENGAGEMENT

In this section, we begin to examine the American Muslim community's political views and behavior. Before doing so, however, we clarify certain aspects of the MAPS surveys. First, the surveys are lacking a measure of denominational affiliation, so it is not possible to investigate major distinctions, such as between Sunni and Shiite Muslim, let alone smaller or regional subtraditions. It may be that the ethnic categories capture these distinctions in a crude way. It is likely, for example, that at least some of the African American Muslims are Nation of Islam, an American denomination.[36] Second, African Americans were set at 20 percent in the 2001 and 2004 MAPS samples, which made them the third-largest ethnic group. South Asians were the most numerous, with one-third of the samples (or some two-fifths excluding African Americans), followed by Arabs (one-fourth and one-third, respectively). The least numerous were Africans (one-twelfth and one-tenth, respectively) and the other Muslims, constituting those not characterized by one of the four preceding distinctions (one-sixth overall and about one-fifth, respectively).

Like other groups of American voters, American Muslims hold very similar views on some issues and diverse opinions on others. Interestingly, the preferences Muslims hold place them close to both traditional Democrat and Republican issue positions (which are often strongly articulated by the parties' presidential candidates). Tables 7.1 and 7.2 look at Muslim opinion on a variety of social welfare, domestic, and foreign policy issues that have been important in presidential elections (the results here are from 2004). Muslim Americans were nearly unanimous (overall and across the ethnic groups) in favoring universal health care, eliminating racism, stricter environmental laws, increased after-school programs for children, more aid to the poor, and foreign debt relief for poor countries. These issues were not the most salient in the 2004 campaign, but they mattered to many Americans, especially those who voted for John Kerry.

A bit more variation occurred on the remaining policy questions, with a distinctive pattern among the ethnic groups. Overall, four-fifths supported limits on gun purchases, where African Americans and other Muslims were the least supportive and the three immigrant groups more so. About two-thirds of the respondents favored stronger laws to fight terrorism. Here African Americans and other Muslims were the least supportive, while the South Asians, Africans, and Arabs were much more so. On this issue there was considerable change between 2001 and 2004, with support for such laws falling by fifteen percentage points overall. Almost two-thirds also favored more income tax cuts (which generally favors the policies championed by George W. Bush), and here the three immigrant categories were most favorable (although this support declined by eight percentage points from 2001). Overall, one-half of the sample supported requiring residents to be fluent in English, a policy also supported by the three immigrant groups and much less so by African Americans and other Muslims. Finally, less than two-fifths supported

Table 7.1:   American Muslims' Stances on Social Welfare and Cultural Issues, 2004

Social Welfare Issues	All	African American	South Asian	African	Arabs	Other
Favor universal health care	96.3	97.8	96.3	97.8	96.1	93.5
Favor eliminating racial discrimination	94.7	96.2	94.4	94.1	94.6	93.5
Favor stricter environment law	94.0	90.3	95.5	94.1	95.9	91.8
Favor increased after school programs	93.7	93.5	93.2	97.8	94.6	90.5
Favor more aid to poor	92.4	91.1	94.7	95.6	92.6	85.7
Favor increased foreign aid	88.4	89.5	89.1	95.6	88.9	79.2
Favor debt relief for poorer countries	88.2	85.2	89.9	91.9	90.3	81.8
Favor limits on buying guns	81.1	73.9	84.3	79.6	86.0	74.9
Favor stronger laws to fight terrorism	68.9	48.0	78.1	85.4	73.8	57.1
Favor more income tax cuts	65.0	57.7	64.6	67.2	72.6	60.6
Favor requiring fluency in English	52.3	30.2	61.1	56.9	57.9	49.4
Favor eliminating affirmative action	37.1	21.6	41.6	38.7	43.4	35.9
Cultural Issues						
Favor banning sale of pornography	75.8	79.2	73.8	73.5	77.0	74.5
Favor faith-based initiative	69.9	80.1	67.2	75.7	70.0	57.1
Favor school vouchers	65.6	80.1	61.1	65.4	63.9	58.4
Favor death penalty	60.8	41.1	66.9	65.4	67.7	58.7
Favor research on stem cells	59.9	48.8	65.0	52.9	61.2	65.4
Favor limiting abortions	55.0	53.9	55.0	56.9	58.2	48.9
Favor Ten Commandments in public	51.1	50.9	47.4	56.9	55.1	48.9
Favor school prayer	47.9	53.4	45.8	44.9	47.9	46.3
Favor doctors-assisted suicide	31.4	18.3	33.3	34.6	34.6	39.0
Favor research on cloning	28.2	11.1	35.9	22.6	30.7	33.0
Favor same-sex marriage	15.0	4.6	17.0	5.9	16.3	28.6

Source: MAPS, 2004.

eliminating affirmative action, with African Americans the most opposed. This strong social welfare liberalism may reflect the minority status of the respondents, in one or another sense of the term. These patterns are interesting given the relatively high social status of these samples, but high status may also explain support for increased tax cuts and law-and-order policies among South Asian, African, and Arab Muslims.

There was considerably more variation on eleven "moral" issues, including policies pertaining to sexuality and public expression of religion (table 7.1). Overall, Muslim Americans tended to hold conservative views on these issues, thereby placing them closer to the positions taken by George W. Bush in 2000 and 2004. For example, 55 percent favored limiting abortion, 85 percent

Table 7.2: American Muslims and Foreign Affairs, 2004

Percent Support/Agree	All	African-American	South Asian	African	Arabs	Other
Support Afghanistan war	39.7	19.9	47.5	55.2	40.4	41.0
Support Iraq war	13.9	9.4	15.7	16.5	12.9	17.1
Iraq war was worth it	16.0	10.3	17.6	23.3	16.2	16.4
More troops to Iraq	10.7	3.6	12.9	22.6	8.2	13.9
Iraq war could mean more terrorism in the U.S.	86.7	86.4	87.2	78.1	87.5	89.0
Iraq war could destabilize the Middle East	87.6	89.0	87.4	81.7	89.4	85.6
Iraq war will bring democracy to Middle East	30.7	37.2	30.2	40.0	26.3	26.3
Terrorism is best combated by reducing inequalities in the world	92.7	93.0	92.1	91.4	92.6	94.9
U.S. should reduce financial support of Israel	89.6	90.9	87.4	80.7	92.1	92.9
U.S. should support a Palestinian state	94.3	90.8	95.0	93.0	97.0	92.6
U.S. should reduce support of undemocratic regimes in the Muslim world	76.8	67.0	78.2	82.6	82.0	72.0
Kashmir is the central dividing issue between Pakistan and India	77.7	65.6	87.8	66.7	75.6	74.2

Source: MAPS, 2004.

opposed same-sex marriage, and three-quarters favored banning the sale of pornography, with only modest variation by ethnicity. Roughly two-thirds favored faith-based social services and school vouchers. Here, African Americans showed the highest level of support, with other Muslims and South Asians the least. The reverse pattern occurred on the death penalty for those convicted of murder. Overall, about three-fifths had favorable views, but it was the three immigrant groups with the highest support and African Americans with the least. A similar pattern held for stem cell research, except that Africans showed a lower level of support and the other Muslims a higher one.

On the moral issues, there were a few changes between 2001 and 2004, including a twenty-two percentage point increase in support for school vouchers, and an eight percentage point drop in support for the death penalty and displaying the Ten Commandments. These changes may reflect the post–September 11 situation. For instance, school vouchers for Muslim children could offer a safe haven from the intolerance experienced in public schools or wider society—a strategy once employed by American Catholics, as David Leege points out in chapter 3, to avoid Protestant-dominated public schools.[37] Likewise, weakened support for display of the Ten Commandments and the death penalty may reflect a growing sense of discrimination.

What about Muslim Americans' views on foreign policy? Table 7.2 shows that Muslim Americans were quite critical of U.S. policy in this regard, thereby clearly breaking with President Bush. Just two-fifths of the sample supported the war in Afghanistan, and there was even less backing for the war in Iraq. On the latter, one-sixth or less believed the Iraq War was worth the cost, supported the war effort, or backed sending more U.S. troops. These patterns reflect the view that the Iraq War could destabilize the region (88 percent), encourage more terrorism in the United States (87 percent), and not bring democracy to the Middle East (71 percent). American Muslims clearly prefer a nonmilitary approach, believing that terrorism is best combated by reducing inequalities in the world (93 percent), a view consistent with the social welfare liberalism shown in table 7.1. There was not a lot of variation on these issues across the ethnic groups, except for the very low level of support for the Afghanistan and Iraq wars by African Americans.

On the Israel-Palestinian conflict, American Muslims overwhelmingly (more than 90 percent) believed that the United States should reduce its financial support of Israel and support the creation of a Palestinian state. And a vast majority supported a reduction of U.S. support for undemocratic regimes (better than three-quarters). Similarly, there is agreement with former secretary of state Colin Powell's view that the main conflict between India and Pakistan is the claim over the state of Kashmir.

How do these patterns aggregate into broader political attachments? Table 7.3 reports the self-identified party and ideology of Muslim Americans. Partisanship shows a substantial change between 2001 and 2004. In 2001, more than two-fifths of Muslim Americans identified as Democrats, a little under one-third as Independents, and the remaining one-quarter as Republicans.[38] A majority of African Americans were Democrats, as was a plurality of every group. Arabs and South Asians were the most Republican. However, these figures were relatively low for recent immigrant groups, which historically have tended to identify strongly with the Democrats.

By 2004, Muslim American partisanship had changed substantially, so that a clear majority (54 percent) identified as Democrats. Meanwhile, Republican identification was cut by one-half, falling to 12 percent. The Democrats made major gains in all the ethnic groups except African Americans, who were already heavily Democratic. The biggest gain was some twenty percentage points among Africans. No doubt these changes reflected the policies of the Bush administration post–September 11. In addition, these changes reveal how malleable partisan identification can be, especially among recent immigrants. To situate these partisan characteristics in the context of American

Table 7.3: American Muslim Party and Ideological Identifications, 2004

	All	African-American	South Asian	African	Arabs	Other
Party Identification, 2001						
Democrat	43.3	59.5	38.2	46.4	32.4	49.3
Independent	30.7	28.0	31.8	23.8	34.9	25.0
Republican	25.1	11.4	28.9	28.6	32.4	25.0
Party Identification, 2004						
Democrat	53.4	59.7	51.8	63.4	46.6	56.3
Independent	33.0	34.2	34.0	28.2	34.8	26.8
Republican	12.7	4.4	14.2	8.5	17.5	14.7
Political Ideology, 2001						
Liberal	31.2	30.1	38.1	33.3	22.9	31.4
Moderate	41.9	38.9	41.2	30.6	47.7	42.8
Conservative	24.2	27.4	18.9	32.4	27.3	22.7
Political Ideology, 2004						
Liberal	33.3	37.5	34.9	25.6	29.3	35.1
Moderate	44.6	38.2	47.6	43.8	48.2	38.6
Conservative	19.9	23.4	15.5	25.6	20.5	22.3

Source: MAPS, 2001, 2004.

religion more generally, in 2004 56 percent of white Evangelicals considered themselves Republican, and a large minority of mainline Protestants affiliated with the GOP (44 percent), as did white Roman Catholics (41 percent).[39]

Muslim ideology differs from party affiliation, and showed less change over time. In 2001, two-fifths of Muslim Americans identified as moderates, a figure that was only slightly higher than in 2004. In both years, about one-third identified as liberal. But some change occurred in conservative identification, which fell from almost one-quarter to about one-fifth overall. Indeed, every group showed at least a small shift away from conservatism toward liberalism.[40] Interestingly, the most Republican ethnic group was not the most conservative: by 2004, Arabs were the most moderate and South Asians, the second-most Republican, were the *least* conservative. In all, the distribution of Muslims on these two key political attachments can be best described as unsettled.

A final set of politically relevant attitudes were views toward civic engagement. Democratic citizenship requires individuals to value civic engagement, and table 7.4 reveals that such values are common among Muslim Americans. Large majorities (four-fifths or more) agreed that Muslims should participate in politics, support social service programs sponsored by non-Muslims, and join interfaith activities. Two-thirds agreed that Muslims should support worthy non-Muslim candidates in elections. Interestingly, agreement with these civic values was always weakest among the groups with large numbers of converts, African Americans and other Muslims, suggesting that conversion may foster greater insularity than immigration. Overall, more than one-half of Muslim Americans claimed it was "very important" for them to be active in politics. More impressive still, more than three-fifths claimed it was very important for their *children* to be politically active. In contrast to the other civic values, here African Americans scored the highest. South Asians scored the lowest on these measures.

To what degree do American Muslims want their religion and religious organizations involved in politics? Table 7.4 reveals strong support for the mixing of religion and politics, which, again, seems to place the community closer to President Bush's policies and campaign strategies, even as Muslims have generally felt alienated by the administration post–September 11.[41] For one thing, a large majority agrees that the "influence of religion and values in the U.S. should increase" (71 percent). This positive view of the role of religion in politics extends to Muslim institutions as well. Overall, three-fifths agree that mosques should express their political views and that Muslims should vote in a bloc. However, there were limits to this political role. For example, fewer respondents were willing to define themselves as part of such a Muslim voting bloc, with just a bare majority agreeing that being a Muslim should be important to how one votes. Further, only two-fifths agreed that Muslim

Table 7.4: American Muslim Views about Democracy and the United States and Religion and Political Participation, 2004

Percent Strongly Agree	All	African American	South Asian	African	Arabs	Other
Very important to be active in politics	53.9	58.8	49.3	64.7	54.2	52.0
Very important for children to be active in politics	62.7	68.6	58.4	63.4	63.5	62.6
Muslims should participate in politics	85.6	80.3	88.1	83.6	89.5	80.4
Muslims should support worthy non-Muslim candidates	68.2	59.9	69.4	69.7	75.2	62.4
Muslims should participate in interfaith activities	80.3	72.7	82.3	85.8	84.3	76.1
Muslims should donate to non-Muslim social service programs	85.5	76.8	88.5	93.4	87.9	81.1
Percent Agree						
Influence of religion and values in the U.S. should increase	71.5	82.0	69.3	72.5	69.3	63.8
Mosques should express their political views	60.6	90.5	47.2	52.3	59.5	56.3
Muslims should vote in a bloc	59.7	66.0	58.1	59.8	62.6	48.3
Being Muslim is very important to vote choice	51.1	66.9	47.2	45.8	50.1	39.9
Right for *Khatibs* to discuss politics in the *Khutbah*	43.6	64.5	32.5	36.7	45.5	41.1
American Muslim Taskforce endorsement is very important to vote choice	42.1	52.1	40.2	47.8	43.1	26.1

Source: MAPS, 2004.

preachers (*khatibs*, who can deliver a Friday sermon) should discuss politics during their sermon. And just two-fifths saw endorsement by the American Muslim Taskforce on Civil Rights and Elections (AMT, a coalition of the ten largest Muslim organizations) as very important for choosing a candidate.

The greatest support for mixing religion and politics comes, not surprisingly, from African Americans, paralleling the view of black Christians.[42] South Asians once again showed the least support for acting in concert with other Muslims; they are the most educated, which tends to encourage individualism. Interestingly, African Americans were the least willing to entertain the influence of a group outside of their Muslim community—they displayed comparatively anemic support for the AMT endorsement. Other ethnic groups were less enthused with the idea of politicking during worship services. Almost a majority of Africans, for instance, appreciated AMT's recommendation, but did not believe in political preaching.

AMERICAN MUSLIM POLITICAL ENGAGEMENT AND PRESIDENTIAL RESPONSIVENESS: BILL CLINTON AND GEORGE W. BUSH

In order to better assess the degree to which presidential action concerning the American Muslim community has been responsive to the needs of this constituency over the previous fifteen years, it is useful to get a sense of the community's self-reported political activity. After all, one of the most logical ways to succeed in receiving political attention is to participate in the electoral system.[43] In 2004, African American Muslims were the most active of the ethnic groups, coming in first on contacting public officials, attending rallies, and participating in boycotts. The other Muslims were likely to "mostly" follow politics, and the Arabs were the most likely to report discussing politics "always" with family and friends. And, although their overall level of activity was low, the Africans scored highest on visiting political websites and being active party members. South Asians did not specialize in any of these activities, although they did score a bit above Africans overall.[44]

In table 7.5, we examine political participation among Muslims, examining first the 2001 data and then the 2004. Participation includes several activities that were included in both surveys: being an active member of a political party, contributing time or money to a candidate, visiting a political website, contacting the media or a politician on an issue, attending a rally for a politician or cause, and participating in a boycott of a product or business. Many of these dimensions of political participation have been shown to be important for other religious communities as well.[45] Importantly, there are quite a few differences between the 2001 and 2004 surveys, which highlight the extent to which the events of September 11 changed the dynamics of political involvement of the American Muslim community.

Given the general degree of political engagement by the American Muslim community in recent years, assessing how the community views responsive efforts by presidents Clinton and Bush, and identifying examples and characteristics of this responsiveness, is worthwhile. Extant research suggests that presidential responsiveness is positively related to a shortened time period to

Table 7.5: American Muslim Political Participation, 2001 and 2004

		All	African American	South Asian	African	Arabs	Other
"Mostly" follow politics	2001	60.3	72.0	50.4	54.7	64.0	63.3
	2004	64.3	72.1	60.1	44.5	65.2	72.2
Contacted politician/media	2001	50.0	62.7	42.3	41.9	48.3	57.4
	2004	54.5	73.6	44.1	31.3	54.2	66.1
Attended a rally	2001	40.2	61.0	29.4	32.3	41.3	38.1
	2004	45.9	67.4	33.8	32.8	46.0	51.7
Discuss politics "always"	2001	35.2	42.8	25.9	32.3	42.1	35.3
	2004	41.7	45.5	31.4	39.6	49.8	47.6
Visited political website	2001	34.1	38.4	30.3	22.5	39.7	32.5
	2004	41.0	32.9	40.4	43.1	42.0	52.4
Boycotted	2001	30.2	51.3	18.5	17.2	31.6	32.3
	2004	36.7	67.5	20.2	10.4	37.6	45.8
Contributed to candidate	2001	33.7	46.1	27.0	32.6	33.2	33.0
	2004	35.6	40.8	31.8	28.5	35.1	43.2
Active member of party	2001	25.9	33.8	22.9	26.6	25.7	21.8
	2004	25.1	31.6	18.8	38.2	21.9	30.4

Source: MAPS, 2001, 2004.

reelection, and is negatively related to increased presidential popularity.[46] At the same time, responsiveness has been considered easier for presidents to undertake when key constituencies are less sure of the policy outcome they desire, thereby allowing the president to explore flexible alternatives to the status quo that do not engender strong resistance.[47] Regarding presidential responsiveness to the American Muslim community, the literature suggest that national political dynamics, especially after September 11, constrain presidential responsiveness.

After all, President Bush's popularity in late 2001, and the general sense of most non-Muslim Americans that the government had a responsibility to do what was necessary to interdict and punish those who would perpetrate terrorist attacks on American soil, would point to a president with fewer options in responding to the needs of the out-group that was arguably the most in need of creative assistance from the chief executive. Given this, we contrast attempts presidents Clinton and Bush made in demonstrating responsiveness to the concerns of the American Muslim community during their respective terms in office. We then juxtapose presidential efforts with how they appear to have been received by the Muslim community.

While it is possible to examine several sources that indicate the direction and tone of administration responsiveness toward American Muslims, public presidential statements are especially useful in that they are generally the best opportunities administrations have to cue interested publics, including political out-groups, to their policy intentions. In other words, public statements allow presidents to actually demonstrate some dimension of responsiveness, even as there may be many more individual efforts taking place behind the scenes. As such, we focus on presidential public statements in our assessment of administrative responsiveness to American Muslims. A second way to consider presidential responsiveness is to assess how executive efforts have been perceived by the American Muslim community. This is where personal interviews prove quite useful. The personal interviews of Pittsburgh Muslims were conducted in late February and early March 2008. Thirteen interviewees identified themselves as Democrats, six as Republicans, and three provided no affiliation. Six were professionals (doctors, college professors, lawyers, etc.), seven held jobs in local businesses, five were university students, two stated that they owned their own business, and two said that they did not work outside of the home. Three of the interviewees were female. All interviewees were Arab. Subjects were put in touch with the authors via assistance from the Islamic Center of Pittsburgh. The interviews were conducted in a long-form, conversational format. The interviewees were asked several general questions concerning their perceived experiences both prior to and after September 11, as well as their sense of how responsive Clinton and George W. Bush have been to community concerns.

Given American preoccupation with the Cold War, there are scant examples of presidents offering public statements on Islam often enough to safely make generalizations concerning presidential responsiveness to the American Muslim community prior to the late 1980s. If anything, presidential recognition of Islam's presence as a factor in political events during the Cold War focused on diplomatic, rather than domestic, policies. Most notable is President Jimmy Carter's brokered peace settlement between Egypt's Anwar El Sadat and Israel's Menachem Begin. Other examples from this era include the Iran hostage crisis, the Marine bombing in Lebanon, the Palestine Liberation Organization (PLO), and the Gulf War, all of which required the sitting administration to acknowledge the difficult position in which the American Muslim community was placed. However, no coherent attempt to reach out to the community was widely pursued by an American president until after the Cold War. This began to change in 1993, given the first attack on the World Trade Center in New York City and President Clinton's strong policy commitment to brokering peace in the Middle East and Bosnia (where Muslim and non-Muslim conflict was raging).

Clinton's initial public statements on Islam came early in his first term at a Democratic National Committee Dinner in October 1993. In his remarks, Clinton addressed Middle East peace and Islam's unfortunate association in the minds of some with terrorism. "Clearly, we know if we could bring peace to the Middle East, it might revolutionize the range of options we have with Muslims all over the world and give us the opportunity to beat back the forces of radicalism and terrorism that unfairly have been identified with Islam by so many people."[48]

Clinton continued to make reference to Islam when discussing issues concerning the Israeli-Palestinian conflict, policies pertaining to the wider Middle East, and genocide in the former Yugoslavia, the latter of which arguably became the most important foreign policy focus of Clinton's second term.[49] Yet it was really only by the end of 2000 that Clinton's public remarks began to acknowledge the presence and unique experiences of *American* Muslims as separate and distinct from the issues confronting their coreligionists around the world. In his comments coinciding with the observance of Ramadan, Clinton stated:

> The rigors undertaken by devout Muslims inspire respect for Islam among people of all faiths. And this can bring hope of greater understanding for good will. It can overflow old boundaries when wholehearted devotion to one's own faith is matched with devout respect for the faith of others. This is why we welcome Islam in America. It enriches our country with Islam's teachings of self-discipline, compassion, and commitment to family. It deepens America's respect for Muslims here at home and around the world, from Indonesia to Pakistan, the Middle East, and Africa.[50]

Though demonstrating more public interest in the American Muslim community than most of his predecessors, Clinton's statements on Islam were less focused on the domestic community's challenges as a political outgroup than his successor's (much of which can be attributed to the events of September 11). Ironically, much of the interview data points to the perception of Clinton's presidency as being more responsive to community needs than Bush's. All twenty-two respondents commented that they believed that Clinton was more interested in helping their community, which may be difficult to accept given Clinton's relatively late recognition of the community in his public statements. That said, the interviewees' favorable impression of Clinton might also be the product of a very negative reaction to Bush. This inverse relationship—a greater sense of responsiveness by the president who said less about their community while in office—may be best explained not by the number of public words Clinton and Bush have offered about Islam, but about the content of those words and the context in which they have been said. Specifically, while Clinton's statements called for peace for all interested parties in various international conflicts, Bush has not only been forced to find ways to show responsiveness to the American Muslim community (a responsibility it is not clear that he relished prior to the September 11), but the themes of his public statements have gone far beyond Clinton's peace message.

While Bush does make mention of international peace in his public statements, Stuckey and Ritter observe that many of Bush's public addresses on Islam, September 11, and various components of U.S. foreign policy, especially in regard to the Middle East, conflate peace and human rights with a neoconservative preference for economic liberalism and free market reforms.[51] In what might be the defining difference between Clinton and Bush's public statements, Stuckey and Ritter point out the striking frequency with which Bush couples the term "human rights" with references to economic liberalism. "He often pairs human rights with the phrase 'free markets.' By linking these terms, Bush's construction of human rights carries with it a strong connection to economic neoliberal ideology and neoconservatism, both of which privilege free enterprise, privatization, deregulation, deterritorialization, and particular economic 'rights' above political 'rights.'"[52]

The authors, drawing on the work of Condit and Lucaites, focus on the role that ideographs (which Stuckey and Ritter define as "culturally bound summary phrases that capture important ideological associations"[53]) play in Bush's rhetoric. As with President Clinton, we draw on President Bush's public statements concerning Islam and related topics since the beginning of his first term, and extending through March 2008. At the risk of sounding redundant, the influence September 11 played in determining the administration's responsiveness to the American Muslim community cannot be overstated. In fact, Bush made no public comments concerning the Muslim community until September 17, 2001, almost nine months after assuming office. In Bush's first address, which was made at the Islamic Center of Washington, he was careful to distance Al-Qaeda from Islam and its followers. He also implied the federal government's protection of Muslims against harassment by other Americans. At the same time, he faintly echoed Clinton's general peace theme while introducing use of the term "evil" (which would become commonplace in almost all Bush administration statements on terrorism).

> The face of terror is not the true faith of Islam. That's not what Islam is all about. Islam is peace. These terrorists don't represent peace. They represent evil and war. . . . America counts millions of Muslims amongst our citizens, and Muslims make an incredibly valuable contribution to our country. Muslims are doctors,

lawyers, law professors, members of the military, entrepreneurs, shopkeepers, moms and dads. And they need to be treated with respect. In our anger and emotion, our fellow Americans must treat each other with respect. I've been told that some fear to leave; some don't want to go shopping for their families; some don't want to go about their ordinary daily routines because, by wearing cover, they're afraid they'll be intimidated. That should not and that will not stand in America.[54]

Of course, the American Muslim community had a particular interest in the U.S. response to the September 11 attacks. How would the United States and its citizens treat Muslims (and people thought to be Muslims because of their appearance)? Nineteen of the twenty-two Pittsburgh Muslims interviewed for this project stated that they felt somewhat comforted by Bush's statement at the Islamic Center on September 17, but all respondents suggested that they retained palpable concern that Bush was using the Islamic community more for its strategic importance in finding potential terrorists associated with continuing plots against the United States.

This feeling was perhaps seen as justified after Bush offered the following statement to reporters on September 16, "This crusade, this war on terrorism, is going to take a while."[55] Bush's characterization of the war of terror as a crusade triggered great discomfort in the Muslim community both at home and abroad, and was seen by twenty of the Pittsburgh interviewees to reflect Bush's true agenda post–September 11. In other words, these twenty respondents all expressed some concern that they were being lied to by Bush—that he and the administration were not interested in showing American Muslims respect and policy responsiveness as much as they hoping to collected vital intelligence from the community. Importantly, this sentiment is somewhat belied not only by Bush's public statements after September 11, which criticized those who would discriminate against Muslims, but also by administration programs to train law enforcement and other officials in cultural sensitivity to Islam and its followers.[56] Yet irrespective of examples where Bush has shown some degree of responsiveness, it is striking that these efforts appear to not to convince the interviewees.

Hence, even though Clinton appeared to forsake consideration of American Muslims as he pursued an international peace agenda, the interviewees appear to view Clinton's preoccupation with those international issues more sympathetically than Bush's overt efforts to demonstrate presidential concern. Despite Bush's discipline in not using the "crusade" term again, the damage to his relationship with American Muslims appears to have been done. Perhaps not helping matters was a perception by sixteen of the interviewees that Bush was not willing to take more affirmative steps to prevent discrimination against Muslims in the weeks following September 11. Whether this is a fair criticism of Bush or not, the policies he pursued in the wake of September 11 left many in the American Muslim community feeling vulnerable—despite his public statements urging respect for Muslims. The feeling of vulnerability was not unfounded. Human Rights Watch found one thousand hate crime incidents reported against Muslims and Arab Americans by November 2001. Concomitantly, American Muslims likely felt pressure from public opinion, which was generally negative toward Muslims post–September 11, and official government antiterrorism policies, of which the Patriot Act was the most conspicuous.[57] Clearly, if there was ever an opportunity for the president to show responsiveness to a community in need, it was during the waning months of 2001.

REJECTING THE RESPONSE

By October 2001, a majority of the respondents to the MAPS survey reported that they or someone they knew had experienced some form of discrimination. Slightly more African American and Arab Muslims reported such negative experiences than South Asians or Africans. In the 2004 survey, the question was separated, asking about discrimination experienced against themselves and against others they knew. Fully two-fifths reported discrimination after September 11, and three-fifths reported knowing a victim of discrimination. Thirty-seven percent reported no discrimination against themselves or others they knew, suggesting a slight increase in such problems since the 2001 survey. By any standard, these figures are shockingly high. They are also corroborated by the Pittsburgh interviewees, all of whom stated that they knew of a fellow Muslim who had been the victim of religious discrimination since September 11. Fully half of the sample stated that they had experienced discrimination to the point of fearing for either their personal safety or continued ability to make a living in their chosen profession in the years immediately following September 11.

Given these reports of discrimination, how did Muslims feel about American society more generally? Is the whole society prejudiced, or just a part of it? Table 7.6 reports relevant answers from the 2001 and 2004 MAPS surveys. In 2001, two-fifths of Muslim Americans agreed with the statement: "In my experience and overall, Americans have been respectful and tolerant of Muslims." On this response, there was some variation by ethnic group. More than one-half of South Asians agreed with this statement, but less one-third of African Americans. By 2004, agreement with this statement had fallen to less than one-third overall, and had declined in every ethnic group (although the inter-group differences remained). By 2004, a plurality of Muslims agreed

Table 7.6:   American Muslim Experience with Discrimination, 2001 and 2004

Percent Strongly Agree	*All*	*African American*	*South Asian*	*African*	*Arabs*	*Other*
I or others experienced discrimination since 9/11 (2001 data)	56.0	61.1	50.0	53.0	60.0	57.7
I have experienced discrimination since 9/11 (2004 data)	40.1	46.8	35.6	36.8	39.3	45.0
Others have experienced discrimination since 9/11 (2004 data)	58.5	61.8	56.2	54.1	58.4	61.9
Type of discrimination...						
Verbal abuse, 2001	25.3	22.0	22.5	23.6	30.9	27.0
Verbal abuse, 2004	43.7	49.3	41.4	33.6	44.4	46.2
Physical abuse, 2001	6.2	5.6	6.3	7.3	5.8	7.1
Physical abuse, 2004	11.9	11.3	10.4	12.7	11.9	16.2
Racial profiling, 2001	8.3	14.2	6.5	4.9	8.0	6.2
Racial profiling, 2004	24.0	22.9	22.7	24.8	25.3	25.7
Denied employment, 2001	2.8	4.5	2.3	2.4	1.6	4.0
Denied employment, 2004	18.0	20.6	17.0	16.4	16.7	20.2

Source: MAPS, 2001, 2004

that "Americans have been respectful and tolerant of Muslims, but American society overall is disrespectful and intolerant of Muslims." One-sixth located the problem in a subset of America, while 12 percent said Americans in general were intolerant.

Table 7.6 also contains a measure of dissatisfaction with American society. Overall, two-thirds of the 2004 sample was dissatisfied and many of those were very dissatisfied, particularly African Americans (84 percent) and the Other Muslims (70 percent). South Asians were the least dissatisfied (54 percent). This dissatisfaction may reflect Muslim perception of the American news media: just one-quarter of Muslims felt the media portrays Muslims fairly. There was some variation between groups, with African Americans the least supportive (18 percent) and South Asians the most (34 percent). However, there was an even more negative perception of Hollywood's portrayal of Muslims and Islam: just 14 percent of respondents said Hollywood's portrayal was fair, with the same distribution of ethnic group support as with the media.

American Muslims also have real doubts about the character and goals of the war on terrorism. When asked if the U.S. effort was a war on "terrorism" or a war on "Islam," one-third of the 2004 sample chose the former and nearly two-fifths the latter (the rest had no opinion). A majority of African

Americans felt it was a war on Islam, a view held by a plurality of Arabs and other Muslims and by a substantial minority of South Asians and Africans. Since the entire sample of Pittsburgh interviewees is Arab, it is not possible to break the group down according to ethnic categories. However, what is interesting about the overall community's basic suspicion that the Bush administration was targeting Islam more than terror is that Bush's rhetoric was, by 2003 and 2004, linking his public interpretation of Islam with democracy and economic liberalism in his ideograph. Here is an example. It is taken from Bush's remarks on the twentieth anniversary of the National Endowment for Democracy.

> Time after time, observers have questioned whether this country or that people or this group are ready for democracy, as if freedom were a prize you win for meeting our own Western standards of progress. In fact, the daily work of democracy itself is the path of progress. It teaches cooperation, the free exchange of ideas, and the peaceful resolution of differences. . . . It should be clear to all that Islam, the faith of one-fifth of humanity, is consistent with democratic rule. Democratic progress is found in many predominantly Muslim countries, in Turkey and Indonesia and Senegal and Albania, in Niger and Sierra Leone. Muslim men and women are good citizens of India and South Africa, of the nations of Western Europe, and of the United States of America.[58]

An example of Bush's more direct coupling of his remarks on peace, human rights, and economic liberalism was found in his remarks to the Asia Society in 2006: "India's middle class is buying air conditioners, kitchen appliances, and washing machines, and a lot of them from American companies like GE and Whirlpool and Westinghouse. And that means their job base in growing here in the United States of America. . . . Today, India's consumers associate American brands with quality and value, and this trade is creating opportunity here at home."[59]

Unfortunately for Bush, it appears that the majority of the American Muslim community associates current American policy relating to terrorism, the Iraq War, and the promotion of democracy with threats to their religious identity, at least in some form. However, this was not the only difficulty Bush encountered in relating to the Muslim community. Reports began to surface in the middle of Bush's first term that the Justice Department was monitoring Muslim communities in major urban centers in an effort to identify terrorism suspects. Reaction from the community at large was not positive toward the administration, and the constitutionality of the administration's monitoring efforts became political fodder during Bush's second term.[60] All of this is highly ironic given how proactive Bush appeared to be in reaching out to American Muslims so quickly after September 11. As the following analysis of the MAPS data shows, Bush's responsiveness efforts were indeed met with large doses of sardonic discontent among American Muslims in 2004.

AMERICAN MUSLIM PRESIDENTIAL VOTE: 2000 AND 2004

Table 7.7 lists reported voting behavior among American Muslims. In 2004, four-fifths of respondents claimed to be registered to vote, up a bit from 2001.[61] As before, African Americans scored highest and Africans lowest. Nearly nine out of ten Muslims said they were likely to vote, a figure that also increased from 2001 and held across the ethnic groups. Note, however, that reported turnout in the 2000 and 2004 elections followed a different pattern. For one thing, reported turnout was *down* in 2004 compared to 2000. The decline was uneven, with African Americans, Africans, and Arabs showing the largest reductions. These differences could result from the survey's measure of turnout,[62] but it could also be that the post–September 11 environment

Table 7.7: American Muslims and Voting Behavior, 2001 and 2004

		All	African American	South Asian	African	Arabs	Other
Registered to vote	2001	78.7	87.7	74.7	74.2	79.2	76.9
	2004	82.6	91	78.8	56.9	85.5	88.7
Very likely to vote	2001	85.3	82.7	87	85.1	85.4	85.5
	2004	89.2	89.2	90.1	88.2	88.2	88.7
Reported Presidential vote	2000	86.7	90.4	84.2	81.1	89.5	85.6
	2004	77.1	81.7	81.1	49.3	80.7	84.8
Reported vote Choice							
Gore	2000	36.0	61.4	31.0	35.6	18.1	42.6
Bush		47.6	22.4	57.7	46.6	60.0	40.5
Nader		13.9	13.3	9.3	15.0	19.3	13.3
Other		2.5	2.9	2.0	2.8	2.6	3.6
		100%	100%	100%	100%	100%	100%
Kerry	2004	82.3	85.4	86.7	86.8	75.5	79.5
Bush		6.7	4.6	7.7	8.7	5.5	9.2
Nader		10.0	8.2	5.3	4.5	17.5	10.7
Other		1.0	1.8	0.3	0.0	1.5	0.6
		100%	100%	100%	100%	100%	100%

Source: MAPS, 2001, 2004

discouraged some Muslims from voting or that Muslims in noncompetitive states were less inclined to participate. Although these data must be viewed with some caution, they do suggest that American Muslims are engaged in the political process.[63]

Turnout aside, estimated presidential vote choice showed a dramatic change in the MAPS surveys.[64] In 2000, almost one-half of Muslim Americans voted for Republican George W. Bush, just over one-third for Democrat Al Gore, and about one-sixth for Ralph Nader (who is of Arab descent) or another candidate. These numbers were impressive for several reasons. As we have seen, most Muslims in 2001 considered themselves Democrats. Also, African American Muslims voted heavily for Gore, giving him two-thirds of their votes. While this was a good bit lower than African Americans as a whole (who voted over 90 percent for Gore), it was quite different than the other Muslim groups: Arabs voted two-thirds for Bush (and nearly one-fifth for Nader) and South Asians backed Bush at nearly the same rate. Nearly one-half of Africans supported Bush, while the other Muslims almost broke even (with a slight edge for Gore). Surely the 2000 Bush campaign's aggressive courting of the Muslim vote explains the pattern.

The 2004 election was strikingly different: President Bush received about 7 percent of the Muslim vote, some forty percentage points less than in 2000. Meanwhile, Democrat John Kerry received more than 80 percent (with the remaining one-tenth going to Nader and others). Arabs and the other Muslims voted a little less strongly for Kerry, but Bush did not reach double digits among any group. The main reason for this turnaround was Bush administration policies after September 11. Although President Bush's positive statements about Islam were no doubt appreciated in the Muslim community, they did little to prevent his sharp decline at the polls. To place the Muslim vote in the context of the larger American religious community in 2004, 78 percent of white Evangelicals, 50 percent of mainline Protestants, and 53 percent of white Catholics voted for Bush, while 73 percent of Jews and 83 percent of black Protestants voted for Kerry.[65]

In table 7.8, we use logistic regression (a statistical procedure that allows us to test for causal relationships between the dependent and independent variables) to estimate what factors distinguish Bush voters from others in both 2001 and 2004, combining non-Bush voters for the sake of simplicity and because the 2004 election was surely a referendum on the administration. In the 2000 election, few explanations distinguish themselves, except for partisanship and ideology working as expected. Converts and African Americans were more likely to vote for a Bush opponent along with those who opposed further restrictions on access to abortion. Even in the 2000 election, those who experienced discrimination were more likely to vote against Bush,

Table 7.8: Determinants of the Muslim Presidential Vote, 2000 and 2004 Elections (logistic regression estimates)

Variable	2000 Election			2004 Election		
	Coeff	(S.E.)		Coeff	(S.E.)	
Convert	-.796	(.332)	**	.206	(.589)	
Immigrant	.072	(.295)		-.636	(.469)	
Religious commitment	.018	(.106)		.249	(.171)	
Partisanship	1.609	(.162)	***	1.379	(.241)	***
Ideology	.313	(.102)	***	.685	(.176)	***
Importance of being Muslim to vote choice	—			-.129	(.218)	
Importance of AMT endorsement	—			.268	(.221)	
War on terror or Islam	.497	(.288)	*	-2.932	(.513)	***
Experienced anti-Muslim discrimination	-.508	(.230)	**	-.873	(.371)	**
Stem cell research	-.002	(.096)		-.007	(.162)	
Abortion restriction	-.159	(.092)	*	.108	(.137)	
Stronger environmental laws	.027	(.144)		.117	(.245)	
Education	.141	(.130)		-.419	(.209)	**
Age	-.008	(.008)		.023	(.011)	**
South Asian	-.387	(.272)		.948	(.413)	**
African American	-.886	(.329)	***	.228	(.652)	
African	-.659	(.489)		2.143	(.771)	***
South	-.230	(.290)		-.858	(.467)	*
Midwest	.283	(.247)		-.244	(.403)	
Constant	-2.322	(.903)		-2.672	(1.579)	
Number of cases	610			670		
Cox and Snell R²	.325			.220		
Pct. correctly predicted	80.6			93.4		

*** $p<0.01$, ** $p<0.05$, * $p<0.10$

Note: The dependent variable is coded 1 if the respondent voted for George Bush and 0 if they voted for anyone else: 45.3 voted for Bush in 2000 (he won a plurality among the sample) and 7.6 percent in 2004.

Source: MAPS, 2001, 2004. See Appendix for variable coding.

though those who believed that the United States was waging a war against Islam instead of terrorism admitted they had voted for Bush in 2000.

That was absolutely not the case in 2004, when those reporting discrimination and believing there was an American war against Islam voted against Bush. Partisanship and ideology worked in the expected directions in 2004.

We also see a rationalization in the vote with the appearance of a flurry of demographic and ethnic effects. The educated were more likely to vote against Bush, while older, South Asian, and African Muslims were more likely to support Bush. Muslims living in the South were more likely to vote against him. This is interesting because the South was Bush's most reliable geographic constituency. Perhaps Muslims living in this region seized on the opportunity to vote against policies and a political culture that they find undesirable, but we are unable to test this possibility at this point.

However, African Americans were no longer the only anti-Bush group, as other ethnic groups came to join them in their opposition to Bush's agenda. Clearly, the personal experiences and mobilization of American Muslims since 2001 determined their votes in 2004.

Taken together, these patterns suggest that the Muslim community will most likely vote as a bloc in the near future. They also suggest that presidential rhetoric in response to community concerns may be an extremely ineffective tool in the face of widespread perception by an out-group that it is being targeted for harassment both by civilians and by their government. Though President Bush likely believed he was getting out in front of the discriminatory wave the Muslim community was beginning to feel in September 2001, his calls for mutual respect and equal treatment were far outweighed by his administration's policies, both foreign and domestic. That a voting bloc with a natural level of agreement with Bush on a variety of political and moral issues turned away from him so dramatically in 2004 leads us to consider implications for how presidential responsiveness as it relates to American Muslims might be studied further.

CONCLUSION AND FUTURE RESEARCH

Obviously, much of the rancor the Muslim community displayed toward President Bush in 2004 can be attributed to the tension stemming from Bush's decision to attack Iraq in 2003 and fallout from the Patriot Act in 2001. Yet one should not underestimate the possibility that Bush's efforts at responsiveness to the Muslim community may be hindered by two vexing realities confronting any president pursuing the same policies. Interestingly, both realities touch on the role rhetoric plays in presidential responsiveness. First, it is far from clear that American Muslims take kindly to having the compatibility of their faith with secular concepts such as trade and democratic process adjudicated so publicly by a non-Muslim (and Western) political leader. This reflects the largely uncertain nature of Islam's relationship with western economic and political concepts.[66] Since there is no significant consensus among the faithful concerning whether Islam is appropriately characterized as prodemocracy and protrade (as they are conceptualized by the West), it is perhaps not surprising that Bush's efforts have met with a strongly negative community reaction. It is here that Bush's rhetoric may have done the most damage to his relationship with American Muslims.

Second, it appears that, at least when addressing the needs of a religious and political out-group, presidents have much less control over how responsiveness efforts are perceived by that group. While some will argue that Bush brought on his difficulties with the American Muslim community, it is likely that future presidents, facing policy constraints due to the actions of their predecessors, may have to make the same choice in promoting the nexus between Islam and democracy through ideographs or other rhetorical devices. Whatever Bush's successors decide to do in terms of responding to the American Muslim community, it is safe to say that group perceptions and administration intentions are not necessarily an easy match. While we have given the issue of presidential responsiveness to the Muslim community general treatment here, much remains to be done in terms of teasing out causal relationships and additional substantive questions relating to both Muslims and other religious out-groups holding political grievances. Scholars might begin to build an argument against presidential responsiveness to certain religious and political out-groups whose assessment of presidential efforts may be so incongruent with the intentions behind the responsiveness to render those policies politically irrational.

Also ready for exploration is the degree to which American Muslims take cues (either tacitly or overtly) from Islamic leaders who criticize U.S. foreign and economic policies. This question is especially important since American Muslims, though an out-group in their country of residence, have a tremendous potential network of elites on whose political and religious guidance they may rely in forming their perceptions of presidential actions. Finally, the differences in subgroups of the Muslim community (as seen in the MAPS results) recommend further assessment as to just how politically cohesive the Muslim community might remain as it grows larger in the coming decades. We encourage research attention for all these items, and believe that insights from this line of research hold enormously useful implications for the presidency and the American public, including and especially its Muslim members.

Chapter 8

Asian Americans, Religion, and the American Presidency

So Young Kim

"At 11:00 on Sunday morning when we stand and sing and Christ has no east or west, we stand at the most segregated hour in this nation." This famous remark by Martin Luther King Jr. may be no better than true for Asian Americans, whose significantly large language differences and relatively recent history of immigration have posed major impediments to their political, social, and economic incorporation and assimilation into the mainstream society of America.[1] In these conditions, religion may well play a larger-than-usual role in the formation of new political and social identity for Asian immigrants, as religion can provide them with physical and spiritual sources of safety and stability upon which they build a notion of a community and a feeling of group identity.

Unfortunately, very little is known about how religion has helped or hampered Asian Americans' integration processes and how religion has influenced (or distorted) their political preferences. Religious institutions of the Asian American community have been shown to perform considerable significant social functions such as the provision of community services, economic assistance, and the socialization of youth groups.[2] Yet many of the existing studies of the political and social roles of religious institutions of the Asian American community have remained largely anecdotal rather than having been grounded upon systematic evidence. One of the notable Asian scholars once called the study of religion and politics of Asian Americans a "doubly marginalized research frontier."[3] In fact, not only is the study of religion and politics of the Asian American community doubly marginalized, but Asian Americans' lives are themselves also doubly marginalized in political and religious terms.

On the political side, Asian immigrants' relatively recent arrival in the United States has no doubt limited their experience in and understanding of

183

the public life of American society, as evidenced in various survey results showing generally low levels of knowledge about American political institutions and processes among Asian immigrants. Active participation in politics and civic life presupposes an acquaintance with political institutions and processes, and therefore it is no wonder that given their level of political knowledge and information, the mass behavior of Asian Americans as political participants is much less pronounced compared to other minority groups.[4] Such limited electoral participation and inactivity in national and local politics has generated a popular perception that Asian Americans do not form a meaningful coherent voting bloc, thus contributing further to marginalizing the voice of Asian Americans.[5]

On the religious side, the Asian American community is highly diverse in its religious beliefs and associations, which range from Christianity to Buddhism, Hinduism, and Islam.[6] This religious diversity sharply contrasts with the dominance of a single religion or religious denomination in other minority groups. For example, Baptists and Catholics account for disproportionately large shares of African Americans and Latinos, respectively. Given such diversity of religions among Asian Americans, one may well expect the effect of religious beliefs on creating a common identity among Asian Americans and stimulating their political activism based on such identity to be less catalyzing than would be the case in other minority communities. In this sense, the role of religion in bonding Asian Americans of different countries of origin is more or less marginalized.

In short, Asian Americans lack significant political influence mostly due to their low levels of political participation. They also lack a substantial degree of religious cohesion to help foster their political and social identity. Asian Americans are truly *the* minority. Some other minorities such as black or Latino Americans can be considered minorities only in number as they hold strong influence on national and local politics. In contrast, Asian Americans are not only a tiny minority in size, comprising only 3.6 percent of the U.S. population according to the 2000 Census (Hispanics comprised 12.5 percent and black Americans 12.3 percent) but are also a weak minority in a political sense.[7]

It is no wonder, then, that not much effort has been devoted to exploring the relationship of religion and politics to Asian Americans. This study aims to fill this gap in the existing research by examining how Asian Americans' religious preferences and intensity influence their political orientations and political behavior as well as how the political effects of religious identity differ in different ethnic groups within the Asian American community.

In examining this triangular relationship of religion, ethnicity, and politics in Asian Americans' public life, the current study draws on a public opinion survey on Asian Americans called the Pilot National Asian American Political Survey 2000–2001 (PNAAPS hereafter).[8] This PNAAPS data analysis is then complemented by the analysis of the American Religious Identification Survey 2001 (ARIS hereafter), another large-scale national survey canvassing religious preferences of the American adult population.[9]

Any attempt to examine the triangular relationship of the religion, ethnicity, and politics of Asian Americans would involve at a minimum a three-dimensional characterization of Asian Americans: Asian Americans as practitioners of religious beliefs, as members of ethnic groups, and as participants in the political arena. The empirical findings of this study reveal several distinctive features of Asian Americans on those three dimensions—religious outlook, ethnic identity, and political preferences—which set them apart from other minority groups.

First of all, there exists great diversity in religious affiliations of Asian Americans; however, individual ethnic groups within the Asian American community are overwhelmingly dominated by a single religion. As an example, Judaic-Christian denominations, the dominant religious tradition for most Americans, account for a tiny share of Asian Americans' religious affiliations as a whole; however, almost 90 percent of Filipino Americans are Catholics. Also, more than 80 percent of Korean Americans are Protestants. Figuratively speaking, the distribution of religious preferences among Asian Americans resembles a mosaic made up of monochrome patches that look very colorful seen from a distance.

This configuration of Asian Americans' religious preferences—with great diversity at the aggregate level and great homogeneity at the level of each ethnic group—sheds light on the formation of Asian Americans' ethnic and political identity. For other racial minorities such as black Americans or Hispanic Americans sharing more or less a common religion,[10] the religion serves as a powerful bond tieing different ethnic groups within the minority community by maintaining and reinforcing cultural practices and customs associated with that religion. It further helps foster common political orientations and facilitates political activism through church-based organizations and activities. In comparison, the aforementioned religious makeup of Asian Americans as a whole suggests that such social and political functions of religion would be far more limited for the Asian American community.

Second, Asian Americans are the *most secular* racial group in American society. A comparison of the PNAAPS and ARIS data shows that the proportion of nonbelievers or seculars is outstandingly higher among Asian Americans (20 percent) than any other racial groups (7 percent for white Americans, 2 percent for black Americans, and 12 percent for Hispanic Americans). As with the aforementioned aggregate-level religious diversity and monolithic dominance of a single religion for individual ethnic groups, the significantly high ratio of nonbelievers among Asian Americans implies that religion has a limited role in establishing their identity on the social and political terrain of American society.

Third, the Asian American community contains a very high ratio of political nonidentifiers, that is, those who do not identify themselves with any political parties, in its distribution of partisan preferences. Twenty-three percent of Asian Americans turn out to identify themselves with no political party, compared to the average of 5 percent nonidentifiers for Americans as a whole. In addition, there is a close relationship between the lack of political party identification and secularism among Asian Americans. For Asian Americans, 37 percent of those who profess no religion are political nonidentifiers, whereas among other Americans, only 10 percent of nonbelievers are nonidentifiers.

In fact, the distinction between believers and nonbelievers proves to be one of the most enduring differences in the degree of political interest, ideological orientation, and presidential vote choice of Asian Americans. Nonbelievers are significantly less likely to take interest in politics, more likely to be politically liberal, less likely to participate in the 2000 presidential election, and more likely to have cast a vote for the Democratic candidate, Al Gore, if they voted. On one hand, these findings confirm the aforementioned limitations in the role of religion in political mobilization and integration in the Asian American community. On the other hand, they suggest some commonalities between Asian American nonbelievers and other American nonbelievers in their political preferences and behavior. Asian American nonbelievers, like their counterparts in the larger American society, tend to be liberal and to prefer a Democratic candidate.

Fourth, while Asian Americans as a whole are predominantly Democrats (43 percent as opposed to 17 percent Republican) and supported Al Gore by a large margin (68 percent versus 32 percent) in the 2000 presidential election, there exists huge variation in political preferences and presidential vote choices within the Asian American community. More specifically, Asian American Christians (including Catholics) turn out to have supported George W. Bush more than non-Christians did. Moreover, non-Catholic Asian American Christians show a higher ratio of Republicans—24 percent as opposed to 17 percent for all Asian Americans. Furthermore, not only religious affiliations but also the level of religiosity seems to matter in ideological leaning and vote choice. Asian Americans who attend religious service frequently turn out to be more politically conservative and more likely to have voted for Bush in 2000.

Finally, there appears to be a close connection between the degree of pan-Asian (or panethnic) identity and the degree of political interest and integration among Asian Americans.[11] Those who view themselves as Asian Americans rather than as members of a specific Asian ethnic group (say, Korean Americans or Vietnamese Americans) show a significantly higher level of interest in American politics as well as a higher voting rate in the 2000 presidential elections. Those with greater panethnic identity are also more likely to associate themselves with the two mainstream political politics rather than to remain Independents or nonidentifiers. The PNAAPS data analysis also shows interesting variations in political attitudes, partisan identification, and presidential vote choices by ethnic groups, which will be introduced in detail later.

Interestingly, however, despite the strong positive association between panethnic identity and political activism among Asian Americans, pan-Asian identity does not appear to pull their partisan preferences or political ideology in one direction or the other. Those with greater panethnic identity are not more likely to be Democrats or Republicans, nor to be more liberal or conservative. Hence, although panethnic identity is clearly linked to greater political interest and activism, it is quite likely to be the case that Asian Americans with greater pan-Asian identity are on opposite sides of the political spectrum, as they are equally likely to be liberal or conservative.

The empirical findings of this study paint a rather bleak picture for the prospect of Asian Americans' integrating themselves fully into the fabric of American society. The Asian American community is not only small in size but also lacks a bond that can tie Asian Americans of different country origins, as they do not share a common religious tradition. Provided that the formation of self-identity in a new society is inherently a fluid process, the relatively recent history of Asian immigration suggests that the minor roles of Asian Americans in various realms of American public life may be improved over time. Yet, given the fact that there exists considerably less commonality among Asian Americans of different religious and cultural backgrounds compared to other minority groups, their integration process may well take longer time and greater effort. It remains to be further explored in future studies how the dynamics of identity construction on the triangular terrain of religion, ethnicity, and politics will play out for Asian Americans.

This study is organized as follows. The next section offers an overview of religious affiliations, ethnic identification, and political attitudes and behavior of Asian Americans based on the descriptive analysis of the PNAPPS and ARIS data. The section following the overview presents the findings of the multivariate regressions disentangling the triangular relationship of religion, ethnicity, and politics of Asian Americans. The final section concludes by discussing the implications of the study and a few suggestions for future research.

ASIAN AMERICANS: RELIGION, ETHNICITY, AND POLITICS

Asian Americans' Religious Makeup

Asian Americans are often called a "model minority" for a variety of reasons, whether good or bad; they are highly educated, relatively richer than other minorities, politically more acquiescent, and so on. Those reasons seemed to be true as shown in table 8.1, which compares four major racial/ethnic groups of the United States. Asian Americans turn out to be most similar to white Americans in a number of categories of comparison including the median age of the population, the gender ratio, homeownership, and median household and family incomes. In particular, educational attainment measured by the percentage of bachelor's degree holders among adults is the highest for Asian Americans in the four major states with a sizable Asian population, which confirms Asians' well-known emphasis on the value of education both as a ladder for upward social mobility and as a means for self-enrichment.[12]

Interestingly, however, the similarity between Asian and white Americans does not extend beyond those socioeconomic and demographic aspects, as Asian Americans are very different in their religious preferences from most other Americans. As illustrated by figures 8.1 and 8.2, the most distinctive feature of Asian Americans' religious preferences is the wide range of religious affiliations they hold in comparison to other racial or ethnic groups in American society. Religious diversity is in fact one of the defining aspects of religious life of Asian Americans, as found in many studies.[13]

In figure 8.1, we find that while Christianity accounts for about half of the total distribution of religious preferences, the rest is well represented by the religious traditions originating in Asia, such as Hinduism and Buddhism. In figure 8.2, we also find that Asian Americans are characterized by much higher level of heterogeneity in their religious affiliations compared to other Americans.

A close look at these two figures reveals a couple of distinct aspects of the religious makeup of the Asian American community. First, while the Asian religions do not themselves take a majority of Asian Americans' religious distribution, they account for a much greater share of the distribution compared to other Americans. About 17 percent of Asian Americans are Buddhists and 7 percent Hindus, while only 0.5 percent and 0.4 percent of other Americans are Buddhists and Hindus, respectively. A counterpart of this finding is that Western religions—especially Christianity—take a relatively small share of the Asian American religious distribution. Christianity including Catholicism accounts for only 52 percent of Asian Americans' religious beliefs, as compared to 76 percent for all other Americans.[14]

Second, the Asian American community contains an astoundingly large segment of seculars or nonbelievers. One in every five Asian Americans sur-

Table 8.1: Asian Americans' Demographic Characteristics

		Asian	Hispanic	Black	White
% Population		3.6%	12.5%	12.3%	75.1%
Median Age		32.8	25.8	30.3	38.6
Sex	Male	48.3%	51.4%	47.5%	48.9%
	Female	51.7%	48.6%	52.5%	51.1%
Average Household Size		3.1	3.6	2.7	2.4
Average Family Size		3.6	3.9	3.3	3
Homeownership		53.5%	45.7%	46.6%	72.4%
Income and Education [Selected States]					
California	Median Household Income	55415	36532	34931	53734
	Median Family Income	61455	35980	39836	65342
	B.A. Holders	28.4%	5.16%	11.5%	21.2%
Illinois	Median Household Income	57394	41047	31704	50218
	Median Family Income	66120	41537	36341	60970
	B.A. Holders	34.2%	5.8%	9.6%	18.3%
New York	Median Household Income	45481	30499	31662	49474
	Median Family Income	49330	31483	36821	60466
	B.A. Holders	24.9%	6.9%	10.2%	17.6%
Texas	Median Household Income	50144	29873	29321	47162
	Median Family Income	57257	30840	33355	57194
	B.A. Holders	27.4%	6.1%	10.7%	20.3%
Hawaii	Median Household Income	54356	37704	41244	49976
	Median Family Income	63488	39416	43090	58952
	B.A. Holders	19.8%	9.2%	14.0%	21.7%

Note: (1) The population percentages are for the single race group only with persons of mixed races excluded except for the Hispanics which is an ethnic category crosscutting races. The Hispanic population percentage here includes Hispanics of any race. For all other tabulations, however, the figures are only for nonwhite Hispanics. (2) B.A. is the share of bachelor's degree holders among adults who are twenty-five years old or older.

Data: 2000 U.S. Census of Population and Housing, Summary File 1 and Summary File 2.

veyed in the PNAAPS confessed no religion, a significantly high ratio compared to 13 percent of nonbelievers among the general American public. In fact, Asian Americans turn out to be the most secular group when compared to other major racial or ethnic groups. According to the tabulation created from the ARIS data (figure 8.3), only 7 percent of white Americans, 2 per-

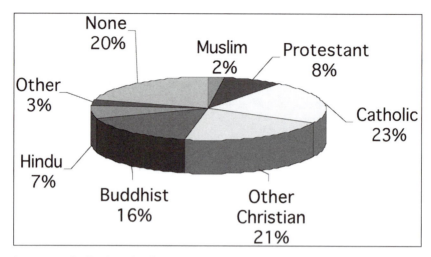

Figure 8.1: Distribution of Religious Preferences among Asian Americans

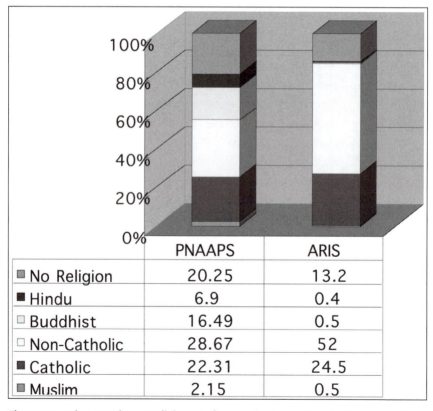

	PNAAPS	ARIS
No Religion	20.25	13.2
Hindu	6.9	0.4
Buddhist	16.49	0.5
Non-Catholic	28.67	52
Catholic	22.31	24.5
Muslim	2.15	0.5

Figure 8.2: Asian Americans' Religious Preferences in Comparison to Other Americans

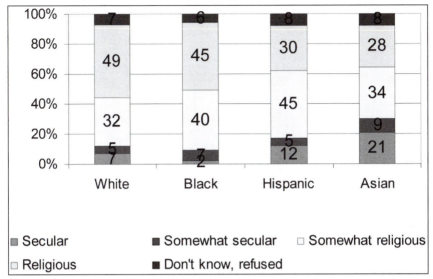

Figure 8.3

cent of black Americans, and 12 percent of Hispanics consider themselves as secular. In contrast, 20 percent of Asian Americans do so.[15]

The great diversity of religious preferences and the comparatively high ratio of nonbelievers among Asian Americans reveal much about the potential impact of religion on their incorporation and adaptation into mainstream society and politics. It is well known in studies of the adjustment and assimilation processes of immigrants that religion more than any other social institution plays a major role in creating, affirming, or promoting social identity of immigrants in a new land.[16] Common religious traditions in immigrant communities also help shape political orientations and attitudes of immigrants by providing an arena for interaction and the communication of political issues and offering a training ground for future community leadership.

The markedly diverse religious preferences and affiliations among Asian Americans shown above, together with the disproportionately high rate of seculars, suggests a much more limited impact of religion on the process of creating political and social identities in a new land, as compared to other minorities that share a common religion and also have comparatively fewer nonbelievers.

Ethnic Differences in Asian Americans' Religious Preferences

Interestingly, while the Asian American community lacks a common religion, most individual ethnic groups within this community have a common religion. Figure 8.4 displays the religious distribution of six ethnic groups of

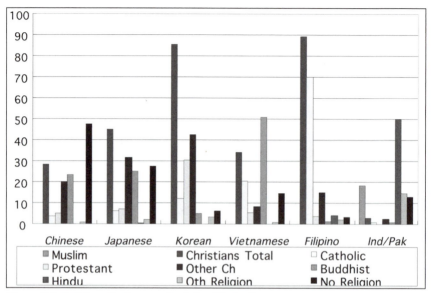

Figure 8.4: Religious Preferences by Asian Ethnic Group

Asian origin. As shown in this figure, each ethnic group is dominated by a single religion, contrary to the heterogeneity of religious affiliations for the Asian American community as a whole.

Two ethnic groups stand out in this table with almost monolithic religious preferences—Filipino and Korean Americans. Almost 70 percent of Filipino Americans are Catholics, and if non-Catholic denominations are included, Christianity accounts for 89 percent of Filipino Americans' religious affiliations. Korean Americans are predominantly non-Catholic Christians (73 percent), and the rate of Christians reaches 85 percent if Catholics are included. All these percentages are much higher than the average rate of Christians among the general American public (76.5 percent) shown in figure 8.2. The monolithic religious distribution for these two particular groups seems largely due to the specific historical circumstances of their home countries. The Filipino case reflects their historical heritage of Spanish colonial rule, whereas the Korean case is mostly due to geopolitical reasons related to the Cold War, which have raised American influence on Korean society.

The so-called Asian religions are most dominant among Asian Americans of Southeast Asian origin. Buddhism and Hinduism each account for half of religious affiliations of Vietnamese and Indian/Pakistani Americans, respectively. Again, this religious makeup of Southeast Asian Americans closely reflects the religious distribution of their home countries.

Not surprisingly, almost half of Chinese Americans are nonbelievers, as a majority of them are immigrants from the mainland China, which as a communist regime officially prohibits religious practice.[17] Japanese Americans are also highly secular; the rate of nonbelievers is about 27.5 percent, which is the second highest after Chinese Americans.

The dominance of a single religion in the individual ethnic groups of the Asian American community is a double-edged sword for Asian Americans' political incorporation and mobilization. On one hand, for the Asian ethnic groups that have a dominant religious tradition (such as Korean and Filipino Americans), the dominant religious institution can fulfill various political and social roles mentioned previously and thus help settle and adjust newcomers to a new society. In particular, many Christian churches allying with specific Asian immigrant groups have linked themselves to mainstream churches that play a significant role in American public life. In doing so, those Asian American churches have alerted their members to salient public policy issues and concerns. These social and political functions of religion for specific Asian immigrant communities are well documented in various ethnographic studies as well as in anecdotal accounts of the immigration and assimilation experiences of different Asian ethnic groups.[18]

On the other hand, the colorful mosaic of diverse religious beliefs among Asian Americans that more or less coincide with the ethnic boundaries of the Asian American community poses a big challenge to the formation of pan-Asian identity and thus to the prospect of political mobilization based on interethnic alliances.

Panethnic or pan-Asian identity refers to the sentiment that Asians are linked to other Asians by the same fate as well as the perception that Asians share a largely similar culture and worldview distinct from other race groups. Pan-Asian identity defined as such has been a central issue in Asian American politics with the increasing tide of Asian immigration since the 1990s. Scholars and researchers of Asian studies have asked whether Asian Americans could form a coherent voting bloc and thus become a meaningful political force in American politics. Panethnic identity is crucial for consolidating different segments of Asian Americans around public policy issues that concern and impact them as a whole group.[19]

If Asian Americans' religious distributions match their ethnic divisions, such a situation would pose a great hurdle for the Asian American community in building interethnic identity.[20]

Asian Americans' Political Preferences and Voting Behavior

Turning to the political preferences of Asian Americans, we find that Asian Americans generally lean toward the Democratic Party. As shown in table

8.2 based on the PNAAPS data, 43.2 percent of Asian Americans identify themselves as Democrats, while 17.4 percent identify as Republicans. This Democratic lead may not be surprising, given that the Democratic Party is historically associated with political and civil rights movements against racial prejudice and discrimination.[21]

Table 8.2 provides further information about the partisan preferences of Asian Americans of different religious beliefs. The columns represent the percentages of Democrats, Republicans, Independents, and nonidentifiers.[22]

Some noticeable patterns of religious and political affiliations are found in this table: (1) the rate of Democrats is the highest among Protestant Christians followed by Catholics, whereas the rate of Republicans is the highest among other Christians, who are mostly evangelical Christians; (2) Muslims are mostly Independents; and (3) those with no religion show the highest rate of nonidentification.

Some of these religious differences in the political preferences of Asian Americans mirror those of the general American public. With figures in parentheses in table 8.2 derived from the ARIS data representing the average rates of partisan preferences for American adults, we can compare the religious and political preferences of Asians and other Americans. Evangelical Christians among Asian Americans are more likely to be Republicans, whereas Protestants and Catholics are closer to the Democratic Party.[23]

Yet there is clear disparity between Asians and other Americans who are nonbelievers. Asian American seculars are predominantly nonidentifiers, whereas seculars among other Americans are generally political Independents.

Table 8.2: Asian Americans' Partisan Preferences by Religion

Religion	Democrats	Republicans	Independents	Nonidentifiers
Muslim	47.62 (35)	19.05 (19)	28.57 (39)	4.76 (7)
Protestant	50	17.5	16.25	16.25
Catholic	46.45 (36)	20.85 (28)	16.11 (30)	16.59 (4)
Other Christians	43.16	24.21	11.58	21.05
Buddhist	33.8 (31)	18.31 (9)	14.79 (48)	33.1 (12)
Other Religions	40	13.33	30	16.67
No Religion	38.51 (30)	6.9 (17)	17.24 (43)	37.36 (10)
Average	*43.22 (31)*	*17.4 (31)*	*16.41 (30)*	*22.98 (8)*

Note: Figures in parentheses are the share of a corresponding partisan group from the ARIS. Not all religious groups have comparable figures from the ARIS.
Data: PNAAPS and ARIS.

Forty-four percent of nonbelievers in the general public are Independents, whereas 17 percent of Asian American nonbelievers are Independents. However, 37 percent of nonbelievers among Asian Americans are nonidentifiers, compared to only 10 percent of nonbelievers among the general public.

This suggests that although American seculars in the general public do not generally align with the two major parties, their understanding of politics still lies on the partisan terrain, as political Independents can be thought as equally distant from either party. By contrast, Asian American nonbelievers remain outside of partisan politics, and as such they are likely to define and think of politics in nonpartisan terms. Together with the aforementioned fact that Asian Americans as a whole are the most secular minority group, the irrelevance of partisan political conceptions to Asian American seculars' political identification implies another challenge for Asian Americans in adapting and integrating themselves into mainstream partisan politics.

Scholars of Asian American politics have long noted that the most basic mode of political participation, voting, which only requires voter registration and turning out to a poll booth, may not be so simple for Asian Americans.[24] Acquiring citizenship, a requirement for voter registration, is a tedious, laborious, and often very complicated process for most immigrants. Asian immigrants are particularly hindered by their language barriers and cultures compared to their European and Latin American counterparts. Figure 8.4 compares Asian Americans' voter turnout rates in the 2000 presidential election by different religious groupings. This figure clearly shows that for most Asian Americans voting is not the simplest or easiest way to participate in politics. The majority of each religious grouping did not vote in the 2000 presidential election, and for Asian Americans as a whole group the voting rate remains at 45 percent.

Interestingly, there is a marked difference between the believers of Christianity and those of other religions; the highest nonvoting rate is found among Muslims (78 percent) whereas the highest turnout rate is found among Christians (48.9 percent for Protestant Christians, 49.1 percent for other—mostly evangelical—Christians, and 45 percent for Catholics).

Turning to candidate preferences, we find that the hotly contested presidential election in 2000 did not present a contentious choice for most Asian Americans. Predominantly they supported the Democratic candidate, Al Gore (68 percent as opposed to 32 percent supporting George W. Bush). However, the support for the two presidential contenders varied greatly among different religious groupings as shown in figure 8.5. There again emerges a distinction between practitioners of Christianity and those of other religions. The support for Gore was generally high among those with non-Christian religious beliefs (75 percent for Hindus and 69 percent for Buddhists).[25] In contrast, Bush won the biggest support from evangelical Christians (40 percent), followed by Protestants (37 percent) and Catholics (33 percent). This rate of support resembles the presidential choices of other American Christians. Interestingly, the highest support rate for Gore was found among nonbelievers (85 percent).

The 2000 presidential choices of Asian Americans conform to the general pattern of Asian American support for Democratic presidential candidates in past elections. This pattern also carries over to the 2004 presidential election. According to one of the exit polls on the 2004 presidential election, Asian Americans cast more votes for the Democratic candidate, John Kerry.[26] In the National Poll of Asian Pacific Islanders (APIs) on the 2004 election, conducted by the New California Media (NCM) in August 2004, Kerry held a 43 percent to 36 percent lead over the Republican candidate, George W. Bush, with 20 percent of APIs remaining undecided. Another exit poll from the National Election Poll reports that 56 percent of Asian Americans voted for Kerry and 44 percent voted for Bush.[27]

PROBING DEEPER: MULTIVARIATE REGRESSION ANALYSIS

This section expands the empirical investigation of the PNAAPS data by employing a multivariate regression technique in exploring the triangular relationship of religion, ethnicity, and political orientation. The descriptive analysis presented in the previous section was mostly concerned with bivariate relationships. The multivariate regression of this section allows us to assess the effects of both religion and ethnicity on the political attitudes and behavior of Asian Americans simultaneously.

From the descriptive findings of the preceding section emerge two sets of predominant religious distinction: one between believers and seculars, and the other between practitioners of Christianity and practitioners of other religions. As shown in the previous descriptive findings, there exists a clear difference in partisan preferences and presidential choices between nonbelievers and believers as well as between Christians and non-Christians.

It is then worth finding out whether these differences would still hold if we take into account other potential influences on such political preferences. One such factor may be religious intensity or religiosity. A conventional observation is that more religious people tend to take more conservative attitudes on various political and social issues. Then we can expect religiosity to correlate with political preferences. Fortunately, the PNAAPS dataset has a survey question asking how often one attends church service, which can be reasonably taken as an indicator of religious intensity.

The other factor that can intervene in the relationship between religious affiliations and political preferences of Asian Americans is the degree of pan-Asian identification. As mentioned earlier, the existence of pan-Asian identity significantly affects the ways Asian Americans perceive their political identity and participate in the political and social arenas. One of the PNAAPS dataset asks whether one has ever thought of oneself as an Asian American rather than an Asian or a member of a specific Asian ethnic group. This question is used in the current multivariate analysis. Also, dummy variables were created from the question asking about an individual ethnic group a respondent belongs to, with the multiple regression analysis employing the category of Indian and Pakistani Americans as the reference group.[28]

FINDINGS

The results of the multiple regression analysis are presented in the following three tables. Table 8.3 shows the regression results examining the effects of religion and ethnicity on Asian Americans' political interest and ideology. Table 8.4 shows the regression results on Asian Americans' partisan affiliations. The three panels of the logistic regressions in this table present the effects of the independent variables on the likelihood of being a nonidentifier, of being an Independent, and of being a Democrat (as opposed to a Republican), respectively. Displayed in table 8.5 are the regressions of Asian Americans' voting behavior during the 2000 presidential election. The dependent variables in the two panels of regressions of this table are the likelihood of participating in voting and of voting for Bush, respectively.

The most visible and consistent difference in Asian Americans' political attitudes and behavior is found between believers and nonbelievers. In all regressions reported in the three tables, the distinction between believers and seculars is almost always significant. Believers are likely to be more interested in politics and more politically conservative than nonbelievers are (table 8.3). Believers also tend to develop stronger partisan identification; the likelihood of being a nonidentifier or of being a political Independent is significantly lower for believers (table 8.4).[29] Finally, believers are more likely to have turned out to a poll booth in the 2000 election and to have voted for the Republican candidate, George W. Bush (table 8.5).

Though not as salient as the distinction between believers and nonbelievers, the difference between Christians and non-Christians is also apparent in Asian Americans' partisanship and electoral participation. Christians among Asian Americans are much less likely to be nonidentifiers (table 8.4), more likely to have participated in the 2000 presidential voting, and more likely to have voted for Bush (table 8.5).

Table 8.3: Religion, Ethnicity, and Political Orientations of Asian Americans

Political Interest [1=not at all interested to 4=very interested]	I	II	III
Believers vs. Nonbelievers	.147*		
Christians vs. Non-Christians		.107	
Religious Attendance			.024
Panethnic Identity	.141**	.144**	.129*
Chinese	-.198	-.280**	-.217**
Japanese	-.369***	-.431***	-.390***
Korean	-.051	-.127	-.069
Filipino	-.460***	-.534***	-.432***
Vietnamese	-.379***	-.413***	-.410***
R²	.033***	.032***	.030***
Number of Obs.	924	924	892

Political Ideology [1=very liberal to 5=very conservative]	I	II	III
Believers vs. Nonbelievers	.148*		
Christians vs. Non-Christians		.106	
Religious Attendance			.056**
Panethnic Identity	.027	.029	.052
Chinese	.436***	.355***	.478***
Japanese	.510***	.448***	.584***
Korean	.590***	.512***	.638***
Filipino	.491***	.416***	.505***
Vietnamese	.389(.009)	.351**	.454***
R²	.031 ***	.029***	.040***
Number of Obs.	850	850	822

Reported figures are the coefficients from the multiple regressions. Positive ones indicate positive relationships of religious variables with political interest (in the first panel) or conservatism (in the second panel). The relationship is significant at the 99 percent level if the coefficient is marked with (***), at the 95 percent level if marked with (**), and at the 90 percent level if marked with (*).

Table 8.4:   Religion, Ethnicity, and Political Partisanship of Asian Americans

Nonidentifiers	I	II	III
Believers vs. Nonbelievers	.619**		
Christians vs. Non-Christians		.678*	
Religious Attendance			.945
Panethnic Identity	.695*	.688**	.664**
Chinese	4.40***	5.76***	4.50***
Japanese	2.36**	2.89**	2.24*
Korean	.888	1.16	.714
Filipino	1.96	2.54**	1.85
Vietnamese	7.01***	7.93	6.50***
Pseudo R^2	.088***	.086***	.084***
N	759	759	733
Independents	*I*	*II*	*III*
Believers vs. Nonbelievers	.892		
Christians vs. Non-Christians		.915	
Religious Attendance			.832**
Panethnic Identity	.571***	.570***	.597**
Chinese	.085***	.091***	.073***
Japanese	.618(.125)	.649	.514**
Korean	.279***	.297***	.293***
Filipino	.490**	.297***	.496**
Vietnamese	.550	.522*	.532*
Pseudo R^2	.077***	.077***	.083***
N	759	759	733
Democrats (vs. Republicans)	*I*	*II*	*III*
Believers vs. Nonbelievers	.513*		
Christians vs. Non-Christians		.809	
Religious Attendance			.699***
Panethnic Identity	.933	.921	.869
Chinese	1.28	1.62	1.02
Japanese	1.39	1.52	.959
Korean	.642	.718	.679
Filipino	.646	.697	.690
Vietnamese	.125***	.141***	.097***
Pseudo R^2	.072***	.065***	.100***
N	450	450	438

Reported are the odd ratios from the logistic regressions with standard errors in parentheses. The odd ratio in each panel of regressions represents the effect of the independent variable on the likelihood of being a nonidentifier, an independent, and a Democrat, respectively. Odd ratios greater than one indicate positive relationships, and those smaller than one negative effects. ***: Significant at the 99 percent level, **: Significant at the 95 percent level, *: Significant at the 99 percent level.

Table 8.5:   Religion, Ethnicity, and Electoral Choice of Asian Americans (2000 Presidential Election)

Participation [1=Yes, 0=No]	I	II	III
Believers vs. Nonbelievers	1.56**		
Christians vs. Non-Christians		1.37*	
Religious Attendance			1.22***
Panethnic Identity	1.54***	1.55***	1.49***
Chinese	1.70**	1.32	1.86**
Japanese	4.31***	3.55***	4.81***
Korean	.994	.787	.852
Filipino	1.63*	1.30	1.61*
Vietnamese	1.54	1.39	1.82*
Pseudo R²	.048***	.046***	.056***
N	932	932	900

Choice [1=Bush, 0=Gore]	I	II	III
Believers vs. Nonbelievers	2.41(.021)		
Christians vs. Non-Christians		1.92(.042)	
Religious Attendance			1.43***
Panethnic Identity	.810	.846	.817
Chinese	.304**	.199***	.366**
Japanese	.358**	.257***	.542
Korean	.498	.317*	.433
Filipino	.467	.296**	.447
Vietnamese	.733	.648	1.07
Pseudo R²	.047***	.043***	.071***
N	322	322	313

Reported are the odd ratios from the logistic regressions with standard errors in parentheses. The odd ratio represents the effect of a given independent variable on the likelihood of casting a vote and that of voting for Bush, respectively. ***: Significant at the 99 percent level, **: Significant at the 95 percent level, *: Significant at the 99 percent level.

Religiosity also matters in Asian Americans' political attitudes and behavior. Those Asian Americans who attend religious service more frequently tend to be more politically conservative and more likely to be Republicans, as seen in the last-column regressions of tables 8.3 and 8.4. Those with higher frequency of church attendance are also more likely to have cast a vote in the 2000 election as well as to have voted for Bush (table 8.5).

As for the ethnic variables, panethnic identity turns out to have important political effects. Those with greater self-identity as Asian Americans rather than as members of a specific Asian ethnic group are not only more interested in American politics but also less likely to become nonidentifiers or Independents (tables 8.3 and 8.4). Asian Americans with greater pan-Asian identity are also more likely to have participated in the 2000 election (table 8.5). Yet strong pan-Asian identification does not seem to make one lean more toward one or the other political party or take more conservative or liberal political views. This implies that while Asian Americans tend to become more interested in mainstream politics as they develop a common identity as members of the Asian American community, this pan-Asian identity does not itself align well with the traditional two-party system of American politics.

Individual ethnic differences in the political orientations and preferences of Asian Americans are also noticeable in various regression results reported in the tables. It turns out that Indian and Pakistani Americans, the reference category group for the regressions, have greater interest in American politics and are at the same time more politically liberal than any other ethnic groups (table 8.3).[30] As for partisan identification, Vietnamese Americans are more likely to be nonidentifiers, followed by Chinese Americans. Vietnamese Americans are also less likely to be Democrats than any other ethnic group in the Asian American community if they develop two-party identification (table 8.4). Finally, among all Asian ethnic groups Japanese Americans are most likely to have voted in the 2000 presidential election. This should come as no surprise given their early naturalization and integration compared to other ethnic groups in the Asian American community. As for presidential candidate support, with controlling for pan-Asian identity and religiosity, the regression results do not show much significant difference among the different ethnic groups. Yet, Chinese Americans turn out to have cast more votes for Bush in 2000 than any other ethnic groups.

DISCUSSION AND CONCLUSION

The fast-growing Asian immigration flows have been one of the signal features of contemporary demographic changes in the U.S. population. Asian immigrants have come from a wide variety of countries and cultures, contributing to greater religious diversity in American society.[31] Apparently, this religious diversity has come at the expense of creating a shared identity for Asian immigrants in a new land. Hindered by a multitude of factors such as high language barriers, significant cultural differences, and heterogeneous religious traditions, Asian Americans have been slow in assimilating and integrating themselves into a new terrain of political and social life. What is worse, the religious makeup of the Asian American communities largely coincides with their ethnic boundaries, thereby reinforcing the difficulty of building a truly panethnic community. In these circumstances, we may expect the well-documented role of a common religion as a bond tying a multiethnic community to be much more limited for Asian Americans.

In addition to these religious characteristics, the Asian American community is highly secular, which would lead us to predict that the growing Asian population in the United States will accelerate the so-called secularization trend characterizing the decades since the 1960s.[32] While Asian American seculars share some commonalities with those in the general American public, they are markedly different in the degree of partisan identification. Asian American nonbelievers tend to be nonidentifiers, while other American seculars are mostly political Independents.

In fact, the believer-secular distinction turns out to make the most consistent and strongest difference in the attitudinal and behavioral patterns of Asian American politics. Asian Americans professing any religion, as opposed to those with no religion, tend to have more interest in American politics and to be more politically conservative. They are also more likely to have participated in the 2000 presidential election, and if they did, they are more likely to have voted for the Republican candidate, George W. Bush. There is also a similar distinction between Christians and non-Christians in various political aspects examined in the preceding analyses. Christians are more likely to develop partisan identification and to have supported for Bush in the 2000 election.

These findings suggest that some of emerging political cleavages between different segments of Asian Americans are attributable to different religious practices and faiths. It needs to be further explored in future research how religion-based political rifts among Asian Americans have evolved and how such religion-driven political cleavages within the Asian American community differ from those of the general public.

The empirical analyses of the current study also demonstrate the importance of pan-Asian identity in developing political interest and activism as well as partisan identification among Asian Americans. Pan-Asian identity is often criticized as a racial concept that is imposed on inherently heterogeneous groups of Asian Americans in an attempt to co-opt them into mainstream politics. Yet this observation cannot negate the fact that any effort to mobilize the mass of Asian Americans politically for a common cause or a public policy issue would not be sustainable without a certain degree of interethnic identification among Asian Americans.

In closing, a few suggestions can be made for further research on Asian Americans' religion and politics. First, we can learn much from comparative studies of the Asian American community and other multiethnic communities such as Latinos, as they would allow us to assess the uniqueness of the Asian American experience.

Second, there is an urgent need for more detailed data collection on both religious and political preferences and practices of Asian Americans.[33] The perennial trade-off between the quality and availability of data is particularly serious in the research on Asian American religion and politics. Those datasets having a rich set of political variables typically lack variables related to religious affiliations and practices, and vice versa. On the other hand, a couple of datasets containing a reasonably good number of both political and religious variables such as the General Social Surveys and the American National Election Studies contain only a very small sample of Asian Americans.

Finally but not least importantly, more theoretical work is needed to better understand the interlinked influences of religious preferences and ethnic self-image on the formation of political identity and the degree of political activism among Asian Americans. This would lead to an enhanced understanding of the dynamic processes of the construction and interaction of threefold identity on the terrain of religion, ethnicity, and politics.

Martin Luther King, Jr., and President Lyndon B. Johnson, 1963.

Chapter 9

African Americans, Religion, and the American Presidency

Melissa V. Harris-Lacewell

Therefore because you trample upon the poor and take from him exactions of wheat, you have built houses of hewn stone, but you shall not dwell in them; you have planted pleasant vineyards, but you shall not drink their wine. For I know how many are your transgressions, and how great are your sins—you who afflict the righteous, who take a bribe, and turn aside the needy in the gate. Therefore he who is prudent will keep silent in such a time; for it is an evil time. Seek good, and not evil, that you may live; and so the LORD, the God of hosts, will be with you, as you have said. Hate evil, and love good, and establish justice in the gate; it may be that the LORD, the God of hosts, will be gracious to the remnant of Joseph . . . let justice roll down like waters, and righteousness like an ever-flowing stream.

—Amos 5:11–15, 24

INTRODUCTION

The relationship between African Americans and the American presidency is tense and complex. Many of the nation's founding fathers were slaveholders. Thomas Jefferson held his own children in bondage while drafting a radical social contract declaring the self-evident nature of Creator-endowed human equality. The new nation not only refused citizenship to enslaved black men and women, it also denied them their full humanity. The nation's first presidents worked to establish an innovative, flexible, and arguably radical democratic republic while simultaneously codifying enslaved blacks as a fraction of a human and relegating them to intergenerational chattel bondage.[1] This system of American slavery was justified through religious reasoning in addition to economic and political expediency.

205

While brutalized by the American state, enslaved blacks retained agency in the face of bondage. Contemporary historiographies of American slavery have increasingly turned away from cataloguing the horrors of southern slavery and have focused more attention on the ways that enslaved persons carved out spaces of humanity, dignity, and social order.[2] The development of unique forms of religious belief and practice was among the most important ways that black men and women resisted the social death of slavery.[3] Emphasizing this point, religion scholar Gayraud Wilmore writes: "Blacks have used Christianity not so much as it was delivered to them by racist white churches, but as its truth was authenticated to them in the experience of suffering and struggle, to reinforce an enculturated religious orientation and to produce an indigenous faith that emphasized dignity, freedom, and human welfare."[4] In this way, enslaved blacks developed religious lives that sustained them throughout slavery and allowed them spaces of resistance and humanity in a system that sought to reduce them to chattel.

At the close of the Civil War, enslaved blacks entered the American polity; they carried their unique religious traditions with them into citizenship and these religious traditions continue to mediate the relationship between black America and the American presidency. This chapter attempts to trace some elements of the interrelationship between black religiosity and black public opinion toward American presidents. First, it argues that black religiosity is constituted in three parts: organizational, cultural, and theological. Then, the chapter maps some contemporary black attitudes toward American presidents. Finally, the chapter uses two case studies to reflect on how black religiosity influences the ways that black Americans think about their presidents.

MULTIPLE DIMENSIONS OF BLACK RELIGION

The African American church developed as a separate institutional structure as early as Reconstruction. Blacks living as freedmen in the North and newly emancipated African Americans in the South constructed the church as a central institution in black life.[5] Lincoln and Mamiya refer to the black church as the womb of the community, giving life to major social, economic, and cultural institutions.[6] Decades of research have investigated the connection between the black church as a central political and social institution and its role in black political thought and action. This research stresses the organizational resources that accrue to black churchgoers, such as the networks, skills, mobilization, and contact opportunities that are nurtured in the church.[7] This work also maps the psychological resources that contribute to the political actions of black church congregants, such as self-esteem and internal efficacy.[8]

This research demonstrates how the black church is crucial in initiating and sustaining political action in black communities. Sociologist Aldon Morris's study of the civil rights movement articulates this position, stating that "the black church functioned as the institutional center of the modern civil rights movement. Churches provided the movement with an organized mass base leadership of clergymen; an institutionalized financial base; and meeting places where the masses planned tactics and strategies and collectively committed themselves to the struggle."[9] There is still debate about whether the black church discourages political action by encouraging followers to focus on the rewards of an afterlife,[10] but there is a good deal of empirical evidence showing that many black churches are actively committed to providing worshippers with the organizational and psychological resources necessary for political action.

The influence of the church in black political life extends beyond its organizational centrality in black communities. The church also directs and influences important elements of black cultural life. Lincoln and Mamiya argue that the black church is deeply embedded in black culture in general, so that the sphere of politics in the African American community cannot be easily separated from it. "The core values of black culture like freedom, justice, equality, an African heritage, and racial parity at all levels of human intercourse, are raised to ultimate levels and legitimated in the black sacred cosmos."[11]

The black church operates as a kind of cultural training ground. Sociologist Mary Patillo demonstrates the "power of church rituals as cultural tools for facilitating local organizing and activism among African Americans."[12] The church is a place where African Americans learn cultural norms and styles that are then employed in secular settings. Patillo's black community residents use prayer, call-and-response interaction, and Christian imagery when coordinating nonreligious activities around issues of youth delinquency and community safety. She finds that "black church culture constitutes a common language that motivates social action."[13]

The black church also offers African Americans unique religious ideas and organic theologies that distinguish black religiosity.[14] These mass-based theologies of the black church are rooted in specific understandings of biblical texts that grow out of black experiences of bondage and oppression. The black church is not only an organizational space that gives rise to unique racial and cultural formations, but is also an interpreter of the black experience in America that gives rise to unique theological formulations. Biblical studies professor Vincent Wimbush argues that African Americans have a distinct approach to reading and interpreting biblical texts. "African Americans used the Bible to make self-assertive claims against a racist America that claimed to be a biblical nation. African Americans were clamoring for realization of the principles of inclusion, equality, and kinship that they understood the Bible to mandate. Beginning in the nineteenth century and extending into the twentieth, African Americans consistently and systematically attempted to make use of the Bible to force 'biblical' America to honor biblical principles."[15] Guided by this hermeneutical key, African American religiosity chooses to emphasize particular elements of the Bible, "the adventures of the Hebrews in bondage and escaping from bondage, and those about the wondrous works, compassion, and resurrection of Jesus. . . and the prophecies, especially the prophetic denunciations of social injustice and the visions of social justice."[16]

African American commitment to and emphasis on Old Testament prophets is important for understanding black public opinion relative to the presidents. I propose that the ideal of the prophet of social justice and equality is the standard against which black America judges American presidents. The Old Testament prophets break from the tribalism of the preceding biblical texts and condemn the injustice and corruption of the rulers of Israel and Judah. They warn that if injustice continues the nation will face political collapse and defeat by foreign enemies. Guided by their specific religious traditions, black Americans judge the president by this standard, asking whether he is willing to voice condemnation of the injustice and inequality that blacks face in American society.

In summary, black religion mediates the relationship between African Americans and the presidency through multiple elements of the black church.

- Black America often communicates with presidential politics through the organizational medium of the black church.
- Black public opinion toward individual presidential candidates and office holders is influenced by the cultural expectations influenced by the church.
- Black attitudes toward the president are strongly influenced by a black folk theology that emphasizes the role of the prophet.

BLACK AMERICA AND THE AMERICAN PRESIDENCY

Constitutionally, the American presidency is a relatively weak office. Article II of the U.S. Constitution grants the president the position of commander-in-chief of the armed forces and allows him, with the consent of Congress, to appoint cabinet members and other executive officials. The president is also responsible for the conduct of foreign affairs, although his treaties and appointments must be approved by the Senate and his expenditures by the House of Representatives. These enumerated responsibilities and capacities are relatively modest compared to executive positions in other world governments and are minimal compared to the extensive powers given to other branches of the U.S. government. But while the office is constitutionally weak, American presidents have often wielded enormous power in governing. This power comes from the capacity of each of the individual presidents to influence or persuade multiple domestic and foreign publics.[17]

The formal powers of the Constitution are not the real basis of presidential power. Instead, the capacity to persuade and wield influence has been the measure of American presidential power, and at times that power has seemed almost boundless. Presidential scholar Michael Nelson argues that strength is the standard for both scholarly and popular evaluations of a president. An "implicit exaltation of presidential strength"[18] underlies our notion of what makes a high-quality president. American presidents hold a constitutionally ill-defined office where persuasion, strength, and charisma are central to success.

As a figure of strength, persuasion, and charisma, the president has come to embody the American state. Presidents are often credited and blamed for many policies and national conditions that are actually the result of forces that are only marginally within their control. For example, the state of the national economy is a powerful predictor of presidential electoral outcomes, even though presidents control very few of the factors that contribute to economic health. Presidents are also the marker for national time. Americans measure the history of the country, in part, by the men occupying the presidency. For example, one might speak of the Roosevelt era or the Reagan years. In contrast, we never speak about the era of the 95th Congress. For many ordinary Americans, the president is the embodiment of American politics.

This is true for African Americans as well. There are important parallels between the relationship of blacks to the presidents and their relationship to the state more broadly. In the years before the Civil War, black America was defined by southern slavery. Although not all blacks were slaves, the reality of southern slavery proscribed and helped define what it meant to be black in America. Thus the relationship of pre–Civil War presidents to slavery is an important lens for understanding how they were connected to black America.

Slavery and the Abolitionist Jeremiad

Many pre–Civil War presidents privately professed to find slavery morally repugnant, but they chose to respond to slavery with thundering silence.[19]

Kenneth O'Reilly writes, "No rut cut by the first president was deeper than the idea that the slave issue ought not intrude on democracy's grand experiment."[20] Washington may have established the presidential forbearance of slavery, but Jefferson's *Notes on the State of Virginia* offered the most vehemently racist justifications of slavery by an early American president. Jefferson, who brought nearly two hundred slaves with him to the capital during his presidency, argued that blacks were biologically and naturally inferior and, therefore, incapable of sustaining emancipation. Jefferson writes:

> Blacks, whether originally a distinct race, or made distinct by time and circumstances, are inferior to the whites in the endowments both of body and mind. It is not against experience to suppose, that different species of the same genus, or varieties of the same species, may possess different qualifications. Will not a lover of natural history then, one who views the gradations in all the races of animals with the eye of philosophy, excuse an effort to keep those in the department of man as distinct as nature has formed them? This unfortunate difference of color, and perhaps of faculty, is a powerful obstacle to the emancipation of these people.[21]

A pattern of presidential racism, silence, or deal making at the expense of enslaved blacks characterized most of the first century of the new nation. Yet in the face of presidential hostility or inaction, African Americans crafted abolitionist political strategies. Black abolitionism was deeply rooted in religious understandings, argument, and rhetoric. Frederick Douglass is most emblematic of this tradition. In 1842, Douglass suggested that moral, not political, action would be most effective in ending slavery, "I ask you, what this legislation has done—was it political action that removed your prejudices and raised in your mind a holy zeal for human rights?"[22] Douglass recognized that because of the utter disfranchisement of free blacks throughout the country his strategy might most fruitfully rest on moral persuasion rooted in unique black religious reasoning: the African American jeremiad.

Wilson Jeremiah Moses describes the black jeremiad as "the constant warning issued by blacks to whites concerning the judgment that was to come from the sin of slavery."[23] Named for the Old Testament prophet Jeremiah, a jeremiad is a form of literature or rhetoric associated with the divine destruction of a wicked people and the deliverance of the children of God. The jeremiad warns that those who have sinned against God or God's chosen people will soon pay the consequences of their sinful actions, and that the chosen people will be led to a land of safety and peace far from the pains of their oppressors. The black jeremiad has been an important form of black political understanding that has helped structure the expectations of black America related to the presidency. The black jeremiad understands African

Americans to be living in a land of oppression similar to the Old Testament experience of ancient Egyptian bondage. As Yahweh delivered His children then, so too would he deliver black America. American presidents are judged by black America, in part, by how they can make use of this narrative of sin, destruction, and deliverance.

Frederick Douglass was a master of the jeremiad as a form of moral persuasion. During the 1840s and 1850s, Douglass spoke before antislavery audiences throughout the North, denouncing slavery as an abomination to God and curse to the nation. Slavery, he contended, posed a dire threat to America's present course. "We shall not go unpunished," he predicted, but "a terrible retribution awaits us." Therefore it was the patriotic duty of blacks "to warn our fellow countrymen" of the impending doom they courted and to dissuade America from "rushing on in her wicked career" along a patch "ditched with human blood, and paved with human skulls," so that "our country may yet be saved."[24]

Douglass exemplifies the early interrelationship between blacks, religion, and the American presidency. Most blacks in America suffered under the crushing weight of slavery while fifteen presidents from different parties, regions, and eras watched in silence or in allegiance to slaveholders. An examination of the life and work of Fredrick Douglass demonstrates that those blacks who did have a voice evoked the prophetic tradition of the Old Testament and generated a unique jeremiad that implored America to end slavery to save itself.

Lincoln, the Prophet President

In the middle of the nineteenth century, the nation was finally forced to confront slavery in the crucible of the Civil War. African Americans found in Abraham Lincoln an American president who acted on racial injustice. Lincoln was drawn into the Civil War because of complex historical forces. His decision to issue the Emancipation Proclamation was prompted as much by war strategy as by abolitionist sentiment. Even knowing that Lincoln was often acting more for the Union than for racial equality, black America developed a sincere adoration of him. Historian Merrill Peterson recounts that black affection for Lincoln began as unyielding gratitude and sense of interconnection. In the eyes of enslaved blacks, Lincoln was a man like them, "His birth like ours was obscure; he was of lowly origins and has toiled from poverty—they had toiled up from slavery."[25]

For nearly one hundred years following emancipation, African Americans remained loyal voters to the "party of Lincoln." This loyalty was sustained even though the party abandoned its positions and politics for blacks soon after Reconstruction. Still, black Americans remained tied to the party of the first American president for whom they felt deep warmth and attachment. Lincoln was the first president that black America could understand in moral terms. Therefore, while the relationship between blacks and Lincoln has been ambivalent and difficult at times, he remains an important icon in black political thought. Lincoln has been the subject of and backdrop for important historical moments in black America. In 1939, Marian Anderson sang before seventy-five thousand Americans in an integrated crowd on the steps on the Lincoln Memorial. In 1957, the NAACP celebrated the third anniversary of the *Brown v. Board of Education* decision at the Lincoln Memorial. In 1963, Martin Luther King Jr. declared, "I have a dream" from the steps of the Lincoln Memorial.

Historian Scott Sandage explains, "Black protesters refined a politics of memory at the Lincoln Memorial. Within the sacred, national space of the memorial, activists perfected a complex ritual of mass politics, one that exploited the ambiguities of cherished American clause to circumvent opposition, unify coalitions, and legitimated black voices in national politics. . . . Blacks strategically appropriated Lincoln's memory and monument as political weapons, in the process layering and changing the public meanings of the hero and his shrine."[26]

Contemporary African Americans view Lincoln with a critical and often ambivalent eye, acknowledging the real contributions he made to the end of slavery, but also criticizing the personal racism that was never fully conquered in his public policies.[27] But even with these criticisms, Lincoln remains the president that black people "loved best and longest."[28] In many ways Lincoln, though only reluctantly and partially, finally fulfilled the role of an Old Testament prophet. In the black imagination, he is remembered as standing with Douglass as a prophet of the black jeremiad. Just as Amos warned Israel that its injustice to men of other nations threatened its status as the elect of Yahweh, so too did Lincoln show America that the evil of slavery could break the union in half and the end the great democratic experiment of the new world. No other president has ever so entirely commanded the trust and respect of African Americans for so long.

Segregation and Communal Faith

Following the Civil War and Reconstruction, black America plunged into the nadir.[29] The prophet president was assassinated and African Americans were abandoned by the federal government in the Hayes-Tilden Compromise of 1877. These presidential politics ushered in a new phase of the relationship between blacks and the presidency. The razor-thin 1876 election race between

Rutherford Hayes and Samuel Tilden generated a congressional deadlock. Congress eventually retreated behind closed doors, where southern Democrats conceded to Hayes's presidency in exchange for the end of Union occupation of the defeated Confederacy. This compromise cleared the path for southern states to institute Jim Crow. Freed from the oversight of the federal government, the South used the rhetoric of states' rights to strip black men of their right to vote, to segregate public accommodations, to provide inferior education to black citizens, and to allow and promote the terrorist rule of lynch-mob violence. Subjected to the vicious retrenchment of states' rights, blacks entered the nadir and returned to a deep collective estrangement from the American presidency. In this context, lynching came to symbolize the position of blacks in America. In the one hundred years following the end of the Civil War, more than five thousand African Americans were lynched and not a single president denounced the atrocities. Once again, presidential silence characterized black America's relationship to the country.[30]

In this difficult period, black religion continued to mediate the relationship between blacks and the American state. From the late nineteenth century to the contemporary period, black America solidified its relationship to the state as communal rather than individual. In this regard, black politics drew heavily from the organizational, cultural, and theological elements of black religiosity. Political scientist Michael Dawson explains, "The communalism of African American public life shared its roots with the communalism of African-American religious thought. One of the critical differences between black and white Protestantism is the African American belief in self-realization of individuality within community. In opposition to the American liberal tradition, African Americans have adopted the worldview that individual freedom can be realized only within the context of collective freedom, that individual salvation can occur only within the framework of collective salvation."[31]

As racial segregation, economic exploitation, and political oppression descended on these new citizens, the church emerged as a center of social and organizational life as well as an interpreter of world affairs and national events. Separate congregations emerged in both the South and in northern cities populated by migrating black workers. In these churches, African Americans developed distinct biblical understandings that mandated collective approaches to religion and to politics. These religious understandings continued to underscore Exodus narratives, prophetic traditions, and readings of the gospels that suggested God related to his people as nations called to special missions. Rather than emphasizing the relationship between God and individual believers, these religious interpretations focused on God in relationship to his people as a collective. Black presidential politics reflect this same sense of collective identity rather than individual interests. "Political responsibility to the African-American community was considered a higher good than the individual's right to act on his or her own preference if those preferences were considered potentially harmful to the black community."[32]

This communal orientation to presidential politics is most visible in black partisanship. African American partisanship is characterized by near unanimous support of a single party, regardless of divisions of income, education, gender, and region. From Reconstruction until the mid-1930s, the African American vote was solidly Republican. Blacks were both tied to the party of the Great Emancipator and wary of the vicious segregationists of the southern Democratic Party. African American disaffection with the Republican Party was widespread, but their votes remained loyal because Democrats were so blatantly hostile. Because millions of black Americans were disenfranchised in the South and discouraged from voting in the urban centers of the North and Midwest, both parties were able to disassociate themselves from blacks with little electoral cost.[33]

It was the presidency of Franklin D. Roosevelt that marked a radical shift in the allegiance of the black electorate. In the early 1930s, African American communities were among the hardest hit in the Great Depression, but because they lacked political power, blacks received far less than their fair share of New Deal program relief. Roosevelt, recognizing the potential growing influence of black voters in hard-hit urban centers, began to shift New Deal policies. By 1935, African Americans had begun to benefit from the jobs of the Works Project Administration (WPA) and in 1936 Roosevelt and the Democrats actively sought the black vote. In an unprecedented and massive shift of partisan allegiance, Roosevelt secured 76 percent of the black vote in the 1936 election.[34] Since 1936, the black vote has further consolidated and more than 85 percent of African Americans have supported the Democratic candidate for the presidency since mid-century.

The shift in black partisanship was precipitated by real economic and political motivations, but there was also a role for black cultural religion in this shift. To locate this role we must look to Eleanor Roosevelt. It was Mrs. Roosevelt, rather than FDR, who was crucial in bringing blacks into the New Deal. The First Lady often appeared in African American churches and church-sponsored schools and daycare centers. She displayed a comfort, ease, and naturalness in interracial setting that resulted in historian Rayford Logan asserting, "Negroes almost worshipped Eleanor Roosevelt."[35] It was Eleanor Roosevelt who functioned as the prophetic voice within FDR's administration. "Free from official responsibilities, and thus able to be more unswervingly moral than Franklin, Eleanor could argue for an action on the grounds that it was right."[36] Economic and political considerations were the engine driving the shift in black partisanship, but the First Lady cemented the relationship between the New Deal and black America. Even with overwhelming economic interests at stake, the communal and moral elements of black presidential politics still required someone in the administration who could tap African Americans' understandings of the prophetic. Eleanor Roosevelt fulfilled this role when FDR could not or would not. She became the moral icon that helped motivate the massive shift in black partisanship.

CONTEMPORARY BLACK ATTITUDES TOWARD THE PRESIDENTS

The contemporary shape of black opinion toward the American presidents is consistent with this history. Among the most important contemporary trends marking African American public opinion is a persistent gulf in attitudes between blacks and whites.[37] An important aspect of the racial gap is the significant animosity of blacks toward the Republican presidents of the past two decades contrasted with their deep affection for and electoral support of President Clinton. This section will trace the attitudes of black America toward the political parties and their presidents and will suggest that support of Democratic presidents in the modern era is mediated by religiously guided expectations for evaluating presidential leadership.

African Americans continue to be strong Democratic partisans. In every election since 1980, less than a quarter of black respondents reveal a partisan preference that is not at least somewhat attached to the Democratic Party.

This partisanship has an enormous influence on assessments of the presidents. Black people gave better than 85 percent of their vote to the Democratic contender in each presidential election since 1980. When asked to report their vote choice in surveys immediately following the election, African Americans report even greater support to the Democratic candidate, even if that candidate lost the general election.[38]

Table 9.1: African American Partisanship

	1980	1984	1988	1992	1996	2000
Strong Democrat	45	33	40	42	44	46
Weak/Leaning Democrat	36	46	43	37	37	38
Independent	7	11	6	13	11	10
Weak/Leaning Republican	5	7	10	6	7	3
Strong Republican	3	3	2	2	1	3

Cells are percent of African Americans reporting partisan affiliation in each survey.
Source: 1980–2000 American National Election Studies.

Table 9.2: Reported Vote Choice and Average Feeling Thermometer Ratings Among African Americans

Survey Year Candidates	Percent of black voters who report voting for candidate	Average warmth score among black respondents
1980		
Carter	93	78
Reagan	7	43
1984		
Mondale	89	77
Reagan	9	38
1988		
Dukakis	90	69
Bush	8	46
1992		
Clinton	91	70
Bush	5	40
1996		
Clinton	97	81
Dole	3	44
2000		
Gore	91	71
Bush	7	48

Source: 1980–2000 American National Election Studies.

African American animosity toward presidents Reagan and Bush, who were well-liked by most whites, was a salient feature of black public opinion throughout the 1980s.[39] Black respondents to national surveys in the eighties reported very cool affect toward presidents Reagan and Bush. When asked to rate their warmth toward Reagan on a scale from 0 to 100, black respondents averaged a rating of forty-three points toward Reagan in 1984. Michael Dawson's 1994 text on contemporary black politics finds that, "having consistently bypassed and denounced the recognized leadership of the black community, [Reagan] was viewed as extraordinarily hostile to black aspirations."[40] In a 1984 volume on blacks in America, Pinkney argues that "the Reagan administration has given increased impetus to the conservative movement in the United States, ranging from such neofacist groups as the Ku Klux Klan to the Moral Majority."[41] While initially somewhat more warmly received than Reagan, Bush ultimately fared poorly within black public opinion. In 1992, Bush averaged a feeling thermometer score of only forty points among African Americans—see table 9.2.

Black attitudes toward Clinton were quite different. In 1992, black respondents averaged a rating of seventy on the feeling thermometer rating toward Clinton. By 1996, the average warmth climbed to eighty-one points. The 1996 rating is the first time in national black public opinion studies that the mean feeling thermometer score for the sitting president (eighty-one) eclipsed the average feeling thermometer score for Jesse Jackson (seventy). In 2000, black respondents reported average warmth toward Gore of seventy-one points. African Americans in the 1980s existed in a political environment dominated by despised presidential figures.[42] In the 1990s, under Clinton, the political landscape changed for African Americans in this regard.

Religion remains an important part of black American life in the contemporary era and continues to be a mediating factor in black opinions toward the U.S. presidents. During the 1980s and 1990s African Americans expressed very high levels of religiosity. In the six American National Election Studies (NES) from 1980–2000, well over 75 percent of African Americans reported that religion provides at least some guidance in their day-to-day living (see figure 9.1). And in each of these surveys, a clear majority reported that religion provided "a lot" of guidance in their daily lives.

This reliance on religion as a source of daily guidance has implications for black American political attitudes (see figure 9.2). As they lean on their religious beliefs, African Americans use religiosity as a lens for judging the po-

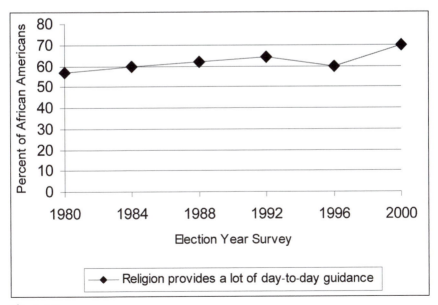

Figure 9.1

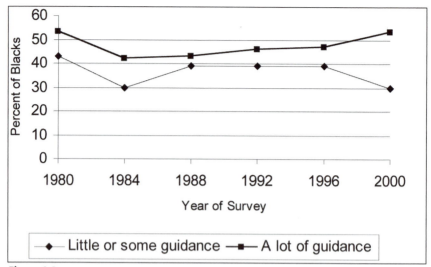

Figure 9.2

litical parties and the presidents. In each election-year NES survey from 1980 to 2000, African American respondents who report that religion provides a lot of daily guidance are more strongly attached to the Democratic Party than those who claim that religion is a more moderate daily influence. Across the past two decades, those who rely most heavily on religious interpretations of daily life are also most strongly attached to the Democratic Party.

This also means that the most religious black Americans rate Democratic presidential candidates and presidents more favorably and Republican presidential candidates and presidents more harshly. Media coverage of the 2004 elections suggested that this pattern may have changed. Casual observers of the 2004 campaign season pointed to high-profile African American ministers who used religious reasoning to undergird their support for the Republican presidential candidates. This was presented as evidence that black Christians were joining the ranks of conservative presidential politics. Data from the Fourth National Survey of Religion and Politics (2004) does demonstrate an increase of 12 percentage points in the black Protestant vote share received by George W. Bush in 2004 compared to 2000. However, too much has been made of the increased percentage of the black vote received by President Bush in the 2004 election. This increase simply reflects the historically low (6 percent) share of the black vote received by Bush in 2000. African Americans have traditionally given 10 to 12 percent of the vote to the Republican presidential candidate. In 1996, Bob Dole received 16 percent of the black vote even running against a popular second-term Bill Clinton. The GOP's religious appeals in 2004 did not increase the black vote share, but only returned it to historic norms after a precipitous decline in 2000. There has been no major exodus of black voters to the Republican Party. In fact, data from the same survey show that black Protestants voted overwhelming for John Kerry (85 percent) and that they made up the single largest group in the Kerry coalition, accounting for 13 percent of the Kerry voters. Conversely, black Protestants constituted only 3 percent of the GOP presidential voting coalition. In the contemporary era, religion continues to provide black people an important lens for viewing the American presidents, and it is a lens that overwhelmingly favors Democratic candidates. To understand the mechanisms that underlie this relationship between religion, blacks, and the American presidency in modern elections we must explore more complex models.

Predicting Presidential Assessments

One way to test how black religiosity is related to attitudes toward American presidents is to posit a simple causal model and test it with available survey data. Data from national random surveys of adult African American populations allow a first cut glimpse at how religiosity influences black attitudes toward the presidents. Table 9.3 reports results from two models estimated using an ordinary least squares regression. The models suggest how religiosity influenced black attitudes toward President Ronald Reagan in 1984 and toward President Bill Clinton in 1994. The dependent variable in both models is constructed from the responses to two questions: (1) Do you approve of how the president is handling his job? and (2) How warmly do you feel toward the president? Responses to these two questions are added together for a scale that represents total feelings toward the president. This is not a perfect measure, but it suggests an overall assessment of the president by combining opinions about job performance with overall affect toward the man.

The model simply hypothesizes that these assessments of the president are a function of (1) individual characteristics, such as gender age, education, and income; (2) partisan identification; (3) racial identification; and (4) religiosity. The model for attitudes toward President Reagan is estimated using data from the 1984 National Black Election Study[43] and the model for attitudes toward President Clinton is estimated using data from the 1994 National Black Politics Study.[44]

Sex is a dichotomous variable with female coded as one. Age is coded in natural years ranging from eighteen to eighty-eight. Education is measured as the highest grade completed, with high school diploma as the modal response category. Income is annual household income measured in nine income categories.

Partisan identification is measured as a five-category variable with lower values indicating strong Republican identification and higher values indicating strong Democratic identification. Previous research shows that partisan identification is the single most important explanatory variable in presidential evaluations. This measure of partisanship is included in the model to control for the powerful effect of partisanship so that the estimation can uncover the independent effects of religiosity.

The model also includes a measure of racial identification. Previous research shows that individuals who perceive their own fate as linked to the fate of the race are systematically different in their political attitudes than those who do not have a sense of racially linked fate.[45] Survey respondents were asked if "what happens to black people affects what happens in my own life." This measure of black-linked fate is coded on a unit range where higher values indicate stronger connection with the fate of the race.

The variables of most interest for this analysis are the religion measures. Both the 1984 model of attitudes toward Reagan and the 1994 model of attitudes toward Clinton include a measure of religious guidance. Respondents are asked how much religion provides guidance in day-to-day living. Higher values indicate the respondent perceives religion as more important in daily life.

The estimated models then include measures of the respondent's connection with politics in the church. In the 1984 model, the only measure available in the data is a question asking if the respondent believes that the church should be involved in politics. Higher values indicate a stronger belief that the church belongs in politics. The 1994 data provide a more nuanced measure. There are two measures of political involvement with the church included in the 1994 model. Using the measures available in the 1994 National Black Politics Study, it is possible to model participation in politicized churches.

Nearly half of respondents report engagement with some form of church-based political discussion. Thirty-four percent reported talking to people about political matters at church. Fifty percent heard a clergy member talk about the need for people to become involved in politics. Thirty-eight percent heard a political leader speak at church and 23 percent heard a church official suggest voting for or against certain candidates. Respondents were somewhat less likely to be engaged in political activity at church than in church-based political discussion, but nearly one-quarter reported some involvement with church-based political action. Twenty-three percent helped in a voter registration drive, 25 percent gave people a ride to the polls on Election Day, 24 percent gave money to a political candidate, 27 percent attended a candidate fundraiser, 23 percent handed out campaign materials, and 42 percent signed a petition supporting a candidate as a part of their regular religious duties in the past two years. For the majority of African Americans, church is not a

Table 9.3:   Models of Attitudes toward Presidents Reagan and Clinton

1984 Attitudes toward Reagan *n=1004* *r2=.07*			*1994 Attitudes toward Clinton* *n=1150* *r2=.11*	
Variable	*Coefficient*	*SE*	*Coefficient*	*SE*
Daily religious guidance	-1.83*	.75	4.12*	2.05
Church should be political	.48	1.6	--	--
Church political action	--	--	7.02**	2.87
Church political discussion	--	--	10.31**	3.73
Partisanship	-25.33*	3.55	13.95**	2.75
Black linked fate	-1.11	.48	-5.1**	1.9
Female	-7.55**	1.7	.08	1.58
Age	.02	.05	.29**	.04
Education	.15	.64	-.19	.24
Income	-.05	.28	.18	.332
Constant	60.9	5.95	40.37	5.2

Coefficients are derived from ordinary least squares regression performed in STATA
*denotes significance at $p<.05$.** denotes significance at $p<.01$.

Sources: 1984 National Black Election Study; 1994 National Black Politics Study.

site of political conversation or action, but a substantial portion of blacks do encounter political ideas and opportunities for involvement in their religious lives. These measures are combined into additive scales of church-based political discussion and church-based political action, and are included to account for earlier findings about the centrality of politicized black churches.

The results reported in table 9.3 show a clear link between religiosity and attitudes toward the presidents among black respondents. In both 1984 and 1994, partisan identification is the most powerful variable. Strong Democrats have much more favorable evaluations of Clinton in 1994 and far more unfavorable ratings of Reagan in 1984. But even after accounting for the powerful effect of partisanship, religiosity continues to have a statistically significant impact on black attitudes toward the presidents. Black people who take significant daily guidance from religion perceive Reagan much more harshly in 1984 and Clinton far more favorably in 1994. Further, in 1994, those African Americans who are involved in either political discussions or political action in their churches have significantly higher evaluations of President Clinton.

These data are only suggestive. They show a clear and independent role for religiosity in influencing black attitudes toward presidents, but they cannot explain the reasons why religion helps solidify the relationship between black Americans and contemporary Democratic presidents. The section below takes up case studies of two modern Democratic presidents: Lyndon Johnson and Bill Clinton. Understanding the similarities and differences in how these men were seen by black America sheds additional light on the question of how religion mediates this complicated relationship.

LBJ, THE FORGOTTEN PROPHET, AND BILL CLINTON, THE FIRST BLACK PRESIDENT?

The statistical analysis above demonstrates the significant gulf in black affection for a contemporary Republican president compared to a contemporary Democratic president. Given the strength of black partisan affiliation, any analysis of presidents from opposing parties will show a similar pattern. Therefore, to really unpack the narratives of presidential assessment it is necessary to compare two modern Democratic presidents. In this way, the analysis "holds constant" the powerful influence of partisan identification and allows us to understand more clearly the perceptions that black Americans have of the president. Presidents Lyndon B. Johnson and Bill Clinton make an ideal pairing for this kind of comparison. Both Johnson and Clinton were southern presidents who shared certain cultural practices and understandings with African Americans. Both had complicated relationships with their black constituencies. Each was judged by black America through a lens of black cultural expectations deeply influenced by black religious practice.

Although he has been characterized as brash, insecure, domineering, and crude, Lyndon B. Johnson could arguably be understood as equivalent to Abraham Lincoln in terms of the sheer impact of his presidency on African American citizenship. When Johnson first assumed the presidency following the assassination of John F. Kennedy, many civil rights leaders believed that the racial progress of the previous decade would come to an end. "A large majority of America's 22 million African Americans admired John F. Kennedy and considered him a sympathetic friend. Many assumed at first that his assassin had been motivated by racial hatred."[46] Johnson was viewed with suspicion. As a southern Democrat with ties to oil interests, Johnson represented the bulwarks of resistance against racial equality.

However, Johnson demonstrated that his commitment to the principles of civil rights paired with his capacity to move legislation through a congressional process he had mastered during his years on the Hill were going to make him a powerful friend of black America. In his early days in office, Johnson took on the mantle of an Old Testament prophet. He chose to make the case for civil rights in compelling moral language. He captured the moment of Kennedy's death to make a messianic appeal to the country and its elected representatives, saying, "No memorial oration or eulogy could more eloquently honor President Kennedy's memory than the earliest possible passage of the civil rights bill for which he fought so long."[47] Johnson's brave and unwavering commitment in his November 1963 address to a joint session of Congress won him the immediate respect of African American political leaders who judged him as a capable of the prophetic work of speaking truth to power.

> There was something else about Johnson's southern roots that the black leaders found significant: any southern white politician who dared take up the cause of civil rights did so knowing full well that his commitment would expose him to rejection by his closest white southern friends and allies. Advocating civil rights could spell defeat in the next election. There was a real cost, political and personally, for a southerner that the northern white politician did not face. Therefore the southerner's commitment demonstrated true courage.[48]

Johnson's finest prophetic moment for racial equality came on March 15, 1965, when he made the moral case to Congress for the passage of the 1965 Voting Rights Act. In his memoir, *Breaking Barriers*, Carl Rowan writes, "Black Americans wanted more than the right to sit next to Whites. . . . They wanted full citizenship, which meant the untrammeled right to vote. . . . I saw in a single day, March 15, 1965, all of God's permutations of Lyndon Johnson as he tried to ensure that his historic appeal to the Congress would not be rejected."[49] In this address, Johnson challenged the nation to face the challenge of racial inequality in order to save its own democratic promise. Only through fulfilling the citizenship demands of African Americans could the nation fulfill the American promise. Johnson argued,

> In our time we have come to live with moments of great crisis. Our lives have been marked with debate about great issues; issues of war and peace, issues of prosperity and depression. But rarely in any time does an issue lay bare the secret heart of America itself. Rarely are we met with a challenge, not to our growth or abundance, our welfare or our security, but rather to the values and the purposes and the meaning of our beloved Nation. The issue of equal rights for American Negroes is such an issue. And should we defeat every enemy, should we double our wealth and conquer the stars, and still be unequal to this issue, then we will have failed as a people and as a nation.[50]

Called to action by the extraordinary times in which he served, Johnson initially rose to the challenge of the prophetic standard that African Americans had long held for the president. Rowan argues that if Johnson "could have had his presidency judged on that speech alone, or on his civil rights record alone, he would today be ranked with Lincoln and FDR as one of the nation's greatest leaders."[51] It was in this moment that LBJ met the litmus test of black religious expectations by fulfilling his prophetic function. Of course, history would not prove kind enough to Johnson to judge him on these moments. Instead, the painful legacy of Vietnam would intervene in Johnson's relationship with America and with black America. As the brutal realities of Vietnam debilitated Johnson's presidency, the moral consistency of Martin Luther King Jr. forced King to speak against the war and to resist the administration that perpetuated it. The war ultimately unraveled the close-knit bond between Johnson and black America, rendering him a forgotten prophet.

Thirty years later, in 1998, Nobel Prize–winning African American author Toni Morrison suggested in a *New Yorker* article about Bill Clinton that, "white skin not withstanding, this is our first black President." Morrison's description of Clinton as black was prompted by his experience of personal, public humiliation at the hands of his political foes. When Morrison labeled Clinton black, she was not making a claim about his genetic heritage, but instead drawing parallels between his public debacle and the historic treatment of black public figures. She was also commenting on his experience with and use of cultural markers that often stand for the denigrated elements of black life in America. "Clinton displays almost every trope of blackness: single-parent household, born poor, working-class, saxophone-playing, McDonald's-and-junk-food-loving boy from Arkansas."[52]

Although Morrison drew a firestorm of responses from African American observers angered by the assertion that these "negative" traits constituted blackness, Morrison had correctly tapped into an important and unique connection between Clinton and African Americans. One of the most fascinating elements of the black president label was that Clinton himself relished it. Clinton acknowledged his "honorary blackness" in a 1999 speech at the Congressional Black Caucus's annual dinner and frequently thereafter. His choice to locate his personal office in Harlem at the close of his presidency confirmed the deep connection he had cultivated with black Americans. Morrison's critics notwithstanding, on the whole African Americans perceived Bill Clinton as a great president and as a friend to the race. Clinton's willingness to pay attention to racial issues and Clinton's "comfort with black people" were among the most frequently cited reasons that blacks assessed him positively.[53] Both the intensity and character of Clinton's popularity among African Americans is unique among modern presidents.

Journalist Dewayne Wickham compiled a fascinating array of interviews with African American leaders and laypersons chronicling the unique relationship between Bill Clinton and black America. Wickham's respondents offer a wide array of anecdotes and reasons why Clinton enjoys a privileged status among blacks. Popular syndicated radio host Tom Joyner recalls Clinton being the only man in a room full of African Americans who knew the words to every verse of the black national anthem "Lift Every Voice and Sing." White House correspondent Bill Douglas was amazed at Clinton's comfort and knowledge while attending a soul food dinner at his home. "He knew how to eat them. He had corn bread on the side. He dipped a little cornbread into the hot sauce and he was just gnawing on those chitlins. He served himself. I just looked at him in amazement."[54] Norma Johnson, a retired woman from Indiana, reasons, "the part of him I do like is the respect that I think he gives black people."[55] Former Atlanta mayor Bill Campbell reports of Clinton that, "the combination of how he grew up, where he grew up, the people he grew up around, but also the fact that he was young enough to really appreciate the African American quest for equality, helped him to connect with us in a way that is rare."[56] New York television reporter April Woodward went so far as to state, "He must have been breast-fed by a black woman because he's so comfortable around us."[57] Civil rights activist Joseph Lowery pointed to Clinton's record of appointments, but also argued that, "the real thing is that the boy blew saxophone. He wasn't no Chew Barry or Sonny Hodges, but the fact that he just blew a saxophone made white folks hate him . . . the saxophone is about as black an instrument as you can get."[58]

The interviews throughout Wickham's text enunciate common themes of shared cultural understanding and genuine personal connection that Clinton exuded to both black leaders and masses. Respondents were critical of some of Clinton's actions and policies, most notably his hasty retreat from Lani Guinier and Jocelyn Elders and his passage of welfare reform and crime legislation, but they also argue that he was more closely aligned with black policy interests than any president in two decades. Black Americans repeatedly cited Clinton's experience as an underdog, publicly embattled by his enemies, as one of the reasons he could relate to the African American experience. Overall, they express significant personal respect and admiration for Clinton as someone who has fondness for African Americans.

Clinton was fully embraced by black America. He was seen as a kindred spirit, a true friend of the race, and an effective champion for black interests. Many observers argue that this affection is misplaced. Many of the political and policy choices Clinton made in office were both symbolically and substantively troubling to black political interests. Clinton abandoned Lani Guinier, his black female nominee for assistant attorney general, when her nomination was attacked by Republicans based on her interest in policies promoting racial democracy. Under President Clinton, the numbers and percentage of incarcerated African Americans grew precipitously. Much of that increase can be traced to the Crime Bill of 1994 that Clinton signed into law.

Clinton supported the 1996 Welfare Reform Act, which most African American leaders understood to be anathema to the interests of poor and working-class blacks. Some question how Clinton could be broadly adored when his policies frequently clashed with community interests.

The interviews in Wickham's text point to the deeply rooted cultural practices that Clinton shared with black America. Among the most important was Clinton's command of and ease with African American religious rhetorical styles. In delineating his support for affirmative action, Clinton spoke of experiences of discrimination and segregation he witnessed while growing up in the American South (July 19, 1995). Clinton made the widely heralded step of offering an apology for the Tuskegee Study on black men in Alabama (May 16, 1997). He used the language of the black national anthem and turned on its head the cheer of southern segregationist in his celebration of the desegregation of Central High School in Little Rock, Arkansas, saying, "Let us resolve to stand on the shoulders of the Little Rock Nine and press on with confidence in the hard and noble work ahead. Let us lift every voice and sing till earth and heaven ring, one America today, one America tomorrow, one America forever" (September 25, 1997).

African American attitudes toward President Clinton pose a special dilemma for the role religion plays in mediating the relationship between black America and the presidents. Some observers argue that Clinton used the style of black religious culture to dupe African Americans into believing he had a prophetic voice when, in truth, his politics failed to promote racial equality. Certainly, Clinton's presidency never produced legislation of the magnitude and importance of Johnson's 1964 Civil Rights Act and 1965 Voting Rights Act, but Johnson left office with far lower approval ratings among blacks than Clinton did when he left office. Clinton forces us to question if religion can be used to obfuscate troubling politics by tapping into black cultural expectations.

Part of how black Americans relate to American presidents is through black religiosity. In its organizational, cultural, and theological permeations, black religion helps to mediate this relationship. Black ministers allow presidential candidates access to their congregations during election season. African Americans respond positively to those presidents, like Bill Clinton, who make use of black religious cultural styles. And African Americans are compelled by presidents, like the early Johnson, who use their power and influence to speak prophetic truths of racial equality. It is unclear whether this partial reliance on religiosity leads to "good" or "bad" political outcomes for black communities, but it seems clear that the mechanism does operate in this complicated relationship between black citizens and their presidents.

LOOKING TO THE FUTURE

For nearly two-and-one-half centuries religion has mediated the relationship between African Americans and the American presidency. It structures beliefs about what makes a good president and expectations for presidents vis-à-vis black people. In 2005, two conferences of black religious leaders hinted about possible future directions of the relationship between black America, religion, and the American presidency. On January 24, 2005, the four black Baptist conventions joined for a momentous meeting that brought these historically antagonistic groups together for a week in Nashville, Tennessee. Together they agreed on an extensive platform reflecting an active and progressive social and political agenda. Their plan called for an end to the Iraq War and to the current tax cuts, an extension of the 1965 Voting Rights Act, opposition to the confirmation of Alberto Gonzales as attorney general, a broad call to end the prison-industrial complex, and a commitment to public education, health care, a national living wage, and development activities in Africa and the Caribbean.

A few days later, more than one hundred black clergy met in Los Angeles, California, to craft the "Black Contract with America on Moral Values." Calling themselves the High Impact Leadership Coalition, these black ministers developed a platform centered on the conservative political agenda of the Republican Party. This group made the issue of gay marriage central, and called for the protection of marriage and family, home and business ownership, and education and prison reform.

Both groups derived their political agendas from interpretations of biblical texts. The Baptist conventions focused on a theology steeped in social justice. The High Impact Leadership Coalition, on the other hand, met at the Reverend Fred Price's Crenshaw Christian Center. Price and his sixteen-thousand-member church are solidly within the tradition of the prosperity gospel, which preaches a clear message of affluence and personal responsibility.

These two meetings of black churches reflect political possibilities. When the black church offers a theology rooted in a social gospel tradition, emphasizing the alleviation of poverty, the advancement of racial and gender equality, and the promotion of peace as moral values, it leads to a progressive political agenda among African Americans. When black churches advance a pervasively individualistic conception of the gospel that breaks the link between moral reasoning and structural inequality, it leads to a conservative political agenda focused exclusively on private morality.

There has never been a single black church or a monolithic black politics. African American religious traditions have always blended concern with social justice and demand for personal righteousness. Black political attitudes have often combined political progressivism with personal conservatism. But in the current political context of highly partisan politics, African Americans may find it difficult to combine these multiple traditions. The agendas of these two summits suggest that we may be at a crossroads in both black religious thought and black political practice.

This chapter has maintained that black assessments of the presidents are rooted in a unique black religiosity that emphasizes the prophetic tradition of the Old Testament and the liberation elements of the New Testament. This form of Christian thought constructs God's relationship to black people communally and contains an explicit critique of inequality and oppression. Presidents are judged, in part, by their willingness to fulfill the role of prophet for social justice.

However, current trends in black religiosity suggest that a new religiosity is gaining prominence among African Americans. Prosperity gospel is a fast-growing theology among black Americans. Preachers like Creflo Dollar and T. D. Jakes have congregations, viewers, and readers numbering in the tens of thousands. The prosperity gospel advances a pervasively individualistic conception of religion. The prosperity gospel asserts God's desire to help his people be financially free and secure. It teaches that God helps individuals who follow certain formulas in their personal and spiritual lives. Christ is an investment strategy and a personal life coach whose power can be accessed by believers to improve their finances, protect their families, strengthen their faith, and achieve personal authenticity. There is some evidence that this individual and instrumental message dampens political activism among African Americans. To the extent the prosperity gospel promotes an individualized, dispositional understanding of the world, it may also change the ways that black people assess future presidents.

If black political communalism is rooted in black religious communalism, then a shift in black folk theology to a more individualized religious practice may change the basis on which American presidents are judged. Black Americans may stop seeking a prophet and seek only a purveyor of individual prosperity.

George W. Bush meets with John DiIulio and Latino Catholic and Protestant clergy and leaders to discuss the faith-based initiatives program at the White House, May 2001. Pedro Windsor, Lisa Treviño-Cummins, Jesse Miranda, Armando Contreras, Luis Cortes, Daniel de Leon, Jim Ortiz, Raymond Rivera, and Rudy Carrasco.

Chapter 10

Latinos, Religion, and the American Presidency

Gastón Espinosa

The seismic growth of the Latino community has made it important in presidential politics. John Kerry's Latino outreach coordinator drove this home when he stated that if the Democratic Party could not keep the Latino Republican vote below 40 percent that it would not win a presidential election in the future.[1] Even if this astonishing statement is not technically true, it drives home the growing saliency of Latinos in American presidential politics.

Although the factors that shape Latino support for particular presidential candidates are as complex and as diverse as they are for any other community, the economy, education, immigration, the wars in Iraq and Afghanistan, and controversial moral issues like homosexual marriage and abortion loom large for different segments of the population. Notwithstanding these important factors, religion is also becoming increasingly important. The Hispanic Churches in American Public Life National Survey (n=2,060) found that 75 percent of Latinos agreed that a political candidate's faith and morals are relevant to their decision to vote for him or her and that 62 percent want their church or religious organization to become more involved in social and political issues. In light of these findings, political candidates across party lines have increasingly realized that clergy, churches, and denominations provide direct access to the hearts and minds of the nation's 46 million Latinos through their pulpits, centers, social programs, magazines, and radio and television programs. Religion has also become more relevant because a growing number of Latino clergy, lay leaders, and faith-based organizations are rising up to fight for social justice. A number of scholars, politicians, and activists are also coming to grips with the scholarship that demonstrates the critical role that religion has played in the lives of some of the most important Latino civil rights leaders over the past

150 years. This new literature is revealing that religion has served as one of the community's most important cultural resources.

This chapter will explore the relationship between Latino religion, politics, and the American presidency by focusing on the changing contours of Latino religious identity and political party identification, election turnout, and voting patterns in the 1996, 2000, and 2004 elections. It will also briefly explore how Clinton and Bush Jr. sought to reach out to the Latino community and how Latinos have in turn sought to influence the presidency.

This study draws on the findings from the Hispanic Churches in American Public Life National Survey U.S. sample (n <=> 2,060) and the Fourth National Survey of Religion and Politics (n <=> 2,750), although it will also draw on results from the Pew Research Post-Election Survey and the National Election Pool.[2] This study analyzes and revises several long-standing perceptions about Latino religious identity and presidential elections. First, it explores the notions that Latino Protestants and other Christian traditions are minor in size and thus always inconsequential in presidential elections; second, that Latino Evangelicals and Pentecostals are Republican; third, that Latino Protestants in general and Evangelicals in particular are monolithic in their political party identification and presidential voting patterns; fourth, that Latino Catholics are much more likely to vote in presidential elections than Protestants in general and Evangelicals in particular; and fifth, that there were no major efforts by non-Catholic Christians to mobilize Latinos for the 2004 election. The findings in this study indicate that the Latino mainline Protestant, Pentecostal, and evangelical communities are very large in number, voted overwhelmingly for Democratic presidential candidates in the 1990s, are as likely or more likely to state they have voted than Catholics, and were effectively mobilized in the 2004 presidential election. Finally, they also indicate that the Latino Protestant and Catholic support for Democratic candidates has slipped steadily from 1996 to 2004 in favor of Republican presidential candidates as a result of Bush's aggressive outreach to Latino religious leaders, denominations, and organizations through his faith-based initiatives and social programs. Republican growth among Latino religious traditions has not been uniform, as Pentecostals are more likely than traditional Evangelicals to vote Democrat.

LATINO RELIGION AND POLITICS IN THE UNITED STATES

American presidents have a long and checkered history of outreach to Latinos. The first large number of Latinos brought into the American political fold were quite literally the spoils of war and American foreign policy.

Although a small number of Spanish, Mexicans, Hispanos, Tejanos, and Latinos in Florida, New Mexico, and Texas fought alongside Euro-Americans in the American Revolution, the War of 1812, and in the struggle for Texas independence, the first significant number of Latinos that were granted U.S. citizenship were brought into the American political system after Spain ceded Florida to President James Monroe in 1821 and after President James K. Polk annexed Texas in 1845 and defeated Mexico in the U.S.–Mexico War of 1846–1848. As a result, Mexico signed the Treaty of Guadalupe Hidalgo and ceded its northern territory (the American Southwest) to the United States. The 80,000 to 100,000 Californios, Hispanos, and other Mexicans living in the Southwest were automatically granted U.S. citizenship. The Spanish-speaking people that had lived in the Southwest since 1598 were now forced to learn a new language and modify their political and cultural orientation to Euro America and its English-based political system and values. A similar imperial and colonial process took place in Puerto Rico after President William McKinley defeated Spain in the U.S.–Spanish War of 1898 and brought the island and its people into the American commonwealth.[3]

Although in theory the peace treaties with Mexico and Spain promised Latinos the same rights and privileges as all other U.S. citizens, in practice the newly created Mexican Americans and Puerto Rican Americans were often looked down upon and discriminated against. President James Buchanan harbored highly derogatory views about Mexicans whom he had previously described as "imbecile," "indolent," and a "mongrel" race. These kinds of sentiments along with the growing nativism in once Mexican and Spanish lands were fed by notions of Manifest Destiny, Euro-American and Protestant exceptionalism, white supremacy, fears of miscegenation, and notions that Mexicans and Puerto Ricans were under the "yoke," "bondage," and "tyranny" of "Papism."[4]

As a result, Mexicans, Puerto Ricans, and other Latinos lost some of their civil rights promised under treaties with Mexico and Spain. Mario Barrera and other scholars argue that Latinos were treated as an internal colony within the United States that was economically, culturally, and politically marginalized, segregated, and exploited. Many of those who resisted suffered political, ecclesiastical, social, and legal marginalization. Fear of revolt against Anglo-American rule in the Southwest resulted in racial-ethnic conflict along the border between 1860 and 1920, during which time hundreds of Mexican Americans and Mexican nationals were lynched, shot, and executed, often without due process or access to a speedy and fair trial. Historians and sociologists have estimated that a minimum of 597 Mexican Americans and Mexican nationals were lynched and killed in the Southwest between 1848 and 1928. In fact, they argue that between 1848 and 1879 more Mexicans were lynched as a percentage of their population in the Southwest than were blacks in the Deep South during this same period. From 1880 to 1930, Mexican Americans and Mexicans shared a similar lynching rate (27.4 per 100,000) with their black counterparts (32.4 per 100,000).[5]

Scholars have argued that Catholic and Protestant churches did little to aid Latinos during this tumultuous period and in some cases tacitly turned a blind eye to the oppressive conditions under which Latinos lived and worked.[6] While it is no doubt true that some clergy did little, if anything, to alleviate the suffering of Latinos, there is also a growing body of evidence to suggest that other clergy fought on their behalf. This scholarship paints a much more nuanced and complicated picture. It suggests that Latino political, civic, and social movements have been influenced and in some cases profoundly shaped by religious leaders, laity, symbols, rhetoric, churches, and ideology. They point out how Latino clergy and lay leaders in particular drew on their faith traditions and status as clergy or lay leaders to protest the oppressive political, economic, and social conditions under which Latinos had to live and work.[7] They used their moral authority and clergy status to call on U.S. society to live up to its ideals of liberty and justice for all.

One of the first U.S. Latinos to do so was Father Antonio José Martínez (1793–1867) of Taos, New Mexico. Drawing upon his experience in helping to organize the New Mexico Territory for the United States in 1848 and his election as president of the New Mexico Constitutional Convention of 1850, where he served three terms in the assembly, he used his moral authority as a priest and his political platform as an assemblyman to criticize Euro-Americans for their ill treatment of Hispanos in New Mexico. Martínez was joined in his protests by other Catholic clergymen like fathers Juan Felipe Ortiz, Lucero, Forane, Manuel Gallegos (a former New Mexico delegate to the U.S. Congress in 1854), Tomás Ortiz, and other priests and lay leaders.[8]

Laity such as José Antonio Navarro and José Ramos de Zuñiga joined Latino Catholic clergy in their faith-based struggle for Latino civil and political rights. In 1854 in San Antonio, Texas, they fought a Know Nothing Party measure to restrict electoral voting to the "free white population." They protested the "spirit of intolerance against all of those who profess the Catholic faith" and the attempt to "exclude the native Catholic population . . . from their inalienable rights." They promised to "resist" all attempts to reduce the Mexican population to what amounted to "political slavery." Similarly, Rafael Romero (1850–1919) publicly criticized the decision of the New Mexico territorial governor Samuel B. Axtell in the 1880s for not granting the Jesuit-sponsored *Colegio de las Vegas* tax-exempt and degree-granting status. He accused the Euro-American provincial governor of being a "misguided" and "pathetic" Pontius Pilate, who not only failed to protect Christ but also joined in his persecution. He chided: "Am I not a Catholic citizen of a Catholic land, New Mexico? And have I not, as a New Mexican Catholic, been grossly insulted by a pathetic public official? What does it mean when a man sent to be the governor of a Catholic land, in an official message directed to Catholic legislators and to our Catholic people, piles insult upon insult against a religious order [Jesuits] of the Catholic Church?" These political activists drew on their Catholic traditions and moral framework to criticize their political and educational marginalization.[9]

As a result of these acts of defiance, the U.S. Catholic hierarchy sided with the American political establishment. Many worked to suppress the native clergy and to stop ecclesiastical and political dissent. In 1851, the Euro-American Catholic hierarchy appointed French-speaking Jean Baptiste Lamy (1814–1888) bishop (and later archbishop) of New Mexico. He moved to silence native Hispano clergy. He excommunicated Father Martínez and other Latino clergy and replaced them with compliant Euro-American, French, and Hispano clergy. He also set out to crush the Penitente Brotherhood, a powerful New Mexican Catholic lay organization that resisted Euro-American political power and its attempt to marginalize the Hispano people in their ancestral lands. Lamy's actions were often followed throughout the American Southwest. This strategy not only muted (although it did not silence) the level of Latino faith-based political, civic, and social action in the early twentieth century, but it also left the Latino community without one of its most important and powerful sets of moral and political advocates. As a result, the community was largely without a Latino moral and religious voice in the face of exploitation, abuse, and discrimination in the American Southwest prior to 1910.[10]

The move to silence and marginalize the native priesthood along with the shift away from National Catholic parishes (ostensibly to avoid segregation and promote assimilation and Americanization) could not have taken place at a more inopportune time. Mob justice and lynching was widespread along the United States–Mexico border. The growth of U.S.-built railroads in Mexico along with U.S. employment opportunities, the Mexican Revolution (1910–1917), and other push-pull social and economic factors propelled more than one million Mexicans across the U.S. border between 1880 and 1920. As a result of nativist fears, the U.S. government set up the Border Patrol in 1924 to prevent illegal entries and laid out strict immigration requirements. Nativism, the Ku Klux Klan, white supremacy, and segregation made life difficult for most Mexican Americans living in the Southwest. Many of their civil rights were systematically denied them through legal segregation and other forms of discrimination in housing, public schooling, and medical services. The Great Depression and scarcity of employment spurred on this nativism as the U.S. government repatriated more than 500,000 Mexicans back to Mexico in the early 1930s, many of which were U.S.-born citizens. During World War II, Latino youth were incarcerated, targeted for abuse, and were accused of instigating the Zoot Suit Riots in Los Angeles in the 1940s. They were swiftly condemned as un-American and as criminals.[11]

The decline in native Latino Catholic clergy together with an increase in Mexican immigration between 1880 and the 1940s created a leadership vacuum in the Latino community that was filled in large part by Catholic lay activists and by Latino mutual aid societies (*mutualistas*), many of which were originally faith-based and supported by Catholic and Protestant churches. They in turn gave birth to and provided leadership training for a growing number of ostensibly secular Mexican American civil rights organizations like the Primero Congreso Mexicanista (1911), La Liga Protectora (1914), the League of United Latin American Citizens (LULAC) (1929), Congreso del Pueblo de Habla Española (1938), and the G. I. Forum (1944). These organizations fought for civil rights. Their work resulted in a number of legal victories such as the *Méndez v. Westminster School District of Orange County* in California (1946) and the *Delgado v. Bastrop Independent School District* in Texas (1948) decisions in which the courts ruled that the segregation of children of Mexican ancestry in public schools was unconstitutional. These decisions paved the way for and were cited by the majority opinion in the landmark *Brown v. Board of Education of Topeka* Supreme Court decision in 1954, which overturned *Plessy v. Ferguson* (1896) by outlawing school segregation on the basis of race.[12]

During this period many of these mutual aid societies and the civil rights organizations that they helped spawn severed their loose ties with churches and faith-based organizations. This diluted their original orientation and religiously infused moral authority. As a result, they lost a key platform from which to critique American society. For this reason, they did not receive the same kind of pervasive and long-term grassroots spiritual formation and infusion of religious values, rhetoric, and leadership as their African American counterparts. The few remaining Latino priests and lack of Latino bishops only accentuated this problem. For these reasons, to this day many Latino civil rights organizations do not have vibrant ties to Latino churches and grassroots faith organizations. This is why since the 1960s a growing number of Latino Catholic and Protestant faith-based civil rights and community organizations like Católicos por la Raza; Las Hermanas; Priests Associated for Religious, Educational, and Social Rights (PADRES); Communities Organized for Public Service (COPS); United Neighborhoods Organization (UNO); the Latino Pastoral Action Center (LPAC); the Alianza de Ministerios Evangélicos Nacionales (AMEN); Nueva Esperanza; the National Hispanic Christian Leadership Conference (NHCLC), and many others have become active in political, civic, and social action and why some participated in recent political mobilization efforts in the 2004 election.[13]

Religion played a key role in shaping at least two and perhaps all four of the principal architects of the Mexican American civil rights movement: César Chávez, Reies López Tijerina, José Ángel Gutiérrez, and Rodolfo "Corky" González. Chávez and Tijerina were profoundly influenced by their Roman Catholic and Pentecostal faith traditions. They were also influenced by Catholic encyclicals on the rights of labor, Mohandas Gandhi's teaching on nonviolent resistance (satyagraha), mainline Protestant teachings on the Social Gospel, Martin Luther King Jr. and African American political protest, and Jewish social activism. The faith-influenced activism during the Mexican American and African American civil rights movements also later indirectly shaped the leaders and the rhetoric in the Sanctuary movement, protests against Proposition 187 in California, the Vieques controversy in Puerto Rico, the Elían González conflict in Miami, and in the 2006 debate over Comprehensive Immigration Reform.[14]

Not all American presidents and presidential candidates have been indifferent to Latino suffering. In fact, many made common cause and fought to uphold their civil rights. One of the first examples in the post-1960 period was President Dwight D. Eisenhower's decision to authorize Operation Pedro Pan in 1961 to work with Protestant, Catholic, and Jewish relief agencies and faith-based social organizations to bring over fourteen thousand Cuban children to the United States in the wake of Fidel Castro's communist revolution. Among these children was Mel Martínez, senator of the key swing state of Florida. Lyndon B. Johnson's civil rights (1964) and voting rights (1965) acts also directly empowered Mexican Americans throughout the Southwest. Robert Kennedy's decision to fly out to California to take communion with César Chávez to end his twenty-five-day spiritual fast during the United Farm Worker's struggle was perhaps the most famous example of mixing religion and politics. President Ronald Reagan's decision to grant what many critics claim amounted to amnesty to 2,700,000 undocumented immigrants in the United States through his Immigration Reform and Control Act in 1986 also helped him garner strong Latino support. Whether or not George W. Bush's decision (along with John McCain, Hillary Clinton, Barack Obama, Ted Kennedy) to use Catholic and faith-based language and moral arguments to push for Comprehensive Immigration Reform will garner any long-term Latino support is uncertain. However, what is clear is that presidential actions are critical in establishing a public and symbolic sense of solidarity with the Latino community. These actions have also had the collateral benefit of reinforcing the longstanding support of Cuban Americans and Mexican Americans for the Republican and Democratic parties.[15]

HISTORIOGRAPHY ON LATINO RELIGION,
POLITICS, AND THE PRESIDENCY

Presidential outreach to the Latino community is a direct product of its seismic numerical growth. However, this growth has not translated into decisive political clout because less than 60 percent of Latinos vote in presidential elections. The poor turnout is shaped by low levels of voter mobilization. Sidney Verba, Kay Lehman Scholzman, and Henry E. Brady argue in their landmark book, *Voice and Equality: Civic Voluntarism in American Society*, that this is because Latinos tend to attend Catholic churches that provide fewer leadership and capacity-building skills and opportunities that can later be transferred into the political arena.[16] They argue that Latino Protestants were more likely to engage in political activities like voter mobilization not because Catholic churches are apolitical but rather because they have fewer small-group activities and other venues in which Latinos can develop skills that can in turn be transferred over into the political arena. Latino Protestants were three times more likely than Catholics to report a "skill learning opportunity," they reported. They hypothesize that this is because Latino Protestants devote twice (2.1 hours versus 1 hour for Catholics) as much time to religious and nonreligious activities (both inside and outside of the church) as Catholics.[17]

Verba, Schlozman, and Brady's findings have been challenged by Michael Jones-Correa and David L. Leal, who argue that recent surveys indicate that Latino Catholics are more likely than Protestant Evangelicals to develop civic skills and to participate in political activities.[18] Louis DeSipio confirms this view and argues that Latinos who practice non-Catholic faiths are less likely to have voted by a margin of about 30 percent. He argues that although it is true that Latino participation is undeniably lower than other racial and ethnic groups in the United States, it is not due to the high rates of Catholic identity. Latino Catholics are more likely than Latino Protestants to report that their churches have become more socially and politically involved in recent years. The change in Latino political preference is "almost exclusively in Protestant voters, who make up one-third of the Latino electorate," he argues.[19] Some scholars believe this is because Latino Evangelical support for Bush "mirrors larger political trends in American politics over the last four decades."[20]

Leal, Barreto, Lee, and de la Garza argue that although Evangelicals did support Bush in 2004, overall Latino religious conservatives did not support Bush in disproportionately large enough numbers to help push the national overall Latino vote to the 44 and 45 percent figures found by the National Election Pool (NEP) and the *Los Angeles Times*. They further argue that non-Catholic Christians constituted only 18 percent of the Latino electorate (a figure at odds with DeSipio's one-third) and that there is no evidence that Latino non-Catholics were highly mobilized. This led them to conclude that it is unlikely that non-Catholics turned out in sufficient numbers to raise Bush's support to 44 or 45 percent.[21]

U.S. LATINO POPULATION, TRENDS, AND RELIGIOUS CLASSIFICATION

In order to determine the influence of religious affiliation on the Latino vote, we first have to ascertain a demographic profile of the size and diversity of the religious community. According to the U.S. Census Bureau, the Latino community has blossomed from 22.4 million persons in 1990 to 46 million in 2008. This does not include 4 million people living on the island of Puerto Rico (all of whom have U.S. citizenship but cannot vote in presidential races) and 10 to 12 million undocumented immigrants. In total, there are 58 to 60 million Latinos living in the United States and Puerto Rico. Latinos surpassed the African American community as the nation's largest minority in 2003. They are now the largest minority in twenty-three states, including every state in New England, the Southwest, and the Pacific Northwest. The population is also rapidly moving into the South and Midwest. The fastest Latino growth rates from 2000 to 2006 were in Arkansas (60.9 percent), Georgia (59.4 percent), South Carolina (57.4 percent), Tennessee (55.5 percent), and North Carolina (54.9 percent). The Pew Hispanic Center in Washington, D.C., projects that people of Latin American and Hispanic descent will make up 29 percent (129 million) of the U.S. population by 2050. The Latino population is hardly monolithic. People of Mexican ancestry make up 64 percent (29.4 million) of all U.S. Latinos, followed by Puerto Ricans (9 percent or 4 million), other Hispanics (7.7 percent or 3.4 million), Central Americans (7.6 percent or 3.4 million), South Americans—primarily Columbians (5.5 percent or 2.4 million), Cubans (3.4 percent or 1.5 million), and Dominicans (2.8 percent or 1.2 million).

One of the most effective avenues to reach the Latino community is through clergy, churches, and faith-based organizations, which have been largely overlooked as a source for political mobilization by presidential candidates until the 1990s. Religious constituencies are especially eager to become involved because most of the attention has focused largely on important secular political organizations like the National Council of La Raza, the League of United Latin American Citizens (LULAC), the Mexican American Legal Defense and Educational Fund (MALDEF), and other organizations. Religious groups are much more open to Republican political, social, and moral views because of the Latino community's culturally and morally conservative views on abortion, same-sex marriage, school vouchers, faith-based initiatives, and other church-state issues.

Interpreting the influence of Latino religion in American presidential politics is fraught with a number of methodological and interpretive difficulties and limitations. This has led to wide range of interpretations on Catholic and Protestant religious affiliation and how these communities vote in presidential politics. While some scholars have argued that the Latino Catholic community has dropped to 50 percent of the U.S. Latino population, others have argued that it is a high as 76 percent. These differences are the direct result of a number of methodological and sampling limitations such as conducting surveys in English only in urban centers and privileging a Euro-American mainline Protestant classification system, all of which skew the findings in favor of second- and third-generation respondents, who are more likely to attend English-language churches that tend to be Protestant. Many of these surveys also do not include a Latino Protestant over-sample for in-depth comparative analyses and do not ask respondents that self-identified as other Christian, something else, other religion, and nondenominational to specify their particular religious tradition. This led to very large groups of Latino respondents being misclassified as non-Christian, secular, or as having no religion.

In order to analyze and overcome these limitations, we will draw upon the Hispanic Churches in American Public Life research project. It fielded three major surveys in cooperation with Virgilio Elizondo and the Mexican American Cultural Center (MACC), Jesse Miranda and the Alianza de Ministerio Evangélicos Nacionales (AMEN), Gastón Espinosa of Claremont McKenna College, and Harry Pachon, Rodolfo O. de la Garza, and Jongho Lee of the Tomás Rivera Policy Institute (TRPI), and included a bilingual national random sample 19-minute, 63-question telephone survey on Latino religion and politics. The HCAPL national survey has several important limitations such as surveying adults eighteen years of age or older that had telephones. Notwithstanding these limitations, it also has a number of important advantages such as being a large (n = 2,060), national, Latino-framed, bilingual survey fielded in urban and rural areas. It also included a large Protestant over-sample for in-depth analyses. Perhaps most importantly, it asked Latinos that self-identified as "independent/non-denominational," "other Christian," "something else," "other religious tradition or denomination," "other religion," and "don't know/unspecified" to specify their particular tradition, if any. Many scholars often assume that these survey respondents are (a) not Protestant, (b) have no religion or are secular, (c) are disenchanted with traditional religion in general and Christianity in particular, and (d) that these disparate groups can be treated and analyzed as one cohort. As a result of being able to identify the religious tradition or spirituality of almost all of the respondents in these categories, we were able to ascertain the religious affiliation of a very large group of respondents normally left out of analyses, unclassified, misclassified or included in with seculars, atheist, agnostics, or those having no religion. In our analyses, we found that the vast majority (50 percent to 77 percent) of these respondents self-identified as born-again Christian, attended church almost every week or more (52 percent to 67 percent), and supported prayer in public schools (59 percent to 87 percent), all views and high rates of participation normally associated with Protestant Evangelical and other conservative forms of Christianity. This problematizes some of the past sociological and political science survey research, analyses, and conclusions because many of these respondents are being inadvertently misclassified as other religion, secular, or as having no religious preference or even no religion when this is often not the case.[22]

In light of the above limitations in classifying Latino religious identity, we created a more refined framework based on the HCAPL national survey findings and over 266 community profile field interviews with people in 45 congregations representing 25 religious traditions in 8 urban and rural areas. We believe that this classification system, although imperfect, nonetheless reflects the Latino community. We found that it was possible to classify virtually every respondent within existing traditions.[23]

We broke Protestants down into three subcategories, because while it is true that in Latin America most Protestants call themselves "evangélicos" regardless of their denominational affiliation, most Protestants in the United States are not immigrants and many second- and third- generation Protestants reflect many of the same complex social views of their Euro-American and African American Pentecostal, evangelical non-Pentecostal, and mainline Protestant counterparts. We also did this because we knew from our field research over the past decade and recent community profile interviews that non-Pentecostal Evangelicals and Pentecostals were the largest subsets of Latino evangelical Christianity and that they differed in their class location and political and social views. While in some cases these distinctions are minor, in other cases they are significant. Perhaps most important, we also separated Jehovah's Witnesses and Mormons into a separate category called alternative Christian for three simple reasons. First, they do not consider themselves Protestants and historic Protestants do not consider them Protestant. Second, because we knew from our field and survey research that Jehovah's Witnesses and Mormons were numerically large in number. They are more numerous than all Baptists and five of the six largest mainline Protestant traditions combined. And third, because they had unusually low rates of political and civic engagement. Thus it would not only be historically, theologically, and sociologically inaccurate to classify them as Protestant, but their large numbers would also bias the findings in favor for "Protestants" in a way that did not reflect the reality of either community.

NATIONAL U.S. LATINO RELIGIOUS PROFILE

In light of this refined classification system and taxonomy, what did we find? The HCAPL national survey found that 93 percent of U.S. Latinos self-identified as Christian or with a Christian tradition, movement, or experience, 6 percent had no religious preference, 1 percent practiced another world religion, and less than one percent were atheist or agnostic.[24]

Despite the high level of homogeneity, the religious marketplace is becoming denominationally diverse and pluralistic. Of those who self-identified as Christian, 70 percent self-identified as Roman Catholic, and 30 percent (13.8 million) reported practicing another tradition or something else.[25] A full 23 percent (10.58 million) self-identified as Protestant (20 percent or 9.2 million) or alternative Christian (Jehovah's Witness, Mormon, other [3 percent]), the latter of which are often mistakenly classified as Protestant or Evangelical. When refined further, the HCAPL survey found that 77 percent of all Latino non-Catholics are Protestant or alternative Christian. Of this group, 85 percent self-identify as Protestant (i.e., mainline, evangelical, Pentecostal). Perhaps more surprising, 88 percent of all Latino Protestants are associated with an evangelical denomination or identify as "born-again" and 64 percent are associated with Pentecostal or Charismatic denominations and/or being Pentecostal, Charismatic, or Spirit-filled.[26]

When the Protestant and alternative Christian groups were broken down further and when we placed those who specified their traditions in their respective categories (e.g., "United Pentecostal" with Pentecostal and "Christian Reform Church" with Evangelical, "United Church of Christ" with mainline, "Buda" with world religion, etc.), we found that 7.72 percent self-identified with evangelical traditions, 7.72 percent self-identified with Pentecostal/Charismatic traditions, 4.4 percent self-identified with mainline Protestant traditions, 3 percent self-identified with alternative Christian traditions like the Jehovah's Witnesses and Mormons, and 1 percent identified with a world religion or metaphysical tradition other than Christianity.

The massive growth of evangelical and Pentecostal Protestantism is consistent with the work of Andrew Greeley, who reported that he found in his analyses of the General Social Survey (GSS) over a twenty-five-year period that one out of seven Hispanics had left the Catholic Church in less than a quarter of a century and that as many as six hundred thousand Latinos may be "defecting" from the Catholic Church every year. He warned that if this "hemorrhaging" continues for the next twenty-five years that half of all American Hispanics will not be Catholic.[27]

The HCAPL survey confirmed these high defection rates. It found that for every one Latino that "recently" returned to Catholicism (5.5 percent of all non-Catholics or 759,000), five "recently left" it (12.4 percent or 3.99 million). Contrary to popular perception, this growth was not largely restricted to what many scholars have described as religiously vulnerable first-generation immigrants seeking acceptance in American society, as 57 percent of all Latinos who said that they had recently converted from Catholicism to Protestantism were second- or third-generation U.S. citizens, a fact that has potential implications for politics and presidential elections. Supporting this demographic shift, Catholic affiliation drops from 74 percent among first-generation Latinos to 62 percent by the third generation. Protestant religious affiliation simultaneously increases from one in six among first-generation Latinos to almost one in three by the third generation. The two main reasons why the overall percentage of Latino Catholics has remained around 70 percent are high Catholic birthrates and high immigration rates from Latin America and especially from Mexico, a country that has one of the highest rates of Catholicism (85 percent) in the world. It is also due to the creative work of Latino priests, Catholic youth programs, social programs aimed at the poor and immigrants, increased lay participation, and especially the growth of the Catholic Charismatic movement.

This study expands Greeley's findings on the religious identity of these Protestants. He reported that almost half of all Latino Protestants "belong to moderate or even liberal Protestant denominations." We found that only 14.8 percent of all Latino non-Catholics self-identified with mainline Protestant traditions and that a high percentage of these said they were born again (43 percent) or Pentecostal, Charismatic, or Spirit-filled (21 percent). The vast majority of Latino Protestants and alternative Christians self-identify with theologically and morally conservative religious traditions, although, as we shall see shortly, not necessarily politically conservative ones. Furthermore, seven of the ten largest Latino-serving non-Catholic denominations and traditions in the United States are Pentecostal, Evangelical, and alternative Christian.[28] Not withstanding these important distinctions, all combined there are now more Latino Protestants (9.2 million) than Jews, Muslims, Episcopalians, or Presbyterians in the United States both in terms of raw percentages and numbers.

Evangelical and Pentecostal spirituality has also influenced Latino Roman Catholicism and mainline Protestantism. The HCAPL survey found that one in four (26 percent) Catholics reported having had a born-again experience with

Jesus Christ and more than one in five (22 percent) reported being Catholic, born-again, and Pentecostal, Charismatic, or Spirit-filled. The overlay between being born-again and Charismatic is strong, with 86 percent of those who said they were born-again also said they were Charismatic. These findings help to explain why 37 percent (17 million) of the U.S. Latino community self-identifies as born-again and 28 percent (12.9 million) as Pentecostal, Charismatic, or Spirit-filled, a figure that matches the percentage (27 percent) of the Pentecostal/Charismatic Christians in Latin America. Today there are more than 150 million Protestant Pentecostals/Charismatics (77 million) and Catholic Charismatics (73 million) in Latin America. Protestant Pentecostals in Latin America attend 1,991 denominations, 1,767 of which are independent and indigenous with no administrative, financial, or organic ties to the United States. Many of these denominations have sent missionaries to the United States (what I call the back-to-the-future phenomenon) to evangelize the nation's 46 million Latinos.[29] These transdenominational religious movements and experiences provide a religious and experiential basis for potential coalition-building across denominational and political party lines that can (because of their large numbers) have significant consequences in American politics and presidential elections. However, our research indicates that this overlap is not likely to be realized, as Latino Catholic Charismatics reflect the voting patterns of their non-Charismatic Catholic rather than their Protestant Pentecostal/Charismatic counterparts. Furthermore, many do not vote.

Nondenominational and independent Christian groups are also driving much of this growth as over 22 percent of all Latino Christians self-identified as nondenominational or other Christian. A clear majority of the nondenominational respondents self-identified as born-again and in many cases Pentecostal or Charismatic, although a small but notable number are also Baptist in history, polity, and orientation. We will see in the pages that follow that employing a more refined and complex religious system and framework challenges several prevailing assumptions about Latino Protestant and evangelical numerical size, diversity, political party affiliation, voter turnout, and presidential election voting patterns.

LATINO POLITICAL IDENTITY AND
VOTING PATTERNS: 1996–2004

Latino Presidential Voting: 1960–1992

The impact of these demographic and religious shifts are being felt in presidential politics. Although Latinos historically favored the Republican Party like their African American counterparts, they likewise underwent a political shift in the 1930s through the coalition-building outreach of Franklin Delano Roosevelt and his New Deal programs aimed at relieving unemployment, poverty, and hopelessness during the Great Depression. Despite Roosevelt's programs, many Latinos did not benefit greatly, either because the jobs gave preference to Euro-Americans or because they could not speak English or pass basic literacy tests. Notwithstanding these limitations, Latinos viewed the Party as a place where their voices and stories increasingly mattered. The key historical events that helped solidify this Democratic orientation among Mexican Americans and Puerto Ricans were FDR's New Deal programs; JFK's Democratic nomination and presidency; Lyndon B. Johnson's land-mark civil rights legislation and the Great Society; and Bobby Kennedy's highly publicized support of César Chávez and the United Farm Workers' struggle in 1968. Some of these factors led to the creation of the famous *¡Viva Kennedy!* clubs in the 1960s, which mobilized a generation of Latinos and persuaded them to join the Democratic ranks and begin participating in presidential politics. As a result, the Democratic Party won the overwhelm-ing support of Mexican Americans and many other Latinos (except Cubans) during the 1960s.

The preference for Democratic presidential candidates began to shift with the candidacy of Richard Nixon, who took 36 percent of the Mexican Ameri-can vote in 1972, largely due to his California credentials, anticommunist rhetoric, and promise to end the war in Vietnam. After the election and in the wake of Watergate, this surge in Latino support returned to the previous 1960s levels with Jimmy Carter, but rebounded again with another Califor-nian, a movie actor turned Cold War warrior named Ronald Reagan. He took 37 percent of the Latino vote in 1980 due to his proposed tax cuts, promise to bring American hostages home from Iran, strong opposition to communism, and because of his strong support for traditional family values— despite hav-ing passed as Governor of California one of the most liberal pro-abortion bills in the United States. His Latino support slipped slightly in 1988 and slightly further still for his successor, George H. W. Bush. However, even Bush was able to take over 30 percent of the Latino vote.[30]

The Republican progress among Latinos was all but washed away in 1992 as Bill Clinton won an overwhelming majority of the Latino vote across ethnic and religious traditions, although still not at the historic levels Latinos gave JFK and LBJ. His youthfulness, gregarious spirit, working-class background, and progressive attitudes toward race, education, social uplift, and church-state limited partnerships to alleviate inner city suffering and hopelessness resonated with Latinos across ethnic lines. Exactly how religion shaped the Mexican American and Latino vote during this pre-2000 period is largely un-

Table 10.1: Latino National Vote, 1960–1992

Year – Latino Electorate	Democratic %	Republican %	Other %
1960 – Mexican American	85	15	0
1964 – Mexican American	90	10	0
1968 – Mexican American	87	10	3
1972 – Mexican American	64	36	0
Mexican American	85	15	0
1976 – Mexican American	92	8	0
Latinos	82	18	0
1980 – Latinos	56	37	7
1984 – Latinos (CBS)	66	34	0
Latinos (NBC)	68	32	0
Latinos (ABC)	56	44	0
1988 – Latinos (CBS)	70	30	0
Latinos (NBC)	70	30	0
Latinos (ABC)	69	31	0
Latinos (LA Times)	62	38	0
1992 – Latinos (VRS)	62	24	14
Latinos (LA Times)	53	31	16

Source: Louis DeSipio, *Counting on the Latino Vote*, 31.

known because the data is very limited, regional, and almost entirely based on English-language surveys, which biases the findings in favor of second- and third-generation Latinos, who tend to be more Protestant. Thus, it is possible that Nixon's and Reagan's high levels of Latino support are inflated due to the methodological sampling limitations noted above. However, even if this were the case, they still would not affect the overall margin of victory every four years.

Latino Presidential Voter Turnout by Religious Tradition, 1996–2004

The first place to begin any analysis of Latino religion and presidential politics is voter turnout. The conventional wisdom is that Latino Catholics are more likely to participate in politics and vote than their Protestant counterparts because they have a longer history of faith-based political, civic, and social action. As we have seen, it is certainly true that Latino Catholics have a rich history of civic engagement. This history has been confirmed by a number of historians and social scientists.

The findings from the HCAPL national survey confirm this view, but also refine and expand our understanding of it by pointing out that Catholics do not vote at higher rates than all Protestants uniformly across all countries of origin, genders, and religious affiliations (see table 10.2). Nationwide, in 2000 only 57 percent of all Latinos reported voting. Voter turnout varied by country of origin, with Cubans (75 percent) having the highest rates followed by Puerto Ricans (60 percent), U.S.-born Latinos (59 percent), other Latinos (57 percent), Central Americans (47 percent), and Mexicans (39 percent), whose low voter rates are due directly to their lower rates of citizenship. The HCAPL survey also found that women (61 percent) were more likely then men (53 percent) to vote in presidential elections and perhaps predictably, third generation Latinos (63 percent) were much more likely to say they voted than first (54 percent) and second (52 percent) generation respondents.

Contrary to some of the previous elections, in 2000 Latino Protestants were slightly more likely (61 percent) to say they voted than their Catholic (59 percent) counterparts if we exclude alternative Christian groups like the Jehovah's Witnesses and Mormons, two traditions that do not self-identify as Protestant. When these findings are analyzed further by religious family groupings (Catholic, mainline, Pentecostal, evangelical non-Pentecostal denominationally affiliated, and alternative Christian), we found that both mainline Protestants (71 percent) and Evangelicals (59 percent) actually re-ported as high or higher rates of voter turnout on Election Day than Catho-lics (59 percent). Pentecostals were only slightly less likely (58 percent) than Catholics to vote on Election Day. The disparity in findings are due to the tendency of many scholars to lump alternative Christians together with other Protestants in general or evangelical or conservative Protestants in particular. This distorts the overall findings because alternative Christians were four or five times less likely (14 percent) to say that they voted than their Protestant counterparts. This is important because they make up size-able percentage (13 percent) of all non-Catholic Christians. When we broke down Latino voter turnout by religious denomination or tradition, we found that Catholics ranked ninth on voter turnout among all Latino religious traditions, behind eight Protestant traditions, five of which were mainline and three of which were Pentecostal and Evangelical. Still another large Pentecostal tradition tied Catholic voter turnout. Furthermore, a number of other large Pentecostal and evangelical traditions had only slightly lower rates of voter participation than Catholics.

What is interesting about these findings is that most Latino mainline Prot-estants were significantly (10–15 percent) more likely to stay that they voted

Table 10.2:   Latino Voter Turnout by Religion

"Did you vote . . . ?"

	Yes	No	Ineligible	Total
Latinos Nationwide	57	36	7	100
Roman Catholic	59	34	7	100
Protestant	60	35	5	100
Mainline Protestant	71	26	3	100
Evangelical-Non-Pentecostal	59	34	7	100
Pentecostal/Charismatic	58	38	4	100
Alternative Christian	14	76	10	100
Independent and Nondenominational	59	35	6	100
Other Religion	60	32	8	100
No Religious Preference	47	41	12	100
Atheist/Agnostic	42	37	21	100
Denomination/Tradition				
Jehovah's Witness	5	78	17	100
Assemblies of God (Pentecostal)	65	33	2	100
Pentecostal Church of God (Pentecostal)	49	49	2	100
Assembly of Christian Churches (Pentecostal)	58	36	6	100
American Baptist	76	24	0	100
Southern Baptist	67	33	0	100
7th-Day Adventist	38	43	19	100
Mormon	29	71	0	100
Apostolic Assembly (Pentecostal)/Oneness	76	16	8	100
Lutheran–All Varieties	100	0	0	100
Methodist–All Varieties	61	33	6	100
Presbyterian–All Varieties	90	10	0	100
Episcopalian	75	25	0	100
Born-Again Protestant	63	32	5	100
Non-Born-Again Protestant	57	41	2	100
Born-Again Catholic	59	37	4	100
Non-Born-Again Catholic	58	35	7	100

Source: HCAPL Survey.

than other Protestant bodies. This is due to higher levels of education and citizenship. However, not all mainline and Pentecostal Protestants shared the same level of political participation in presidential elections. Latino Methodists only equaled the national average. Large Pentecostal bodies like the Apostolic Assembly and Assemblies of God founded in the Southwest with a large Mexican American/Southwestern base, were more likely to vote than both Catholics and Puerto Rican-origin Pentecostal traditions like the Pentecostal Church of God and the Assembly of Christian Churches. This may be due to the fact that these movements are chronologically older in age and can tap into larger Euro-American (General Council of the Assemblies of God, United Pentecostal Church) and African American (Pentecostal Assemblies of the World) parent or sister denominations, along with their acculturating institutions, literature, and resources.

Somewhat counterintuitive, the HCAPL survey found that Latino Protestants who self-identified as born-again Christian were also more likely (63 percent) to report having voted than either born-again Catholics (59 percent) or non-born-again Catholics (58 percent). If being born-again is considered one of defining marks of being Evangelical, then this finding along with those above indicate that Latino Protestants in general and Evangelicals in particular are as likely or more likely to report having voted in a presidential election than Catholics. However, it is interesting to note that being born-again only slightly increased the likelihood of voting among born-again Catholics. Their voting patterns largely resembled non-Charismatic Catholics, leading us to conclude that being Charismatic does not always result in any major trans-denominational coalition building or voting patterns. This could, of course, change in the future.

Latino Religion and Political Party Identity, 2000–2004

Although Latinos have a long record of voting Democrat, there were major deviations from this pattern for Nixon and Reagan. These deviations re-emerged again in 2000 despite Clinton's overwhelming success and favorability among Latinos. That year Latino Democratic Party affiliation shifted to 47 percent (see table 10.3). However, this did not translate into a direct benefit for Republicans as only 15 percent chose to self-identify with the party of Lincoln. The biggest surprise is that almost 38 percent of Latinos self-identified as politically independent or something else. Despite this, the Democratic Party maintained a decisive three-to-one advantage among Latino mainline Protestants (51 percent) and Catholics (50 percent) and more than a two to one advantage among Latino Pentecostals and Evangelicals—far surpassing Democratic support by their Euro-American mainline Protestant and Catholic counterparts. What is equally interesting is that a plurality of Latino Evangelicals (43 percent) and Pentecostals (47 percent) also self-identified as Democrat. The higher rates of Pentecostal Democratic Party affiliation is in large part shaped by the fact that Latino Pentecostals have higher rates of poverty (49 percent versus 41 percent) and lower levels of educational attainment than their evangelical counterparts (33 percent versus 45 percent for grade school or less), both of which are often correlated with greater Democratic partisanship.

It is interesting to note that in 2000 party affiliation did not differ by more than four percentage points between Catholics, mainline Protestants, and Pentecostals. This challenges the notion that Latino Evangelicals and Pentecostals are Republicans as a plurality of Pentecostals self-identified as Democrats and only 20 percent as Republican. Despite this high degree of party affiliation across religious family groupings, it is not true to therefore say that religion had no impact on party affiliation. Jehovah's Witnesses were, for example, four or five times more likely than Evangelicals to say that they did not affiliate with either Democrats or Republicans. Democratic Party affiliation wavered considerably by religious traditions with Presbyterians reporting the highest affiliation (76 percent) and Witnesses offering the lowest (10 percent). The differences for Latino Republican Party affiliation were much smaller, with Latino Mormons having the highest party affiliation (33 percent) and the Jehovah's Witnesses the lowest (3 percent). Despite the relatively strong affiliation with the Democratic Party, overall party support was much softer than one might have imagined coming off the Clinton presidency. Although counterintuitive, the relatively low levels of Latino Democratic Party affiliation by religious family grouping and individual denominations did not translate into significant Republican gains. In fact, less than one in five Latinos in the major religious groupings considered themselves Republican.

What factors contributed to the low levels of Democratic and Republican Party identification? The first is the fact that 35–38 percent of all U.S. Latinos are immigrants and are thus new to the American political system. Second, while Democrats reflect the Latino commitments to civil rights, social and economic justice, and racial equality, Republicans reflect many of their attitudes and values on abortion, same-sex marriage, vouchers, prayer in school, and charitable choice/faith-based initiatives. Third, Bush was a relatively unknown candidate in the U.S. Latino community outside of Texas. These factors may help to explain why a very high percentage of Latinos nationwide self-identified as politically independent or something else (38 percent) in 2000. A significant percentage of Latino Catholics (37 percent), traditional Evangelicals (37 percent), Pentecostals (33 percent), and mainline Protestants (32 percent) self-identified as being politically independent or something else. An overwhelming number of alternative Christians (63 percent) reported being independent or

Table 10.3:   Latino Political Party Preference by Religion, 2000

	Democrat	Republican	Independent	Something Else
Latinos Nationwide	47	15	34	4
Roman Catholic	50	13	33	4
Protestant–two response options	67	33	0	0
Mainline Protestant	51	17	30	2
Evangelical–Non-Pentecostal	43	20	31	6
Pentecostal/Charismatic	47	20	30	3
Alternative Christian Denomination/Tradition	23	14	45	18
Jehovah's Witness	10	3	59	28
Assemblies of God	43	22	31	4
Pentecostal Church of God	50	15	33	2
Assembly of Christian Churches	55	15	28	2
American Baptist	55	29	16	0
Southern Baptist	49	24	27	0
7th-Day Adventist	50	12	21	17
Mormon	43	33	24	0
Apostolic Assembly/Oneness	62	25	13	0
Lutheran–All Varieties	34	8	58	0
Methodist–All Varieties	47	13	33	7
Presbyterian–All Varieties	72	14	14	0
Episcopalian	57	29	14	0
Independent/Non-Denominational	44	20	36	2
Other Christian	40	27	32	1
Something Else	43	18	32	7
Other Religion	44	7	30	19
World Religions	70	15	15	0
Born-Again	45	19	33	3
Non-Born-Again	50	12	33	5
Pentecostal & Charismatic	49	14	34	3
Non-Pentecostal & Charismatic	44	18	32	6

Source: HCAPL Survey

something else as well, but these data are skewed because Jehovah's Witnesses, who make up the majority of the alternative Christian sample, are discouraged from participating in politics lest they become attached to worldly pursuits. For this reason they often refuse to participate in politics, the military, and swear allegiance to the flag or their home country. Another counterintuitive finding is that a plurality of Latino born-again Catholics and Protestants self-identified as Democrats, thus challenging the widely held view that conservative born-again religiosity is automatically correlated with the Republican Party. Although it has long been understood that 20–30 percent of the Euro-American born-again community is Democrat in party affiliation and/or voting patterns, we now see that Latino born-again Christians have an even higher level of Democratic Party affiliation than their Euro-American counterparts.

Latino born-again voters (aggregate) made up a large and significant component of both the Democratic and Republican voting constituencies. Not only did 45 percent of all Latino born-again Christians self-identify as Democrat in 2000, but they also made up 40 percent of all Latino Democratic voters. They were even more critical to the Latino Republican voting bloc in 2000, where they made up 55 percent of the vote. Despite the high percentage of Latino Republican votes, only 19 percent (less than one in five) of Latino born-again Christians nationwide self-identified as Republican. More than one third of all Latino voters self-identified as Independent or something else. A similar pattern was true for Pentecostal/ Charismatic/Spirit-filled Christians, although the margin increased to three-to-one in favor of the Democratic Party. In short, Latino born-again and Pentecostal, Charismatic, and Spirit-filled Christians were much more likely to self-identify as Democrats rather than Republicans. However, because such a high percentage of this community self-identifies as independent or something else and because born-again and Pentecostals/Charismatic Christians tend to be morally and socially conservative, the Democratic Party remains vulnerable to inroads not only among those in the Party, but also among Independents.

The findings from the HCAPL national survey also challenge the perception that Republicans attract most Latinos of faith. Although 64 percent of Latino Republicans reported attending church every week or more, more than half (54 percent) of all Latino Democrats also reported the same. Furthermore, Latinos who self-identified as politically independent (49 percent) and something else (55 percent) also reported attending church every week or more. Democrats were also more likely to attract women (59 percent versus 41 percent for men) than Republicans (50 percent versus 50 percent) and a plurality of first (40 percent), second (53 percent), and third (56 percent) generation voters. Although counterintuitive at first, first generation (52 percent) Latinos rather than second (14 percent) or third (33 percent) made up a majority of all Latino Republicans. This challenges the long-standing perception that second and third generation assimilated Latinos make up the majority of Latino Republicans. When analyzed by country of origin and four response options (Republican, Democrat, independent, or something else) in the months leading up the 2000 election, we found that Puerto Ricans (69 percent) were more likely to self-identify as Democratic than other Latinos (50 percent), Central Americans (45 percent), Mexicans (34 percent), and Cubans (20 percent). Republican representation was predictably strongest among Cubans (57 percent) and then dropped considerably for Puerto Ricans (15 percent), other Latinos (13 percent), Mexicans (7 percent), and Central Americans (4 percent). We also found a very high percentage of Latinos of Mexican (59 percent), Central American (51 percent), U.S. (31 percent), Cuban (23 percent), and Puerto Rican (16 percent) ancestry who reported being either independent or something else. Although exit polls taken after the 2000 election indicate that most voted Democrat, the mere fact that so many self-identified as independent/something else is one of the reasons why they are often seen as a potential swing vote.

Latinos, Religion, and the 1996 Presidential Election: Bill Clinton and Bob Dole

The massive demographic upswing in the Latino population in the United States during the 1980s and early 1990s attracted growing attention from presidential candidates. This upsurge was due to immigration and high birth rates, guest worker programs, the civil wars in El Salvador, Guatemala, and Nicaragua, and, perhaps ironically, Ronald Reagan's 1986 Immigration Reform and Control Act, which gave amnesty to millions of immigrants who arrived in the United States prior to January 1, 1982. Reagan's conservative message of God, country, and family resonated with many Americans and Latinos. Despite Reagan's program and the high levels of Latino political party independence, in 1992 and again in 1996 Clinton captured an overwhelming majority of the Latino vote (see table 10.4). He took 62 percent of the U.S. Latino vote in 1992 and 76 percent in 1996. In 1996, he received decisive support from Latino women (82 percent versus 69 percent of men), first- (73 percent versus 18 percent), second- (82 percent versus 12 percent), and third-generation Latinos (76 percent versus 16 percent), Latinos in lower (86 percent versus 10 percent), middle (76 percent versus 17 percent), and upper ($50,000+) (64 percent versus 18 percent) income brackets, and among people of Mexican (86 percent versus 11 percent), Puerto Rican (75 percent versus 16 percent), Central American (69 percent), and even Cuban (53 percent versus 37 percent) ancestry, something many later regretted because of Clinton's handling of the Elían González and Vieques controversies, two facts that may explain why Gore's support from these communities slipped in 2000.

Clinton's strong support translated across religious family groups, where he won a decisive majority of the Latino Catholic (83 percent), mainline Protestant (78 percent), Pentecostal (69 percent), and Evangelical (53 percent) vote. He split the alternative Christian vote with Dole 43 percent to 43 percent. Bob Dole did well only among alternative Christians (43 percent) and Evangelicals (36 percent), but poorly among Pentecostals (18 percent), Catholics (11 percent), and mainline Protestants (13 percent). Ross Perot, whom many accuse of serving as a Republican spoiler, took a small percentage of the alternative Christian (14 percent), Pentecostal (9 percent), Evangelical (7 percent), mainline Protestant (6 percent), and Catholic (4 percent) votes. The remainder voted for someone else. If it is true that two-thirds of Perot's vote would have gone Republican, then it could be argued that Republican support was uniquely low.

Contrary to the stereotype that Latino Evangelical and born-again Christians vote overwhelmingly for Republican candidates, we have seen that Latino born-again Christians supported Clinton across denominational lines by large margins. His ability to talk about his Southern Baptist evangelical faith and born-again conversion experience, social justice, and the years he spent attending a Catholic parochial school and Georgetown University enabled him to take a decisive majority of Latino born-again Catholics (87 percent) and born-again Protestants (63 percent). They viewed him as a man of faith with a social-economic background not unlike their own. A similarly high percentage of Latinos who self-identified as Pentecostal, Charismatic, and Spirit-filled gave Clinton 78 percent of their vote. This is due largely to the fact that the Pentecostal and Charismatic movement largely drove the born-again identity.

Despite his overall strong support across religious traditions, Clinton found the strongest support (89 percent) among those Latinos who said that a candidate's personal faith and morals were not very relevant in their voting decision rather than among those who said it was very relevant (65 percent). He similarly was more likely to take an overwhelming majority of those Latinos who said they never read the Bible (86 percent) than those who said they read it almost every day (60 percent). He also did much better among those who said they attend church once a year or less (81 percent) than those who attend once a week or more (72 percent), although by a much smaller margin. He also took a decisive majority of those who agreed that religious leaders should influence public affairs (79 percent), approved of prayer in public schools (72 percent), opposed same-sex relationships (69 percent), and those who said that religion provided that a great deal of guidance in their day-to-day living (74 percent). Clinton did exceptionally well on topics that are normally considered Republican issues and this may help explain why he was able to capture such a high level of support across religious lines.

Table 10.4: Latino Presidential Vote by Religion, 1996

	Dole	Clinton	Perot	Someone Else
Latinos Nationwide	16	76	5	3
Roman Catholic	11	83	4	2
All Protestants	23	66	7	4
Mainline Protestant	13	78	6	3
Evangelical–Non-Pentecostal	36	53	7	4
Pentecostal	18	69	9	4
Alternative Christian	43	43	14	0
Independent and Nondenominational	35	53	6	6
Other Religion	8	77	8	7
Other Christian	28	60	12	0
Something Else	18	64	14	4
Denomination/Tradition				
Jehovah's Witness	50	50	0	0
Assemblies of God	24	62	7	7
Pentecostal Church of God	19	81	0	0
Assembly of Christian Churches	4	80	12	4
American Baptist	9	91	0	0
Southern Baptist	33	56	6	5
7th-Day Adventist	14	86	0	0
Mormon	50	25	25	0
Apostolic Assembly/Oneness	17	67	16	0
Lutheran–All Varieties	18	73	0	9
Methodist–All Varieties	14	72	14	0
Presbyterian–All Varieties	17	67	16	0
Episcopalian	0	67	17	16
Born-Again Protestant	25	63	7	5
Non-Born-Again Protestant	13	76	9	2
Born-Again Catholic	11	87	1	1
Non-Born-Again Catholic	11	82	5	2
Pentecostal & Charismatic	15	78	5	2
Non-Pentecostal/Charismatic	22	67	8	3

Source: HCAPL Survey.

Religion and the 2000 Presidential Election:
George W. Bush and Al Gore

Although Al Gore actively drew on the Clinton economic mantle to promote his presidential candidacy, in the 2000 election he did not receive the same level of Latino support as his predecessor. The HCAPL survey found that his support dropped off significantly in the months prior to the election as 44 percent of those Latinos who planned to vote for Bush in 2000 had voted for Clinton in 1996. As we shall see in the final section of this chapter, one of the reasons why Bush did so well among Latinos is that his election team decided to make religion one of the primary vehicles for reaching out to the community. This strategy was neither new to presidential politics (as we saw with Robert Kennedy in the 1960s) or to Bush's campaigns for governor of Texas. His recent adult conversion in the 1990s also served him well among born-again Catholics and Protestants, despite the fact that Gore stated that he too once had a born-again experience. This fact, along with Bush's promise to promote prayer in school, faith-based initiatives, and school vouchers for Catholic, Protestant, religious, and secular schools, also gained traction among Latinos confronted with inner city gang violence, rising rates of teenage pregnancy, and alarmingly high drop-out rates in poorly equipped schools. Bush strategically picked winning issues among Latinos as they overwhelmingly supported prayer in school (74 percent), charitable choice (70 percent), and school vouchers (60 percent).

Bush's strategy resulted in his doubling Bob Dole's Latino vote in just one election cycle. Although scholars are quick to point out that this simply re-turned the Republican share of the Latino vote to the levels during the Reagan years, it was not a foregone conclusion that any Republican candidate would double Dole's support. The HCAPL national survey (which was conducted August through October 2000), found that in a three way contest prior to the election, 38 percent of likely Latino voters nationwide stated that they planned to give their vote to George W. Bush, while 57 percent planned to give their support to Al Gore (see table 10.5). Gore's support dropped by 19 percentage points over Clinton's 76 percent in 1996. When analyzed by Protestant and Catholic identity, 33 percent of Latino Catholics planned to vote for Bush while 63 percent planned to vote for Gore. Despite losing the general Latino Protestant vote, Bush did receive a decisive majority of the Latino born-again *Protestant* vote (53 percent) over Al Gore (44 percent). Born-again Catholics broke ranks with their Protestant counterparts, giving Gore (61 percent) a higher percentage of their vote than they gave Bush (36 percent). Nationwide, 49 percent of Latino born-again Christians (aggregate) across denominational lines voted for Gore, while 48 percent voted for Bush. This was a significant drop-off from Clinton's high level of support from born-again Catholics (87 percent) and Protestants (63 percent) in 1996. Similarly, Gore's level of support from Latino Charismatic Catholics (61 percent) and Latino Pentecostal/ Charismatic Protestants (44 percent) also dropped off significantly from their support for Clinton in 1996.

However, these figures do not tell the whole story. When the fall 2000 HCAPL survey is analyzed further by religious family groups, Al Gore's level of support also declined among Catholics (63 percent), mainline Protestants (63 percent), alternative Christians (47 percent), Pentecostals (46 percent), and Evangelicals (40 percent). Gore's loss was largely Bush's gain as a majority of Evangelicals (56 percent), alternative Christians (53 percent), and Pentecostals (50 percent) indicated that they planned to vote for him in 2000. While some of them may have switched back over to vote Democrat on Election Day, these findings nonetheless signal an important shift and a trend in Republican support. By contrast, only 33 percent of the Latino Catholics and 27 percent of Latino mainline Protestants said they planned to vote for Bush, thus indicating that religious identity was a factor.

Bush was also polling more than one-third of all Latino Pentecostals/ Charismatics (39 percent), but not as well as Gore (57 percent). Gore was polling a majority of Latino Protestant Pentecostals (49 percent versus 46 percent) and Latino Catholic Charismatics (62 percent versus 35 percent). This underscores the fluidity and volatility of the Latino Catholic and Protestant electorates. It also reveals that there is not any pan-Pentecostal and Charismatic voting coalition.

Although the cell count is small and thus the findings for the smaller religious traditions must be viewed with caution and as tentative rather than conclusive, when the presidential voting pattern was further analyzed by denomination and religious tradition, Bush polled a majority of Latinos who self-identified as other Pentecostal (100 percent), Mormon (64 percent), other evangelical (62 percent), Apostolic Assembly (57 percent), Assemblies of God (56 percent), other Christian (55 percent), Southern Baptist (52 percent), and independent/nondenominational Protestant (51 percent). However, Al Gore was polling well among mainline, evangelical, and Pentecostal traditions such as Episcopalians (100 percent), Seventh-day Adventists (71 percent), American Baptists (68 percent), the Pentecostal Assembly of Christian Churches (64 percent), Methodists (64 percent), Presbyterians (57 percent), other Lutherans (55 percent), the Pentecostal Church of God (52 percent), and even the Jehovah's Witnesses (50 percent). Gore polled a plurality of those who self-identified as other religion (47 percent versus 35 percent) and something else (47 percent versus 43 percent). Although it is not surprising to note that Gore polled well among all major Latino mainline Protestant tradi-

Table 10.5:   Latino Presidential Vote by Religion, 2000

"If the presidential election were held today, would you vote for . . . ?"

	Bush	Gore	Someone Else
Latinos Nationwide	38	57	5
All Christian Groups	39	57	4
Roman Catholic	33	63	4
Protestant	47	48	5
Mainline Protestant	27	63	10
Evangelical–Non-Pentecostal	56	40	4
Pentecostal	50	46	4
Alternative Christian	53	47	0
Independent and Nondenominational	51	38	11
Other Pentecostal	100	0	0
Other Evangelical	62	38	0
Other Religion	35	47	18
Other Christian	55	38	7
Something Else	43	47	10
Denomination/Tradition			
Jehovah's Witness	33	50	17
Assemblies of God	56	36	8
Pentecostal Church of God	45	52	3
Assembly of Christian Churches	36	64	0
American Baptist	32	68	0
Southern Baptist	52	48	0
7th-Day Adventist	29	71	0
Mormon	64	36	0
Apostolic Assembly/Oneness	57	43	0
Lutheran–All Varieties	18	55	27
Methodist–All Varieties	27	64	9
Presbyterian–All Varieties	29	57	14
Episcopalian	0	100	0
Born-Again Across All Traditions	48	49	3
Born-Again Protestant	53	44	3
Non-Born-Again Protestant	26	65	9
Born-Again Catholic	36	61	3
Non-Born-Again Catholic	32	63	5
Pentecostal/Charismatic–All Traditions	39	57	4
Pentecostal/Charismatic Protestant	46	49	5
Non-Pentecostal/Charismatic	52	41	7
Pentecostal/Charismatic Catholic	35	62	3
Non-Pentecostal/Charismatic	20	70	10

Source: HCAPL Survey.

tions, it is interesting and counter-intuitive to note that he polled a majority of Latinos in two of the three largest Latino Pentecostal bodies, the fifth-largest Latino evangelical tradition, and the largest alternative Christian tradition, all of which are theologically and morally conservative—thus defying the stereotype that Democratic candidates cannot do well among Pentecostals and Evangelicals.

Bush polled better than Gore in the national average (38 percent) among those who reported that religion provides a great deal of guidance in their day-to-day living (43 percent versus 53 percent), that they were very interested in politics (43 percent versus 52 percent), that they had a lot of influence over governmental decisions (41 percent versus 56 percent), that religious leaders should try to influence public affairs (52 percent versus 42 percent), that reported high weekly church attendance (44 percent versus 52 percent), and that held an official position in their church or religious organization (43 percent versus 52 percent). He also polled well above his national share of the Latino vote among those Latinos who supported prayer in school (44 percent versus 53 percent) and opposed same-sex relations (45 percent versus 51 percent). Bush's strongest support came from those who considered themselves born-again Christians (48 percent versus 49 percent) and those who said that a political candidate's faith and morals were relevant to their decision to support him or her (49 percent versus 48 percent) (see table 10.6). Despite this, Gore received a higher level of support than Bush in virtually every category.

In the fall of 2000, the HCAPL national survey found that a clear majority of Latinos of Central American (76 percent), other Latin-American (71 percent), Mexican (68 percent), and U.S. (57 percent) origin planned to vote for Gore (see table 10.7). By contrast, a majority of Cubans (82 percent) and half of Puerto Ricans (48 percent versus 48 percent) indicated that they planned to vote for Bush. Gore polled a decisive majority of Latinos holding U.S. citizenship (57 percent versus 38 percent for Bush), women (60 percent versus 36 percent for Bush), men (52 percent versus 41 percent for Bush), and Latinos across the first (56 percent versus 42 percent), second (59 percent versus 35 percent), and third (56 percent versus 37 percent) generations, although all well below Clinton's 1996 levels. Gore also polled very well among Latinos who attended church every week or more (44 percent to 52 percent) and people in all three income categories ($24,999 or less [65 percent versus 30 percent], $25,000–$49,000 [57 percent versus 39 percent], $50,000+ [46 percent versus 43 percent]). Finally, a majority of Latinos of Mexican (49 percent) and Central American (52 percent) ancestry indicated that they planned to vote for Gore, while he split those of Puerto Rican (30 percent) and lost those of Cuban origin (13 percent), perhaps because of the Vieques and Elían González controversies.

Table 10.6: Latino Religious Practices, Political Efficacy, and Social Views, 2000

	All Latinos	Bush	Gore	Someone Else
How often do you attend church?				
Once a week or more	45	44	52	4
Almost every week	8	37	56	7
Once or twice a month	18	33	61	6
A few times a year	16	33	62	5
Once a year or less	6	32	63	5
Never	7	35	59	6
How often do you read the Bible?				
Almost every day	18	50	45	5
A few times a week	18	48	47	5
A few times a month	14	36	59	5
Once a month or less	27	33	63	4
Never	23	28	65	7
How much guidance does religion provide?				
A great deal	53	43	53	4
Quite a bit	22	38	57	5
Some	18	26	65	9
No guidance at all	7	40	52	8
How relevant is a politician's faith and morals?				
Very relevant	45	49	48	3
Somewhat relevant	31	33	62	5
No very relevant	9	28	65	7
Not relevant at all	15	26	66	8
Do you approve of prayers in public schools?				
Approve	74	44	53	3
Disapprove	26	23	68	9
What do you think of same-sex relations?				
Always wrong	65	45	51	4
Almost always wrong	6	30	63	7
Wrong only sometimes	7	34	55	11
Not wrong at all	22	28	66	6

Source: HCAPL Survey.

Table 10.7: Latino Vote by Gender, Generation, Income, Country of Origin, 2000

	Bush	*Gore*	*Someone Else*
U.S. Citizenship	38	57	5
Gender			
Male	41	52	7
Female	36	60	4
National Average	38	57	5
Generation			
First	42	56	2
Second	35	59	6
Third	37	56	7
Income			
$0–24,999	30	65	5
$25,000–$49,999	39	57	4
$50,000 and up	43	46	11
Country of Origin			
Mexico	31	68	1
Puerto Rico	48	48	4
Cuba	82	16	2
Central America	24	76	0
Other Latino	26	71	3

Source: HCAPL Survey.

Religion and the 2004 Presidential Election: George W. Bush and John Kerry

During Bush's first term as president, he worked harder than any previous American president to develop one of the most successful long-term outreach campaigns to the Latino community. He took a three-pronged approach. First he targeted Latino Catholic, mainline, evangelical, and Pentecostal clergy and lay leaders. Second, he worked directly with Latino faith-based community organizations, associations, and councils to promote a "faith-friendly," "pro-family" domestic program. Third, he appointed Latinos with open ties to the faith community to his administration. His threefold strategy to secure their support was through (1) his faith-based initiative program, (2) his administration's objection to same-sex marriage, stem cell research, partial birth abortion, and his support for his Hispanic healthy marriage initiative, and (3) developing relationships with high-profile Latino leaders like Mexican president Vicente Fox, giving speeches in Spanish, and celebrating Latino community and cultural events by decree and at the White House. These factors, along with his strong Latino support base in Texas, gave him a natural entrée into the U.S. Latino community and enabled him to secure not only a larger share of the overall Latino vote in 2004, but also a decisive majority of the Latino Protestant vote, something that Republicans were unable to secure in 1996 and barely won in 2000.

The role of Latinos in the 2004 election was decisive. The National Election Pool (NEP)—ABC, Associated Press, CSB, CNN, FOX, and NBC—and the *Los Angeles Times* national exit polls respectively reported that Bush took 44 and 45 percent of the national Latino vote. A number of scholars, institutes, and think tanks were surprised by these findings since they are two very reliable sources. They examined these findings and came to the conclusion that there must have been sampling errors and other factors to explain these unusually high figures. First, they stated that these figures were unprecedented because according to most exit polls Bush only won 35 percent of the Latino vote in 2000. Second, they point out that a Zogby International/ *Miami Herald* poll showed Bush polling around 33 percent just days before the election and a study of ten polls put Bush's support from a low of 29 percent for Bendixen and Associates (September 20, 2004) and to a high of 38 percent for the Gallup Poll (June 30, 2004). Third, Latino support for Kerry was reportedly strong across a wide range of respondents. And fourth, they claimed that the religion gap only helped Bush among Latino Protestants and regular churchgoers, where Bush beat Kerry by 19 percent among Protestants and 22 percent among weekly church-goers. They also argue that a 44 percent margin would only be possible if Latino religious conservatives had supported Bush in "disproportionately large numbers." However, they argue that since the non-Catholic Latino electorate constitutes "only 18" percent of the electorate, that it was simply too small to help Bush to reach the 44 percent figure. Finally, they argue that there is no evidence that Latino non-Catholics were highly mobilized for Bush.[31]

These are all excellent points. However, there are also a number of other factors that may support Bush receiving approximately 40 to 44 percent of the U.S. Latino vote. First, two of the most highly reliable exit polls in the nation put Bush's support at 44 and 45 percent respectively. These same polls are often cited by the same scholars as reliable sources of data for other findings and analyses. Second, the fact that two very independent and otherwise reliable sources reached similar findings also shows that this was not simply the sampling error of one study group. Third, the HCAPL national survey put the Latino Republican vote at 38.35 percent in 2000—nearly the same figure (38 percent) that the Gallup Poll (another highly reliable source) put it at four years later. Making a jump from 38 to 44 percent in one election cycle is much more realistic than 33 percent to 44 percent. Fourth, we have seen that a very high percentage of Latinos across religious traditions self-identified as politically independent and this could in part (especially given their size) explain how they deviated from their normal voting trajectory. Fifth, the Latino Protestant vote swung by more than 31 percentage points between 2000 and 2004 according to the National Survey of Religion and Politics. This is very relevant given the fact that we have seen that most national surveys and analyses significantly undercount the percentage and raw number of Latino Protestants and other socially and politically conservative religionists. Sixth, just because the Latino community voted or polled in one direction in past elections or weeks prior to an election does not mean that there cannot or will not be unexpected last-minute vote swings, as we saw with Obama's projected ten-point victory over Hillary Clinton in the 2008 New Hampshire primary. Seventh, Latino Protestant voter turnout was higher (49 percent) than Latino Catholic (43 percent) voter turnout. Eighth, Latino Catholic support for Bush increased by seven percentage points between 2000 and 2004. And ninth, there was a high level of Latino Protestant and evangelical political mobilization between 2000 and 2004, as will be pointed out later in this chapter, thus possibly providing the resources needed to get out the vote.[32] Despite these countervailing points, it is impossible to know for certain if 44 percent of Latinos nationwide voted for Bush. Regardless, it is clear that the Democratic strategists and pollsters cited at the beginning of this chapter believe he took a much higher percentage of the Latino vote than in 2000.

The Fourth National Survey of Religion and Politics (NSRP) (n <=> 2,730) found that Latino political party identity had solidified a little since 2000 among both Catholics and Protestants. However, Bush's outreach to Protestants resulted in a much higher level of support. In 2004, a clear majority of Latino Protestants self-identified as Democrat (44 percent), although followed closely by Republican (39 percent). Latino Catholic political party identity increased to a decisive majority for Democrats (61 percent), with very little Republican growth (15 percent). However, more than one-sixth (17 percent) of all Latino Protestants and almost one-fourth (24 percent) of Latino Catholics continued to self-identify as politically independent. Together they make up a sizeable portion of the Latino electorate and one that both parties will have to fight hard to secure.[33]

The NSRP found that in a two-party race in the 2004 election, George W. Bush took 63 percent of the Latino Protestant vote to Kerry's 37 percent (table 10.8). The overall impact of the Latino Protestant vote was heightened slightly by the fact that they turned out on Election Day in higher percentages (49 percent) than Latino Catholics (43 percent), thus magnifying their influence disproportionate to their numbers. However, Kerry still took a decisive majority of the Latino Catholic vote (69 percent) over Bush (31 percent). Green, Smidt, Guth, and Kellstedt argue that his increased Protestant support represented a 31 percent increase between 2000 and 2004. Although it is true that Latino Catholics supported Kerry by a decisive margin, it is not true that Bush did not make inroads here as well. They also point out that Bush increased his share of the Latino Catholic vote by 7 percent between 2000 and 2004. When these two increases are combined, they make for a notable increase in Bush's overall share of the Latino religious vote over 2000. These gains were significant because blacks and Latinos together made up one-fifth of Kerry's vote.[34]

One of the reasons why Bush flipped the Protestant vote in his favor in 2004 is that he was proactive in reaching out to Latinos across the nation. He did this through traditional strategies and by seeking the support of Latino faith leaders. The NSRP found that almost one in six (15 percent) Latino Protestants nationwide said they had been contacted by the Bush campaign versus only 9 percent for the Kerry camp. In key battleground states, Bush's get out the vote proved decisive as 41 percent of Latinos in these states reported having been contacted by the Bush team versus 0 percent by the Kerry team. Another 12 percent reported being contacted by both Bush and Kerry. That Bush focused his energy on Protestants is clear when we look at his campaign outreach to Catholics. Only 4 percent of Latino Catholics reported having been contacted by the Bush camp as compared to 9 percent having been contacted by the Kerry team, with 10 percent saying that both camps contacted them. This advantage was increased in key battleground states, where 21 percent of Latino Catholics reported having been contacted by the Kerry camp in contrast to only 5 percent from the Bush camp. Twenty-three percent of Latinos in these states reported that both camps contacted them. Despite these efforts, the Pew Research Center Post-Election Survey found that Latino Catholics were almost three times more likely than Latino Protestants to have been contacted by telephone (61 percent versus 20 percent) and in-person (17 percent versus 6 percent). The same study found that 29 percent of Latino Catholics and 21 percent of Latino Protestants reported that their churches provided voter information for parishioners. Latino Catholic congregations were in some cases three times more likely than their Protestant counterparts to say that they were provided information on ballot issues (31 percent versus 8 percent) and were given more guidance and cues by clergy about who to vote for or how to view a

Table 10.8:   Latino Political Party Preference and Vote by Religion, Church Attendance, Gender, and Generation, 2004

Latino Political Party Preference	Republican	Democrat	Independent
Latino Protestant	39	44	17
Latino Catholic	15	61	24
Latino Vote by Religion	*Bush*	*Kerry*	*Vote Gap*
Latino Protestants	63	37	26
Latino Catholics	31	69	38
All Non-Latino Catholics	53	47	
All Non-Latino Mainline Protestants	50	50	
All Non-Latino Evangelical Protestants	78	22	
Black Protestants	17	83	
Jews	27	73	
Entire Electorate	51	49	
Attendance Gap by Religious Tradition			
Latino Protestants	57	43	
Weekly Attending Latino Protestants	65	35	
Less Observant Latino Protestants	45	55	
Latino Catholics	37	63	
Weekly Attending Latino Catholics	38	62	
Less Observant Latino Catholics	36	64	
Latino Religion, Gender, and 2004 Vote			
Latino Protestants	45	55	
Latino Male	57	43	
Latino Female	55	45	
Latino Catholics	50	50	
Male	40	60	
Female	33	67	
Latino Religion, Age, and the 2004 Vote			
Latino Protestants Under 40	52	48	
Latino Protestants Over 40	62	38	
Latino Catholics Under 40	31	69	
Latino Catholics Over 40	42	58	

Sources: 2004 NSRP; 2004 National Election Pool; Green, *The Faith Factor*, 60, 63, 88, 93, 95, 98, 101.

candidate's political and social views. This indicates that Catholic congregations and churches are much more politically minded and provide much more political guidance than their evangelical and Pentecostal Protestant counterparts. This is surprising given the tendency to argue that evangelical Protestants are much more likely to politicize their pulpits. In this case, it is the Democratic Party that is the most effective in politicizing and leveraging Latino Catholic parishioners and churches. When the total campaign and congregational contacts are added up, Latino Catholics (84 percent) are significantly more likely than Protestants (58 percent) to report some kind of political contact.[35]

What factors shaped the Latino Catholic and Protestant vote in 2004 (see table 10.9)? The 2004 National Election Pool (NEP) found that Latino Catholics who attended church on a weekly basis or more rated economic policies as the top priority (57 percent), followed by foreign policy (30 percent) and moral values (13 percent). Latino Protestants also listed economic policy as their number one concern (36 percent), although only slightly more than moral values (32 percent) and foreign policy (29 percent). These findings indicate that Latino Protestants are two times more likely than Catholics to list moral values as a top priority in shaping their choice for a presidential candidate. The saliency of moral values becomes much clearer when we realize that 92 percent of those Latino Protestants who said moral values were a top priority voted for Bush as compared to 8 percent for Kerry. This may have been due to Kerry's reported 100 percent voting record in favor of what many conservatives saw as pro-abortion policies along with his support for stem cell research and concerns that he would support (despite his statements to the contrary) same-sex marriage. Bush attracted 64 percent of Latino Protestants who said foreign policy was the top issue, compared to Kerry's 36 percent. The tragedy of 9/11, wars in Iraq and Afghanistan, and conservative Swift Boat attacks on Kerry all appear to have helped Bush win over some Latinos.[36]

Despite Bush's attacks on Kerry, the latter still took an overwhelming majority (80 percent) of those Protestant voters who said that the economy was their top concern. Bush took only 20 percent. Kerry took a majority of Latino Catholics who said the economy (75 percent to Bush's 25 percent) and foreign policy (54 percent to 46 percent) were the top issues facing Americans. Not surprisingly, however, Bush took an overwhelming majority of Latino Catholics who said that moral values (70 percent to 30 percent) were a top priority, and this may in part explain how he was able to increase his share of the Latino Catholic vote by 7 percentage points between 2000 and 2004, especially among those who regularly attended worship services. Same-sex marriage was also a strategic wedge issue for Latinos as only one-fifth of

Protestants (20 percent) and one-fourth of Catholics (25 percent) supported same-sex marriage. Furthermore, over half (54 percent) of all Latino Protestants and almost one-third of all Latino Catholics (31 percent) opposed same-sex marriage. Similarly, only a minority of Latino Protestants (15 percent) and Catholics (35 percent) supported abortion. Catholics were more than two times more likely than Protestants to support a pro-choice position. Most Latino Protestants (57 percent) and over one-third of Latino Catholics (37 percent) said that abortion should be illegal in all or most cases except rape, incest, or when it endangers the mother's life (table 10.9).[37] Latino Catholics (63 percent) were much more likely than Protestants (43 percent) to say that abortion should be legal in most or all cases.

When it came to foreign policy, a clear majority of Latino Protestants (62 percent) said they strongly approve (37 percent) or somewhat approve (25 percent) of the war in Iraq in contrast to Latino Catholics (49 percent), who were less likely to strongly (25 percent) or somewhat strongly (24 percent) support the war. One of the reasons why there was such widespread opinion on the matter may be related to the fact that Latino Protestants overwhelmingly saw it as part of the war on terrorism (61 percent versus 39 percent) in contrast to Latino Catholics (33 percent versus 67 percent). Both Latino Protestants (65 percent) and Catholics (75 percent) were very concerned about health care. These political, moral, and social views were not strictly driven by ideology, as Latinos tended to fall evenly along the ideological spectrum. Latino Protestants were about one-third conservative (36 percent), one-third moderate (38 percent), and slightly less liberal (26 percent) than Catholics, who, although equally conservative (35 percent), were nonetheless slightly less moderate (29 percent) and almost ten points more liberal (36 percent). It is interesting to note that Latino Protestants tended to be much less conservative (36 percent) than Euro-American Evangelicals (64 percent), Catholics (49 percent), and mainline Protestants (46 percent) who attend church on a weekly basis, while Latino Catholics were significantly more conservative (35 percent) than every other constituency in the Democratic coalition, including blacks (33 percent), less observant Catholics (32 percent), the unaffiliated (24 percent), Jews (22 percent), and other faiths (19 percent).[38]

Gender remains an important variable in Latino voting patterns in presidential elections. A clear majority of Latino Protestants are women (55 percent) rather than men (45 percent). This is in contrast to Catholic women (50 percent) and men (50 percent) who are evenly split. A majority of Latino Protestant men (57 percent) and women (55 percent) voted for Bush in 2004. Kerry performed well, taking almost half of women (45 percent) and men (43 percent). Not surprisingly, Kerry took a decisive majority of Latino Catholic men (60 percent) and women (67 percent), although he did much better

Table 10.9:   Latino Voting Issue Priorities: Gay Marriage, Abortion, Iraq War, Political Ideology, 2004

Issue Priorities	Moral Values	Foreign Policy	Economic Policy
Latino Protestants	35	29	36
Latino Catholics	13	30	57

Views on Homosexual Marriage	No legal union	Civil Unions	Legally Marry
Latino Protestants	54	26	20
Latino Catholics	31	44	25

Views on Abortion	Illegal in most or all cases	Legal in most or all cases	
Latino Protestants	57	43	
Latino Catholics	37	63	

War in Iraq: Approve or Disapprove?	Approve	Disapprove	
Latino Protestants	62	38	
Latino Catholics	49	51	

War in Iraq: Part of War on Terrorism or a Separate Issue?	Part of War	Separate Issue	
Latino Protestants	61	39	
Latino Catholics	33	67	

Political Ideology, 2004	Conservative	Moderate	Liberal
Latino Protestants	36	38	26
Latino Catholics	35	29	36

Sources: 2004 National Election Pool; 2004 NSRP; Green, *The Faith Factor*, 67–89.

among women than men. Bush took only one-third of women (33 percent) and two-fifths (40 percent) of men. Interestingly enough, Bush took more Latino Protestants who attend church on a weekly basis (52 percent) under the age of 40 than did Kerry (48 percent), although the margin was modest. However, Kerry took more Latino Catholics under the age of 40 (69 percent) and over the age of 40 (58 percent) than Bush (31 percent and 42 percent).[39]

PRESIDENTIAL OUTREACH: CLINTON AND BUSH

Presidents Bill Clinton and George W. Bush made significant efforts to reach out to the Latino community. Clinton's contact with the Latino community began while campaigning for George McGovern in 1972 in San Antonio, Texas, where he met congressman Henry B. Gonzalez, who served in that capacity from 1961 to 1999. Clinton developed his contacts with Mexican Americans and the League of United Latin American Citizens (LULAC) and took 66 percent of the Latino vote in the presidential primaries in 1992. He also persuaded the U.S. Congress to pass the North American Free Trade Agreement (NAFTA) and to help Mexico avoid financial collapse by guaranteeing an $18 billion financial bailout, a plan that worked. Clinton also promoted his charitable choice initiative to Latinos in 1996. The goal was to provide direct government funding to inner-city churches and organizations that provided social services. Latino churches and clergy overwhelmingly supported the initiative. He sought to secure Latino faith-based support by inviting Latino leaders like Father Virgilio Elizondo (co-founder of the Mexican American Cultural Center [MACC]) and Rev. Jesse Miranda (founder and president of the Alianza de Ministerios Evangélicos Nacionales [AMEN]) to the White House. Clinton effectively used this outreach and that of others to reach Latino clergy, churches, and faith-based organizations.

Despite Clinton's efforts, there were setbacks. In 1999, when Rev. Jesse Miranda and AMEN decided to cohost the annual convention with the National Association of Evangelicals (NAE) in Washington, D.C., they had arranged for vice president Al Gore to address the delegates at the White House. This meeting was unexpectedly cancelled without explanation. Instead, U.S. Ambassador-at-Large for International Religious Freedom Robert Seiple was brought in to give a lecture to his fellow Evangelicals. The American Baptist leader proceeded to berate his listeners for their lack of social and global concerns. The large delegation of Latino clergy and denominational leaders were surprised by Seiple's condescending tone and because of a number of assumptions he made about Latino Evangelicals, despite the fact that most all of them were loyal Democrats that had voted for Clinton in 1992 and again in

1996. The assumption that Latino Evangelicals mirror their white counterparts politically is a common stereotype and miscalculation Democrats continue to make to this day. Latino Evangelicals and Pentecostals tended to vote more like their African American rather than their Euro-American counterparts in the 1990s. Regardless of these political facts on the ground, many Latino clergy and denominational leaders were offended by their shoddy treatment. Over the course of the next few years, the news spread through various sectors of the Latino Protestant community and did little to help Gore on Election Day in 2000. It was one small but important factor that contributed to the shift in Latino Protestant support for Bush between 2000 and 2004.[40]

Despite this misstep, Clinton and his administration worked closely with Latino faith leaders to help address and alleviate the problems in the inner city. Latino clergy leaders like Seventh-Day Adventist evangelist José Vicente Rojas served as a behind-the-scenes Latino resource for President Bill Clinton and his administration in the late 1990s. Rojas attended many Latino Protestant events, where he sought to inform Latino evangelicals, Pentecostals, mainline Protestants, and Catholics about the president's policies. President Clinton also met with Mexican American scholars such as Father Virgilio Elizondo, former rector of the historic San Fernando Cathedral in San Antonio, Texas, and professor of Hispanic theology at the University of Notre Dame.[41]

In addition, President Clinton courted the Latino community by appointing a number of Latinos to his administration, such as Bill Richardson (UN ambassador and secretary of energy), Federico Peña (secretary of energy), Henry G. Cisneros (secretary of housing and urban development), and many others. Richardson's service during the Clinton administration helped lay the foundation for his bid for the Democratic nomination for the presidency of the United States in 2008.

President George W. Bush first began working with Latino organizers and faith leaders in Texas. Like Clinton, he used their denominational and organizational ties to court the Latino faith vote at the state and national levels. After he became President, he called a meeting of a large number of Latino Catholic and Protestant religious leaders to the White House in May 2001. In a press conference, he lauded the important role that Latino clergy played in undergirding American life and stated that it was important for political leaders to work together with Latinos for social change. President Bush and John DiIulio met with Catholics and Protestants such as Armando Contreras, Rev. Jesse Miranda, Rev. Daniel de Leon, Rev. Pedro Windsor, Rev. Raymond Rivera, Rev. Luis Cortes, Lisa Treviño-Cummins, Rudy Carrasco, and others to discuss President Bush's faith-based initiatives. Miranda and Elizondo were invited to a five-minute audience with President Bush at the White House to discuss trends in American religion and politics. Although Elizondo could not attend due to a prior engagement, Miranda met with Bush and shared with him the recent findings from the HCAPL national survey on U.S. Latino religion and politics that he and Elizondo were codirecting. The findings were also shared with Democrats. In a targeted effort to reach out to Latino Catholics, Bush called a White House meeting of Latino Catholic bishops, priests, and theologians. However, this event, which Elizondo had flown to Washington to help lead, was cancelled due to the 9/11 attacks on the World Trade Center and the Pentagon.[42]

In addition to this Catholic outreach, Bush also made high-profile appointments, such as *Pedro Pan* Catholic refugee Mel Martínez to the Department of Housing and Human Development (HUD). He served as a senator of the key swing state of Florida. His administration also appointed Lisa Treviño-Cummins to work in the White House Office for Faith-Based Initiatives. She helped lay the foundation for many of the initiative's nonlegislative strategies and was key in engaging the leadership of the African American and Latino faith communities.

On May 2–4, 2002, Jesse Miranda, Virgilio Elizondo, and Gastón Espinosa directed the Hispanic Churches in American Public Life National Conference on Capitol Hill in Washington, D.C. The conference revealed the findings from the Hispanic Churches in American Public Life National Survey, religious leaders and civic leaders surveys (n=434), the results of the 266 people interviewed in the community profiles, and sixteen scholarly research studies commissioned to explore Latino religion, politics, and civic activism in the United States. Over 150 scholars, denominational executives, politicians, and other national leaders across religious and political lines attended the historic two-day conference. At this event, several speakers urged Latinos to work across denominational and party lines to form coalitions to engage in political, civic, and social action.

On May 16, 2002, Rev. Jesse Miranda of AMEN and American Baptist minister Rev. Luis Cortes of Nueva Esperanza organized the first National Hispanic Presidential Prayer Breakfast in Washington, D.C. Cortes, who also attended the HCAPL National Conference, invited President George W. Bush, Senator Joseph Lieberman, television show host Chris Matthews, and many other dignitaries. They addressed 750 Latino religious leaders from forty-nine states (except Alaska). Bush, Ted Kennedy, Nancy Pelosi, Rahm Emanuel, Tom Ridge, Hillary Clinton, Barack Obama, and many others have since spoken at this annual event. This has been a strategic place for members of both parties to secure direct face-to-face access to over 750 clergy, civic leaders, and faith-based activists and the tens of thousands of Latinos they represent. This event also serves as a mobilizing event as Rev. Cortes asks the participants to go out in groups to meet with their respective state congresspersons on Capitol Hill to push for Latino-informed social, educational, immigration, and family issues. This is a bipartisan and inter-religious event, although the vast majority of participants are evangelical, Pentecostal, and mainline Protestant, though many Catholics attend as well. As a result of Cortes's leadership, Nueva Esperanza won an $11 million grant in 2004 from the Department of Labor to launch the Esperanza Trabajando [Hope is Working] project, which was a nine-city, three-year project working with at-risk and adjudicated youth.

At the 2007 National Hispanic Prayer Breakfast, Bush praised the "Hispanic American pastors and priests and community leaders and faith-based activists" from all over the United States for "their compassion" and "abiding faith in the power of prayer." He also thanked them for supporting his call for humane comprehensive immigration reform. He ended by stating that he was proud of the fact that Hispanic Americans who were the grandsons of migrant workers could stand in front of the president of the United States and talk about the "promise of America." That, Bush declared, is the "beauty of America." As he waved good-bye, he looked out over the audience and said "Y también, que Dios les bendiga."[43]

Bush's outreach to the Latino community paid off in 2004 not only with Protestants but also Catholics. However, his level of support also grew because of his regular speeches in Spanish, frequent meetings with Mexican President Vicente Fox, highlighting his sister-in-law's Latina identity, and decision to appoint a number of Latinos to high-profile administrative posts, including Mel Martínez (HUD), Miguel Estrada (U.S. Court of Appeals), Alberto González (attorney general), Gaddy Vasquez (Peace Corps), and others.

Another one of Bush's primary strategies was to seek Latino support for his administration's position on controversial church-state and social issues, which Latinos tend to support. He was aware of the fact that the HCAPL and Pew Forum national surveys found that 74 percent of Latinos support prayer in schools, 60 percent support school vouchers, 70 percent support charitable choice, and 66 percent do not support homosexual sex relations. Given the fact that the South is becoming increasingly Republican and that Latinos constitute a growing swing vote in critical electoral states like Florida, New Mexico, Arizona, Nevada, and Colorado, this southwestern political strategy proved effective in 2004.[44]

Bush's outreach to Latino clergy and religious leaders has met with mixed reviews. Many point out Bush's perceived inconsistencies in his administration's views on immigration, big business, and other economic, social justice, and civil rights issues. Some were highly skeptical of Bush's motives and saw his policies as little more than crass opportunism. Still other Latinos worried about losing their prophetic voice and moral authority in society if they secured government funding because it might mute or undermine their prophetic critiques of the U.S. government and society. The fact that Bush has been able to attract Latinos to his cause is one reason for his push for bipartisan Comprehensive Immigration Reform in 2006, a struggle that attracted grassroots support not only from MACC, AMEN, and Nueva Esperanza, but also from new organizations like the National Hispanic Christian Leadership Conference (NHCLC), led by Rev. Samuel Rodríguez, an ordained minister in the Assemblies of God. Inspired by the work of Jesse Miranda, AMEN, and others, the politically progressive Rodríguez worked with Senator Ted Kennedy and Senator John McCain on Capitol Hill to push for a humane immigration reform bill, although without securing the legal victory they had hoped.[45] Regardless of Bush's motives for working with Latinos in 2000 and 2004, it is clear that Latino clergy, lay leaders, churches, and faith-based civil rights organizations are being sought out by political leaders to support their public policies and presidential races as never before.

CONCLUSION

This analysis of the changing and dynamic relationship between Latinos, religion, and the presidency has explored the growing importance of clergy, churches, and faith-based organizations in American politics. We have seen that contrary to popular opinion there are differences in party affiliation and presidential voting by religious affiliation and identity. In this respect, religion matters. We have also seen that Latino evangelicalism is less politically homogeneous than its Euro-American counterpart. The U.S. Latino Catholic and Protestant evangelical and Pentecostal communities are much larger, diverse, and politically mobilized than hitherto realized. Latino Protestants and Evangelicals are more likely than Latino Catholics to vote on Election Day, especially after we separate Jehovah's Witnesses and Mormons from Protestants. We have also seen that when we further break down the Latino Protestant vote that Pentecostals were more likely to support Democratic candidates than Republicans and both supported Bill Clinton by decisive margins in the 1990s, before shifting their support to another born-again Christian governor named George W. Bush in 2004. Clinton's pervasive support was a result of his strategic efforts to reach out to the Latino faith community through clergy, churches, and faith-based organizations. Bush also took this approach and worked harder and more systematically than any previous president in history to court the U.S. Latino vote in general and the Latino Catholic and Protestant votes in particular. These efforts were largely successful and resulted in possibly garnering 40 to 44 percent of the U.S. Latino vote, though the former more likely than the latter. All of these political shifts point to the fact that the Latino vote is highly volatile and responds to direct political canvassing by American presidents and presidential candidates.

The shift from calling Latinos "a mongrel race" to a "beautiful people" who represent the spirit of America is remarkable, if not long overdue. Although Latinos have come a long way from their fight with the Know-Nothings in the 1850s to the Bush White House in 2008, they have a long way to go to fully realize the president's proclamation that they represent the "promise of America."

Chapter 11

Religion, Race, and the 2008 Presidential Election

Gastón Espinosa

Religion and race played critical roles in the 2008 Presidential election. Barack Obama beat John McCain by increasing his margin of victory over John Kerry's 2004 results in almost every major religious and racial-ethnic minority group by 4 to 14 percentage points.[1] Although Obama's economic recovery plan and hopeful optimism proved critical in helping people vote for him on Election Day, there was no single factor that explained his victory, although the economy came as close as any. Instead, his victory was due to his more persuasive plan for economic recovery; aggressive outreach to Catholics, Evangelicals, Latinos, and people of all faiths and none at all; outreach to Latinos in key swing states; and the fact that he did not openly support gay marriage, which split the two key moral issues that often influence religious voters.[2]

THE 2008 ELECTION BY SOCIAL, ECONOMIC AND POLITICAL FACTORS

Obama won the 2008 election by winning a majority of voters in almost every major racial, religious, and gender category, except among Euro-Americans. The economic crisis trumped all traditional Republican moral wedge issues in the 2008 election. The vast majority of people who were concerned about the economy, health care, the war in Iraq, and energy voted by Obama. McCain only took an overwhelming majority of those worried about terrorism. McCain's economic plan; modest outreach (in comparison with Bush in 2004 and Obama in 2008) to Latinos, Catholics, Evangelicals, and other people of faith; and efforts to reassure the nation that the economy was strong and that economic recovery was around the corner proved unpersuasive. Obama took the overwhelming majority of voters who believed that economic conditions would hurt their families. This was significant because over 80 percent of the American people were worried about the economy and 75 percent believed it was going in the wrong direction (75% vs. 20%, 5% no answer).

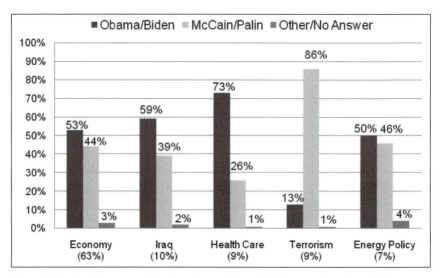

Figure 11.1: Most Important Election Issues. Note: Findings are from the 2008 National Election Pool (NEP). Number in parenthesis is the share of the 2008 electorate. Some percentages do not add to 100% due to rounding.

THE 2008 ELECTION RESULTS BY RELIGION AND RACE

Obama's aggressive outreach to Evangelicals, Catholics, Jews, Latinos, and other faith and ethnic communities enabled him to beat McCain by a margin of seven percentage points nationwide on Election Day, 53 to 46 percent, or by 8.5 million votes. He won a majority of the national aggregate male (49% vs. 48%) and female (56% vs. 43%) vote. This was largely due to racial-ethnic minority men and women, who made up 26 percent of the electorate. They voted for him by overwhelming margins. His victory was also the result of securing three (18–29, 30–44, 45–64) of the four age groups across all ethnicities, which made up 84 percent of the electorate. McCain beat Obama only with the oldest age group (65+).

Despite McCain's lackluster support across all four age groups in the national aggregate, white men (57% vs. 41%) and women (53% vs. 46%) voted decisively for him. He won a majority of white men in three of the four age

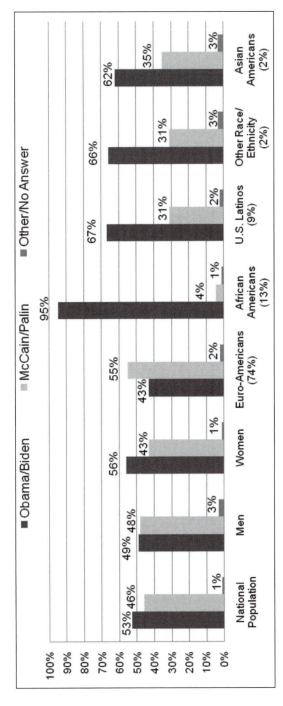

Figure 11.2: National 2008 Election by Gender and Race/Ethnicity. Note: Findings are from the 2008 National Election Pool (NEP). Number in parenthesis is the share of the 2008 electorate.

groups, with Obama taking just the eighteen- to twenty-nine-year-olds. This loss was offset by his winning African Americans, Latinos, and all other major racial-ethnic minorities in all four age groups. He also won a majority of Americans across the economic spectrum, including people in the lowest, middle, and highest income brackets. The fact that more voters self-identified as Democrat (39%) rather than Republican (32%) in 2008 and that Obama won a majority of independents (52%), who made up 29 percent of the electorate, also contributed to his victory. Despite Obama's support in these age categories, McCain not only won the oldest voters (65+), who make up 16 percent of the aggregate electorate, but he also tied (49% vs. 49%) Obama with the forty- to forty-nine-year-old voters (21% of the electorate) and just barely lost (50% vs. 49%) the fifty- to sixty-four-year-old voters, the largest segment of the electorate (27%), again in large part due to Obama's overwhelming support among racial-ethnic minorities.

However, these findings obscure the fact that Obama lost a majority of the aggregate national Protestant vote (45% vs. 54%), which made up 54 percent of the U.S. electorate. It also hides the fact that white Protestants (65% vs. 34%) and white Catholics (52% vs. 47%) voted for McCain by wide margins. These losses were offset by Obama winning a majority of racial-ethnic minority Catholics and Protestants, the latter of which are largely Evangelical. This is significant because all combined, white Protestants and Catholics make up 61 percent of the electorate. McCain also took a majority of white Evangelicals across all denominations, although not at Bush's rates (74% for McCain in 2008 vs. 78% for Bush in 2004).

Obama was able to offset McCain's support by taking 83 percent of white Jews, 67 percent of white other non-Christian religious practitioners, 71 percent of whites that practiced no religion, and 79 percent of nonwhite religious people—who made up 26 percent of the electorate. Equally important, he also took 67 percent of all nonwhite Evangelicals, largely Latinos, Asian Americans, and mixed racial-ethnic minorities. Most surprising, given rhetoric by some conservatives about Obama being a Muslim or a anti-Evangelical liberal Protestant, was the fact that Obama took 24 percent of the total aggregate white born-again vote across all Christian traditions compared to Kerry's 21 percent in 2004. They made up 26 percent of the electorate. More surprisingly, Obama also took more than one in four (26%) of all white Protestant born-again voters. His growing support among all white born-again voters in general and white born-again Protestant voters in particular is very important because they make up 23 percent and 26 percent of the electorate respectively, making them larger than the white Catholic (19%) and white mainline Protestant (19%) electorates. Obama's ability to increase his support among Evangelicals was emblematic of his overall success in 2008 and is politically significant.[3]

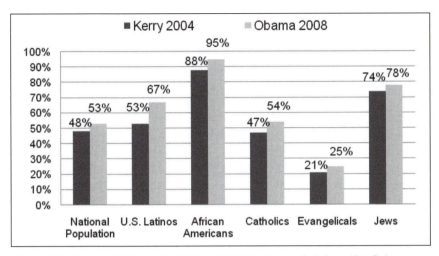

Figure 11.3: Kerry and Obama in 2004 and 2008 by Race/Ethnicity and Religion.
Note: Findings are from the 2004 and 2008 National Election Pool (NEP) exitpolls and
are aggregates for all races/ethnicities.

Although Obama won voters that reported attending church once a month
or more (53% vs. 46%), he lost those that attended church once a week or
more (43% to 55%). He also lost Protestants (32% vs. 67%) and Catholics
(49% vs. 50%) nationwide who reported attending church—once a week or
more. All combined, they made up 42 percent of the electorate. By contrast,
Obama won the vast majority of seculars (67% vs. 30%), people with no
religion (75% vs. 23%), and gays and lesbians (70% vs. 27%), the latter of
which make up less than 2 percent of the U.S. population.

Latinos in general and Catholics and Protestants in particular also proved
critical to Obama's success. He won 67 percent of their vote to McCain's 31
percent, with 2 percent refusing to answer the exit poll survey. He won the
vast majority of Latino men (64% vs. 33%) and women (68% vs. 30%) across
all four age groups. By October, Obama led McCain among Latino Catholics
(63% vs. 24%), Latino Protestants (50% vs. 34%), and even Latino born-
again Evangelicals (46% vs. 38%). On Election Day, he won 57 percent of the
Latino Protestant vote, thus reversing the growing trend of Latino Protestants
voting Republican. He returned them to around their Democratic share in
2000.[4] He also arrested the small trend of Latino Catholics voting Republican
over the past three election cycles, which fell precipitously from 83 percent in
1996 to 58 percent (or approximately 54% according to the National Election
Pool and *Los Angeles Times* exit polls) in 2004. Obama won 69 percent of
Latino Catholics in 2008.

One of the keys to Obama's success among Latinos was his ability to win over a plurality of moderates and even the most religious voters—those that opposed abortion, gay marriage, and read the Bible; prayed; and attended church once a week or more. By publicly stating that he supported traditional marriage and yet also supporting abortion, Obama split the Latino moral vote, which gave moderate and conservative Catholics and Protestants another reason to vote him because they could reason that at least Obama supported one of their key moral issues. This combined with his race, youthfulness, and optimism won over religious voters.

Was this a mere political expediency, since gays and lesbians make up only two percent of the U.S. population according to the 2008 National Election Pool (NEP), versus the almost half of the population that opposes abortion in one form or another? Perhaps. But that was the compromise that helped pave the way to Obama's victory. It was a shrewd political ploy and precisely the kind of proof that Obama cited to cast doubt on the charges that he was nothing more than a cultural and religious liberal.[5] By supporting traditional marriage and appearing to oppose gay marriage, Obama also stole the thunder from those conservatives that might have otherwise more vehemently opposed his candidacy than they did on moral and religious grounds.

All of these findings indirectly challenge the long-standing view that being morally conservative leads people to automatically vote Republican. This simply isn't always true for racial and ethnic minorities. This election found that religiously and morally conservative voters will vote for a Democrat if the candidate addresses their economic and social issues, is respectful of faith, does not have a voting record that openly contradicts all of his or her stated moral and religious views, and adopts a moderate to conservative point of view on at least a few key public policy issues like faith-based initiatives and gay marriage. In short, as long as a candidate runs a campaign with moderate to conservative leanings, they can and will vote for him or her. This can't be a strictly political ploy, because voters have the uncanny ability to sift through motives. Obama was able to present himself as a genuine centrist candidate on many religious issues (some might even say right of center on issues like faith-based initiatives and traditional marriage) because in many respects he is. Like many other African Americans, his views, ideas, and policies are a blend of right and left of center impulses that resonate with the attitudes and values of many Americans. He recognized what many Democrats do not, that, in the words of Bill Clinton, although the American electorate is "operationally progressive," it is nonetheless "philosophically moderate conservative."[6]

The simple reason why this strategy works so well is that while many Americans hold conservative moral and social views, there is nonetheless no single moral or religious issue that decides their vote. In most cases, they take a holistic view of a candidate. They place the candidate along with his or her social and political views in a larger socio-religious context that takes into account a constellation of other factors. For example, Evangelical pastor Wilfredo De Jesus, Obama's Latino Protestant faith outreach advisor and pastor of the 4,000 member New Life Covenant Church of the Assemblies of God in South Chicago, stated that he was impressed that Obama spoke out about the "mistreatment of illegal immigrants" and that he "understood the importance of justice issues such as Health Care, Education and Immigration within the Hispanic faith community."[7] As a result, he decided to join Obama's campaign team because despite supporting past Republican candidates, being pro-life, and opposing gay marriage, he believed these other issues were also important to the Latino community.

The fact that McCain did not effectively use traditional Republican wedge issues like abortion and gay marriage to his political advantage is one of the reasons why he was unable to highly mobilize his base and the religious community—Euro-American and Latino. He decided to remain relatively silent on traditional moral issues in order to win over enough moderates and independents to win—a strategy that sounded good in theory but that ultimately failed in practice. This strategy created the impression that there wasn't a great deal of difference between the candidates on faith and moral issues and led a growing number of Evangelicals, especially racial-ethnic minorities, Evangelical progressives, and younger students, to take a second look at Obama. Bishop Harry R. Jackson, Jr., an African American and pastor of Hope Christian Church in Washington, D.C., summed up this perception when he stated in October 2008 that McCain's "relative silence on conservative social issues has motivated evangelicals to take a second look at Obama." The result, he went on, was "tremendous apathy" among Evangelicals because they felt "betrayed" and "left out." All of which "worked to Obama's advantage," Jackson argued.[8] In the end, McCain played the moderate on Democratic turf—and lost.

Despite their conservative views, this did not lead religious conservatives to automatically vote for McCain. Obama and his team ran a brilliant campaign by outflanking McCain on key traditional Republican issues and also by courting Catholic, Evangelical, and Pentecostal leaders; defining many of the campaign issues; taking the initiative on promoting faith and social justice issues; and responding rapidly and effectively to McCain's critiques, thus neutralizing Republican rallying points. McCain, by contrast, was reluctant to personally address some of these issues, although his surrogates certainly raised the banners when and where they could secure media attention. His unwillingness to personally promote these issues contributed to the perception that McCain ran a largely secular campaign, at least when compared to Bush in 2000 and especially 2004. This perception was confirmed by Rich Cizik, vice president for governmental affairs of the National Association of Evangelicals (NAE), who lamented in October 2008 that although the NAE had "been receiving weekly communication from the Obama camp," they received "nothing from McCain." He stated that Obama was the first Democratic presidential candidate to request a meeting with an NAE official in twenty-eight years.[9] Clearly Obama was—at least at one level—breaking new ground. Although McCain did in fact reach out to religious voters, it was limited in scope and vision and was not covered well in the media. More importantly, many believed that he lacked genuine passion on faith and moral issues.[10]

One of the larger factors that shaped Obama's successful outreach to Catholics and Protestants was not only his enormous funding base, but also his ability to talk openly and warmly about his Christian faith. Although neither candidate claimed to be born-again, at least Obama's African American black church faith expressions resonated with people of faith. It enabled him to speak with the cadence, heart, and energy of Evangelicalism without having to necessarily affirm all of its politics, morality, or theology.

The perception that Obama was a person of genuine faith and a religious moderate was driven home by his strong and outspoken support of church-state partnerships aimed at addressing inner-city poverty, crime, and drug abuse. This was a direct byproduct of his African American religious heritage; the influence of Reverend Jeremiah Wright's teaching on social justice, empowerment, and community transformation; and his work as a community organizer. Obama made his views clear in his autobiography, *The Audacity of Hope: Thoughts on Reclaiming the American Dream*. He wrote that after he graduated from Harvard Law School he moved to Chicago to work in the inner city with churches as a community organizer to address joblessness, drugs, and hopelessness. As a result, he recognized the link between faith and progressive social change. Sounding more like George W. Bush giving a speech in defense of faith-based initiatives, Obama wrote: "Religious sentiment and religious activism have sparked some of our most powerful political movements, from abolition to civil rights to the prairie populism of William Jennings Bryan."[11] The connection between religion and social transformation, especially in the Black church, was one of the reasons why he was attracted to and eventually converted to the Christian faith. He stated:

> I was drawn to the power of the African American religious tradition to spur social change. Out of necessity, the black church had to minister to the whole person. Out of necessity, the black church rarely had the luxury of separating

individual salvation from collective salvation. It had to serve as the center of the community's political, economic, and social as well as spiritual life; it understood in an intimate way the biblical call to feed the hungry and clothe the naked and challenge powers and principalities . . . I was able to see faith as more than just a comfort to the weary or a hedge against death; rather, it was an active, palpable agent in the world.[12]

His spiritual journey was one that could resonate with many Americans of all races and denominations. His comments captured the reason why many people were attracted to the Christian faith and ministry in the first place.

At the African Methodist Episcopal Church Convention in July 2008, he argued for a link between faith, morality, and social transformation when he declared:

Our faith cannot be an idle faith. It requires more of us than Sundays at church. It must be an active faith, rooted in the most fundamental of all truths: that I am my brother's keeper . . . The challenges we face today—war and poverty, joblessness and homelessness, violent streets and crumbling schools—are not simply technical problems in search of a 10-point plan. They are moral problems.

Going one step further than JFK, but still echoing Democratic presidents like FDR and Clinton before him, Obama chided secularists for asking religious believers to leave their faith and morality at the door of American public life and because they told people they shouldn't inject their personal morality into public-policy debates.[13] Sounding more like a sojourner-style Evangelical prophet than a liberal Protestant, Obama argued that many of America's greatest reformers were shaped by if not driven by their faith and morality in their efforts to bring about social justice. He wrote:

Secularists are wrong when they ask believers to leave their religion at the door before entering the public square; Frederick Douglass, Abraham Lincoln, William Jennings Bryan, Dorothy Day, Martin Luther King, Jr.—indeed, the majority of great reformers in American history—not only were motivated by faith but repeatedly used religious language to argue their causes. To say that men and women should not inject their "personal morality" into public-policy debates is a practical absurdity; our law is by definition a codification of morality, much of it grounded in the Judeo-Christian tradition.[14]

He went on to state that the U.S. government needed to partner with faith-based programs to "feed the hungry, reform the prisoner, rehabilitate the drug addict, and keep the veteran employed," an idea that resonated with former Democratic presidents like FDR and Bill Clinton.[15] Although he also strongly supported the separation of church and state and argued that religious pluralism required people to accept Americans of all faiths or none at all, this was still no doubt off-putting to some American secularists. This, however, was precisely the kind of emotive reasoning that attracted Americans from all faiths and walks of life to his campaign. Many Catholics, Protestants, Jews, and others resonated with this line of reasoning because of their long-standing traditions of faith-based activism and because Catholic Charities, Lutheran Social Services, and Latino faith-based organizations like Nueva Esperanza received federal funding, including from Bush's faith-based initiatives program, which was originally initiated by Clinton as Charitable Choice.[16]

Perhaps the most compelling reason why Catholics, mainline Protestants, Evangelicals, Latinos, and others were comfortable with voting for Obama was because he was very open and public about his personal conversion to the Christian faith. Although many have charged that he spoke about it only to counter changes that he was a Muslim and to distance himself from Reverend Jeremiah Wright, in fact he began speaking about his faith journey (no doubt anticipating future criticisms) long before the campaign formally began. He won over many Americans by declaring that, "I let Jesus Christ into my life" because I "learned that my sins could be redeemed and if I placed my trust in Jesus, that he could set me on a path to eternal salvation."[17] This kind of conversion narrative about accepting Jesus Christ into his life resonated with Evangelical and Catholic Christians across the nation and from many denominational traditions.[18]

Aware that his personal faith journey could serve as an asset and as a point of contact with racially and socially progressive Evangelicals, Obama argued that Democrats in general and he himself in particular were not inherently anti-Evangelical and anti-faith. He promised to correct this misperception: "Evangelicals have come to believe often times that Democrats are anti-faith. Part of my job in this campaign, something that I started doing well *before* this campaign, was to make sure I was showing up and reaching out and sharing my faith experience with people who share that faith. Hopefully we can build some bridges that can allow us to move the country forward" (emphasis in the original).[19] As a result of this commitment and outreach, he held closed-door meetings with top white, black, and Latino Evangelical, Pentecostal, and Catholic leaders like Bishop T. D. Jakes, Franklin Graham, Rick Warren, Bishop Charles Price, Doug Kmiec, Samuel Rodríguez, Luis Cortes, and others.[20] This forward-looking strategy proved effective. His conversion story, outreach to Catholics and Evangelicals, contact with the NAE, and decision to appoint the twenty-six-year-old African American Pentecostal pastor Joshua DuBois to lead his 2008 campaign faith outreach, along with closed-door meetings with Evangelical and Pentecostal megachurch pastors to listen to their concerns, caught the attention of faith leaders. Samuel Rodríguez, president of the National Hispanic Christian Leadership Conference (NHCLC), stated: "It's good to see a Democratic Nominee engage Evangelical leaders. For too long the Democratic party seemed hostile to Evangelicals."[21]

In the end, Obama's victory in 2008 was due to the economy, Latinos in key swing states, his bipartisan and optimistic vision to bring about positive social change and recovery, his support for traditional marriage, his youth vote, and his 4–14 percent increase over Kerry's 2004 support among religious, racial-ethnic minority, and women voters. His vision attracted voters from all walks of life because it seemed to provide hope for a better tomorrow. Whether or not this will enable him to match or surpass Clinton's historic support in 1996 in the 2012 Election remains to be seen, although momentum, optimism, and energy are—at least at this moment—on his side.

Variable Coding for MAPS Data

Religious commitment: 1 <=> lowest quartile on religious commitment scale, 2 <=> second-lowest quartile, 3 <=> second-highest quartile, 4 highest quartile.

Ideology: "Which description best represents your political ideology?" 1 <=> progressive/very liberal, 2 <=> liberal, 3 <=> moderate, 4 <=> conservative, 5 <=> very conservative. Libertarians were excluded.

Convert and Immigrant: 1 <=> yes, 0 <=> no.

War on terror or Islam?: "Do you feel the U.S. is fighting a war on terrorism or a war against Islam?" 1 <=> terrorism, 2 <=> Islam.

Experienced discrimination: coded 1 if either the respondent and/or friends and family experienced discrimination after 9/11 and coded 0 if neither did.

Education: 1 <=> non-high school graduate, 2 <=> high school, 3 <=> some college, 4 <=> college graduate.

Female: 1 <=> male, 2 <=> female.

Importance of being Muslim to vote choice: "How important is being Muslim in your decision for whom to vote?" 1 <=> very important, 2 <=> important, 3 <=> not important.

Importance of AMT endorsement: "If the American Muslim Taskforce (AMT) endorses one of the Presidential candidates, how important would it be in your decision for whom to vote?" 1 <=> very important, 2 <=> important, 3 <=> not important.

Partisanship: 1 <=> Democrat, 2 <=> Independent, 3 <=> Republican.

Important to participate: "How important is it for you to participate in politics?" 1 <=> very important, 2 <=> important, 3 <=> not important.

Political discussion: "How often do you discuss politics with family and friends?" 1 <=> always, 2 <=> sometimes, 3 <=> hardly ever, 4 <=> never.

Follow politics: "How often would you say you follow what's going on in government?" 1 <=> most of the time, 2 <=> some of the time, 3 <=> only now and then, 4 <=> hardly at all.

Community organizations: an additive index ranging from 0 to 10, giving one point for some participation (the options are donated time, donated money, served as an officer, and a combination of these) in each of the following groups: school or youth programs; any arts or cultural organization; any neighborhood, civic, or community group; any organization to help the poor, sick, elderly, or homeless; any professional organization; any mosque or religious organizations; any trade or labor unions; any veteran's or military service organization; any ethnic organizations; any Muslim political action or public affairs organization.

Satisfied with the way things are going in American society: "How satisfied are you overall with the way things are going in American society today?" 1 <=> very satisfied, 2 <=> satisfied, 3 <=> somewhat dissatisfied, 4 <=> very dissatisfied.

Political participation: an additive index giving one point (range is 0 to 6) for participation in each of the following activities: active member of political party, contribution of time or money to candidate, visiting political website, contacting the media or a politician on an issue, attending a rally for a politician or cause, participating in a boycott of a product or business.

Children under 17: ranges from 0 to 6 (where 6 stands for six or more).

Questions for Pittsburgh Interviewees

Describe your feelings regarding President Clinton. How would you characterize his responsiveness to the needs of the Muslim community in America?

Describe your feelings regarding President Bush. How would you characterize his responsiveness to the needs of the Muslim community in America?

Describe your feelings about September 11, 2001.

How do you think President Bush handled his job in the months following September 11, 2001?

What was your reaction to President Bush's appeals to Americans to treat Muslims with dignity and respect?

What was your reaction to President Bush's use of the term "crusade" in the days following September 11?

Do you know a fellow Muslim who was the victim of discrimination as a result of September 11? If so, what kind of discrimination did they face?

Were you the victim of discrimination as a result of September 11? If so, what kind of discrimination did you face?

Survey Information

I. Pilot National Asian American Political Survey (PNAAPS), 2000–2001
    Principal Investigator: Pei-te Lien (University of Utah)
    This study is a multicity and multilingual survey undertaken to gauge the political attitudes and behavior of Asian Americans. The survey drew on a semirandom sample of households from the six major Asian American ancestries selected to approximate the size of the ethnic population among Asian Americans according to the 1990 census. The telephone surveys were collected for the households of Los Angeles, New York, Honolulu, San Francisco, and Chicago, based on a dual-frame approach consisting of random digit dialing at targeted Asian zip code densities and listed-surname frames.

II. American Religious Identification Survey (ARIS), 2001
    Principal Investigators: Barry A. Kosmin and Egon Mayer
    Study Director: Ariela Keysar (The Graduate Center of the City University of New York)
    This is a survey of religious distribution of the American adult population. This 2001 survey is a follow-up study to the 1990 survey named the National Survey of Religious Identification. Both surveys were initiated because the U.S. Census does not provide questions on religious profiles. These surveys are claimed as the most extensive surveys of religious identification of American adults in the second half of the twentieth century. The 2001 study employed a random digit dialed telephone survey of 50,281 American residential households in the forty-eight continental states.

Notes

CHAPTER 1

1. Our analysis begins with the concept of religious tradition, measured in terms of religious affiliation or belonging. A religious tradition is a set of "religious communities that share a ... distinctive worldview"; the building blocks of these religious traditions "are the specific religious communities to which individuals typically belong," the most common of which are denominations. Lyman Kellstedt, John Green, James Guth, and Corwin Smidt, "Grasping the Essentials: The Social Embodiment of Religion and Political Behavior," in *Religion and the Culture Wars: Dispatches from the Front*, ed. John Green, James Guth, Corwin Smidt, and Lyman Kellstedt (Lanham, MD: Rowman & Littlefield, 1996), 176.

The advantage in using the concept of religious traditions is very simple. Rather than employing some categorical entity (e.g., conservative Christian or "born-again" voters), whose members are unified only by certain arbitrary criteria specified by the analyst, this approach more fully captures a sociological reality, as members of a religious tradition are more likely to interact socially with others in that tradition, and more likely to fall within the same communication and informational networks. Thus, the beliefs and values shared by the religious bodies within a tradition are further reinforced and made more salient through these social factors. For a fuller discussion of the concept of religious tradition, see Corwin E. Smidt, "Evangelical and Mainline Protestants at the Turn of the Millennium: Taking Stock and Looking Forward," in *From Pews to Polling Places in the American Religious Mosaic*, ed. Matthew Wilson (Washington, DC: Georgetown University Press), 29–51.

2. Robert Johnson, "American Evangelicalism: An Extended Family," in *The Variety of American Evangelicalism*, ed. Donald Dayton and Robert Johnson (Knoxville: University of Tennessee Press, 1991), 260–63.

3. Richard Coleman, *Issues of Theological Conflict*, rev. ed. (Grand Rapids, MI: Eerdmans, 1980), 12.

4. Mark Noll, "Forward: American Past and World Present in the Search for Evangelical Identity," in *Pilgrims on the Sawdust Trail: Evangelical Ecumenism and the Question for Christian Identity*, ed. Timothy George (Grand Rapids, MI: Baker Academic, 2004), 11–18.

5. William McLoughlin, "Introduction, the American Evangelicals: 1800–1900," in *The American Evangelicals, 1800–1900*, ed. William McLoughlin (New York: Harper and Row, 1968), 1.

6. Noll, "Forward: American Past," 12.

7. Joel Carpenter, *Revive Us Again: The Reawakening of American Fundamentalism* (New York: Oxford, 1997).

8. Noll, "Forward: American Past," 12–13.

9. D. G. Hart, "Mainstream Protestantism, 'Conservative' Religion, and Civil Society," in *Religion Returns to the Public Square*, ed. Hugh Heclo and Wilfred McClay (Washington, DC: Woodrow Wilson Center Press, 2003), 201.

10. Winthrop Hudson, *Religion in America*, 3rd ed. (New York: Charles Schribner's Sons, 1981), 442–45; Richard Ostling, "Evangelical Publishing and Broadcasting," in *Evangelicalism and Modern America*, ed. George Marsden (Grand Rapids, MI: Eerdmans, 1984), 46–55.

11. Martin Marty, "Transportations: American Religion in the 1980s," *Annals of the American Academy of the Political and Social Sciences* 480 (July 1985): 13–14.

12. Dean Kelley, *Why Conservative Churches are Growing* (New York: Harper and Row, 1972).

13. Wade Clark Roof and William McKinney, "Denominational America and the New Religious Pluralism," *Annals of the American Academy of the Political and Social Sciences* 480 (July 1985): 24–38.

14. As a result of the 1989 National Election Study Pilot Study, a new measure of religious affiliation produced a large increase in the size of the secular population in the 1990s. In order to address this problem, respondents who say they "never" attend church are part of the secular group in the period before 1990. Then, following 1990, it is necessary to make a small adjustment in order to produce roughly similar percentages to those obtained prior to 1990. As a result, after 1990, a secular individual is one who claims no affiliation, never attends church, *and* says that religion is unimportant to his or her life.

15. Raymond Wolfinger and Steven Rosenstone, *Who Votes?* (New Haven: Yale University Press, 1980).

16. For purposes of this analysis, the South was defined as the eleven states of the old confederacy, plus the states of Kentucky and Oklahoma.

17. Wolfinger and Rosenstone, *Who Votes?*

18. Sidney Verba, Kay Scholzman, and Henry Brady, *Voice and Equality: Civic Volunteerism in American Politics* (Cambridge, MA: Harvard University Press, 1995).

19. Verba, Scholzman, and Brady, *Voice and Equality*, 282–83.

20. There are those, however, who would argue that the hierarchical ecclesiastical structure of a church may not be as much of an obstacle to the development of civic skills as Verba and his colleagues have contended. See, for example, Mark Warren,

"Faith and Leadership in the Inner City: How Social Capital Contributes to Democratic Renewal," in *Religion as Social Capital: Producing the Common Good*, ed. Corwin E. Smidt (Waco, TX: Baylor University Press, 2003), 49–68.

21. See, for example, table 3.1 in Wade Clark Roof and William McKinney, *American Mainline Religion: Its Changing Shape* (New Brunswick, NJ: Rutgers University Press, 1987), 83–84.

22. Lyman Kellstedt and Mark Noll, "Religion, Voting for President, and Party Identification: 1948–1984," in *Religion & American Politics: From the Colonial Period to the 1980s*, ed. Mark Noll (New York: Oxford University Press, 1990), 371.

23. Marty, "Transportations: American Religion," 14.

24. Over the past century, Evangelicals have mounted several different waves of political engagement. See James Davison Hunter, *American Evangelicalism: Conservative Religion and the Quandary of Modernity* (New Brunswick, NJ: Rutgers University Press, 1987), 117–30.

25. For other scholars, the almost simultaneous fall of prominent televangelists such as James Bakker and Jimmy Swaggart as a result of sexual and financial improprieties and the collapse of Pat Robertson's bid for the 1988 GOP presidential nomination ended this phase of evangelical political engagement. See Steve Bruce, *The Rise and Fall of the New Christian Right: Conservative Protestant Politics in America, 1978–1988* (Oxford: Oxford University Press, 1988). Although one could argue that a fourth wave of evangelical activism began in the 1990s, it is just as easy to contend that we are still in the third wave of evangelical engagement discussed above.

26. It should be noted that this data is based on respondents' verbal report that they turned out to vote. Obviously, such data are somewhat problematic. This can be seen from the fact that the data in the tables presented here suggests that voter turnout increased over the past three decades, while the level of voter turnout actually declined over that period of time.

27. If proclivities to provide false reports of voting are randomly distributed across all religious traditions in proportion to the numbers within the ranks of each tradition, then the extent to which false reporting occurs is proportional, allowing one to assess the relative level of differences across religious traditions, even if one can not assume that the absolute level of voter turnout within the tradition is a correct figure. In that light, Evangelicals continue to trail most other religious traditions in terms of their level of voter turnout.

28. Byron Shafer, "The New Cultural Politics," *PS: Political Science & Politics* 18 (Spring 1985): 221–31; David Leege, Kenneth Wald, Brian Krueger, and Paul Mueller, *The Politics of Cultural Differences: Social Change and Voter Mobilization Strategies in the Post-New Deal Period* (Princeton, NJ: Princeton University Press, 2002).

29. Lyman Kellstedt, John Green, James Guth, and Corwin Smidt, "Religious Voting Blocs in the 1992 Election: The Year of the Evangelical?" in *Religion and the Culture Wars: Dispatches from the Front*, ed. John Green, James Guth, Corwin Smidt, and Lyman Kellstedt (Lanham, MD: Rowman & Littlefield, 1996), 273.

30. Kellstedt, Green, Guth, and Smidt, "Religious Voting," 273.

31. This list was compiled from different reports. See, for example, Philip Yancey, "Breakfast at the White House," *Christianity Today*, February 7, 1994, 37; Rick Lowry, "Clinton's Revelation," *National Review*, March 7, 1994, 52–54. Some others involved were Roberta Hestenes, president of Eastern College; Mark Noll, professor of history, Wheaton College; and John Perkins, Voice of Calvary Ministries.

32. Peter Steinfels, "Evangelicals Lobby for Oppressed Christians," *New York Times*, September 16, 1996, 26A.

33. Andrew Heffmann, "White House Issues Guidelines on School Prayer," *Chicago Sun-Times*, September 2, 1995, 17A.

34. "Clinton Speaks to Prayer Breakfast," *The Boston Globe*, September 12, 1998, A2.

35. "Clinton Freed by Forgiveness: Thank You, America," *The Herald* [Glasgow], August 12, 2000, 1.

36. Rob Boston, "Preachers, Politics, and Campaign," *Church & State*, September 2000, 12.

37. Boston, "Preachers, Politics, and Campaign," 12.

38. "Faith-based Groups Said to be Backed by Bush," *The Christian Century*, January 3, 2001, 9–10.

39. Rob Boston, "God and Election 2000," *Church & State*, December 2000, 4.

40. Boston, "God and Election 2000," 4.

41. Andrew Ferguson, "Bush Shouldn't Be 'Misunderestimated,'" *Los Angeles Business Journal*, October 8, 2001, 51.

42. Ryan Lizza, "Write Hand," *The New Republic*, May 21, 2001, 14–16.

43. Stephen Goode, "Working in the Eye of the Storm," *Insight on the News*, May 20, 2002, 36.

44. Jim VandeHei, "Pipeline to the President for GOP Conservatives," *The Washington Post*, December 24, 2004, A15.

45. Rob Boston, "President Pushes Ahead with Religion-Funding Schemes as a Way to 'Save Americans One Soul at a Time,'" *Church & State*, March 2004, 7–12.

46. "Evangelicals Decry Bush Use of Churches," *The Christian Century*, July 27, 2004, 14–15.

47. It should be noted that the turnout figure for the 2004 data reflect a statistically adjusted, or "corrected," turnout figure.

48. Assume, for example, that evangelical Protestants comprise about 20 percent of all voters. If 4 percent of all evangelical Protestants shift in the partisan direction of their voting preferences, there would be a shift of one percentage point in the overall vote (.20 <x> .04 <=> .01). Consequently, even with this small shift in the overall numbers of Evangelicals, what was a 51 percent to 49 percent win in 2004 would become a 50 percent to 50 percent "tie" in total votes in the next election.

CHAPTER 2

1. Richard E. Neustadt, *Presidential Power and the Modern Presidents: The Politics of Leadership From Roosevelt to Reagan* (New York: Free Press, 1990), 33–34.

2. George C. Edwards III, *At the Margins: Presidential Leadership of Congress* (New Haven, CT: Yale University Press, 1989), 109.

3. But see Robert S. Alley, *So Help Me God: Religion and the Presidency, Wilson to Nixon* (Richmond, VA: John Knox, 1972); Mark J. Rozell and Gleaves Whitney, eds., *Religion and the American Presidency* (New York: Palgrave Macmillan, 2007); Gary Scott Smith, *Faith and the Presidency: From George Washington to George W. Bush* (New York: Oxford University Press, 2006); Jeff Walz, "Religion and the American Presidency," in *In God We Trust: Religion and American Political Life*, ed. Corwin E. Smidt (Grand Rapids, MI: Baker Academic, 2001).

4. See Samuel Kernell, *Going Public: New Strategies of Presidential Leadership*, 4th ed. (Washington, DC: CQ Press, 2007).

5. Wade Clark Roof and William McKinney, *American Mainline Religion: Its Changing Shape and Future* (New Brunswick, NJ: Rutgers University Press, 1987); Robert Wuthnow, *The Restructuring of American Religion: Society and Faith Since World War II* (Princeton, NJ: Princeton University Press, 1988).

6. Jerry Park and Samuel Reimer, "Revisiting the Social Sources of American Christianity, 1972–1998," *Journal for the Scientific Study of Religion* 41 (2002): 735–48; Christian Smith and Robert Faris, "Socioeconomic Inequality in the American Religious System: An Update and Assessment," *Journal for the Scientific Study of Religion* 44 (2005): 95–104; Robert Wuthnow and John H. Evans, eds., *The Quiet Hand of God: Faith-based Activism and the Public Role of Mainline Protestantism* (Berkeley: University of California Press, 2002).

7. Roger Finke and Rodney Stark, *The Churching of America, 1776–1990: Winners and Losers in Our Religious Economy* (New Brunswick, NJ: Rutgers University Press, 1992); Phillip Hammond, *The Protestant Presence in Twentieth-Century America: Religion and Political Culture* (Albany: State University of New York Press, 1992); Laurence R. Iannaccone, "Why Strict Churches are Strong," *American Journal of Sociology* 99 (1994): 1180–1211; Dean M. Kelley, *Why Conservative Churches Are Growing: A Study in Sociology of Religion* (San Francisco: Harper, 1977); Robert Wuthnow, *The Crisis in the Churches* (New York: Oxford University Press, 1996).

8. Andrew M. Greeley, "The Ethnic Miracle," *The Public Interest* 45 (1976): 20–36; Andrew M. Greeley, "Protestant and Catholic: Is the Analogical Imagination Extinct?" *American Sociological Review* 54 (1989): 485–502.

9. Robert N. Bellah, Richard Madsen, William M. Sullivan, Ann Swidler, and Steven M. Tipton, *Habits of the Heart: Individualism and Commitment in American Life* (San Francisco, CA: Harper, 1985); Robert Booth Fowler, Allen D. Hertzke, Laura R. Olson, and Kevin R. den Dulk, *Religion and Politics in America: Faith, Culture, and Strategic Choices*, 3rd ed. (Boulder, CO: Westview, 2004); Eugene V. Gallagher, *The New Religious Movements Experience in America* (Westport, CT: Greenwood, 2004); Pew Forum on Religion & Public Life, *U.S. Religious Landscape Survey: Summary of Key Findings*, 2008, http://religions.pewforum.org/reports/.

10. Allen D. Hertzke, *Representing God in Washington: The Role of Religious Lobbies in the American Polity* (Knoxville: University of Tennessee Press, 1988); Allen D. Hertzke, "An Assessment of the Mainline Churches Since 1945," in *The Role*

of Religion in the Making of Public Policy, ed. James E. Wood, Jr. and Derek Davis (Waco, TX: J. M. Dawson Institute of Church-State Studies, 1991).

11. Fowler et al., *Religion and Politics*.

12. Robert Wuthnow, "The Moral Minority," *The American Prospect*, May 22, 2000; Wuthnow and Evans, *Quiet Hand*.

13. Martin E. Marty, *Righteous Empire: The Protestant Experience in America* (New York: Dial, 1970); H. Richard Niebuhr, *Christ and Culture* (New York: Harper and Row, 1951); Wuthnow, *Restructuring of American Religion*.

14. Pew Forum on Religion & Public Life, *U.S. Religious Landscape Survey*.

15. James L. Guth, John C. Green, Corwin E. Smidt, Lyman A. Kellstedt, and Margaret M. Poloma, *The Bully Pulpit: The Politics of Protestant Clergy* (Lawrence: University Press of Kansas, 1997); Corwin E. Smidt, ed., *Pulpit and Politics: Clergy in American Politics at the Advent of the Millennium* (Waco, TX: Baylor University Press, 2004).

16. Andrew Kohut, John C. Green, Scott Keeter, and Robert C. Toth, *The Diminishing Divide: Religion's Changing Role in American Politics* (Washington, DC: Brookings Institution, 2000); Wuthnow, *Restructuring of American Religion*.

17. Jackson W. Carroll, Barbara G. Wheeler, Daniel O. Aleshire, and Penny Long Marler, *Being There: Culture and Formation in Two Theological Schools* (New York: Oxford University Press, 1997); Guth et al., *Bully Pulpit*; Wuthnow, *Restructuring of American Religion*.

18. Jeffrey K. Hadden, *The Gathering Storm in the Churches* (Garden City, NY: Doubleday, 1969); Guth et al., *Bully Pulpit*; Harold E. Quinley, *The Prophetic Clergy: Social Activism among Protestant Ministers* (New York: Wiley, 1974).

19. James L. Adams, *The Growing Church Lobby in Washington* (Grand Rapids, MI: Eerdmans, 1970); Hertzke, *Representing God*; Ted G. Jelen, *The Political World of the Clergy* (Westport, CT: Praeger, 1993); Norman B. Koller and Joseph D. Retzer, "The Sounds of Silence Revisited," *Sociological Analysis* 41 (1980): 155–61.

20. Guth et al., *Bully Pulpit*; Quinley, *Prophetic Clergy*; Wuthnow, *Restructuring of American Religion*; Wuthnow and Evans, *Quiet Hand*.

21. Adams, *Growing Church Lobby*; Paul A. Djupe and Christopher P. Gilbert, *The Prophetic Pulpit: Clergy, Churches, and Communities in American Politics* (Lanham, MD: Rowman & Littlefield, 2003); Guth et al., *Bully Pulpit*; Hadden, *Gathering Storm*; Koller and Retzer, "Sounds of Silence"; Jelen, *Political World*; Laura R. Olson, *Filled with Spirit and Power: Protestant Clergy in Politics* (Albany: State University of New York Press, 2000); Laura R. Olson, Sue E. S. Crawford, and Melissa M. Deckman, *Women with a Mission: Religion, Gender, and the Politics of Women Clergy* (Tuscaloosa: University of Alabama Press, 2005); Wuthnow, *Restructuring of American Religion*; Wuthnow, "Moral Minority"; Wuthnow and Evans, *Quiet Hand*.

22. Guth et al., *Bully Pulpit*; Marty, *Righteous Empire*; Wuthnow, *Restructuring of American Religion*.

23. Marty, *Righteous Empire*; Niebuhr, *Christ and Culture*; Wuthnow, *Restructuring of American Religion*.

24. Ernest Q. Campbell and Thomas F. Pettigrew, *Christians in Racial Crisis: A Study of Little Rock's Ministry* (Washington, DC: Public Affairs Press, 1959); James

F. Findlay, *Church People in the Struggle: The National Council of Churches and the Black Freedom Movement, 1950–1970* (New York: Oxford University Press, 1993); Michael B. Friedland, *Lift Up Your Voice Like a Trumpet: White Clergy and the Civil Rights and Antiwar Movements, 1954–1973* (Chapel Hill: University of North Carolina Press, 1998).

25. Mitchell Hall, "CALCAV and Religious Opposition to the Vietnam War," in *Give Peace a Chance: Exploring the Vietnam Antiwar Movement*, ed. Melvin Small and William D. Hoover (Syracuse, NY: Syracuse University Press, 1992); Quinley, *Prophetic Clergy*.

26. Hertzke, *Representing God*; Christian Smith, *Resisting Reagan: The U.S. Central America Peace Movement* (Chicago: University of Chicago Press, 1996).

27. Wuthnow, "Moral Minority"; Wuthnow and Evans, *Quiet Hand*.

28. For a broad discussion of the work that these offices undertake, see Hertzke, *Representing God*; Daniel J. B. Hofrenning, *In Washington but Not Of It* (Philadelphia: Temple University Press, 1995); Laura R. Olson, "Mainline Protestant Washington Offices and the Political Lives of Clergy," *Quiet Hand*, Wuthnow and Evans.

29. Ram A. Cnaan, *The Newer Deal: Social Work and Religion in Partnership* (New York: Columbia University Press, 1999); Ram A. Cnaan, *The Invisible Caring Hand: American Congregations and the Provision of Welfare* (New York: New York University Press, 2002); Sue E. S. Crawford and Laura R. Olson, "Clergy as Political Actors in Urban Contexts," in *Christian Clergy in American Politics*, ed. Sue E. S. Crawford and Laura R. Olson (Baltimore: Johns Hopkins University Press, 2001); Djupe and Gilbert, *Prophetic Pulpit*; Olson, *Filled with Spirit*; Olson, Crawford, and Deckman, *Women with a Mission*; Mark R. Warren, *Dry Bones Rattling: Community Building to Revitalize American Democracy* (Princeton, NJ: Princeton University Press, 2001); James K. Wellman Jr., *The Gold Coast Church and the Ghetto: Christ and Culture in Mainline Protestantism* (Urbana: University of Illinois Press, 1999); Wuthnow and Evans, *Quiet Hand*.

30. Kohut et al., *Diminishing Divide*; David C. Leege, Kenneth D. Wald, Brian S. Krueger, and Paul D. Mueller, *The Politics of Cultural Differences: Social Change and Voter Mobilization in the Post–New Deal Period* (Princeton, NJ: Princeton University Press, 2002); Amy Sullivan, *The Party Faithful: How and Why Democrats Are Closing the God Gap* (New York: Scribner, 2008).

31. The American National Election Studies (ANES), Center for Political Studies, University of Michigan. Electronic resources from the ANES website (www.umich .edu/~nes) (Ann Arbor, MI: University of Michigan, Center for Political Studies [producer and distributor], 1995–2004). These materials are based on work supported by the National Science Foundation under Grant Nos. SBR-9707741, SBR-9317631, SES-9209410, SES-9009379, SES-8808361, SES-8341310, SES-8207580, and SOC77-08885. Any opinions, findings, conclusions, or recommendations expressed in these materials are those of the authors and do not necessarily reflect those of the National Science Foundation.

32. For a useful discussion of how to classify survey respondents by religious affiliation, see Brian Steensland, Jerry Z. Park, Mark D. Regnerus, Lynn D. Robinson,

W. Bradford Wilcox, and Robert D. Woodberry, "The Measure of American Religion: Toward Improving the State of the Art," *Social Forces* 79 (2000): 291–318.

33. David C. Leege, "Methodological Advances in the Study of American Religion and Politics," (presentation at the Annual Meeting of the American Political Science Association, Philadelphia, PA, 2003); David C. Leege and Lyman A. Kellstedt, eds., *Rediscovering the Religious Factor in American Politics* (Armonk, NY: M. E. Sharpe, 1993).

34. Wuthnow and Evans, *Quiet Hand.*

35. William H. Flanigan and Nancy H. Zingale, *Political Behavior of the American Electorate*, 10th ed. (Washington, DC: CQ Press, 2002); Katherine Tate, *From Protest to Politics* (Cambridge, MA: Harvard University Press, 1994).

36. See also John C. Green, *The Faith Factor: How Religion Influences American Elections.* Westport, CT: Praeger, 2007.

37. Karen M. Kaufmann and John R. Petrocik, "The Changing Politics of American Men: Understanding the Sources of the Gender Gap," *American Journal of Political Science* 43 (1999): 864–87; Margaret C. Trevor, "Political Socialization, Party Identification, and the Gender Gap," *Public Opinion Quarterly* 63 (1999): 62–78.

38. Cal Clark and Janet M. Clark, "The Gender Gap in 1996: More Meaning than a 'Revenge of the Soccer Moms,'" in *Women in Politics: Outsiders or Insiders?* 3rd ed., ed. Lois Duke Whitaker (Upper Saddle River, NJ: Prentice-Hall, 1998).

39. See also Karen M. Kaufmann, "The Gender Gap," in *Beyond Red State, Blue State: Electoral Gaps in the Twenty-First Century American Electorate*, ed. Laura R. Olson and John C. Green (Upper Saddle River, NJ: Prentice Hall, 2008).

40. Wendy Cadge, "Vital Conflicts: The Mainline Protestant Denominations Debate Homosexuality," in *Quiet Hand*, Wuthnow and Evans.

41. Amy R. Gershkoff, "The Marriage Gap," in *Beyond Red State, Blue State*, Olson and Green; Laura Stoker and M. Kent Jennings, "Life Cycle Transitions and Political Participation: The Case of Marriage," *American Political Science Review* 89 (1995): 421–36.

42. See Anand Edward Sokhey and Paul A. Djupe, "The Generation Gap," in *Beyond Red State, Blue State*, Olson and Green.

43. Paul Allen Beck and M. Kent Jennings, "Family Traditions, Political Periods, and the Development of Partisan Orientations," *Journal of Politics* 53 (1991): 742–63; M. Kent Jennings and Gregory B. Markus, "Partisan Orientations over the Long Haul: Results from the Three-Wave Political Socialization Panel Study," *American Political Science Review* 78 (1984): 1000–18; Richard G. Niemi and M. Kent Jennings, "Issues and Inheritance in the Formation of Party Identification," *American Journal of Political Science* 35 (1991): 970–88.

44. Bruce Keith, David B. Magleby, Candice J. Nelson, Elizabeth Orr, and Mark C. Westlye, *The Myth of the Independent Voter* (Berkeley: University of California Press, 1992).

45. Angus Campbell, Philip E. Converse, Warren E. Miller, and Donald E. Stokes, *The American Voter* (New York: Wiley, 1960); Flanigan and Zingale, *Political Behavior*; Seymour Martin Lipset, *Political Man* (New York: Doubleday, 1960); Sidney Verba and Norman H. Nie, *Participation in America: Political Democracy*

and Social Equality (Chicago: University of Chicago Press, 1972); Sidney Verba, Kay Lehman Schlozman, and Henry E. Brady, *Voice and Equality: Civic Volunteerism in American Politics* (Cambridge, MA: Harvard University Press, 1995).

46. Park and Reimer, "Revisiting"; Smith and Faris, "Socioeconomic Inequality"; Wuthnow and Evans, *Quiet Hand*.

47. Data on regions was not yet available in the advance release of the 2004 ANES dataset.

48. Wuthnow, *Restructuring of American Religion*.

49. V. O. Key Jr., *Southern Politics in State and Nation* (New York: Knopf, 1949).

50. Earl Black and Merle Black, *The Rise of Southern Republicans* (Cambridge, MA: Belknap Press of Harvard University Press, 2002).

51. Green, *Faith Factor*; Kohut et al., *Diminishing Divide*; Geoffrey Layman, *The Great Divide: Religious and Cultural Conflict in American Party Politics* (New York: Columbia University Press, 2001); Laura R. Olson and John C. Green, "The Worship Attendance Gap," in *Beyond Red State, Blue State*, Olson and Green.

52. Leege et al., *Politics of Cultural Differences*.

53. Kenneth W. Starr, *The Starr Report: The Findings of Independent Counsel Kenneth W. Starr on President Clinton and the Lewinsky Affair* (Washington, DC: Public Affairs, 1998).

54. For an extended treatment of the Lewinsky matter and the subsequent impeachment charges brought against the president, see Bill Clinton, *My Life* (New York: Knopf, 2004).

55. Clinton, *My Life*, 30.

56. Clinton, *My Life*, v.

57. Clinton, *My Life*; Hillary Rodham Clinton, *Living History* (New York: Simon and Schuster, 2003).

58. See J. Philip Wogaman, *An Unexpected Journey: Reflections on Pastoral Ministry* (Louisville, KY: Westminster John Knox, 2004), for a fascinating account of the Clintons' involvement at Foundry United Methodist Church from their pastor's perspective.

59. Clinton, *My Life*, 563.

60. Clinton, *My Life*, 810–11. See also J. Philip Wogaman, *From the Eye of the Storm: A Pastor to the President Speaks Out* (Louisville, KY: Westminster John Knox, 1998); Wogaman, *Unexpected Journey*.

61. Wogaman is now retired. He is past interim president of the Iliff School of Theology (Denver) and professor emeritus of Christian ethics at Wesley Theological Seminary (Washington, D.C.). For an in-depth look at the history and significance of the congregation Wogaman served for a decade, Foundry United Methodist Church, see Wogaman, *Unexpected Journey*.

62. Cal Thomas, "Politics and the Pastor," *The Washington Times*, April 23, 1995; Mark Tooley, "The President's Pastor," *Faith and Freedom*, Spring 1995.

63. Jim Naughton, "Picking a Church When You're President-Elect," Beliefnet. com, January 18, 2001, www.beliefnet.com/story/61/story_6159_1.html; Wogaman, *Unexpected Journey*.

64. J. Philip Wogaman, *To Serve the Present Age: The Gift and Promise of United Methodism* (Nashville, TN: Abingdon Press, 1995); J. Philip Wogaman, *Christian Perspectives on Politics* (Louisville, KY: Westminster John Knox, 2000); Wogaman, *Unexpected Journey.*

65. Wogaman, *To Serve*; Wogaman, *Christian Perspectives*; Wogaman, *Unexpected Journey.*

66. Hadden, *Gathering Storm*; Guth et al., *Bully Pulpit*; Quinley, *Prophetic Clergy.*

67. Wogaman, *Unexpected Journey.*

68. Wogaman, *To Serve*, 21–22.

69. Wogaman, *To Serve*; Wogaman, *Christian Perspectives*; Wogaman, *Unexpected Journey.*

70. Wogaman, *Unexpected Journey*, 70.

71. Wogaman, *From the Eye of the Storm*, 42. Emphasis in original.

72. Wogaman, *From the Eye of the Storm.*

73. Thomas, "Politics and the Pastor"; Tooley, "President's Pastor."

74. Fowler et al., *Religion and Politics*; Olson, "Mainline Protestant."

75. David Aikman, *A Man of Faith: The Spiritual Journey of George W. Bush* (Nashville, TN: W Publishing Group, 2004); Deborah Caldwell, "An Evolving Faith," Beliefnet.com, October 30, 2004, www.beliefnet.com/story/121/story_12112_1.html; Alan Cooperman, "Openly Religious, To a Point," *The Washington Post*, September 16, 2004; Paul Kengor, *God and George W. Bush: A Spiritual Life* (New York: HarperCollins, 2004).

76. Stanley A. Renshon, *In His Father's Shadow: The Transformations of George W. Bush* (New York: Palgrave Macmillan, 2004), 143–44.

77. See Kernell, *Going Public.*

78. Green, *Faith Factor.*

79. Aikman, *Man of Faith*, 33–34; George W. Bush, *A Charge to Keep* (New York: William Morrow, 1999), 19.

80. Stephen Mansfield, *The Faith of George W. Bush* (New York: Penguin, 2003), 60.

81. David Aikman recounts a private meeting Bush had with an evangelist named Arthur Blessit in Midland, Texas on April 3, 1984. During this meeting, both men prayed and discussed the topic of personal faith in Jesus Christ. Although Blessit made a positive impression on Bush, it appears that Bush's social lifestyle did not change drastically after his encounter with Blessit. See Aikman, *Man of Faith*, 69–73.

82. Bush, *Charge to Keep*, 136.

83. Kengor, *God and George W. Bush*, 24–25.

84. Fred I. Greenstein, ed., *The George W. Bush Presidency: An Early Assessment* (Baltimore: Johns Hopkins University Press, 2003).

85. Greenstein, *George W. Bush Presidency*, 40.

86. Bryan Hilliard, Tom Lansford, and Robert P. Watson, *George W. Bush: Evaluating the President at Midterm* (Albany: State University of New York Press, 2004), 107; Kengor, *God and George W. Bush*, 41–42; Minutaglio, *First Son: George W.*

Bush and the Bush Family Dynasty (New York: Times Books, 1999), 289–90; see also Marvin Olasky, *Compassionate Conservatism: What It Is, What It Does, and How It Can Transform America* (New York: Free Press, 2000).

87. Wuthnow and Evans, *Quiet Hand.*

88. Aikman, *Man of Faith*, 112–13.

89. Kengor, *God and George W. Bush*, 78.

90. Mansfield, *Faith of George W. Bush*, 117.

91. Amy E. Black, Douglas L. Koopman, and David K. Ryden, *Of Little Faith: The Politics of George W. Bush's Faith-Based Initiatives* (Washington, DC: Georgetown University Press, 2004).

92. Greenstein, *George W. Bush Presidency*, 254; Stephen V. Monsma, *Putting Faith in Partnerships: Welfare-to-Work in Four Cities* (Ann Arbor: University of Michigan Press, 2004), 4.

93. Jon Kraus, Kevin J. McMahon, and David M. Rankin, *Transformed by Crisis: The Presidency of George W. Bush and American Politics* (New York: Palgrave Macmillan, 2004).

94. George W. Bush, Agency Responsibilities with Respect to Faith-Based and Community Initiatives, Executive Order 13198 (29 January 2001), *Federal Register* 66, no. 21, 8497–98.

95. George W. Bush, Establishment of White House Office of Faith-Based and Community Initiatives, Executive Order 13199 (29 January 2001), *Federal Register* 66, no. 21, 8499–500.

96. Greenstein, *George W. Bush Presidency*, 60.

97. Gary L. Gregg II and Mark J. Rozell, eds., *Considering the Bush Presidency* (New York: Oxford University Press, 2004), 41.

98. Black, Koopman, and Ryden, *Of Little Faith*, 194.

99. Colin Campbell and Bert A. Rockman, eds., *The George W. Bush Presidency: Appraisals and Prospects* (Washington, DC: CQ Press, 2004), 171.

100. Black, Koopman, and Ryden, *Of Little Faith*, 194–95.

101. Quoted in Kraus, McMahon, and Rankin, *Transformed by Crisis*, 111.

102. Greenstein, *George W. Bush Presidency*, 59.

103. Gregg and Rozell, *Considering the Bush Presidency*, 40.

104. George C. Edwards III and Stephen J. Wayne, *Presidential Leadership: Politics and Policy Making*, 7th ed. (Belmont, CA: Thomson/Wadsworth, 2006), 288–89.

105. Green, *Faith Factor*; Guth et al., *Bully Pulpit*; Kohut et al., *Diminishing Divide*; Layman, *Great Divide*; Leege et al., *Politics of Cultural Differences*; Wuthnow, *Restructuring of American Religion.*

106. Will Herberg, *Protestant-Catholic-Jew* (Garden City, NY: Doubleday, 1955).

107. Leege et al., *Politics of Cultural Differences.*

108. See also Sullivan, *Party Faithful.*

109. John C. Green, Mark J. Rozell, and Clyde Wilcox, eds., *The Values Campaign? The Christian Right and the 2004 Elections* (Washington, DC: Georgetown University Press, 2006), 67.

110. Robert N. Bellah, "Civil Religion in America," *Daedalus* 96 (1967): 1–21.

CHAPTER 3

1. Jay P. Dolan, *The American Catholic Experience* (New York: Doubleday, 1985), 72.

2. Dolan, *American Catholic Experience*, 97.

3. Dolan, *American Catholic Experience*, 105.

4. William Prendergast, *The Catholic Voter in American Politics* (Washington, DC: Georgetown University Press, 1999), 24.

5. Paul Kleppner, "Coalitional and Party Transformations in the 1890s," in *Party Coalitions in the 1980s*, ed. S. M. Lipset (San Francisco: Institute for Contemporary Studies, 1981).

6. David C. Leege and Paul D. Mueller, "How Catholic Is the Catholic Vote?" in *American Catholics and Civic Engagement: A Distinctive Voice*, ed. Margaret O'Brien Steinfels (Lanham, MD: Rowman & Littlefield, 2004), 213–50.

7. Andrew Greeley, *The American Catholic: A Social Portrait* (New York: Basic Books, 1977).

8. See the arguments in David C. Leege, Kenneth D. Wald, Brian S. Krueger, and Paul D. Mueller, *The Politics of Cultural Differences: Social Change and Voter Mobilization Strategies in the Post–New Deal Period* (Princeton: Princeton University Press, 2002); Thomas B. and Mary D. Edsall, *Chain Reaction: The Impact of Race, Rights, and Taxes on American Politics* (New York: Norton, 1991); and Martin Gilens, *Why Americans Hate Welfare* (Chicago: University of Chicago Press, 1999).

9. Samuel G. Freedman, *The Inheritance: How Three Families and America Moved from Roosevelt to Reagan and Beyond* (New York: Simon & Schuster, 1996).

10. David C. Leege, "Catholics and the Civic Order: Parish Participation, Politics, and Civic Participation," *Review of Politics* 50, no. 4 (1988): 704–36.

11. E. J. Dionne, Jr., "There Is No Catholic Vote—and It's Important," in *American Catholics and Civic Engagement: A Distinctive Voice*, ed. Margaret O'Brien Steinfels (Lanham, MD: Rowman & Littlefield, 2004), 251–60.

12. Robert D. Woodberry, "The Missing Fifty-Percent: Accounting for the Gap between Survey Estimates and Head Counts of Church Attendance" (master's thesis in sociology, University of Notre Dame, 1997).

13. Leege et al., *Politics of Cultural Differences*, 132–34, 160–68.

14. Leege et al., *Politics of Cultural Differences*, 132–34, 160–68.

15. Leege and Mueller, "How Catholic Is the Catholic Vote?"

16. See Leege et al., *Politics of Cultural Differences*; Alan I. Abramowitz and Kyle L. Saunders, "Is Polarization a Myth?" *Journal of Politics* 70, no. 2 (2008): 542–55; J. Matthew Wilson, "The Changing Catholic Voter: Comparing Responses to John Kennedy in 1960 and John Kerry in 2004," in *A Matter of Faith: Religion in the 2004 Presidential Election*, ed. David E. Campbell (Washington DC: Brookings Institution Press, 2007), 180–98; and Steven Mockabee, "Cultural Conflict, Religion, and Party Support: The Catholic Vote, 1952–2002" (paper presented to the annual meeting of the American Political Science Association, Chicago, 2004).

17. David L. Leal, Matt A. Barreto, Jongho Lee, and Rodolfo de la Garza, "The Latino Vote in the 2004 Election," *P. S.: Political Science and Politics* 38, no. 1 (January 2005): 41–49.

18. Peter Steinfels, *A People Adrift: The Crisis in the Roman Catholic Church in America* (New York: Simon & Schuster, 2003), 87–88.

19. Steinfels, *A People Adrift*, 90.

20. See J. Quin Monson and J. Baxter Oliphant, "Micro-Targeting and the Instrumental Mobilization of Religious Conservatives," in *A Matter of Faith*, ed. David E. Campbell, 95–119; David E. Campbell and J. Quin Monson, "The Case of Bush's Reelection: Did Gay Marriage Do It?" in *A Matter of Faith*, ed. David E. Campbell, 120–41.

21. Corwin E. Smidt and James M. Penning, eds., *Sojourners in the Wilderness: The Christian Right in Comparative Perspective* (Lanham, MD: Rowman & Littlefield, 1997), 97–168.

22. David C. Leege, "Catholics and the Civic Order"; Michael R. Welch, David C. Leege, Kenneth D. Wald, and Lyman A. Kellstedt, "Are the Sheep Hearing the Shepherds? Cue Perceptions, Congregational Responses, and Political Communication Processes," in *Rediscovering the Religious Factor in American Politics*, ed. David C. Leege and Lyman A. Kellstedt, (Armonk, NY: M. E. Sharp, 1993), 235–54.

23. Ted G. Jelen and Clyde Wilcox, *Public Attitudes toward Church and State* (Armonk, NY: M. E. Sharpe, 1995).

24. Andrew Kohut, John C. Green, Scott Keeter, and Robert C. Toth, *The Diminishing Divide: Religion's Changing Role in American Politics* (Washington DC: Brookings Institution Press, 2000).

CHAPTER 4

1. The term *secular* is employed throughout this chapter but should be interpreted to mean *relatively secular*. Even atheists, who can be considered to be antireligious, will exhibit some degree of religiosity. "Unaffiliated" is another option that is sometimes employed, but the analysis that follows will show that there is a group of affiliated respondents who show no signs of religiosity—the nominal religionists.

2. Glenn M. Vernon, "The Religious 'Nones': A Neglected Category," *Journal for the Scientific Study of Religion* 7 (1968): 219–29.

3. Gerhard Lenski, *The Religious Factor* (Garden City, NY: Anchor Books, 1963); Charles Glock and Rodney Stark, *Religion and Society in Tension* (Chicago: Rand McNally, 1965); Charles Glock and Rodney Stark, *Christian Beliefs and Anti-Semitism* (New York: Harper and Row, 1966); and Rodney Stark and Charles Glock, *American Piety* (Berkeley and Los Angeles: University of California Press, 1968).

4. John M. Benson, "The Polls: A Rebirth of Religion?" *Public Opinion Quarterly* 45 (1981): 576–85; Norval D. Glenn, "No Religion Respondents," *Public Opinion Quarterly* 51 (1987): 293–315; and Andrew M. Greeley, *Religious Change in America* (Cambridge, MA: Harvard University Press, 1989).

5. Peter L. Berger, *The Sacred Canopy* (Garden City, NY: Anchor Books, 1967).

6. Greeley, *Religious Change*, 128.

7. Rodney Stark and William Bainbridge, *The Future of Religion* (Los Angeles: University of California Press, 1985); and Rodney Stark and William Bainbridge, *A Theory of Religion* (New York: Peter Lang, 1987).

8. The difficulty results from the fact that religious affiliation question wording varies from survey to survey. For example, the General Social Surveys (GSS) asks the following: "What is your religious preference? Is it Protestant, Catholic, Jewish, some other religion, or no religion?" Probes for specific Protestant denominations follow (although the probes were minimal prior to 1983). At least this question allows one to follow the "no religion" response percentages over time. On the downside, however, such a question may encourage a respondent to name a religious category, like "Protestant," even when no such predilection exists.

The National Election Studies (NES) has changed its religious affiliation question over the years. From 1952 to 1964, the following was asked: "Is your church preference Protestant, Catholic, or Jewish?" (Since 1960, a follow-up question has been asked to ascertain specific denominational affiliation, with the codes for denominations brought up to date in 1990.) In 1966 and 1968 the question was changed to "Are you Protestant, Catholic, or Jewish?" From 1970 to 1988, it was asked in this way: "Is your religious preference Protestant, Catholic, Jewish, or something else?" In 1990 and in years following another wording change was made: "Lots of things come up that keep people from attending religious services even if they want to. Thinking about your life these days, do you ever attend religious services, apart from occasional weddings, baptisms, or funerals?" If respondents said "yes," they were asked, "Do you mostly attend a place of worship that is Protestant, Roman Catholic, Jewish, or what?" Probes followed to obtain specific denominational preferences. For those who said that they did not attend services, the following question was posed, "Regardless of whether you now attend any religious services do you ever think of yourself as part of a particular church or denomination? (IF YES:) Do you consider yourself Protestant, Roman Catholic, Jewish or what?" Again, appropriate probes followed to obtain specifics. The post-1990 wording changes had some effect on frequency distributions, dramatically increasing the percentage of respondents in the "none" category, as conceded in the NES codebook. Manza and Brooks discuss this problem but offer no solution to it. Suffice it to say that use of the NES surveys to determine the size of the secular population is fraught with difficulty, given the changes in question wording over the years. Otherwise excellent scholarship by Layman and Leege and colleagues ignore this problem.

A preferable affiliation question offers a broader set of response categories that do not encourage the naming of a religious "preference" when there is none. In the 2004 NSRP, we use the following: "Do you think of yourself as part of a religious tradition, for example, do you consider yourself as Christian, Jewish, Muslim, other non-Christian, agnostic or atheist, nothing in particular, or something else?" The greater options, when compared with GSS and NES, produce higher percentages in a "no affiliation" category. Detailed probes follow for specific denominational attachments.

There is one study, *The Dimensional Divide* by Andrew Kohut and colleagues, that makes more than a token effort to come to grips with changes in the size of all religious groups in the population, including seculars. Comparisons are made between a Gallup survey conducted in 1965 (on occasion, the 1964 NES is used) and surveys conducted by the Pew Center for the People and the Press in the 1980s and 1990s. Both atheist or agnostic and "no preference" categories are used, showing an increase of almost seven percentage points in a combination of the two between 1965 and 1996. However, the "no preference" category combines those who express no preference as well as nominal religionists who express a preference but exhibit no religious behaviors or beliefs. Kohut and colleagues argued that individuals with nominal affiliations looked very much like those with no affiliation, at least in terms of social-demographic characteristics.

9. Barry Kosmin and Seymour Lachman, *One Nation Under God* (New York: Harmony Books, 1993).

10. Will Herberg, *Protestant, Catholic, Jew* (Garden City, NY: Anchor Books, 1955).

11. Andrew Kohut et al., *The Diminishing Divide: Religion's Changing Role in American Politics* (Washington, DC: Brookings Institution Press, 2000).

12. Kosmin and Lachman, *One Nation*.

13. Michael Hout and Claude S. Fischer, "Why More Americans Have No Religious Preference: Politics and Generations," *American Sociological Review* 67 (April 2002): 165–90.

14. Pew Forum on Religion and Public Life, *Reports: Summary of Key Findings*, 2008, http://religions.pewforum.org/pdf/report-religious-landscape-study-full.pdf.

15. Kathleen McCourt and D. Garth Taylor, "Determining Religious Affiliation Through Survey Research: A Methodological Note," *Public Opinion Quarterly* 40 (1976): 124–27; and Wade Clark Roof, "The Ambiguities of 'Religious Preference' in Survey Research—A Methodological Note," *Public Opinion Quarterly* 44 (1980): 403–7.

16. Kohut, *Diminishing Divide*.

17. Lyman A. Kellstedt and Nathan J. Kelly, "Seculars and Political Behavior: The Neglected Segment of the U.S. Population" (Prepared for delivery at the Annual Meeting of the American Political Science Association, Boston, September 3–6, 1998).

18. The life after death item (POSTLIFE) was not asked in 1972, 1974, 1977, and 1985 GSS surveys, and, as a result, these years were excluded from the analysis. The inclusion of only one belief item and one religious practice item, church attendance (ATTEND), for determining nominals is unfortunate. Frequency of prayer (PRAY) was not asked until 1983, and was not included in either the 1986 or 1991 surveys. A Bible item was not asked until 1983, making it unavailable for analysis throughout the time series. Similarly, a belief in God item (GOD) was not asked until 1988 and was included on an irregular basis thereafter. This item allows the analyst to distinguish atheists and agnostics from each other and from other nonaffiliates, but its infrequent inclusion rules it out in analysis over time. In addition, there is no religious salience measure, although a strength of affiliation item (RELITEN) is included throughout the time series. Including the latter in efforts to categorize nominals proved fruitless.

There is another difficulty in using the GSS data to categorize nominals. Large numbers of respondents were coded 70 (No denomination given or nondenominational church) on the follow-up question directed at Protestants (DENOM) in an attempt to ascertain their specific denominational affiliation. There are also large numbers of respondents to the same question coded 60, or "other." The latter were followed up with a probe (OTHER) but many still could not be classified. In addition, there were others who responded to the original affiliation question (RELIG) with answers like "Christian," and "Inter-Nondenominational," response categories added in 1996. All of these groups were placed in a "Protestant No Further Specifics" category. Many of them turned out to be nominal religionists and were so assigned. Details of these coding procedures can be obtained from the author.

19. Unfortunately, the National Survey on Religion and Politics did not distinguish between atheists and agnostics but placed them in one category. Their number is relatively small, which mitigates the problem, but the theoretical differences between the two groups—one antagonistic toward religion and the other dubious about religion—suggests that they should be separated.

20. Religious modernists, as suggested in the text, hold heterodox or modernist positions in terms of belief and rank rather low in religious practice. They are also inclined to identify with liberal, progressive, and ecumenical religious movements. In the analysis that follows, they are limited to the three largest white religious traditions in the United States: evangelical and mainline Protestantism and Roman Catholicism. This is done for two reasons: (1) other traditions do not tend to exhibit the internal belief and practice differences that characterize evangelical and mainline Protestants and Anglo Catholics and (2) their numbers are often too small to permit detailed subgroup analysis. Modernists are examined in some depth in order to determine if they belong with the secular groups included in the analysis. Details for classifying religious modernists can be obtained from the author.

21. Kohut, *Diminishing Divide*, 156–57.

22. Kohut, *Diminishing Divide*, 75.

23. Kohut, *Diminishing Divide*, 83.

24. For similar findings from the NES, see David C. Leege et al., *The Politics of Cultural Differences* (Princeton, NJ: Princeton University Press, 2002).

25. Greeley, *Religious Change*, 33 and Wade Clark Roof and William McKinney, *American Mainline Religion* (New Brunswick, NJ: Rutgers University Press, 1987).

26. The GSS data did not have a sizeable number of "unaffiliated but religious." The paucity of religious measures in most of the years in the GSS data set precluded a serious effort to create this category.

27. Ideally, atheist and agnostic should be given separate codes, the practice of the NES surveys. However, the numbers in both groups have been too small to capitalize on the practice, although affiliation questions that explicitly mention these groups as possibilities should increase their percentages. Of course, in larger samples the absolute numbers would increase. And in time series, survey years can be combined to increase *n*s.

28. Kohut, *Diminishing Divide*, 37.

29. James L. Guth et al., "Onward Christian Soldiers?" *Books & Culture*, July/August 2005, 20–21.

30. Kohut, *Diminishing Divide*, 55.

31. Kohut, *Diminishing Divide*, 117.

CHAPTER 5

1. Anonymous, "Jewish Giving: Women's Issues," *Moment*, April 1999.

2. Sandra Baxter and Marjorie Lansing, *Women and Politics: The Visible Majority*. Women and Culture Series (Ann Arbor: The University of Michigan Press, 1983); Carole Kennedy Chaney, R. Michael Alvarez, and Jonathan Nagler, "Explaining the Gender Gap in U.S. Presidential Elections, 1980–1992," *Political Research Quarterly* 51, no. 2 (1998): 311–39; Darlisa Y. Crawford, "Women Voters Key in 2004 Presidential Election," in *U.S. Election System*, ed. Paul McCaffrey. The Reference Shelf (New York: H. W. Wilson, 2004); Michael X. Delli Carpini and Ester R. Fuchs, "The Year of the Woman? Candidate, Voters, and the 1992 Election," *Political Science Quarterly* 108, no. 1 (1993): 29–36; Jeff Manza and Clem Brooks, "The Gender Gap in U.S. Presidential Elections: When? Why? Implications?" *The American Journal of Sociology* 103, no. 5 (1998): 1235–66.

3. Robert Booth Fowler, Allen D. Hertzke, and Laura R. Olson, *Religion and Politics in America: Faith, Culture, and Strategic Choices*, 2nd ed. (Boulder, CO: Westview Press, 1999); John Green, Mark Rozell, and Clyde Wilcox, *Prayers in the Precincts: The Christian Right in the 1998 Elections* (Washington, DC: Georgetown University Press, 2000); Allen Hertzke, *Representing God in Washington: The Role of Religious Lobbies in the American Polity* (Knoxville: University of Tennessee Press, 1988); Daniel Hofrenning, *In Washington but Not of It: The Prophetic Politics of Religious Lobbyists* (Philadelphia: Temple University Press, 1995); David Leege and Lyman Kellstedt, *Rediscovering the Religious Factor in American Politics* (New York: M. E. Sharpe, 1993), James E. Wood and Derek Davis, eds., *The Role of Religion in the Making of Public Policy* (Waco, TX: J. M. Dawson Institute of Church-State Studies, 1991).

4. Richard A. Seltzer, Jody Newman, and Melissa Voorhees Leighton, *Sex as a Political Variable: Women as Candidates and Voters in U.S. Elections* (Boulder, CO: Lynne Rienner Publishers, 1997).

5. Baxter and Lansing, *Women and Politics: The Visible Majority*.

6. Chaney, Alvarez, and Nagler, "Explaining the Gender Gap in U.S. Presidential Elections"; Kristin Kanthak and Barbara Norrander, "The Enduring Gender Gap," in *Models of Voting in Presidential Elections: The 2000 U.S. Election*, ed. Herbert F. Weisberg and Clyde Wilcox (Stanford, CA: Stanford University, 2004); Georgie Ann Weatherby, "Gender, Religion, and Politics: An Empirical Study" (Seattle: University of Washington, 1990).

7. Crawford, "Women Voters Key in 2004 Presidential Election."

8. Manza and Brooks, "The Gender Gap in U.S. Presidential Elections"; Robert Putnam, *Bowling Alone: The Collapse and Revival of American Community* (New York: Simon and Schuster, 2000).

9. Delli Carpini and Fuchs, "The Year of the Woman?"

10. Karen M. Kaufmann and John R. Petrocik, "The Changing Politics of American Men: Understanding the Sources of the Gender Gap," *American Journal of*

Political Science 43, no. 3 (1999): 864–87; Seltzer, Newman, and Leighton, *Sex as a Political Variable*.

11. Delli Carpini and Fuchs, "The Year of the Woman?"

12. Alan Crawford, *Thunder on the Right: The "New Right" and the Politics of Resentment* (New York: Pantheon Books, 1980); Sara Diamond, *Not by Politics Alone: The Enduring Influence of the Christian Right* (New York: The Guilford Press, 1998); David Domke, *God Willing? Political Fundamentalism in the White House, the "War on Terror," and the Echoing Press* (Ann Arbor, MI: Pluto Press, 2004); Clyde Wilcox, *Onward Christian Soldiers? The Religious Right in American Politics*. Dilemmas in American Politics (Boulder, CO: Westview Press, 1996).

13. Diamond, *Not by Politics Alone*.

14. Cal Thomas and Ed Dobson, *Blinded by Might: Can the Religious Right Save America?* (Grand Rapids, MI: Zondervan Publishing House, 1999); Wilcox, *Onward Christian Soldiers?*

15. Seltzer, Newman, and Leighton, *Sex as a Political Variable*.

16. Domke, *God Willing?*

17. Melissa M. Deckman et al., "Clergy and the Politics of Gender," *Journal for the Scientific Study of Religion* 42, no. 4 (2003): 621–31; Laura R. Olson, Sue E. S. Crawford, and James L. Guth, "Changing Issue Agendas of Women Clergy," *Journal for the Scientific Study of Religion* 39, no. 2 (2000): 140–53.

18. Lynn Resnick Dufour, "Sifting through Tradition: The Creation of Jewish Feminist Identities," *Journal for the Scientific Study of Religion* 39, no. 1 (2000): 90–106; Christel J. Manning, *God Gave Us the Right: Conservative Catholic, Evangelical Protestant, and Orthodox Jewish Women Grapple with Feminism* (New Brunswick, NJ: Rutgers University Press, 1999).

19. The 1976 survey lacks important religious variables. In particular, the 1976 survey does not ask the question, "Is religion an important part of your life?" which makes it impossible to compare religious and nonreligious women and men.

20. These questions only begin to scratch the surface of this fascinating aspect of voting behavior and leave many interesting, yet unanswered questions. For example, are religious women more or less interested in politics than these other groups? What political issues concern religious women compared to these other groups?

21. The vote is "intended" because the NES survey data used for the analysis is taken before the election and asks respondents who they intend to vote for in the upcoming presidential election.

22. Samuel Kernell, *Going Public: New Strategies of Presidential Leadership*, 3rd ed. (Washington, DC: CQ Press, 1997); Thomas E. Patterson, *Out of Order* (New York: Alfred A. Knopf, 1993).

23. Norman Nie, Sidney Verba, and John R. Petrocik, *The Changing American Voter* (Cambridge, MA: Harvard University Press, 1976).

24. George Lakoff, *Moral Politics: How Liberals and Conservatives Think*, 2nd ed. (Chicago: The University of Chicago Press, 2002).

25. Robert Huckfeldt and John Sprague, *Citizens, Politics, and Social Communication: Information and Influence in an Election Campaign* (New York: Cambridge University Press, 1994); Samuel Popkin, *The Reasoning Voter: Communication*

and Persuasion in Presidential Campaigns (Chicago: University of Chicago Press, 1991).

26. Dufour, "Sifting through Tradition."

27. Baxter and Lansing, *Women and Politics.*

28. Leege and Kellstedt, *Rediscovering the Religious Factor in American Politics.*

29. James L. Guth et al., *The Bully Pulpit: The Politics of Protestant Clergy* (Lawrence: University of Kansas Press, 1997).

30. Admittedly, this variable only captures religious belief for Catholic, Protestant, and Jewish believers; however, respondents from other religious traditions make up only a minute fraction of the total sample.

31. Robert E. Denton Jr., "Religion, Evangelicals, and Moral Issues in the 2004 Presidential Campaign," in *The 2004 Presidential Campaign: A Communication Perspective*, ed. Robert E. Denton, Jr. (Lanham MD: Rowman & Littlefield Publishers, 2005), John C. Green, Mark J. Rozell, and Clyde Wilcox, *The Values Campaign? The Christian Right and the 2004 Elections* (Washington, DC: Georgetown University Press, 2006).

32. Mark J. Rozell and Debasree Das Gupta, "'The Values Vote'? Moral Issues and the 2004 Elections," in *The Values Campaign? The Christian Right and the 2004 Elections*, ed. John C. Green, Mark J. Rozell, and Clyde Wilcox (Washington, D.C.: Georgetown University Press, 2006), Katherine Stenger, "Religiously Motivated Political Action and Same-Sex Marriage," in *Church-State Issues in America Today: Religious Convictions and Practices in Public Life*, ed. Ann W. Duncan and Steven L. Jones (Westport: Praeger Perspectives, 2008).

33. Richard J. Powell and Mark D. Brewer, "Constituencies and the Consequences of the Presidential Vote," in *A Defining Moment: The Presidential Election of 2004*, ed. William Crotty (Armonk: M.E. Sharpe, 2004).

34. Baxter and Lansing, *Women and Politics*; Wendy J. Deichmann Edwards and Carolyn De Swarte Gifford, eds., *Gender and the Social Gospel* (Chicago: University of Illinois, 2003).

35. Susan M. Hartmann, "Expanding Feminism's Field and Focus: Activism in the National Council of Churches in the 1960s and 1970s," in *Women and Twentieth-Century Protestantism*, ed. Margaret Lamberts Bendroth and Virginia Lieson Brereton (Chicago: University of Illinois, 2002).

36. Baxter and Lansing, *Women and Politics.*

37. Edwards and Gifford, *Gender and the Social Gospel.*

38. Dale E. Soden, "The Women's Christian Temperance Union in the Pacific Northwest: A Different Side of the Social Gospel," in *Gender and the Social Gospel*, ed. Wendy J. Deichmann Edwards and Carolyn De Swarte Gifford (Chicago: University of Illinois, 2003).

39. Carolyn De Swarte Gifford, "'The Woman's Cause Is Man's'": Frances Willard and the Social Gospel," in *Gender and the Social Gospel*, ed. Wendy J. Deichmann Edwards and Carolyn De Swarte Gifford (Chicago: University of Illinois, 2003), 26.

40. Kim A. Lawton, "Whatever Happened to the Religious Right?" *Christianity Today*, December 15, 1989, 44.

41. Ruth Murray Brown, *For a "Christian America": A History of the Religious Right* (Amherst, MA: Prometheus Books, 2002).

42. Diamond, *Not by Politics Alone*.

43. Clyde Wilcox, Matthew DeBell, and Lee Sigelman, "The Second Coming of the New Christian Right: Patterns of Popular Support in 1984 and 1996," *Social Science Quarterly* 80, no. 1 (1999): 181–92.

44. Diamond, *Not by Politics Alone*.

45. Brown, *For a "Christian America."*

46. Brown, *For a "Christian America."*

47. Brown, *For a "Christian America."*

48. Brown, *For a "Christian America."*

49. Wilcox, DeBell, and Sigelman, "The Second Coming of the New Christian Right."

50. Hartmann, "Expanding Feminism's Field and Focus"; Roberta Grimm and Kathleen S. Hurty, "Prayer, Power, and Prophetic Action: Church Women United," in *A Tapestry of Justice, Service, and Unity: Local Ecumenism in the United States, 1950–2000*, ed. Arleon L. Kelley (Tacoma, WA: National Association of Ecumenical and Interreligious Staff Press, 2004).

51. Grimm and Hurty, "Prayer, Power, and Prophetic Action," 95–96.

52. Grimm and Hurty, "Prayer, Power, and Prophetic Action"; Hartmann, "Expanding Feminism's Field and Focus."

53. Grimm and Hurty, "Prayer, Power, and Prophetic Action," 76.

54. Faith Rogow, *Gone to Another Meeting: The National Council of Jewish Women, 1893–1993*, ed. Leon J. Weinberger, Judaic Studies Series (Tuscaloosa: The University of Alabama Press, 1993).

55. Rogow, *Gone to Another Meeting*.

56. Rogow, *Gone to Another Meeting*.

57. B'nai B'rith International is a Jewish organization founded in 1843 for the purpose of advocating on behalf of the State of Israel and combating anti-Semitism.

58. Marlin Levin, *Balm in Gilead: The Story of Hadassah* (New York: Schocken Books, 1973).

59. Levin, *Balm in Gilead*.

60. Afaf Lutfi al-Sayyid Marsot, "Entrepreneurial Women in Egypt," in *Feminism and Islam: Legal and Literary Perspectives*, ed. Mai Yamani and Andrew Allen (New York: New York University Press, 1996).

61. Fareed H. Numan, *The Muslim Population in the United States* (American Muslim Council, 1992 [cited February 11 2005]), www.islam101.com/history /population2_usa.html. This figure is disputed by many scholars of religion and politics. Green, Djupe, and Calfano in this volume argue that a more accurate figure is 1.6 to 28 million Muslims.

62. David Truman, *The Governmental Process* (New York: Knopf, 1951).

63. *Azizah*, "Muslim Women's League," Spring 2002.

64. Larry B. Stammer, "First Lady Breaks Ground with Muslims," *Los Angeles Times*, May 31, 1996.

65. *Azizah*, "Kamilat," Spring 2002.

66. Jim Wallis, *God's Politics: Why the Right Gets It Wrong and the Left Doesn't Get It* (San Francisco: HarperCollins, 2005).

67. Margaret Lamberts Bendroth and Virginia Lieson Brereton, eds., *Women and Twentieth-Century Protestantism* (Chicago: University of Illinois, 2002), xiii.

CHAPTER 6

1. David G. Dalin and Alfred J. Kolatch, *The Presidents of the United States and the Jews* (Middle Village, NY: Jonathan David Publishers, Inc., 2000).

2. Jonathan D. Sarna, *American Judaism: A History* (New Haven, CT: Yale University Press, 2004), 38; this correspondence is also discussed in Jonathan D. Sarna and David G. Dalin, *Religion and State in the American Jewish Experience* (Notre Dame, IN: University of Notre Dame Press, 1997), 77–78.

3. Sarna, *American Judaism*, 38.

4. Sarna, *American Judaism*, 38. This letter is quoted in some detail in Dalin and Kolatch, *The Presidents of the United States and the Jews*, 7–8. It is reprinted in its entirety in Sarna and Dalin, *Religion and State in the American Jewish Experience*, 78–79.

5. Sarna, *American Judaism*, 38–39; and Sarna and Dalin, *The Presidents and the Jews*, 80.

6. Sarna, *American Judaism*, 39.

7. Sarna, *American Judaism*, 39.

8. Dalin and Kolatch, *The Presidents and the Jews*, 89.

9. Dalin and Kolatch, *The Presidents and the Jews*, 112–13.

10. Dalin and Kolatch, *The Presidents and the Jews*, 113.

11. Jonathan D. Sarna, *Jacksonian Jew: The Two Worlds of Mordecai Noah* (New York: Holmes & Meier, Publishing, Inc., 1981), 27.

12. Sarna and Dalin, *Religion and State*, 89.

13. Sarna and Dalin, *Religion and State*, 90.

14. Sarna, *Jacksonian Jew*, 28.

15. Belmont's political career in nineteenth-century Democratic politics is discussed in considerable detail in Irving I. Katz, *August Belmont: A Political Biography* (New York: Columbia University Press, 1968).

16. Judah P. Benjamin's life and political career is discussed and analyzed in illuminating detail in Eli N. Evans, *Judah P. Benjamin: The Jewish Confederate* (New York: The Free Press, 1989).

17. Simon Wolf's life and political career is discussed and analyzed in Esther L. Panitz, *Simon Wolf: Private Conscience and Public Policy* (Cranberry, NJ: Associated University Presses, Inc., 1887); his political career and role as a political confidant and adviser of every Republican president from Abraham Lincoln to William Howard Taft is also discussed in his autobiographical memoir, *The Presidents I Have Known, From 1860–1918* (Washington, DC: Byron S. Adams, 1918).

18. Dalin and Kolatch, *The Presidents and the Jews*, 107.

19. Wolf, *The Presidents I Have Known*, 111.

20. Dalin and Kolatch, *The Presidents and the Jews*, 117–18. Although he was at first reluctant to accept the nomination, Straus concluded that "my destiny" was to return to Constantinople, and he wrote McKinley that "I deem it my patriotic duty to you and to the country to accept." Dalin and Kolatch, *The Presidents and the Jews*, 118.

21. Oscar S. Straus, *Under Four Administrations: From Cleveland to Taft* (New York: Houghton Mifflin Company, 1922), 210.

22. Richard F. Fenno Jr., *The President's Cabinet* (Cambridge, MA: Harvard University Press, 1959), 67–87; Anthony J. Bennett, *The American President's Cabinet: From Kennedy to Bush* (New York: St. Martin's Press, 1996); and Henry J. Abraham, *Justices, Presidents and Senators: A History of U.S. Supreme Court Appointments from Washington to Clinton*, new and revised edition (Lanham, MD: Rowman & Littlefield, 1999).

23. Naomi W. Cohen, *A Dual Heritage: The Public Career of Oscar S. Straus* (Philadelphia: The Jewish Publication Society of America, 1969), 147.

24. Cohen, *A Dual Heritage*, 148.

25. Cohen, *A Dual Heritage*, 150.

26. Cohen, *A Dual Heritage*, 150.

27. Arthur Hertzberg, *The Jews in America: Four Centuries of an Encounter; A History* (New York: Simon and Schuster, 1989), 282.

28. Henry L. Feingold, "Jewish Leadership During the Roosevelt Years," in *Bearing Witness: How America and the Jews Responded to the Holocaust* (Syracuse, NY: Syracuse University Press, 1995), 241.

29. Dalin and Kolatch, *The Presidents and the Jews*, 168.

30. Geoffrey C. Ward, *A First-Class Temperament: The Emergence of Franklin Roosevelt* (New York: Harper and Row Publishers, 1989), 254.

31. Kissinger's life and career as a Harvard University professor of government, as a foreign policy adviser to New York governor (and presidential hopeful) Nelson Rockefeller, and as President Nixon's special assistant for National Security Affairs and Secretary of State, is discussed and analyzed in much critical and illuminating detail in Walter Isaacson's comprehensive biography: Walter Isaacson, *Kissinger: A Biography* (New York: Touchstone Books, 1992). His role in the Nixon administration is also discussed in Dalin and Kolatch, *The Presidents and the Jews*, 219–22.

32. J. J. Goldberg, *Jewish Power: Inside the Jewish Establishment* (Reading, MA: Addison-Wesley, 1996), 238.

33. Dalin and Kolatch, *The Presidents and the Jews*, 240–41.

34. Dalin and Kolatch, *The Presidents and the Jews*, 241–43.

35. Dalin and Kolatch, *The Presidents and the Jews*, 246.

36. Dalin and Kolatch, *The Presidents and the Jews*, 247.

37. The political background, role, and ideas of these neoconservative intellectuals is discussed in John Ehrman, *The Rise of Neoconservatism: Intellectuals and Foreign Affairs, 1945–1994* (New Haven, CT: Yale University Press, 1995); Peter Steinfels, *The Neoconservatives: The Men Who Are Changing America's Politics* (New York: Simon and Schuster, 1979); Gary Dorrien, *The Neoconservative Mind: Culture and the War of Ideology* (Philadelphia: Temple University Press, 1993); Mark Gerson,

The Neoconservative Vision: From the Cold War to the Culture Wars (Lanham, MD: Madison Books, 1996); and Edward S. Shapiro, "Right Turn? Jews in the American Conservative Movement," in *Jews in American Politics*, ed. L. Sandy Meisel and Ira N. Forman (Lanham, MD: Rowman & Littlefield, 2001), 195–211.

38. The role and experience of these and other Jewish appointees to foreign policy positions in the Reagan administration is discussed in Dalin and Kolatch, *The Presidents and the Jews*, 252–54; John Ehrman, *The Rise of Neoconservatism: Intellectuals and Foreign Affairs, 1945–1994*; Kenneth W. Thompson, ed., *Foreign Policy in the Reagan Presidency: Nine Intimate Perspectives* (Lanham, MD: University Press of America, 1993); Elliott Abrams, *Undue Process: A Story of how Political Differences Are Turned into Crimes* (New York: The Free Press, 1993); Richard Pipes, *VIXI: Memoirs of a Non-Belonger* (New Haven, CT: Yale University Press, 2003); Dov S. Zakheim, *Flight of the Lavi: Inside a U.S.-Israeli Crisis* (Washington, DC: Brassey's, Inc., 1996); and James Mann, *Rise of the Vulcans: The History of Bush's War Cabinet* (New York: Penguin Books, 2004).

39. Elliott Abram's experiences in the Reagan administration are recounted, in considerable detail, in his memoir *Undue Process: A Story of Political Differences Are Turned into Crimes* (New York: The Free Press, 1992).

40. Wolfowitz's government career during the 1970s and during the Reagan administration is discussed in James Mann, *Rise of the Vulcans.*

41. Dalin and Kolatch, *The Presidents and the Jews*, 247.

42. Dalin and Kolatch, *The Presidents and the Jews*, 247.

43. Dalin and Kolatch, *The Presidents and the Jews*, 247.

44. The history and experiences of the Kirkpatrick mission to the United Nations during the first Reagan administration is recounted by Allan Gerson, Ambassador Kirkpatrick's legal counsel to the UN Mission, in his memoir. Allan Gerson, *The Kirkpatrick Mission: Diplomacy Without Apology: America at the United Nations, 1981–1985* (New York: The Free Press, 1991).

45. This "battle" between the American Jewish community and the Reagan White House over the sale of AWACS to Saudi Arabia is discussed in Edward Tivnan, *The Lobby: Jewish Political Power and American Foreign Policy* (New York: Touchstone Books, 1987), 135–61; Jerome A. Chanes, "Who Does What? Jewish Advocacy and Jewish 'Interest,'" in *Jews in American Politics*, ed. L. Sandy Maisel and Ira N. Forman, 111 and 117; Wolf Blitzer, *Between Washington and Jerusalem* (New York: Oxford University Press, 1985), 135–37, 195–97, and 244–47; Steven L. Spiegel, *The Other Arab-Israeli Conflict: Making America's Middle East Policy, from Truman to Reagan* (Chicago: The University of Chicago Press, 1985), 407–11; and Peter Golden, *Quiet Diplomat: Max M. Fisher—A Biography* (New York: Cornwall Books, 1992), 427–29 and 431–32.

46. Jerome A. Chanes, "Who Does What?" 117.

47. James Mann. *Rise of the Vulcans*, 113.

48. Although the House of Representatives voted against the AWACS sale by a margin of 301 to 111, "the Jewish community's effort to stop the AWACS sale failed," when the Senate voted in favor of the sale, by a margin of 52-48. Chanes, "Who Does What?" 117.

49. Dalin and Kolatch, *The Presidents and the Jews*, 247–48.

50. Dalin and Kolatch, *The Presidents and the Jews*, 248.

51. Dalin and Kolatch, *The Presidents and the Jews*, 248.

52. Marshall Breger, "Reagan: Big Steps Altered Jewish Politics," *Forward*, June 10, 2004.

53. Dalin and Kolatch, *The Presidents and the Jews*, 250.

54. Dalin and Kolatch, *The Presidents and the Jews*, 252.

55. Dalin and Kolatch, *The Presidents and the Jews*, 252.

56. Max Kampelman discusses his role in these human rights efforts on behalf of Soviet Jewish emigration during the Reagan administration in Deborah Hart Strober and Gerald S. Strober, *Reagan—The Man and His Presidency: The Oral History of an Era* (Boston: Houghton Mifflin Company, 1998), 230–31, 338.

57. In his autobiographical memoir, *Fear No Evil*, Sharansky recounts his nine years as a prisoner in the Soviet Union, his release from prison in 1986, and his subsequent emigration to Israel. Natan Sharansky, *Fear No Evil* (New York: Random House, 1988).

58. Dalin and Kolatch, *The Presidents and the Jews*, 250; and Sharansky, *Fear No Evil*, 422.

59. Quoted in Strober and Strober, *Reagan—The Man and His Presidency*, 349.

60. Breger, "Reagan: Big Steps Altered Jewish Politics."

61. Quoted in Strober and Strober, *Reagan—The Man and His Presidency*, 251.

62. Breger, "Reagan: Big Steps Altered Jewish Politics."

63. Seymour Martin Lipset and Earl Raab, *Jews and the New American Scene* (Cambridge, MA: Harvard University Press, 1995), 157.

64. This point has recently been made by Jay Lefkowitz, who has noted that since the founding of the State of Israel in 1948, "a key factor for Jewish voters has been their perception of which candidate will best attend to the security needs of the Jewish state and best deal with the terrorism that has been directed against it." Jay Lefkowitz, "The Election and the Jewish Vote," *Commentary*, February 2005, 62.

65. Steven L. Spiegel, "Israel and Beyond: American Jews and U.S. Foreign Policy," in *Jews in American Politics*, ed. Maisel and Forman, 264.

66. Spiegel, "Israel and Beyond," 264.

67. Benjamin Ginsberg, *The Fatal Embrace: Jews and the State* (Chicago: University of Chicago Press, 1993), 218.

68. Ginsberg, *The Fatal Embrace*, 222.

69 "The U.S. vs. Israel," *Wall Street Journal*, March 6, 1992, quoted in Ginsberg, *That Fatal Embrace*, 222.

70. Ginsberg, *The Fatal Embrace*, 223.

71. Spiegel, "Israel and Beyond," 264.

72. Spiegel, "Israel and Beyond," 264; and Fred Barnes, "They're Back!: Neocons for Clinton," *New Republic*, August 3, 1992, 12–14.

73. Lipset and Raab, *Jews and the New American Scene*, 165.

74. Dennis Ross recounts his role as President Clinton's special Middle East coordinator and negotiator and as the point man for the Clinton administration in shaping U.S. involvement in the Middle East peace process in his memoir. Dennis Ross, *The*

Missing Peace: The Inside Story of the Fight for Middle East Peace (New York: Farrar, Straus, and Giroux, 2004).

75. Neoconservative Republican critics of the Clinton administration's foreign policy initiatives, especially, argued that the Middle East peace process had been decidedly unsuccessful. The views and critiques of many of these neoconservative critics of the Clinton-Ross peace efforts in the Middle East are contained in Neal Kozodoy, ed., *The Middle East Peace Process: An Autopsy* (San Francisco: Encounter Books, 2001). The conservative Israeli author and political analyst Shmuel Katz critiques Ross's role in shaping U.S. involvement in the Middle East peace process in Shmuel Katz, "Dennis Ross Confesses," *Jerusalem Post*, July 11, 2001.

76. Dalin and Kolatch, *The Presidents and the Jews*, 286–87.

77. Quoted in Natalie Weinstein, "Clinton, Dole Backers Debate: Who's Best for Jews?" *Jewish Bulletin of Northern California*, June 14, 1996.

78. Dalin and Kolatch, *The Presidents and the Jews*, 272–78.

79. Dalin and Kolatch, *The Presidents and the Jews*, 261–67.

80. President Clinton's nomination of Zoe Baird as attorney general, the controversy over the nomination, and the eventual withdrawal of her nomination are discussed in Bennett, *The American President's Cabinet: From Kennedy to Bush*, 207–8.

81. Robert A. Burt, "On the Bench: The Jewish Justices," in *Jews in American Politics*, ed. Maisel and Forman, 66.

82. The history of the Supreme Court appointments and judicial careers of these five Jewish justices is recounted in Jennifer M. Lowe, ed., *The Jewish Justices of the Supreme Court Revisited: Brandeis to Fortas* (Washington, DC: The Supreme Court Historical Society, 1994). The role of anti-Semitism in the Supreme Court appointments of these five Jewish justices is discussed in Thomas Karfunkel and Thomas W. Ryley, *The Jewish Seat: Anti-Semitism and the Appointment of Jews to the Supreme Court* (Hicksville, NY: Exposition Press, 1978). Comparative studies of the Supreme Court appointments and judicial careers of justices Louis Brandeis and Felix Frankfurter are found in the dual biographies Leonard Baker, *Brandeis and Frankfurter: A Dual Biography* (New York: Harper and Row, 1984); and Richard A. Burt, *Two Jewish Justices: Outcasts in the Promised Land* (Berkeley: University of California Press, 1988). The Supreme Court appointments and judicial careers of the Jewish justices are also analyzed in the following judicial biographies: Alpheus Thomas Mason, *Brandeis: A Free Man's Life* (New York: Viking, 1946); Melvin I. Urofsky, *Louis D. Brandeis and the Progressive Tradition* (Boston: Little, Brown and Company, 1981); Philippa Strum, *Louis D. Brandeis: Justice for the People* (Cambridge, MA: Harvard University Press, 1984); Lewis J. Paper, *Brandeis* (Englewood Cliffs, NJ: Prentice Hall, 1983); Andrew L. Kaufman, *Cardozo* (Cambridge, MA: Harvard University Press, 1998); Liva Baker, *Felix Frankfurter* (New York: Coward-McCann, 1969); H. N. Hirsch, *The Enigma of Frankfurter* (New York: Basic Books, 1981); Michael E. Parrish, *Felix Frankfurter and His Times* (New York: Free Press, 1982); Bruce Allen Murphy, *Fortas* (New York: William Morrow and Company, 1988); and Laura Kalman, *Abe Fortas* (New Haven, CT: Yale University Press, 1990).

83. President Clinton's appointments of Ruth Bader Ginsburg and Stephen G. Breyer to the Supreme Court are discussed in Abraham, *Justices, Presidents and Senators*, 317–

25; and in Ruth Bader Ginsburg, "From Benjamin to Breyer: Is There a Jewish Seat?" *The Supreme Court Historical Society Quarterly* 24 (November 3, 2003): 1 and 4–6.

84. Henry J. Abraham, *Justices, Presidents and Senators*, 299.

85. Robert A. Burt, "On the Bench: The Jewish Justices," 55.

86. Ginsburg, "From Benjamin to Breyer," 6.

87. Bill Clinton's appointments of Martin Indyk as ambassador to Israel and Daniel Kurtzer as ambassador to Egypt are discussed in Dalin and Kolatch, *The Presidents and the Jews*, 268–69.

CHAPTER 7

1. Some of the material in this chapter first appeared in Paul A. Djupe and John C. Green, "The Politics of American Muslims," in *From Pews to Polling Places: Faith and Politics in the American Religious Mosaic*, ed. J. Matthew Wilson (Washington, DC: Georgetown University Press, 2007), 213–50, and is included here with permission. The authors gratefully acknowledge the cooperation of Richard Brown and his colleagues at Georgetown University Press.

2. Tom W. Smith, "Religious Diversity in America: The Emergence of Muslims, Buddhists, Hindus, and Others," *Journal for the Scientific Study of Religion* 41, no. 3 (2002): 577–85.

3. Tom W. Smith, *Estimating the Muslim Population in the United States* (New York: The American Jewish Committee, 2001).

4. Michael A. Hogg, "Social Identity," in *Handbook of Self and Identity*, ed. Mark R. Leary and June P. Tangney (New York: Guilford Press, 2003), 422–79; Henri Tajfel, *Social Identity and Intergroup Behavior* (Cambridge: Cambridge University Press, 1982); Hugh Goddard, "Christian-Muslim Relations: A Look Backwards and a Look Forwards," *Islam and Christian Muslim Relations* 11, no. 2 (2000): 195–212.

5. Ronald Inglehart and Pippa Norris, "The True Clash of Civilizations," *Foreign Policy* 135 (March–April 2003): 62–70.

6. Gabriel A. Almond and Sidney Verba, *The Civic Culture* (Boston: Little, Brown, and Company, 1963); Norman Nie, Jane Jun, and Kenneth Stehlik-Barry, *Education and Democratic Citizenship in America* (Chicago: University of Chicago Press, 1996); Alexander Keyssar, *The Right to Vote: The Contested History of Democracy in the United States* (New York: Basic Books, 2000).

7. Zogby International made the 2001 and 2004 MAPS surveys available at cost. We owe a special thanks to John Zogby and Zogby International for allowing access to these data.

8. Yvonne Yazbeck Haddad and Adair T. Lummis, *Islamic Values in the United States: A Comparative Study* (New York: Oxford University Press, 1987).

9. Karen Isaksen Leonard, *Muslims in the United States: The State of Research* (New York: Russell Sage Foundation, 2003).

10. Leonard, *Muslims in the United States*, 44.

11. It is worth noting that ARIS found that 62 percent of American Muslims claimed to belong to a mosque, a figure that supports the MAPS sampling strategy.

However, ARIS also found that African Americans made up 27 percent of American Muslims, more than the MAPS assumption of 20 percent.

12. Data provided to authors by the Islamic Center of Pittsburgh, March 9, 2008.

13. M. Arif Ghayur, "Muslims in the United States: Settlers and Visitors," *Annals of the American Academy of Political and Social Science* 454 (March 1981): 150–63.

14. Ilyas Ba-Yunus and Kassim Kone, "Muslim Americans: A Demographic Report," in *Muslims' Place in the American Public Square: Hopes, Fears, and Aspirations*, ed. Zahid H. Bukhari, Sulayman S. Nyang, Mumtaz Ahmad, and John L. Esposito (New York: Alta Mira, 2004).

15. Association of Statisticians of American Religious Bodies (ASARB), *Religious Congregations & Membership in the United States 2000* (Nashville, TN: Glenmary Research Center, 2002).

16. Smith, *Estimating the Muslim Population in the United States*.

17. Pew Research Center, "Muslim Americans: Middle Class and Mostly Mainstream," http://pewforum.org/surveys/muslim-american (accessed March 23, 2008).

18. Data courtesy of *The Washington Post*, www.washingtonpost.com/wp-dyn /politics/elections/2004/ (accessed March 19, 2008).

19. The Zogby 2004 Post Election Survey had ten thousand cases and the Muslim figures were made available by Tom Perriello of the Progressive Faith Media. The National Surveys of Religion and Politics were conducted at the University of Akron 1992 to 2004 (with a total of some fourteen thousand total cases and four thousand in 2004). According to Scott Keeter, survey director for the Pew Research Center, the Muslim figures came from pooling the thirty-five thousand cases in the 2004 surveys.

20. Barry A. Kosmin, Egon Mayer, and Ariela Keysar, "American Religious Identification Survey: 2001" (New York: The Graduate Center for the City University of New York, 2001).

21. Jane I. Smith, *Islam in America* (New York: Columbia University Press, 1999).

22. Council on American-Islamic Relations Research Center, "American Muslim Voters: A Demographic Profile and Survey of Attitudes" (Washington, DC: 2006).

23. While other attempts at national surveys of the American Muslim community have been made (the CAIR study being just one example), we believe the methodology used in the MAPS surveys to be inherently superior in capturing a more accurate national sample of Muslims than has been the case previously.

24. California voter population estimates courtesy of the California Secretary of State, www.sos.ca.gov/elections/ror/60day_presprim/hist_reg_stats.pdf (accessed March 19, 2008).

25. Leonard, *Muslims in the United States*.

26. Amaney Jamal, "The Political Participation and Engagement of Muslim Americans," *American Politics Research* 33 no. 4 (2005): 521–44.

27. Sylviane Diouf, *Servants of Allah: African Muslims Enslaved in the Americas* (New York: New York University Press, 2004).

28. Ghayur, "Muslims in the United States," 153.

29. Leonard, *Muslims in the United States*, 6–7.

30. Leonard, *Muslims in the United States*, 19–44.

31. Leonard, *Muslims in the United States*, 13–14.

32. Leonard, *Muslims in the United States*, 9–12.

33. Diouf, *Servants of Allah*, 268–69.

34. Diouf, *Servants of Allah*, 272.

35. Leonard, *Muslims in the United States*, 41.

36. Contact Calfano for variable coding information from MAPS data.

37. We made several attempts to ascertain an estimate of the Nation of Islam's membership size, especially in terms of the percentage of African-American Muslims holding group membership. In correspondence, Mark Potok, director of the Southern Poverty Law Center's Intelligence Project, which monitors the size and affairs of various hate groups within the United States, suggested that no accurate estimate of the group's membership exists, and that the Nation of Islam itself likely does not know how many members it has (correspondence with Calfano, March 19, 2008).

38. Jay P. Dolan, *The American Catholic Experience: A History from Colonial Times to the Present* (Notre Dame, IN: University of Notre Dame Press, 1992).

39. ARIS found that 35 percent of Muslim Americans were Democrats in 2001, 39 percent were Independents, and 19 percent were Republicans (ARIS 2001). However, the ARIS data were collected well before September 11 and the MAPS data afterward.

40. John C. Green, Corwin E. Smidt, James L. Guth, and Lyman A. Kellstedt, "The American Religious Landscape and the 2004 Presidential Vote: Increased Polarization," http://pewforum.org/publications/surveys/postelection.pdf, 2004 (accessed March 15, 2008).

41. The 2004 National Survey of Religion and Politics found that 35 percent of the American public identified as conservative, 43 percent as moderate, and 22 percent as liberal.

42. John W. Ayers, "Changing Sides: 9/11 and the American Muslim Voter," *Review of Religious Research* 49, no. 2 (2007): 187–98.

43. Andrew Kohut, John C. Green, Scott Keeter, and Robert C. Toth, *The Diminishing Divide: Religion's Changing Role in American Politics* (Washington, DC: Brookings Institution, 2000).

44. Sidney Verba, Kay Lehman Schlozman, and Henry E. Brady, *Voice and Equality: Civic Volunteerism in American Politics* (Cambridge, MA: Harvard University Press, 1995).

45. The low rate of African participation may reflect the fact that the 2004 sample contained more recent immigrants than the 2001 sample.

46. Paul A. Djupe and J. Tobin Grant, "Religious Institutions and Political Participation in America," *Journal for the Scientific Study of Religion* 40, no. 2 (2001): 303–14.

47. Brandice Canes-Wrone, Michael C. Herron, and Kenneth W. Shotts, "Leadership and Pandering: A Theory of Executive Policymaking," *American Journal of Political Science* 45 (July 2000): 532–50; Jeff Manza and Fay Lomax Cook, "The Impact of Public Opinion on Public Policy: The State of the Debate," in *Navigating Public Opinion: Polls, Policy, and the Future of American Democracy*, ed. Jeff Manza, Fay Lomax Cook, and Benjamin I. Page (Oxford: Oxford University Press, 2002).

48. Margaret G. Hermann, "Leaders, Leadership, and Flexibility: Influences on Heads of Government as Negotiators and Mediators," *Flexibility in International Negotiation and Medication, Annals of the American Academy of Political and Social Science* 542 (November 1995): 148–67.

49. Contact Calfano for information on interview questions.

50. William J. Clinton, remarks at a Democratic National Committee dinner, October 21, 1993, text provided by the American Presidency Project, www.presidency.ucsb.edu (accessed March 9, 2008).

51. William J. Clinton, address to Arab nations, December 19, 1998, text provided by the AmericanPresidency Project, www.presidency.ucsb.edu (accessed March 9, 2008).

52. William J. Clinton, videotape remarks on the observance of Ramadan, November 22, 2000, text provided by the American Presidency Project, www.presidency.ucsb.edu (accessed March 9, 2008).

53. Mary E. Stuckey and Joshua R. Ritter, "George Bush, Human Rights, and American Democracy," *Presidential Studies Quarterly* 37, no. 4 (2007): 646–66.

54. Stuckey and Ritter, "George Bush and American Democracy," 647.

55. Stuckey and Ritter, "George Bush and American Democracy," 648.

56. George W. Bush, remarks at the Islamic Center of Washington, September 17, 2001, text provided by the American Presidency Project, www.presidency.ucsb.edu (accessed March 9, 2008).

57. Peter Ford, "Europe Cringes at Bush's 'Crusade' Against Terrorists," *The Christian Science Monitor*, September 19, 2001.

58. Jacky Rowland, "Muslim Stereotypes Challenged in US," *BBC News*, http://news.bbc.co.uk/2/hi/americas/3454115.stm (accessed March 19, 2008); George W. Bush, remarks at the Islamic Center of Washington, September 17, 2001.

59. Wendy Cho, James G. Gimpel, and Tony Wu, "Clarifying the Role of SES in Political Participation: Policy Threat and Arab American Mobilization," *Journal of Politics* 68, no. 4 (2006): 977–91; Ayers, *Changing Sides*, 188; Human Rights Watch, "World Report 2002: United States Hate Crimes," http://www.hrw.org/wr2k2/us.html#Hate%20Crimes (accessed March 23, 2008).

60. George W. Bush, remarks on the twentieth anniversary of the National Endowment for Democracy, November 6, 2003, text provided by the American Presidency Project, www.presidency.ucsb.edu (accessed March 9, 2008).

61. George W. Bush, remarks to the Asia Society, February 22, 2006, text provided by the American Presidency Project, www.presidency.ucsb.edu (accessed March 9, 2008).

62. David E. Kaplan, "Nuclear Monitoring of Muslims Done without Search Warrants," *U.S. News and World Report*, December 22, 2005, http://www.usnews.com/usnews/news/articles/nest/051222nest.htm (accessed March 9, 2008). John Solomon, "FBI Provided Inaccurate Data for Surveillance Warrants," *The Washington Post*, March 27, 2007, http://www.washingtonpost.com/wp-dyn/content/article/2007/03/26/AR2007032602073.html (accessed March 9, 2008).

63. ARIS found that four-fifths of the entire population was registered to vote in 2001, but just 44 percent of Muslims were registered to vote. The higher levels of

registration may reflect overreporting, but also the higher social status of the MAPS samples.

64. For the 2001 MAPS, the measure of turnout was a recall measure of 2000 turnout; for 2004, it was anticipated turnout in 2004. Like many other survey measures of turnout, these figures certainly contain a high level of overreporting.

65. All these reported levels of activism are high compared to the population at large, and this may reflect some overreporting on the part of the respondents. However, the questions asked if the respondent *ever* participated in these ways, and in addition, these individuals have high social status, a factor strongly associated with political participation.

66. For the 2001 MAPS, the recall of 2000 presidential vote choice was used. The 2004 MAPS had a measure of anticipated presidential vote choice because the survey occurred before the 2004 election. These data were adjusted to reflect the final presidential vote in the Zogby 2004 Post Election Survey.

67. Paul A. Djupe and Laura R. Olson, eds., *The Encyclopedia of American Religion and Politics* (New York: Facts on File, 2003).

68. David Lerner, *The Passing of Traditional Society: Modernizing the Middle East* (New York: The Free Press, 1968); Raymond Hinnebusch, "Authoritarian Persistence, Democratization Theory and the Middle East," *Democratization* 13, no. 3 (2006): 373–95; Brian Robert Calfano and Emile Sahliyeh, "Determining Democracy among Members of the Organization of the Islamic Conference," *Social Science Quarterly* 89, no. 3 (forthcoming).

CHAPTER 8

1. Asians began immigrating to the United States en masse with the 1965 Immigration Act, which repealed the discriminatory national origin quota system. However, Asian migration to America goes back to a much earlier period. It is commonly dated to the arrival of the Chinese in 1849 in the midst of the California Gold Rush. While these Chinese laborers contributed to building the American West with their physical looks and lifestyles, they were too visible and were considered to menace the predominantly Anglo society. Such antagonistic sentiments resulted in the Chinese Exclusion Act of 1882, subsequently curtailing the size of Chinese and other Asian immigration. Pei-te Lien, "Religion and Political Adaptation among Asian Americans: An Empirical Assessment from the Pilot National Asian American Political Survey," in *Asian American Religions: The Making and Remaking of Borders and Boundaries*, ed. Tony Carnes and Fenggang Yang (New York: New York University Press, 2004).

2. Andy Aoki and Don T. Nakanishi, eds., "Symposium on Asian Pacific Americans and the New Minority Politics" *PS: Political Science and Politics* 34, no. 3 (2001): 605–44 and Bruce B. Lawrence, *New Faiths, Old Fears: Muslims and Other Asian Immigrants in American Religious Life* (New York: Columbia University Press, 2002).

3. Pei-te Lien, "Religion and Political Adaptation among Asian Americans: An Empirical Assessment from the Pilot National Asian American Political Survey," in

Asian American Religions: The Making and Remaking of Borders and Boundaries, ed. Tony Carnes and Fenggang Yang (New York: New York University Press, 2004).

4. Although mass-based electoral participation of Asian Americans became a possibility with the liberalization of the immigration policy in 1965, Asian Americans' involvement in electoral politics has been led by prominent elite politicians rather than mass-based organizations. (Lien, "Religion and Political Adaptation among Asian Americans.") This elite-centered political engagement is one of the major barriers to mass political participation by Asian Americans.

5. Aoki and Nakanishi, "Symposium"; Wendy Tam Cho, "Naturalization, Socialization, and Participation: Immigrants and (Non-)Voting," *Journal of Politics* 61, no. 4 (1999): 1140–55; John W. Lee, ed., *Asian-American Electoral Participation* (New York: Novinka Books, 2002); Janelle Wong, "The Effects of Age and Political Exposure on the Development of Party Identification Among Asian American and Latino Immigrants in the United States," *Political Behavior* 22 (December 2000): 341–71.

6. Carnes and Yang, *Asian American Religions*; Jane Naomi Iwamura and Paul Spickard, eds., *Revealing the Sacred in Asian and Pacific America* (New York: Routledge, 2003); Pyong Gap Min and Jung Ha Kim, *Religions in Asian America: Building Faith Communities* (Walnut Creek, CA: AltaMira Press, 2002).

7. If Asians who identify themselves with more than one race are included, the percentage of Asian Americans increases to 4.2 percent. The Census Bureau concedes that the count of Asians as a racial group may have underestimated the Asian population size by about two percentage points in 2000 (see www.census.gov/Press-Release /www/2001/cn03attach.pdf).

8. Pilot National Asian American Political Survey, 2000–2001 (Principal Investigator: Pei-te Lien). This study is a multicity and multilingual survey on the political attitudes and behavior of Asian Americans. The survey drew on a semirandom sample of households from one of the six major Asian-American ancestries, collected for the households of Los Angeles, New York, Honolulu, San Francisco, and Chicago.

9. American Religious Identification Survey, 2001 (Principal Investigators: Barry A. Kosmin and Egon Mayer), The Graduate Center of the City University of New York. This is a survey of religious distribution of the American adult population. This 2001 survey is a follow-up study to the 1990 survey named the National Survey of Religious Identification. These surveys are claimed as the most extensive surveys of religious identification of American adults in the second half of the twentieth century. The 2001 study employed a random digit-dialed telephone survey of 50,281 American residential households in the forty-eight continental states.

10. Hispanic is not really a racial grouping, for it crosscuts different racial groups. Hispanics emerged as the largest minority group in the 2000 census.

11. Panethnic or pan-Asian identity is a political and cultural construct rather than a concept indicating an existing condition. It is not an inevitable coalition but a product of social and political processes Mari Matsuda, *Where Is Your Body?* (Boston: Beacon Press, 1996).

12. Asians are the most established minority in Hawaii for historical reasons. Since the descendents of Asian immigrants who receive tertiary education mostly live and

work in continental states, the percentage of bachelor's degree holders among Asians is lower than is actually the case in Hawaii.

13. Ho-Youn Kwon, Kwang Chung Kim, and R. Stephen Warner, eds., *Korean Americans and their Religions: Pilgrims and Missionaries from a Different Shore* (University Park: Pennsylvania State University Press, 2001); Lawrence, *New Faiths, Old Fears*; Min and Kim, *Religions in Asian America*; David K. Yoo, ed., *New Spiritual Homes: Religion and Asian Americans* (Honolulu: University of Hawaii Press, 1999).

14. Another interesting finding is that the distribution of Catholic and non-Catholic Christians is relatively equal (22 percent versus 29 percent) among Asian Americans, whereas the latter is more dominant among the general American public (24.2 percent versus 52 percent).

15. These percentages were obtained from the question asking "When it comes to your outlook, do you regard as secular, somewhat secular, somewhat religious, or religious?" Though the question was about the general outlook, the percentage of those who said "secular" in this survey is very much similar to the percentage who said "no religion" in the PNAAPS survey. Kosmin et al., p. 22. Barry Kosmin, Egon Mayer, and Ariela Keysar, *American Religious Identification Survey* (New York: The City University of New York, 2001), p. 22.

16. R. Stephen Warner and J. G. Wittner, eds., *Gathering in Diaspora: Religious Communities and the New Immigration* (Philadelphia: Temple University Press, 1998); Carnes and Yang, *Asian American Religions*.

17. Chinese immigration has taken place in several waves, each marked by people of different social strata and of different regions of China. Mainland Chinese after the communist revolution could not emigrate until the restoration of the diplomatic relationship during the Nixon administration. Since then, mainland Chinese immigrants have overwhelmed Taiwanese immigrants in number and political influence.

18. Janelle Wong, "The Role of Community Organizations in the Political Incorporation of Asian American and Latino Immigrants" (paper presented at the Conference on Race and Civil Society, Racine, WI, 2000); Yang, *Chinese Christians in America*.

19. Researchers of Asian American politics have found the degree of panethnic identity to vary significantly among different ethnic groups of the Asian American community. Japanese Americans are most likely to identify themselves as Asian Americans, whereas Korean and Chinese Americans are least likely to do so (Lien, "Religion and Political Adaptation among Asian Americans"). Japanese Americans, the first Asian group to immigrate to the United States in large numbers, initially settled in Hawaii, expanding later to continental regions. Since the early decades of the 1900s, Japanese American politicians who held high offices in Hawaii and in other states have been the most ardent advocates of Asian interests and causes in American politics.

20. There have been some efforts to create panethnic religious gatherings, however. Jeung (2004) tracks the emergence of panethnic churches among Asian Americans around western cities such as San Francisco and Los Angeles. Russell Jeung, *Faithful Generations: Race and New Asian American Churches* (New Brunswick, NJ: Rutgers University Press, 2005).

21. As in other cases of nonwhite rights movements, political activists of the Asian American movement have formed an affiliation with the Democratic Party since the civil rights era.

22. Nonidentifiers are those who do not think politics in partisan terms at all, whereas Independents are those who have other political affiliations than the Republican or Democratic Party.

23. Michael Corbett and Julia Mitchell Corbett, *Politics and Religion in the United States* (New York: Garland Publishers, 1999); Kenneth J. Heineman, *God is a Conservative: Religion, Politics, and Morality in Contemporary America* (New York: New York University Press, 1998); William B. Prendergast, *The Catholic Voter in American Politics: The Passing of the Democratic Monolith* (Washington, DC: Georgetown University Press, 1999); Kenneth D. Wald, *Religion and Politics in the United States* (Washington, DC: CQ Press, 1997).

24. John W. Lee, ed., *Asian-American Electoral Participation* (New York: Novinka Books, 2002).

25. Muslims' support for Bush (60 percent) is somewhat surprisingly high in this regard. However, the number of Asian American Muslims who said they voted in 2000 was extremely small, which makes the percentage of their candidate support highly unreliable.

26. Note, however, that the presidential candidate support rates varied greatly by individual ethnic group. Most notably, a majority of the Vietnamese gave their support to Bush.

27. The Asian American Legal Defense and Education Fund (AALDEF) exit polls were conducted in November 2004 on about eleven thousand Asian American voters in eight states with large Asian populations. According to these polls, Asian Americans favored Kerry over Bush by a three to one margin (74 percent to 24 percent), with 2 percent voting for other candidates. However, this result may not be truly representative of Asian American voters, since the poll sample was weighted heavily towards large metropolitan areas.

28. Individuals' political attitudes and behavior are well-known to vary with socioeconomic and demographic characteristics such as age, gender, education, and income. The current multivariate analysis leaves out these variables, however. One of the reasons is that not only political variables but also religious and ethnic variables in the analysis are affected by those same background variables. Hence the inclusion of such demographic variables would generate very high correlations among the independent variables. Known as collinearity, such high correlations pose a problem for statistical estimation.

29. Yet having a religion does not itself lead one to lean more towards one or the other political party, as can be seen in the insignificant coefficient estimate on the believers dummy variable in the last panel regression of table 8.4.

30. In table 8.3, the coefficients on all other ethnic group dummy variables are significantly negative in the regressions of political interest. This indicates that the members of these groups are less interested in politics than those of the reference group. The coefficients on the ethnic variables in the regressions of political ideology are all significantly positive, suggesting that these ethnic group members are more

politically conservative than Indian/Pakistani Americans. Among all ethnic groups, Korean Americans turn out to be most politically conservative, which in part reflects the ideological tension in their home country, where Protestant churches have aligned with the political right.

31. According to the ARIS data, between 1990 and 2001 the proportion of Asian Americans who are Christian has dropped from 63 percent to 43 percent, whereas those professing other religions such as Buddhism or Islam have risen from 15 percent to 28 percent. For example, there are more than three times as many Hindus in the United States today as there were in 1990.

32. Harvey G. Cox, *The Secular City: Secularization and Urbanization in the Theological Perspective* (New York: Macmillan, 1965).

33. See Lien, "Religion and Political Adaptation among Asian Americans," 231–45 for an excellent overview of currently available survey datasets on Asian American political behavior.

CHAPTER 9

1. The three-fifths compromise of 1787 was enacted by delegates to the constitutional convention in Philadelphia. The plan was offered by James Madison for determining a state's representation in the U.S. House of Representatives. The issue of how to count slaves split the delegates into two orders. The northerners regarded slaves as property who should receive no representation. Southerners demanded that blacks be counted equally with whites. The compromise reflected the strength of the proslavery forces at the convention. The "three-fifths compromise" allowed a state to count three-fifths of each black person in determining political representation in the House.

2. Some sources on the issue of slave resistance include Ira Berlin et al., *Remembering Slavery: African Americans Talk About Their Personal Experiences of Slavery and Freedom* (New York: The New Press, 1998); Richard D. E. Burton, *Afro-Creole: Power, Opposition, and Play in the Caribbean* (Ithaca, NY: Cornell University Press, 1997); Kim D. Butler, *Freedoms Given, Freedoms Won: Afro-Brazilians in Post-abolition, Sao Paulo and Salvador* (New Brunswick, NJ: Rutgers University Press, 1998); Paul D. Escott, *Slavery Remembered: A Record of Twentieth-Century Slave Narratives* (Chapel Hill: University of North Carolina Press, 1979); John David Smith, *Black Slavery in the Americas: An Interdisciplinary Bibliography, 1865–1980* (Westport, CT: Greenwood Press, 1982).

3. Orlando Patterson, *Slavery and Social Death: A Comparative Study* (Cambridge, MA: Harvard University Press, 1985); Gayraud S. Wilmore, *Black Religion and Black Radicalism: An Interpretation of the Religious History of African Americans* (Maryknoll, NY: Orbis Books, 1998); Carlyle Fielding Stewart III, *Black Spirituality and Black Consciousness: Soul Force, Culture and Freedom in the African-American Experience* (Trenton, NJ: Africa World Press, Inc, 1999); Earl Riggens, *Dark Symbols, Obscure Signs: God, Self, and Community in the Slave* Mind. Maryknoll (New York: Orbis Books, 1993); Albert B. Cleage Jr., *The Black Messiah: The Religious Roots of Black Power* (New York: Sheed and Ward, 1969); Katie Can-

non, *Katie's Canon: Womanism and the Soul of the Black Community* (New York: Continuum, 1995).

4. Wilmore, *Black Religion and Black Radicalism*, 25.

5. E. Franklin Frazier, *The Negro Church in America* (New York: Schocken Books, 1974); C. Eric Lincoln, *The Black Church Since Frazier* (New York: Schocken Books, 1974).

6. C. Eric Lincoln and Lawrence H. Mamiya, *The Black Church in the African American Experience* (Durham, NC: Duke University Press, 1990).

7. Doug McAdam, *Political Process and the Development of Black Insurgency, 1930–1970* (Chicago: University of Chicago Press, 1982); Aldon D. Morris, *The Origins of the Civil Rights Movement: Black Communities Organizing for Change* (New York: The Free Press, 1984); Henry Brady, Sidney Verba, and Kay Lehman Schlozman, *Voice and Equality: Civic Voluntarism in American Politics* (Cambridge, MA: Harvard University Press, 1996).

8. Frederick C. Harris, *Something Within: Religion in African-American Political Activism* (Oxford: Oxford University Press, 1999); Christopher G. Ellison, "Religious Involvement and Self-Perception among Black Americans," *Social Forces* 71, no. 4 (1993): 1027–55; Allison Calhoun-Brown, "African American Churches and Political Mobilization: The Psychological Impact of Organizational Resources," *The Journal of Politics* 58, no. 4 (1996): 935–53.

9. Morris, *Origins of the Civil Rights Movement*, 4.

10. This critique is leveled by researchers of the black church who argue that religion works as a means of social control offering African Americans a way to cope with personal and societal difficulties and undermining their willingness to actively challenge racial inequalities. Works in this tradition include Gary T. Marx, *Protest and Prejudice: A Study of Belief in the Black Community* (New York: Harper and Row, 1969); E. Franklin Frazier, *The Negro Church in America*; Adolph Reed, *The Jesse Jackson Phenomenon: The Crisis of Purpose in Afro-American Politics* (New Haven, CT: Yale University Press, 1986).

11. Lincoln and Mamiya, *The Black Church in the African American Experience*, 7.

12. Mary Patillo-McCoy, *Black Picket Fences: Privilege and Peril Among the Black Middle Class* (Chicago: University of Chicago Press, 1998), 767.

13. Pattillo-McCoy, *Black Picket Fences*, 768.

14. Some have argued that the black church does not have a distinct theology or did not have one until the mid-1960s. James H. Cone and Gayraud S. Wilmore, eds., *Black Theology: A Documentary History, Volume One: 1966–1979* (New York: Orbis Books, 1993). In the introduction, Cone and Wilmore argue that "when blacks separated themselves from White denominations and organized their own churches in the late eighteenth and early nineteenth centuries they did not perceive their actions as being motivated by theological differences. They accepted without alteration the church doctrines and politics of the White denominations from which they separated" (89). In some ways this assertion is an overstatement, one that does not credit the distinct worship styles and religious emphases that distinguished slave religion from the Christianity of white Americans, but it does reflect the lack of a fully articulated academic theological perspective to guide black Christian worship. I am making a

claim of a more organic form of theology built around commonly held understandings of religious texts that circulate in black churches.

15. Vincent Wimbush, *The Bible and African Americans: A Brief History* (Minneapolis: Augsburg Fortress Press, 2003), 40–41.

16. Wimbush, *The Bible and African Americans*, 24.

17. Richard Neustadt, *Presidential Power and the Modern Presidents: The Politics of Leadership from Roosevelt to Reagan* (New York: Free Press, 1991).

18. Michael Nelson, *The Presidency and the Political System* (Washington, DC: Congressional Quarterly, 1995), 9.

19. Kenneth O'Reilly, *Nixon's Piano: Presidents and Racial Politics from Washington to Clinton* (New York: The Free Press, 1995).

20. O'Reilly, *Nixon's Piano*, 17.

21. Thomas Jefferson, *Notes on the State of Virginia* (Richmond, VA: J. W. Randolph, 1853).

22. National Anti-Slavery Standard, Feb 24, 1842, as cited in Charles Wesley, "The Participation of Negroes in Anti-Slavery Political Parties," *The Journal of Negro History* 29, no. 1 (January 1944), 43.

23. Wilson Jeremiah Moses, *Black Messiahs and Uncle Toms: Social and Literary Manipulations of a Religious Myth* (University Park: Pennsylvania State University Press, 1993).

24. David Howard-Pitney, "Wars, White America, and the Afro-American Jeremiad: Frederick Douglass and Martin Luther King, Jr.," *The Journal of Negro History* 71, no. 1. (Winter–Autumn 1986): 23–37.

25. Merrill D. Peterson, *Lincoln in American Memory* (New York: Oxford University Press, 1994).

26. Scott Sandage, "A Marble House Divided: The Lincoln Memorial, the Civil Rights Movement, and the Politics of Memory, 1939–1963," *Journal of American History* 80, no. 1 (1993): 135–67.

27. Lerone Bennett, *Forced into Glory: Abraham Lincoln's White Dream* (Chicago: Johnson Publishing Company, 2000).

28. Peterson, *Lincoln in American Memory*.

29. Historians classify the post-Reconstruction era, especially following *Plessy v. Ferguson* (1896), as the nadir of American race relations. By deferring to states' rights throughout post-Reconstruction, the federal government and Supreme Court allowed the persistent and deliberate destruction of black civil rights momentarily gained in the Reconstruction amendments. The prospect of permanent confinement to a second-class status made post-Reconstruction America the nadir moment for blacks.

30. President Franklin D. Roosevelt did denounce lynching following an incident of a white person being murdered by mob violence. He did not draw specific parallels to the black experience of lynching. For more on this see Nancy Weiss, *Farewell to the Party of Lincoln: Black Politics in the Age of FDR* (Princeton, NJ: Princeton University Press, 1983).

31. Michael Dawson, *Behind the Mule: Race and Class in African-American Politics* (Princeton, NJ: Princeton University Press, 1994), 99–100.

32. Dawson, *Behind the Mule*, 99.

33. Walton Hanes, *Black Political Parties: An Historical and Political Analysis* (New York: Free Press, 1972).

34. Weiss, *Farewell to the Party of Lincoln.*

35. Weiss, *Farewell to the Party of Lincoln,* 122.

36. Weiss, *Farewell to the Party of Lincoln,* 129.

37. Perhaps the most comprehensive study of change in U.S. racial attitudes, Howard Schuman, Charlotte Steeh, Lawrence D. Bobo, and Maria Krysan's *Racial Attitudes in America* (Cambridge, MA: Harvard University Press, 1998), uncovers a significant and persistent gap in contemporary attitudes of white and black Americans. They find "large differences in the perspectives of blacks and whites about the causes of black disadvantage. Blacks emphasize continuing discrimination; whites stress low motivation on the part of blacks. This disagreement in perceptions of causality sets the stage for many other differences" (275).

38. There is always some difference in self-reported data in postelection surveys and the actual counts from voting localities. However, surveys of white Americans typically create a bandwagon effect where survey respondents overreport having voted for the election winner. The fact that African Americans overreport support for the Democratic candidate, even when that candidate fails to win the election, is indicative of the strength of the attachment to the party and its candidates.

39. For more on this trend and its relevance for contemporary black politics see the following sources: Lucius Barker and Ronald Walters, eds., *Jesse Jackson's 1984 Presidential Campaign: Challenge and Change in American Politics* (Urbana: University of Illinois Press, 1989); Michael Dawson, *Behind the Mule*; Michael Dawson, Ronald Brown, and Cathy Cohen, *Political Parties and African American Unemployment* (unpublished manuscript, 1990); Katherine Tate, *From Protest to Politics: The New Black Voters in American Elections* (Cambridge, MA: Harvard University Press, 1994); Ronald Walters, "The Emergent Mobilization of the Black Community in the Jackson Campaign for President," in *Jesse Jackson's 1984 Presidential Campaign,* eds. Barker and Walters.

40. Dawson, *Behind the Mule,* 117.

41. Alphonso Pinkney, *The Myth of Black Progress* (New York: Cambridge University Press, 1984), 178.

42. There was one important factor that complicated presidential politics for black Americans in the 1980s. Although the presidency was held by Republicans whom African Americans largely reviled, 1984 and 1988 ushered in the Democratic primary bids of Reverend Jesse Jackson Sr. Jackson's presidential bids had an important influence on black involvement in presidential politics by increasing voter registration and turnout among blacks and by affecting the attitudes that blacks held toward the Democratic Party. For full treatment of these issues see the following sources: Barker and Walters, eds., *Jesse Jackson's 1984 Presidential Campaign*; Tate, *From Protest to Politics*; Reed, *The Jesse Jackson Phenomenon.*

43. The National Black Election Study survey focuses on the attitudes and political preferences of the black electorate during the 1984 and 1988 presidential elections. Questions regarding party identification, political interest, and preferences and choices for president were asked. In addition, respondents were asked about their

feelings concerning Jesse Jackson's campaigns for the presidency in 1984 and 1988 and the effect his campaigns had on the elections. Information on race and gender issues, economic matters, quality of life, government spending, political participation, and religion and church politics is also included. Demographic information on respondents includes sex, age, education, marital status, income, and occupation and industry. The principal investigator was James Jackson.

44. The data from the National Black Politics Study come from a probability sample of all African American households, yielding 1,206 respondents who are African Americans eighteen years or older. The survey was conducted between November 20, 1993, and February 20, 1994, with a response rate of 65 percent. The survey was administered through the University of Chicago with principal investigators Ronald Brown of Wayne State University and Michael Dawson of the University of Chicago.

45. Richard Shingles, "Black Consciousness and Political Participation: The Missing Link," *The American Political Science Review* 75, no. 1 (1981): 76–91; Dawson, *Behind the Mule*; Tate, *From Protest to Politics.*

46. Nick Kotz, *Judgment Days: Lyndon Baines Johnson, Martin Luther King, Jr., and the Laws that Changed America* (New York: Houghton Mifflin Company, 2005).

47. Speech of President Lyndon B. Johnson to joint session of Congress on November 27, 1963.

48. Speech of President Lyndon B. Johnson to joint session of Congress, November 27, 1963, 24.

49. Carl T. Rowan, *Breaking Barriers: A Memoir* (New York: Perennial, 1992).

50. Speech of President Lyndon B. Johnson to joint session of Congress on March 15, 1965.

51. Rowan, *Breaking Barriers.*

52. Toni Morrison, "The Talk of the Town," *The New Yorker*, October 5, 1998.

53. Lawrence Bobo and Michael Dawson, "Poles and Polls Apart: Blacks and Whites Divided on the Clinton Legacy," preliminary report from joint project of Dubois and Center for the Study of Race, Politics, and Culture (CSRPC), 2001.

54. Dewayne Wickham, *Bill Clinton and Black America* (New York: Ballantine Books, 2002), 80.

55. Wickham, *Bill Clinton and Black America*, 35.

56. Wickham, *Bill Clinton and Black America*, 58.

57. Wickham, *Bill Clinton and Black America*, 64.

58. Wickham, *Bill Clinton and Black America*, 26.

CHAPTER 10

1. The author heard this comment at the "Rebranding the Democratic Party" event in Los Angeles County in spring 2005. The author wishes to thank the Pew Charitable Trust for funding the HCAPL research project and So Young Kim for her assistance in analyzing the Hispanic Churches in American Public Life National Survey data.

2. For a detailed discussion of the HCAPL national survey methodology see Gastón Espinosa, "Methodological Reflections on Social Science Research on Latino Religions," in *Rethinking Latino/a Religions and Identity*, ed. Miguel de la Torre and Gastón Espinosa (Cleveland, OH: Pilgrim Press, 2006), 13–45. For a discussion of the survey by Green, Smidt, Guth and Kellstedt and Green's methodology see John C. Green, *The Faith Factor: How Religion Influences American Elections* (Westport, CT: Praeger Publishers, 2007), xv–xvi, 189, n. 34. The discussion of Latinos, religion, and the 2004 election will draw extensively on the findings in this book.

3. F. Arturo Rosales, *Chicano! The History of the Mexican American Civil Rights Movement* (Houston, TX: Arte Público Press, 1997), 2–109.

4. Reginald Horsman, "Scientific Racism and the American Indian in the Mid-Nineteenth Century," *American Quarterly* 27, no. 2 (May 1975): 165n54, 166nn59, 61; Michael H. Hunt, *Ideology and U.S. Foreign Policy* (New Haven, CT: Yale University Press, 1987), 60; David R. Roediger, *The Wages of Whiteness: Race and the Making of the American Working Class* (New York: Verso Books, 1999), 141; Moises Sandoval, *On the Move: A History of the Hispanic Church in the United States* (Maryknoll, NY: Orbis Books, 1991).

5. William D. Carrigan and Clive Webb, "The Lynching of Persons of Mexican Origin or Descent in the United States, 1848–1928," *Journal of Social History* 37, no. 2 (2003): 411–38.

6. Rodolfo Acuña, *Occupied America: A History of Chicanos* (San Francisco, CA: Canfield Press, 1972), 144, 147–49.

7. See Gastón Espinosa, Virgilio Elizondo, and Jesse Miranda, eds., *Latino Religions and Civic Activism in the United States* (New York: Oxford University Press, 2005), passim.

8. Sandoval, 1991, 10–40; Espinosa, Elizondo, and Miranda, eds., *Latino Religions and Civic Activism in the United States*, 7–14, 19–33; Timothy Matovina and Gerald E. Poyo, *¡Presente! U.S. Latino Catholics from Colonial Origins to the Present* (Maryknoll, NY: Orbis Books, 2000), 45–89.

9. Matovina and Poyo, 67–68, 73–76.

10. Sandoval, *On the Move*, 30–37.

11. Rosales, *Chicano!* 28–86, 96–109.

12. Rosales, 28–109; Moises Sandoval, *Fronteras: A History of the Latin American Church in the USA Since 1513* (San Antonio, TX: Mexican American Cultural Center, 1983), 233–35, 262–63.

13. Espinosa, Elizondo, and Miranda, eds., *Latino Religions and Civic Activism in the United States*, 77–126, 298–300; Gastón Espinosa, "Today We Act, Tomorrow We Vote": Latino Religions, Politics, and Activism in Contemporary U.S. Civil Society," *The Annals of the American Academy of Political and Social Science* 612 (July 2007): 152–71.

14. Espinosa, Elizondo, and Miranda, eds., *Latino Religions and Civic Activism in the United States*, 13–75, 159–73, 187–88, 249–78.

15. Espinosa, Elizondo, and Miranda, eds., *Latino Religions and Civic Activism in the United States*, 13–14, 187–88, 249–78.

16. Sidney Verba, Key Lehman Schlozman, and Henry E. Brady, *Voice and Equality: Civic Voluntarism in American Politics* (Cambridge, MA: Harvard University Press, 1995); Rodolfo O. de la Garza, *Ethnic Ironies: Latino Politics in the 1992 Elections* (Boulder, CO: Westview Press, 1996); Rodolfo O. de la Garza, Louis DeSipio, F. Chris García, John A. García, and Angelo Falcón, *Latino Voices: Mexican, Puerto Rican, and Cuban Perspectives on American Politics* (Boulder, CO: Westview Press, 1992); Peggy Levitt, "Two Nations under God? Latino Religious Life in the United States," in *Latinos Remaking America*, eds. Marcelo M. Suárez-Orozco and Mariela M. Páez (Berkeley: University of California Press, 2002), 150–64.

17. Verba, Schlozman, and Brady, *Voice and Equality*, 230–31, 245–47, 320–32.

18. Michael Jones-Correa and David L. Leal, "Political Participation: Does Religion Matter?" *Political Research Quarterly* 54 (2001): 751–70.

19. Louis DeSipio, "Power in the Pews? Religious Diversity and Latino Political Attitudes and Behaviors," in *From Pews to Polling Places: Faith and Politics in the American Religious Mosaic*, ed. J. Matthew Wilson (Washington, DC: Georgetown University Press, 2007), 161–84.

20. Verba, Schlozman, and Brady, *Voice and Equality*; de la Garza, *Ethnic Ironies*; de la Garza, DeSipio, F. Chris García, John A. García, and Falcón, *Latino Voices*; Levitt, *Latinos Remaking America*, 150–64; Jones-Correa and Leal, 751–70.

21. David L. Leal, Matt A. Barreto, Jongho Lee, and Rodolfo O. de la Garza, "The Latino Vote in the 2004 Election," *PSOnline* (2005): 41–49; DeSipio, "Power in the Pews?" 181.

22. For a more detailed discussion and analysis of misclassifying the religious identity of Latinos in social science research, see Espinosa, "Methodological Reflections of Social Science Research on Latino Religions." For the association of born-again Christianity with evangelicalism, see Wade Clark Roof, *The Spiritual Marketplace: Baby Boomers and the Remaking of American Religion* (Princeton, NJ: Princeton University Press, 1999), 129, 303, 319. For a discussion of classifying those with ambiguous religious identities, see Michael Hout and Claude S. Fischer, "Why More Americans Have No Religious Preference: Politics and Generations," *American Sociological Review* 67 (2002): 165–90; Darren E. Sherkat, "Tracking the Restructuring of American Religion: Religious Affiliation and Patterns of Religious Mobility, 1973–1988," *Social Forces* 79, no. 4 (2001): 1462; Brian Steensland, Jerry Z. Park, Mark D. Regnerus, Lynn D. Robinson, W. Bradford Wilcox, and Robert D. Woodberry, "The Measure of American Religion: Toward Improving the State of the Art," *Social Forces* 79, no.1 (September 2000): 291–318.

23. We realize that all taxonomies and classification systems are imperfect and fraught with all kinds of limitations noted in the anthropological, sociological, theological, and religious studies literature. Religious boundaries are porous, fluid, and combinative. However, we also realize that social scientists are nonetheless required and forced by the very nature of their profession and methodology to place small numbers of religious respondents together into larger pools of respondents in order to statistically analyze their religious views and how they in turn shape their political, civic, and social views. We see this classification system as simply one of many potential starting points and research tools that should be revised and developed as

the needs and contours of the Latino community change. Espinosa, Elizondo, and Miranda, 2003, 13.

24. Respondents in the HCAPL national survey category "no religious preference" come from the screening question (S #4) rather than the religious identity question (Q #23). Because we only asked respondents to specify their tradition for the religious identity question rather than from the religion screening question (where "no religious preference" is found), we are unable to know how or if these individuals could or would self-identify with a religious tradition. We believe that many would if we had provided the "specify" option for the screening question. However, because we did not ask them to specify their tradition we also cannot classify them or break them down further into an existing religious tradition and have no intention of doing so. The number of Latinos self-identifying with other religious traditions, world religions, other, or something else is much lower in the HCAPL national survey than in most other surveys because respondents were able to specify their precise tradition or spirituality. The majority of these respondents specified an identifiably Christian denomination or tradition.

25. These calculations are based on imputing the raw percentages from the HCAPL national survey response options into raw numbers and projections based on the 2008 U.S. Census Bureau figures, which indicate that the number of Latinos in the United States is 46 million. All estimates in this study are rounded up to the nearest hundred thousand or million.

26. In the HCAPL national survey, a large number of Latinos self-identified with the following traditions below. These figures are not membership or Spanish-language district statistics, which are limited to largely first generation Latinos, but rather how Latinos self-identify across all generations including those that attend English-language "Euro-American" congregations. These figures should also not be considered strict denominational figures because people can and do self-identify with a religious tradition without necessarily attending a church or tradition on a regular basis for a whole host of reasons, including holding multiple jobs, job transfers, multiple religious identities, and alienation or indifference with a tradition that they still recognize as their own religious tradition. Twelve of the largest non-Catholic Latino-serving Christian traditions in the United States include the Jehovah's Witnesses (2.26 percent of the U.S. Latino population), Assemblies of God (2.17 percent), Pentecostal Church of God (2.02 percent), Assembly of Christian Churches (1.99 percent), American Baptist (1.50 percent), Southern Baptist (1.21 percent) Seventh-Day Adventist (0.83 percent), Mormon (0.75 percent), Apostolic Assembly (Pentecostal) (0.52 percent), Lutheran (ELCA & Missouri Synod) (0.52 percent), Methodist (United & Free) (0.51 percent), and Presbyterian (0.30 percent).

27. Andrew M. Greeley, "Defection Among Hispanics," *America*, July 30, 1988, 61–62; Andrew M. Greeley, "The Demography of American Catholics: 1965–1990," in *The Sociology of Andrew W. Greeley* (Atlanta, Georgia Scholars Press, 1994), 545–64; Andrew M. Greeley, "Defection Among Hispanics (Updated)," *America*, September 27, 1997, 12–13.

28. Greeley; "Defection"; Greeley; "Defection . . . (updated)."

29. Gastón Espinosa, "The Pentecostalization of Latin American and U.S. Latino Christianity," *Pneuma: The Journal of the Society for Pentecostal Studies* 26, no. 2 (2004): 262–92.

30. Table I information as cited in Louis DeSipio, *Counting on the Latino Vote: Latinos as a New Electorate* (Charlottesville: University Press of Virginia, 1996), 31.

31. Leal, Barreto, Lee, and de la Garza, "The Latino Vote in the 2004 Election."

32. Leal, Barreto, Lee, de la Garza, "The Latino Vote in the 2004 Election," 43; Green, *The Faith Factor*, 154; Espinosa, Elizondo, and Miranda, *Latino Religions and Civic Activism in the United States*, 279–306.

33. The findings for the 31 percent vote swing and how Latinos voted in 2004 draw on the NSRP and Green, *The Faith Factor*, 87–89.

34. The Fourth National Survey of Religion and Politics sample size was large (n = 2730), random, and nationally representative. For more on the methodology and findings, see John C. Green, Corwin E. Smidt, James L. Guth, and Lyman A. Kellstedt, *The American Religious Landscape and the 2004 Presidential Vote: Increased Polarization* (The Pew Forum on Religion and Public Life: 2004), http://pewforum .org/publications/surveys/postelection.pdf. Green, *The Faith Factor*, 88. Many of these findings are cited in Green, *The Faith Factor*, passim. The NEP found that Bush won 57 percent of the Latino vote while Kerry won 43 percent.

35. The NSRP as cited in Green, *The Faith Factor*, 18, 147, 149.

36. The NEP and NSRP as cited in Green, *The Faith Factor*, 14–16, 72–75.

37. The NEP and NSRP as cited in Green, *The Faith Factor*, 14–16, 72–75, 79–81.

38. The NEP and NSRP as cited in Green, *The Faith Factor*, 9, 11, 15, 80–86.

39. The NSRP and Green, *The Faith Factor*, 63–66, 92–96.

40. I was a witness to these events because I was invited by Rev. Miranda and the AMEN Board to give a series of scholarly lectures on trends and demographic shifts in U.S. Latino religion and politics. I had no prior association with AMEN or the NAE. This is where I also met a Latino (who shall remain nameless) who confided to me that he was a "Democratic operative" working in the Latino faith community on behalf of the Democratic Party and then-presidential candidate Al Gore. He showed several photographs of himself with President Clinton at White House functions. He asked me to work on the election team. I declined the invitation and all other such Democratic and Republican invitations. That he was a low-ranking operative is clear because he too was surprised by Gore's decision not to address the clergy, despite the fact that he strongly encouraged him to do so.

41. José Vicente Rojas, *José: God Found Me in Los Angeles* (Hagerstown, MD: Review and Herald Publishing Association, 1999). This section is also based on personal conversations and interviews with the Rojas.

42. The information in this paragraph is based on the following sources and conversations with Father Virgilio Elizondo and Jesse Miranda. Espinosa, Elizondo, and Miranda, eds., *Latino Religions and Civic Activism in the United States*, 298–302; Bill Clinton, *My Life* (New York: Alfred A. Knopf, 2004), 197, 394, 546–47, 641–45, 792, 896, 928; Rojas, *José*, 97, 146–47.

Gastón Espinosa, Virgilio Elizondo, and Jesse Miranda, *Hispanic Churches in American Public Life: Summary of Findings No. 2*, Interim Reports (Notre Dame, IN:

University of Notre Dame Institute for Latino Studies, 2003), 14–16; Rojas, *José*, 97, 138–47. See the photo of President Bush's meeting with Latino clergy and lay leaders in Espinosa, Elizondo, and Miranda, *Latino Religions and Civic Activism in the United States*, 281. Other observations in the following paragraphs are based on confidential interviews with Latino political leaders, clergy, and lay leaders. For evidence of the 2004 presidential election findings see Roger Simon, "Second Act," *U.S. News and World Report, Special Election Edition*, November 5, 2004, 30, especially 24; Dan Gilgoff, "The Morals and Values Crowd," *U.S. News and World Report*, November 15, 2004, 42; Ricardo Alonso-Zaldivar, "Bush Snags Much More of the Latino Vote, Exit Polls Show," *Los Angeles Times*, November 4, 2004, A30; Green, Smidt, Guth, and Kellstedt, *The American Religious Landscape and the 2004 Presidential Vote*; President George W. Bush, "President Bush Attends National Hispanic Prayer Breakfast," Office of the Press Secretary, June 15, 2007, www.whitehouse.gov/news/releases/2006/06/20060608-1.html, 1–3.

43. President George W. Bush, "Remarks at the National Hispanic Prayer Breakfast," Washington, D.C., June 15, 2007.

44. Espinosa, Miranda, and Elizondo, *Hispanic Churches in American Public Life: Summary of Findings*, 17–22.

45. Espinosa, "Today We Act, Tomorrow We Vote," 163–69.

CHAPTER 11

1. The findings in this study are based on the National Election Pool (NEP), the Latino Religions and Politics (LRAP) national survey, and other post-election studies. The NEP poll was conducted by Edison/Mitofsky and was funded and sponsored by ABC, CNN, the Associated Press, CBS, Fox, and NBC. The 2008 NEP was conducted at three hundred polling places across the United States. It polled the attitudes of 17,836 Election Day voters. The polling places were selected as a stratified probability sample of each state and a subsample was selected at the proper proportions for the national exit poll. In addition, absentee or early voters in all fifty states were interviewed in a preelection telephone poll. Absentee or early voters and voters at the polling places on Election Day were asked the same questions, and the results were combined in approximately the correct proportions. Exit polls are arguably as or more reliable than post-election surveys because people are more likely to respond in the latter that they voted for the winning candidate. The LRAP national survey, which was conducted from October 1 through 7, 2008, was based on a nationwide bilingual Spanish/English, thirty-nine-question telephone survey of 1,104 Latinos that were either citizens or permanent residents or had nonresident status (covering all of the possibilities). These adults were all eighteen years of age or older, Latino, and declared that their religious preference was either Catholic or Protestant/other Christian. The margin of error for the 1,104-Latino sample is +/-2.9 percentage points. The margin of error for the 700 registered voters and 700 Protestants interviews is +/-3.7 percent, and for the 400 Latino Catholic interviews (half registered voters) is +/-4.9 percent. The margin of error for the 200 Latino Catholic registered voters is +/-6.9 percent-

age points at a 95 percent confidence level. The margin of error for the 500 Latino Protestant registered voters is +/-4.4 percentage points at a 95 percent confidence level. Although this study will occasionally refer to the other surveys and other LRAP samples (1,104 national sample, 500 Protestants, 400 Catholics), unless otherwise indicated, this study will focus exclusively on the 700 Latino registered voters, 500 of which were Protestant and 200 Catholic. These voters were all eighteen years of age or older, Latino, registered, and either Catholic or Protestant/other Christian. The raw totals were weighted by Rick Hunter and SDR Consulting according to the national percentage of Latino Catholics (68%) and Protestant/other Christians and Others (32%) in the United States as noted in the Pew Hispanic Project and Pew Forum study *Changing Faiths: Latinos and the Transformation of American Religion.*

2. For evidence of Obama's outreach to and meetings with religious leaders throughout the nation see the following Pew Religion Forum on Religion and Public Life link: http://pewforum.org/religion08/profile.php?CandidateID=4. Latino Catholic theologian Dr. Miguel Díaz of St. John's University (MN) and Pentecostal pastor Wilfredo De Jesus of the four thousand–member New Life Covenant Church in Chicago were brought on to Obama's campaign team as his Latino Catholic and Protestant 2008 election advisors to help spread his message throughout the Latino faith community. De Jesus is vice president of social justice for the NHCLC. Obama recently appointed Díaz to serve as ambassador to the Vatican. Obama's campaign held a number of conference calls and face-to-face meetings with Latino Evangelical leaders, including one conference call with thirty leaders in July 2008. Obama also meet with 150 Latino Evangelical leaders on February 29 to listen to their concerns and issues in at an invitation-only event at the University of Texas–Brownsville. David Brody wrote: "Obama's faith based team was on the call along with the campaign's Latino Vote Director. As for the groups represented, the National Hispanic Christian Leadership Conference was on the call along with pastors from New York, Florida, Colorado, Texas, Indiana, Pennsylvania, Ohio, and DC/Baltimore" (David Brody, "Hispanic Evangelical Pastors Meet with Obama Campaign," CBNnews.com, www.cbn.com/cbnnews/406193. aspx). NHCLC, "National Hispanic Evangelical Leader, Rev. Wilfredo De Jesus, Meets with Obama, Hispanics Embracing 'Change' Message," www.nhclc.org/about/news/mar2008_1.html. See Michelle A. Vu, "Obama Connects with Hispanic Evangelicals in Texas," *Christian Post*, March 3, 2008, www.christianpost.com/article/20080303/obama-connects-with-hispanic-evangelicals-in-texas.htm; Leslie Sanchez, "Courting Hispanic Evangelicals," June 11, 2008, CNN Political Contributor, http://ac360.blogs.cnn.com/2008/06/11/courting-hispanic-evangelicals/; Arian Campos-Flores and Jessica Ramirez, "Power in the Pews: Latino Evangelicals Are In-Demand Group This Fall," *Newsweek*, October 7, 2008; Lawrence Schumacher, "Event of a Lifetime: Several Central Minnesotans Will Attend the Historic Inauguration," *St. Cloud Times*, January 18, 2009; Pamela Brogan, "Locals Witness History in D.C.," *St. Cloud Times*, January 21, 2009; Hispanic Theological Initiative, "HTI Fellow Present as Religious Advisor at Historical Inauguration," *Journeys*, March 2009, 1; Peter Wallsten, "Obama Leads in Battle for Latino Vote," *Los Angeles Times*, June 6, 2008; Kevin Eckstrom, "Inaugural Prayers," *Religion News Service*, January 7, 2009. For evidence that immigration is a key factor in shaping how Latinos vote see the following report, National Survey on

Latino Protestants, "Immigration and the 2008 Election," October 16, 2008. For the link see: http://blog.faithinpubliclife.org/upload/2008/10/LATINO%20PROTESTANT %20POLL%20REPORT%20--%20Embargoed%20until%2010%2016%2008%20at% 201%2000%20pm%20EDT.pdf.

3. Ted Olsen, "The Evangelical Electoral Map (Updated)," *Christianity Today* on-line edition, November, 5, 2008, http://blog.christianitytoday.com/ctpolitics/2008/11/ the_evangelical.html; Joe Von Kanel, "Exit Polls: The Religion Factor," CNNPolitics. com, November 4, 2008; "Exit Polls: 78% of Jews Voted for Obama," *Jerusalem Post* online edition, November 5, 2008, www.jpost.com/servlet/Satellite?pagename=JPost/ JPArticle/ShowFull&cid=1225715346628.

4. For the 2000 figures, see John C. Green and Mark Silk, "The New Religion Gap," special supplement to *Religion in the News* (Fall 2003): 1–7. There is some debate about the Latino vote for Bush in 2004. The 2004 NEP placed Bush's Latino support at 57 percent in a two-way vote while the Fourth National Survey of Religion and Politics, directed by John C. Green at the University of Ohio–Akron, placed Bush's support at 63 percent. See Green, *The Faith Factor: How Religion Influences American Elections* (Westport, CT: Praeger Publishers, 2007), 7, 9, 11, 60, 63, and 189 n. 34.

5. Stephen Mansfield wrote: "There's no question Obama is a Christian, but he is definitely a postmodern, liberal, and to some small extent, black liberation theology perspective." Stephen Mansfield, *The Faith of Barack Obama* (Nashville, TN: Thomas Nelson Publishing House, 2008).

6. Gastón Espinosa, "Religion and the Presidency of William Jefferson Clinton," in *Religion and the American Presidency: George Washington to George W. Bush with Commentary and Primary Sources*, ed. Gastón Espinosa (New York: Columbia University Press, 2009), 451; Bill Clinton, *My Life* (New York: Random House, 2004), 632.

7. John W. Kennedy, "Preach and Reach: Despite His Liberal Record, Barack Obama Is Making a Lot of Evangelicals Think Twice," *Christianity Today* online edition, October 6, 2008, www.christianitytoday.com/ct/2008/october/18.26.html.

8. Kennedy, "Preach and Reach."

9. Kennedy, "Preach and Reach." One source inside the McCain camp said that McCain felt it was wrong to use his faith to win votes and that he simply wasn't comfortable talking about his personal faith on the campaign trail. It was a "private matter." David Brody, "McCain Religious Advisor: Using Your Faith for Election Is Wrong," CBNnews.com, April 15, 2008, www.cbn.com/cbnnews/357703.aspx Some Evangelicals were very critical of Obama's outreach to Evangelicals and said his outreach to conservatives was "a fraud" because his faith forums really didn't address key moral issues from a conservative perspective. Sarah Pullman, "Minnery Disappointed by Religious Outreach, not Thrilled with McCain," *Christianity Today* politics blog, August 27, 2008, http://blog.christianitytoday.com/ctpolitics/2008/08/ minnery_disappo.html.

10. Justin Ewers, "McCain and Obama's Religious Outreach Experts," *U.S. News & World Report* political blog, August 24, 2008, www.usnews.com/articles/news/ campaign-2008/2008/08/24/mccain-and-obamas-religious-outreach-experts.html.

11. Barack Obama, *The Audacity of Hope* (New York: Three Rivers Press, 2006), 199, 206.

12. Obama, *Audacity of Hope*, 207, 218; Marjorie Miller, "Economic Strife Drives Latino Vote," *Los Angeles Times*, October 26, 2008; Patrick Whelan, The Catholic Case for Obama (Boston, MA: Catholic Democrats, 2008), 1–54, online version http://209.85.173.132/search?q=cache:EOWAnWmy6IoJ:www.catholicdemocrats. org/cfo/pdf/Catholic_Case_for_Obama_booklet.pdf+Latinos+see+social+and+econo mic+justices+issus+on+par+with+abortion&cd=20&hl=en&ct=clnk&gl=us&client= safari. Pew Forum on Religion and Public Life: http://pewforum.org/religion08/pro-file.php?CandidateID=4. For evidence that immigration was a key factor in shaping how Latinos voted see the previously cited *National Survey on Latino Protestants: Immigration and the 2008 Election*, October 16, 2008; Hispanic Newswire, "National Hispanic Evangelical Leader, Rev. Wilfredo De Jesus, Meets with Obama, Hispanics Embracing 'Change Message,'" *Hispanic Newswire*, March 4, 2008. This document stated: "'The meeting went very well and the Senator really understands the importance of justice issues such as Health Care, Education and Immigration within the Hispanic faith community,' declared DeJesus."

13. Clinton stated: "There is a great debate . . . about the extent to which people of faith can seek to do God's will as political actors. I would like to come down on the side of encouraging everybody to act on what they believe is the right thing to do [based on] the grounds of their faiths. I encourage them to speak out . . . People should not be embarrassed to say that they advocate a course of action simply because . . . they believe it is dictated by their faith, by what they discern to be, with their best efforts, the will of God." He went on to declare: "It is high time we had an open and honest reaffirmation of the role of American citizens of faith . . . We are a people of faith . . . Let us instead respect one another's faiths, fight to the death to preserve the right of every American to practice what ever convictions he or she has . . . [and] bring our values back to the table of American discourse to heal our troubled land." Clinton, *My Life*, 558; Espinosa, "Religion and the Presidency of William Jefferson Clinton," 449. For evidence of FDR and Carter doing the same see chapters 5 and 9 of Espinosa, *Religion and the American Presidency*.

14. Obama, *Audacity of Hope*, 218.

15. Kennedy, "Preach and Reach"; Clinton, *My Life*, 558; Espinosa, "Religion and the Presidency of William Jefferson Clinton," 449. For evidence of FDR and Carter doing the same see chapters 5 and 9 of Espinosa, *Religion and the American Presidency*.

16. Gastón Espinosa, Virgilio Elizondo, and Jesse Miranda, eds. *Latino Religions and Civic Activism in the United States* (New York: Oxford, 2005); Catherine Wilson, *The Politics of Latino Faith: Religion, Identity and Urban Community* (New York: New York University Press, 2008).

17. Kennedy, "Preach and Reach."

18. Andrew Greeley, "Defections Among Hispanics (Updated)," *America*, September 27, 1997: 12–13; Gastón Espinosa, Virgilio Elizondo, and Jesse Miranda, *Hispanic Churches in American Public Life Summary of Findings*, no. 2 (Notre Dame, IN: Institute for Latino Studies, University of Notre Dame, 2003), 15–16,

27; Gastón Espinosa, "Latinizing American Christianity: Pluralism, Pentecostalism and the Future of American Catholicism," *Conscience: The Newsjournal of Catholic Opinion* (Summer 2007): 28–31; Gastón Espinosa, "Methodological Reflections on Social Science Research on Latino Religions," in *Rethinking Latino/a Religions and Identity*, ed. Miguel de la Torre and Gastón Espinosa (Cleveland, OH: Pilgrim Press, 2006), 33–42.

19. Emphasis added. Robin Mazyck, "Obama Reaches out to Young Evangelicals," CBN News.com political blog, June 10, 2008, www.cbn.com/cbnnews/388364.aspx. Obama stated of DuBois, "Josh is a great friend and has really led the way for Democrats in terms of faith outreach. The grassroots conversations we've held across the country, our landmark evangelical meetings . . . are helping to change our nation, person by person" (Amy Chozick, "Young Clergyman Leads Obama's Drive to Attract 'Faith Voters,'" *Wall Street Journal*, WSJ.com, August 16, 2008). For an excellent summary of DuBois's background and relationship to Obama see Alex Altman, "Joshua DuBois: Obama's Pastor-in-Chief," *Time*, February 6, 2009.

20. Obama, *Audacity of Hope*, 216. For more evidence, see endnotes 3, 4, and 10.

21. Hispanic Christian Newswire, "Obama Meets with America's Leading Christian Leaders including National Hispanic Christian Leadership Conference, President, Rev. Samuel Rodriguez," *Hispanic Christian Newswire*, www.nhclc.org/about/news/jul2008_2.html.

Index

Abortion, 280–81, 338

Abrams, Elliot, xxvi, 140, 143, 144, 303n39

Adelman, Kenneth, 140

African Americans: and Al Gore, 217; and American presidents, xvii, xxv, 205; approach to church and state, 79; and Bill Clinton, 215, 217, 219, 220, 221, 222, 224, 225, 226; as black Protestants, 6, 8, 9, 28, 87; voter turnout, 11, 21; church-based political discussion, xxiv, 220; and civil rights, 61, 207; conflict with Catholics, 61; congregational organization, 29, 32; as constituency, xvii; communal relationship to presidency, 213, 214; and Eleanor Roosevelt, 214, 215; and Franklin Delano Roosevelt, 214, 316n30; and George W. Bush, 20, 218; and George H.W. Bush, 216, 217; jeremiad tradition, 210, 211, 212; and John F. Kennedy, 222; and John Kerry, 23, 219; and lynching, 213; and Lyndon Johnson, 222, 223, 224, 226; misinterpreted support for Republican candidates, 218; models of attitudes toward Presidents

Reagan and Clinton, 219, 220, *221* table 9.3, 222; partisan identities, 96; partisanship, 214, *215* table 9.1, 220, 221, 222; and presidential power, 208, 209; and presidential silence, 213; progressive communitarian principles versus prosperity Gospel message, 227, 228; and prophets of social justice and equality, 208, 228; and prosperity gospel, 228; and public opinion, 215, 216, 217; reported vote choice and average feeling thermometer ratings, *216* table 9.2, 217; resistance to slavery, 209; and Ronald Reagan, 213, 219, 220, 221; and Robert Dole, 218; as Muslims, 159, 161, 168; working with mainline Protestants demanding justice, 31. and Barack Obama, 278, 280–82, 284; *See also* Nation of Islam

African Methodist Episcopal Church, 283

Aikman, David, 290n79, 290n81

Albright, Madeleine, 148

American Baptist Churches (USA), 29; frontier revivalist roots, 30; including Southern Baptists, 30; separation

341

About the Editor and Contributors

Brian Robert Calfano is assistant professor of political science at Missouri State University. He is the author of articles and book chapters on topics as diverse as clergy political behavior, the effect of religious heuristics on voting behavior, religion in state politics, and Middle East democratization.

David G. Dalin is professor of history and political science at Ave Maria University in Florida and the Taube Research Fellow in American History at Stanford University. He is the author or coauthor of ten books, including *The Presidents of the United States and the Jews* (2000), *Religion and State in the American Jewish Experience* (1997), and *American Jews and the Separationist Faith: The New Debate on Religion in Public Life* (1992). An ordained rabbi, he studied at the Jewish Theological Seminary and received his PhD from Brandeis University.

Paul A. Djupe is associate professor of political science at Denison University. He is coauthor of *The Political Influence of American Churches* (2008), *The Prophetic Pulpit: Clergy, Churches, and Community in American Politics* (2003), and *Religious Institutions and Minor Parties in the United States* (1999).

Gastón Espinosa is associate professor of religious studies at Claremont McKenna College. He is the past project manager of the $1.3 million Hispanic Churches in American Public Life research project funded by Pew Charitable Trusts, one of the largest studies in U.S. history on Latino religions and politics. He is the editor or coeditor of *Religion and the American Presidency: George Washington to George W. Bush with Commentary and Sources* (2009),

Mexican American Religions: Spirituality, Activism, and Culture (2008), and *Latino Religions and Civic Activism in the United States* (2005). He is coeditor of the Columbia University Press Series on Religion and Politics.

John C. Green is a senior fellow in religion and American politics at the Pew Forum on Religion and Public Life. He also serves as director of the Ray C. Bliss Institute of Applied Politics and is Distinguished Professor of Political Science at the University of Akron. Green is the author or coauthor of five books and more than sixty scholarly articles, including *The Faith Factor: How Religion Influences American Elections* (2007). The *Los Angeles Times* described Green as the nation's "preeminent student of the relationship between religion and American politics."

Melissa V. Harris-Lacewell is associate professor of politics and African American studies at Princeton University. She is author of *Barbershops, Bibles, and BET: Everyday Talk and Black Political Thought* (2004). Professor Harris-Lacewell's writings have been published in the *Chicago Tribune*, *Los Angeles Times*, and *New York Newsday*. She has provided expert commentary on U.S. elections, racial issues, religious questions, and gender issues.

Lyman A. Kellstedt is visiting professor of political science at Furman University. He is the author, coauthor, or coeditor of five books, including *Political Science: American Politics and Government* (2000), *The Bully Pulpit: The Politics of Protestant Clergy* (1997), *Religion and the Culture Wars* (1996), and *Rediscovering the Religious Factor in American Politics* (1993).

So Young Kim is assistant professor of political science at Florida Atlantic University. She studied at Seoul National University, Korea, and received a PhD from Northwestern University. Her scholarly work focuses on East Asian politics, international political economy, Asian American politics and religion, and quantitative political methodology. She has conducted research on U.S. ethnic, Asian American, and Latino religions and the American presidency.

David C. Leege is professor emeritus of political science from the University of Notre Dame and coauthor of eighteen books and reports including *The Politics of Cultural Differences* (2002) and *Rediscovering the Religious Factor in American Politics* (1993). He writes on voting behavior, religion and politics, and sociology of religion. He is former board chair of the American National Election Studies (NES). He currently coedits the Cambridge Studies in Social Theory, Religion, and Politics.

Laura R. Olson is professor of political science at Clemson University. She is the coauthor, coeditor, or author of eight books, including *Religion and Politics in America: Faith, Culture, and Strategic Choices* (2004), *The Encyclopedia of American Religion and Politics* (2003), *Filled with Spirit and Power: Protestants in Politics* (2000), and *Women with a Mission: Religion, Gender, and the Politics of Women Clergy* (2005).

Corwin Smidt is director of the Paul Henry Institute for the Study of Christianity and Politics and professor of political science at Calvin College. He is the author, editor, or coauthor of ten books on religion and public life, including *Pulpit and Politics: Clergy in American Politics at the Advent of the Millennium* (2004), *In God We Trust? Religion and American Political Life* (2001), and *Religion and the Culture Wars* (1996). He served as director of the religion and politics section of the American Political Science Association (APSA).

Katherine E. Stenger is assistant professor of political science at Gustavus Adolphus College. Her research focuses on the role of women and religious interests groups in American politics.

Adam L. Warber is associate professor of political science at Clemson University. He has coauthored works on religion and the American presidency. He is the author of *Executive Orders and the Modern Presidency: Legislating from the Oval Office* (2006).